IN THIS SERIES . . .

Helping the Visually Handicapped Child in a Regular Class

Anthony J. Pelone

Helping the Trainable Mentally Retarded Child

Bernice B. Baumgartner

Administration of Special Education Programs

Leo E. Connor

Guiding the Physically Handicapped College Student

Herbert Rusalem

An Experimental Curriculum for Young Mentally Retarded Children

Frances P. Connor and Mabel E. Talbot

Education of Homebound or Handicapped Children

Frances P. Connor

Terminology and Concepts in Mental Retardation

Joel R. Davitz, Lois J. Davitz, and Irving Lorge

Edouard Seguin: A Study of an Educational Approach to the Treatment of Mentally Defective Children

Mabel E. Talbot

TC series in SPECIAL EDUCATION

FRANCES P. CONNOR, EDITOR

An Experimental Curriculum for
Young Mentally Retarded Children

FRANCES P. CONNOR

Professor of Education
Department of Special Education
Teachers College, Columbia University

MABEL E. TALBOT

Assistant Professor of Education
Department of Special Education
Teachers College, Columbia University

TEACHERS COLLEGE PRESS

Teachers College, Columbia University

New York

MENTAL RETARDATION PROJECT

TEACHERS COLLEGE, COLUMBIA UNIVERSITY

1957 - 1961

Director of the Study	Maurice H. Fouracre, Ph.D.
Assistant Director	I. Ignacy Goldberg, Ed.D.
Steering Committee	Frances P. Connor, Ed.D.
	Maurice H. Fouracre, Ph.D.
	I. Ignacy Goldberg, Ed.D.
	Irving Lorge, Ph.D.*
Teachers College Technical Advisory Group	Millie G. Almy, Ph.D.
	Max R. Brunstetter, Ph.D.
	Gertrude P. Driscoll, Ph.D.
	Paul E. Eiserer, Ph.D.
	Anne S. McKillop, Ph.D.
	Ernest G. Osborne, Ph.D.*
	Jane Beasley Raph, Ed.D.
	Rosalea A. Schonbar, Ph.D.
	Elizabeth C. Stobo, Ed.D.
	Kenneth D. Wann, Ed.D.
	Paul W. F. Witt, Ed.D.
	Jane D. Zimmerman, Ph.D.

*Deceased

This work represents the curriculum developed as part of a comprehensive study, The Effects of a Preschool Program upon Young Mentally Retarded Children. The research reported was performed pursuant to a contract with the United States Office of Education, Department of Health, Education and Welfare, #SAE6444.

Library of Congress Catalog Card Number 64-13899. Manufactured in the USA.
THIRD PRINTING 1970

ACKNOWLEDGMENTS

This curriculum was developed as part of a five-year study to determine the influence of group experience upon a sample of young educable mentally retarded children and has involved a large number of individuals and organizations. Our indebtedness to each of them is gratefully acknowledged, although only a few can be individually specified.

Gratitude is expressed to Dr. Maurice H. Fouracre, who served as Director of the Study, for his consistent encouragement and support in the curriculum's development, and to Dr. I. Ignacy Goldberg, the Project's Assistant Director during its last four years, whose interest and participation were of prime importance to its realization. Mr. Godfrey Stevens served in this latter capacity during the first year and assisted in the organization and initiation of the Study.

The late Dr. Irving Lorge, Research Associate for the evaluation, contributed extensively to the Study from the time of its initiation until his death in January, 1961. The sudden termination of his participation was a grievous loss to the Study as well as to all those who worked with him.

Particularly helpful also were Dr. John V. Hottel and Dr. Martin B. Miller who served for briefer periods as Research Associates for the overall study and, finally, Dr. M. Leigh Rooke, whose editorial talents were used to bring the Project report to fruition.

The curriculum is the direct result of the creative efforts and contributions of the teachers who worked with the project classes. Those who assumed major leadership over an extended period were Mrs. Elizabeth Badgeley, Dr. Joan McDaniel Fairchild, Dr. Mabel Talbot, and Mrs. Comilda Weinstock. They, together with Mrs. Carolyn Asterita and Miss Catherine Sailor, gave an enthusiasm as well as a devotion to the children while in the process of curriculum development. We also wish to thank Miss Joan Miller, Mrs. Manijeh Alborz Ghazi, and Mrs. Elaine Fried for their participation at various times during the five years. Each of these teachers met in regularly scheduled sessions to design and analyze the curriculum materials as well as to report on the program's implementation.

Closely associated with the important contribution of the teachers was the work of Mrs. Cornelia Belinkoff, social worker; Dr. Ruth Bockner and Mrs. Ruth A. Lipsky, psychologists; Sam Harrison and Miss Rebecca Haskel, language developmentalists; Charles C. Bovee, Dr. Mortimer Kreuter, and Dr. Elizabeth Webster, observers; Mrs. Jeanne Ludwig, music consultant; Dr. Virginia A. Powell, pediatrician; and Mrs. Gwen Moskowitz, nurse.

This list would not be complete without a special word of appreciation to Mrs. Ursula Burns, secretary and office manager for the Project, whose constant attention to every detail and whose efficiency and perceptive understanding were a major contribution throughout the duration of the Study.

In addition to the Project staff, sincere gratitude is expressed to the following:

Bellevue Hospital and the staff of the Hearing and Speech Clinic. The Project is indebted for their untiring cooperation in providing all of the audiological evaluations for the children in the experimental programs.

Flower and Fifth Avenue Hospitals and Babies Hospital, Columbia Presbyterian Hospital, for their cooperation and assistance in obtaining referrals of subjects.

The City of New York Department of Health and its staff, who cooperated in the establishment and approval of the Project school as a licensed private school.

The City of New York Board of Education, Dr. John J. Theobold, Superintendent of Schools, and especially the Bureau of Children with Retarded Mental Development and the Bureau of Child Guidance. Special appreciation is given to Miss Katherine D. Lynch, head of the CRMD Bureau, and to her associates, without whose assistance and cooperative efforts the securing of comparison subjects in the public schools and the follow-up of Project children who transferred to these schools would not have been possible.

The New York City Council of Social Agencies as well as the many individual public and private agencies and organizations who assisted so ably in the work of locating subjects and who maintained a consistent interest in this activity despite the additional demands it made upon their time and energies.

The Reliable Transportation Company and its owners, Mr. and Mrs. Harry Berliner, who provided dependable safe transportation for pupils and cooperated in making necessary reports and in giving services beyond those of their contractual agreement.

The Musician's Emergency Fund of New York City, which graciously donated to the Study the able services of the music consultant.

Paul Byers, who took many photographs of the Project activities.

Dr. Elizabeth P. Hagen, Professor of Education, Teachers College, and Dr. Stanley V. Smith, Program Specialist, State Statistical Services, Office of Education, U.S. Department of Health, Education and Welfare, both of whom gave valuable advice and suggestions, contributing not only extensive knowledge in research and statistics but also knowledge of educational methods and practices.

To each of these and to other resource persons not specifically named, the Project has been indebted for services rendered, for cooperation, and for information.

And, finally, the services, facilities, and unending assistance and support of the administration, faculty, and staff of Teachers College, Columbia University, made the Mental Retardation Project possible. One of these College contributions was the consultant services of the members of the Technical Advisory Group, who individually and as a committee provided a valuable specialized resource. Another College contribution was the number of graduate students who, from time to time, served in a variety of capacities as technical assistants.

Particular appreciation is extended to the children and their parents from whom we learned so much and without whom the Project would not have been possible.

Frances P. Connor
Head, Department of Special Education
Teachers College, Columbia University

TABLE OF CONTENTS

Page

Acknowledgements   v

Introduction   ix

Chapter I. The Curriculum Base   1

Development - The Process   1

Curriculum Structure and Content   2

Educational Methodology   5

References   10

Chapter II. The Curriculum Guide and Its Programming   14

The Curriculum Guide as a Rating Form   14

The Curriculum Guide as Base for Programming   15

The Curriculum Guide, Revised Form   18

Programming:

Intellectual Development   34

Imagination and Creative Expression   66

Social Development   84

Emotional Development   103

Manipulative Development   108

Motor Development   138

Self Help   153

Chapter III. Settings for Curriculum Implementation   203

Overview   203

The Physical Space and General Plan   203

Discussion Periods   207

Music Experiences   209

Group Handwork Projects   214

Page

Free Play 215

Juice Time 218

Playground and Gymnasium Activities 221

Story Telling 222

Swimming 224

Cooking 225

Trips 227

Chapter IV. Cross-sectional Considerations 230

Introduction 230

Activity Sequences 235

Time Sequences as a Cross-sectional Unit 236

Subject Matter Sequences as a Cross-sectional Unit 237

Reading Readiness as a Conceptual Sequence 262

Child-Parent-Teacher Relations as a Cross-sectional Unit 264

Chapter V. Program Organization and Management 270

Scheduling Arrangements 270

In-Class Structures 271

Observations 274

Chapter VI. Evaluations 279

Individual Log Excerpts as Bases for Curriculum Guide Ratings 280

Mean Scores on Selected Curriculum Guide Items 283

Chapter VII. A Concluding Statement 298

Summary 298

Conclusions 299

This curriculum report is a description of the special education program for preschool educable mentally retarded children together with an account of its development in experimental classes in New York City. The experimental curriculum was the independent variable of a United States Office of Education - Teachers College, Columbia University cooperative research project to study the effects of group experience upon young retardates.

The first two of the over-all Project objectives are covered in this curriculum report. They were as follows:

1. To discover the amount and kinds of learning within the classroom; e.g., activities of daily living, academic learning and readiness, social and emotional adjustment, speech development, listening skills, oral comprehension, and vocabulary growth.

2. As a consequent of 1, above, to determine appropriate curriculum and teaching methods in classroom settings for preschool educable mentally retarded children.

The other objectives were:

3. To evaluate the subsequent adjustment at or near age 7 - 8 years, after admission to a public school program in the same range of activities specified in 1, above.

4. To evaluate periodically learnings and adjustments of 4 and 5 year old mentally retarded children attending the classroom program.

5. To evaluate periodically the learnings and adjustments of the children who attended the experimental classroom program at 6, 7 and 8 years while they are attending the public school program for the mentally retarded.

6. To evaluate growth and development of these children as a function of the degree of parental acceptance of the children's deviation.

7. To compare the developmental sequence of educable mentally retarded children with that of the so-called normal. Particular attention to be given to physical, social-emotional and speech developmental patterns.

According to the research plan, children's growth was to be evaluated in a cross-sectional longitudinal matrix through periodic medical evaluations, psychometric appraisals, measurements of personality and social maturity variations, language development reports, academic readiness inventories and measures of parental acceptance. The results of the study are on file in the United States Office of Education. Descriptions of the curriculum and the classroom technique are reported in the present volume.

To conduct such a study, it was necessary to obtain pupils for participation in the group experience, to develop an appropriate curriculum, to carry out the necessary testing and interviewing, and to devise means of reporting the data. The Project called for two classes of fifteen children each, one of kindergarten age, the other of first-grade age. There was to be no charge for tuition or transportation.

Criteria for admission to the preschool groups included the following:

1. Residence: within reasonable travel time from the college.

2. Chronological Age: between the ages 4 years 9 months and 6 years 9 months as of September 1st of the school year he was admitted to the Project.

3. Sex: both boys and girls.

4. I.Q.: between 50 and 75 at the time of the psychometric examination as administered by the Project psychologist.

5. Physical Status: a) in good general health, b) able to walk without assistance, c) free from physical disorders which would require restriction of activities (e.g., heart disease, major convulsive disorders, asthma), d) toilet trained, e) free of major visual and auditory handicaps, and f) free of major speech and language dysfunction.

6. _Emotional Status_: Evidence of severe emotional disturbance or psychosis disqualified children for the study.

7. _Family Participation_: cooperation assured
for studying the background and developmental
history of each child as well as the family constel-
lation; application for admission to the preschool
to be made by the parents.

Case Finding

One of the major difficulties encountered by
the Project staff was the securing of subjects.
Despite Kirk's earlier difficulty in locating preschool educable retarded children, the Project
designers were assured of more than an adequate
eligible population in metropolitan New York City.
The subjects were sought through agency referral
and no mass community testing process was to be
used.

However, to obtain the minimum number of
children for classroom participation, direct contact was made with over 900 organizations, including schools, in New York City. Each agency received material describing the Project and criteria
for admission to the experimental classes.
In addition project staff visited hospitals to
examine files on young children. Hundreds of phone
calls were made to key people in clinics, agencies,
child health stations, community centers and
housing projects. Mass media such as newspapers
and professional journals were used. Letters
were sent to pediatricians, ministers, priests and
rabbis. Apparently, the usual educable mental
retardate is not easily discernible until he fails
in school subjects or when he has difficulty with
abstract and symbolic learnings. The children
in the Project represent those whose deviant or
retarded development is noticeable at an early
age. Because of the inability to locate subjects,
the earlier conceived project design had to be
altered to eliminate control and null groups.

Screening

A lengthy questionnaire was sent to the parents
upon initial application for admission of their
child to the experimental program. Among the
topics covered on the form were the usual family
data, mother's medical history, birth and ob-
stetrical history, early developmental history,
and other information about the child such as his
activities at home, his fears, nervous habits,
parents' estimation of child's functioning and behavior. If the social worker upon reviewing the
returned form deemed the child eligible for further

screening, the parents were invited to the college
for an interview. The psychologist then administered the Stanford-Binet Form L test to the child
and also made a tentative estimate for potential
inclusion in the group situation. The social worker interviewed the mother.

If the child met the psychological criteria, he
was referred for a medical examination. When
accepted after staff review, he was admitted on
a probationary basis. Final admission was contingent upon adjustment to the group situation.

The Experimental Classroom

Thirty children for each of three years were
divided into two groups: the younger, ages 4 years
9 months to 5 years 9 months and the older, 5
years 9 months to 6 years 9 months. During the
fourth year, only an older group participated. The
daily class sessions were 2-1/2 hours in length;
the two groups shared the use of the Project
classroom. For each group of 15 children, there
were 2 teachers. An observer was assigned to the
one-way vision booth equipped with sound. The
booth also accommodated college students and
other visitors wishing to observe the classes.

THE CURRICULUM REPORT

Curriculum development was the major focus
of the teachers during the four years. A minimum of two scheduled meetings were held per
week to discuss what was happening in the classroom, what should have been happening, how to
make it happen, and why.

The purposes of this report are to describe
1) the setting and process for the curriculum
development, 2) the curriculum guide and its
implementation, and 3) the observed behavior
and growth of the children. The curriculum is
one prepared and used by the teachers in the
experimental classes; the Guide, developed
during the first year, served as a basis for
activity planning and evaluation for the remaining three years.

In Chapter I a point of view is presented
through reference to supporting literature and
through a chronology of the development of the
various aspects of the curriculum.

Chapter II contains the detailed Curriculum
Guide, with the observed five-step sequences of
behavior for 190 items in seven areas of development, and the expanded form of the Guide,
giving programming for the five levels of each
Curriculum Guide item.

To emphasize the use of the Guide as a guide rather than as a limiting factor in the curriculum, Chapter III is devoted to the Action Settings, the arenas for experiences represented by the scheduled daily activity periods. Included here are descriptions of teacher preparation for the experiences, materials and equipment used, the variety of activities, and the nature of the children's participation.

Chapter IV consists of a series of illustrations. It is a presentation of the manner in which the long range goals and the curriculum guide items were implemented in the action settings. It is a cross-sectional description of two sets of directions: those for the teachers and those for the children. Included are discussions of the teachers' long range behavioral goals and the children's operational patterns of time, subject matter, conceptualization and personal relationships. Samples of five kinds of teachers' records and reports serve to illustrate, interpret, and give perspective to the Curriculum Guide items as they appear and reappear in the action settings.

In Chapter V are discussed the various aspects of organization and management of the preschool program for children with retarded mental development. The conduct of the daily program is illustrated by comparisons of teacher plans and observer's notes.

Chapter VI is a description of individual and composite teacher evaluations based on anecdotal records of observed child behavior in the program. Sample records illustrate use of the five point curriculum scale in noting progress, identifying strengths and weaknesses and indicating program emphases. Included in this chapter are the composite ratings on Curriculum Guide items for three Project Groups.

Chapter VII summarizes the curriculum design and highlights areas for further study.

It must be emphasized that although the curriculum was developed for young children diagnosed as mentally retarded, it is envisioned that the material presented here lends itself to upward extension for older and more mature children. It is strongly believed that it can also be modified to apply to children with a variety of disabilities. It represents an *approach* to curriculum development and teaching methodology. It is not meant to be a course of study. It is not static.

CHAPTER 1

THE CURRICULUM BASE

DEVELOPMENT - THE PROCESS

The process of curriculum development required reeducation of teaching personnel as well as the obtaining of their creative contributions to content and methodology. Reeducation and the production of a curriculum document in the unexplored area of educational planning and programming for preschool children diagnosed as educable mentally retarded involved the teacher as a person and as a professional worker. According to Lewin and Grabbe (1945) change must give recognition to cognitive structure including the person's perception of his physical and social worlds, the degree of his control over his physical and social movements, and the modification of his valences and values including reactions to groups and their standards, status differences and personal evaluation.

The Project's teaching staff came into this new situation with different backgrounds, both experiential and pedagogical. Of the four, two had worked previously with slightly older retarded children and with the "normal" child; one had a long and varied experience in regular nursery schools; and the fourth had worked with young deaf and deaf-blind children. Each teacher had acquired in previous settings patterns of successful classroom operation and management. The preschool retarded children were a unique group and previously tried and proven guide-lines were less than adequate. Teachers met a minimum of four hours weekly in scheduled curriculum sessions to determine and set down the kinds of learnings to take place, the appropriate curriculum and effective methodology. Differences in perception of the program abounded. These had to be accepted and the strength that each possessed within these differences incorporated. Likewise, similarities were recognized and broadened.

As noted in small group action generally, attention was turned to the development of an informal social organization including a group code and role differentiation (Olmstead, 1959). Bales (1950) indicates the advantage to each individual in a group

of stabilizing the potential activity of others toward him, favorably if possible, but in any case in such a way that he can predict it. He refers to the social structure of groups as a system of solutions to the functional problems of interaction which become institutionalized to reduce tensions growing out of uncertainty and unpredictability in the actions of others. In working with the Project's curriculum participants, each of whom viewed himself and was viewed by others as a specialist in light of both academic preparation and experience, cognizance was given to Bales' (1950) four dimensions or axes of role differentiation which in varying degrees affected the group's productivity. These elements of the social structure which were important in determining the process of curriculum development are the following: (1) access to resources, (2) control over persons, (3) status in the stratified scale of importance or prestige, and (4) solidarity or identification with the group as a whole.

In light of the diverse factors operative in the curriculum development, the coordinator viewed the process in terms of (1) group cohesion, (2) individualization through free expression of diverse opinions and (3) recombination for a new purpose with more complete understanding.

Festinger et al (1950) have viewed the problem of group cohesion as the total field of forces which act on members to remain in the group. Back (1952) in discussing influence through social communication identified cohesiveness as the product of, among other factors, group prestige and task interest. Smith, Stanley and Shores (1957) have categorized the forces to be dealt with in curriculum as follows: (1) those that are crucial, for example, those that may threaten highly regarded educational and social values; (2) those restraining forces that can be reduced with the least effort and whose conquest promotes a sense of accomplishment; (3) those resisting forces that can be changed in direction, possibly through clarification and highlighting the role of the personally valued elements which further the attainment of the commonly accepted goals, and (4) those augmenting forces that can be increased as relationship between these forces and the proposed curriculum direction is noted. They feel that leadership efforts are preferably directed toward reducing resisting forces rather than increasing the augmenting forces and, wherein teacher morale is low, focusing on teacher problems rather than on the curriculum per se. Upon a background of success in the group's social structure, many problems more difficult to solve can be tackled. Thus, the logical point of curriculum initiation was the immediate problem of classroom management. Since many of the children responded hyperactively and with quickly dropped interest in the usual nursery-kindergarten setting, specific focus on individual children and suggestions for their improved function served as the base for group cohesion.

At this point, attention was directed toward identification of the areas of teacher concern, later identified as long range goals for the children in the group situations. The following problem-centered categories were defined to cover those areas in which children should establish competence: (1) daily living skills, (2) cognitive and sensory-motor skills adequate for participation in subsequent school programs, (3) communication skills adequate for group conversation, cooperative planning, and evaluation of experiences, (4) tolerance of a variety of simultaneously presented stimuli through selection and sustained interest in one stimulus, (5) understanding and ability to accept teacher values and interests different from their own, (6) extra-curricular social adjustment patterns for safe participation in activities such as swimming, field trips and playing in the park.

With the overt acceptance of the goals and recognition of the need for a concentrated effort to promote related changes in child behavior, the teachers felt freer to express their opinions relative to observed child characteristics, program content and classroom procedures. In the regular informal teacher meetings, analysis was made of teacher-learner behavior. Apparent to all were the ideas and problem solutions emerging from the group which would not have been considered by the individual in isolation (Kelley and Thibaut, 1954). Quality of response improved as inhibitions faded and each person was dealing with coworkers whose points of view were recognized and respected.

Despite the direction provided by the teachers' long range goals, developmental steps were sought to fill in the beginning framework. Children were observed, reports were accumulated, the materials and equipment selected before the children's arrival were tested for function, and teaching methods were dissected; professional literature was

surveyed and reported; questioning, listening and debating took place. Concurrently, teachers were registered in advanced courses in child growth and development, bringing to the curriculum sessions new learnings and energies from other contacts. Weber and Traeltsch (1947) found that individuals return to assigned tasks with renewed energy subsequent to their experiencing personal satisfactions outside the sphere of the assigned charge.

The insights gained called for reorganization of the curriculum development activity. Teachers envisioned guidelines around which school experiences could be selected and provided. A structured curriculum guide was to serve three purposes: teacher direction, program balance and assessment of child and group status. The initial stated task of developing a curriculum guide was the teachers' charge to themselves. They had a common purpose and sought the optimum content regardless of which teacher contributed the ideas.

The curriculum materials presented in this publication were prepared by the teachers and the curriculum coordinator for their use in the experimental classes. Without leadership, the small group meetings, the vehicles for curriculum development, might have been little more than scheduled sessions with production the result of isolated efforts. Designated responsibility for group leadership was obviously imperative. Jennings (1952), Berkowitz (1955), and Bales (1955) have emphasized, however, the need for compatibility in the roles of the task specialist and the social-emotional specialist who transmutes negative affect into positive affect. These roles may rest in either one or several of the group members but it is not enough either to direct the task or to create the environment. The functions appear interdependent and essential to group solidarity and productivity.

CURRICULUM STRUCTURE AND CONTENT

In developing curriculum materials for preschool children diagnosed as mentally retarded, the need for a teacher's guide was paramount. Existing courses of study were not adequate; the preconceived curriculum for the young children was inappropriate. Questions were raised concerning the basis for selection and use of some materials, the discard or postponement of others, results expected from the group and from individuals and programming to assure the child's growth.

Goodlad (1960) reported curriculum as threefold: (1) as a design or plan of institutionalized education, (2) as comprised of the actual learning opportunities provided at a given time and place and (3) as an instrument for bringing about psychological changes in learners as a result of their activities in an educational institution. The curriculum seemed related to the plan or design - the structure envisioned by those creating it. This foundation, however, and the content as provided for the children were governed by the objectives and interpretations of those implementing the program.

Structure

As stressed by Dewey (1902) the child does not develop entirely from within himself. His development requires a development of experience and a development into experience of that which is really wanted; the problem of direction is the problem of adult selection of appropriate stimuli for instincts and impulses selected for use in the gaining of new experience. Thus is emphasized the need for awareness of the development expected in the child and for the educator's providing a setting with the selected elements (stimuli) to promote the child's forging ahead in areas deemed essential. It was upon this premise that the Project's curriculum team identified major areas of focus and determined steps through which to foster child movement toward competence, maturity and independence. Chronologically, the group was homogeneous; functionally, they were diverse.

An early assignment was observation of classroom behavior to note the lowest level of function among the children and, from there, to identify increasingly complex operations. Pertinent to the study was Bruner's (1961) summary of the three stages of the child's intellectual development as noted by Piaget (1952) and others. The first stage, essentially the pre-kindergarten period, is identified as one in which the child's mental work consists principally in noting relationships between action and experience. In this pre-operational period, deemed relevant to the preschool population under study, the child learns how to represent the external world through symbols, but has yet to learn the manipulation of those symbols. A major teacher task, then, was the assistance of the child in his movement toward concrete operations in which he could develop an internalized structure through which new knowledge could be learned. Maritain (1957) sees the fundamental task of the teacher as one of liberation, and laying stress on inwardness and the internalization of the educational influence. To him, the extent to which the tendency toward objects or knowledge to be grasped is set free and the intellect becomes accustomed to grasping, seeing, and expressing the objects toward which it tends is the extent to which intuitive power is liberated and strengthened.

Implications for curriculum planning were also inherent in Argyris' (1957) propositions about human behavior in organization. In the development of self in our culture, Argyris suggests seven areas of movement, including the tendency to develop from a state of passivity as an infant to activity, from dependence to relative independence, from behaving in a few ways to behaving in many ways, from erratic, casual, shallow, quickly dropped interests to deepening interests, from short term perspective to long term view, from subordinate position in family and society to equal and/or superordinate position to peers and from lack of awareness of self to awareness and control. It was assumed that, through a planned curriculum and selection of experiences based on the learners, the content to be learned and the organizing elements (Goodlad, 1960), young children diagnosed as educable mentally retarded would be enabled to close some of the "inevitable" gaps in development.

Supported also by Goodlad and Anderson (1959) were the identification and viewing of a set of longitudinal threads or organizing elements of both behavior and content, running vertically through the curriculum. Around these threads could be developed the learning activities and settings for action. These organizing elements were viewed as the teacher's guide against which to view the child's movement, the program's balance and the sequence of elements to be added in the planned activities. Such organization together with systematic programming appeared compatible with Skinner's (1954) case for a program which moves forward through a series of progressive approximations to the final complex behavior desired. It related also to the Estrans' (1959) findings of need for both differentiation and syntheses in the school program for young children while the Project's concept of action settings supported their conclusion that growth occurs as the child develops increased ability to make detailed and analytical examination of closely related ideas.

Early Childhood Programs

Kindergarten programs have developed from the Froebel and Montessori concepts of the "children's garden" as a happy place for growing. The consistent emphasis on its educational purposes and the expressed goals, similar to those of education generally, are reflected in evidence of reported systematic progression of experiences and recognition of less than conforming behavior (Read, 1955). Structure was noted also in the curriculum for realization of the goals stated specifically and the activities described by early childhood specialists. For example, Langford (1960) includes: the encouragement of vigorous physical activity, the practice of manipulative skills, increasing of physical independence and self-confidence, the stimulation of independent thinking, experimentation, problem solving, the use of imagination and the development of ideas and curiosity as well as the laying of a foundation for dealing with adult authority and the formation of acceptable social techniques. Almy (1950) draws attention to preschool experiences with print forms. She found, for example, a significant positive relationship between success in beginning reading and early opportunities which permit interest in words, letters and numbers. Fuller, (1961) however, generalizing from research in the field, supports a broad kindergarten curriculum to provide a broad base of experience drawn from many samplings of knowledge, skills and appreciations. She believes this aim would suggest to teachers the questioning of set curricula or courses of study which would structure this orientation year in the way upper grades are structured, a view consistent with the Stratemeyer et al (1957) proposal that curriculum represents a process of designing, never a fixed design.

In early childhood programs, avenues of development have been promoted in many contexts. One, for example, is through concentration on the experience areas proposed for five and six year olds by Sheehy (1954), namely dramatic play, building, the arts, music dance and games; language, arts and literature; reading, writing and arithmetic; science and social living. Leavitt (1958) views the program as fostering the developmental tasks of young children, not as assigned work, but recognizing that unless satisfactory development takes place, subsequent progress will be markedly impaired. The defined tasks include: learning skill in controlling his own body; increasing stability of bodily processes (maturation); discovering himself as an independent, self-determining person; accepting limitations and developing a conscience; acquiring skills in relating to other people; developing language skills and learning about the world in which he lives. In light of the studies on sensory deprivation as related to child growth and development (Padilla, 1935; Riesen, 1949; Nissen and others, 1951), the applicability of Leavitt's hypothesis to the education of children with retarded development seemed clear.

Emphasis on starting habits of thought is paramount in Ward's presentation of resources for young children's learning. Although enrichment is evident in the children's experiences cited, the learnings highlighted are listed as building judgment, learning cause and consequence of behavior, building clarity of concept, and finding food for thought. Initiation of habits of thought has proved feasible in working with very young children, children developing accuracy of sensory perception and conceptualizations. Verification that retarded children learn as other children learn, but are slower in establishing channels for functional thought processes became increasingly important to the Project's teachers in their program development.

Special Education Programs

Guidelines for curriculum content for young children are found in areas other than early childhood education as such.

General statements with minimal reference to preschool mentally retarded children have been presented by Inskeep (1926), Descoeudres (1928), Duncan (1932), Martens (1950), Kirk and Johnson (1951), Ingram (1953), Lloyd (1953), Smith (1954), Wallin (1955), and Cleugh (1957). These presentations, however, are essentially focused on school-age children. Although Kirk (1958) conducted an extensive study on the effects of a preschool program for the mentally retarded, reference to the enrichment systematically offered to the children is limited.

Some relevant curriculum bases were provided by Stratemeyer et al, (1957), Stevens (1958), Goodlad and Anderson (1959), and Kaya (1961). Kaya suggests, for example, (1) that the importance of psychological operations determines the curricular sequence, (2) that intellectual operations receive a good deal of emphasis in developing curriculum theory and (3) that when sequence is developed, it should take into account individual differences in rates of learning and therefore focus away from grade levels. His conclusions are consistent with planning a curriculum based on a clearly outlined developmental sequence as indicated in Goodlad and Anderson's (1959) proposal for an ungraded primary unit and Bruner's (1961) hypothesis that any subject can be taught effectively in some intellectually honest form to any child at any stage of development with implementation of a "spiral curriculum" approach. Emphasized again, for the experimental program, was an identification of general and specific content and determination of the settings to assure child growth.

Stratemeyer and her colleagues (1957) offer a program designed to assist children to meet persistent life situations which has, to a major degree, laid the foundation for Stevens' (1958) proposed curriculum focus for children who are mentally retarded. Stevens suggests that the child's learning be directed toward maintaining a state of physical well-being, living safely, understanding himself, getting along with others, communicating ideas, using leisure time, traveling and moving about, earning a living and being a home-maker. These areas should receive attention throughout the child's school life and be related to the degree and kind of skill and knowledge required at each stage of development.

Introductory units in curriculum guides for the mentally retarded such as those for city public school programs, are heavily weighted in the direction of concentration on the family and home. Considered by the Project staff was the challenge to this restriction of content noted in Crowder's (1958) study of the extensive out-of-school experiences of young children and their subsequent insights beyond the near-at-hand. Particularly influential, for example, in expanding the common experiences of the young children in the Mental Retardation Project were the experiential bases provided by television and modern transportation.

The total review of materials relevant to the group under study suggested a broad curriculum foundation and a need for specific guidelines for the teachers. To determine the program elements, the teachers identified freely as many as possible of the short term goals toward which they were consciously or unconsciously working in their classrooms. These were then studied, categorized, broken down into short term goals and stated in a series of steps through which the child appeared to go to attain the desired and expected more complex behavior.

The broad categories under which specific curriculum items were grouped and studied for child development sequence were as follows: (1) intellectual development, (2) imaginative and creative expression, (3) social development, (4) emotional development, (5) manipulative development, (6) gross motor development and (7) self-help skills. The area of language development was omitted from the headings, not because it was deemed unimportant, but because the language developmentalist assumed major responsibility for defining the area and evaluating children's status and progress. Language development was considered, by the teaching team, therefore, as a cross-sectional emphasis inherent in all the activities.

Under the seven categories were designated 190 curriculum items, areas of directed growth. For each item, teachers defined the lowest level of function observed and projected the highest achievement expected. Through concentrated study of literature on each item, observed behavior of the children in the classrooms, and operative teaching-learning processes, a five point developmental scale was evolved in the regularly scheduled curriculum meetings. Prior to group acceptance of the sequences agreed upon in the discussion sessions, additional check was made by the teachers in the school setting as they observed and tested the developmental sequence through which children seemed to progress. Subsequent teacher reports on observed behavior, comparisons of children's function, reactions and production, as well as questions on applicability of the sequence as originally presented resulted in either the item's modification or its support. The resultant 190 items comprised the teacher's curriculum guide which was in use early in the Project's second year. Three times annually each child was rated on each item; referents for ratings were the child's observed levels of function in the action settings, not in a one-to-one testing situation. Although presence of stimuli such as other children, routines and materials, had both favorable and deleterious effects, the ratings were deemed representative of internalized behavior patterns manifest in the school settings arranged by the teachers. The curriculum guide was for the teacher's use; the children were directed by the action settings and use of the common elements of physical space, time, people and tangible materials.

EDUCATIONAL METHODOLOGY

Bases of classroom methodology are inherent in Mowrer's (1960) theory that all learning is conditioning of which solution learning or problem solving is a derivative. In his proposal he stresses the essentially emotional (motivating and reinforcing) nature of conditioned responses. Behavior is viewed as a continuous, on-going function of the informational feedback from all senses, internal and external; it is a function of the total psychological field. Actions, therefore, are continually being guided and corrected by new information and new stimuli brought to bear on the child in the situation.

The Action Setting

Piaget (1952) points out that "the progress of knowledge never proceeds by a mere addition of items or of new levels, as if richer knowledge were only a complement of the earlier meagre one." It requires also a perceptual reformation of previous points of view by a process which moves backwards and forward, continually correcting both the initial errors and those arising along the way. He insists that educators need to utilize systematically the child's spontaneous mental development.

Inhelder (1957) stresses the integral relationship of perception and movement and views the first manifestations of problem solving as founded on this interrelation. Also relating problem solving and learning sets and the experiences of children is Hunt (1961) as he examines intelligence and experience. Strauss and Lehtinen (1947) in dealing with brain-injured children emphasize too the need for directed action to reduce undue hyperactivity and distractibility, concluding that as children carry out activities with understanding, the area of successful performance is enlarged and disturbances diminish proportionately. The major objective, however, is the child's internal control rather than the externally regulated conditions.

With older children, use of the whole method within an action setting has been viewed as effective by Harap and Mapes (1934), Hildreth (1942) and Havland (1951). Their experiments with an activity program yielded better pupil achievement than did more traditional assignment-recitation programs which were essentially subject-centered. The Estrans (1959) concluded that learning experiences for young children should be organized in short, relatively simple units which stress relationships between structure and function. They see growth occurring as the child learns to see and study related ideas, to place them in a space and time setting and to integrate them with other bodies of knowledge. Goldstein and Kass (1961) express belief that retarded children's ability to abstract has been underestimated and call for more emphasis on their learning to reason as well as on their dealing with concrete manipulative tasks. Iscoe and Giller (1959) stress the need for continuous training and stimulation for the mentally retarded to reduce the possibilities for private, noncommunicable systems of conceptualization to develop.

Pertinent in methodology for the education of young children is recognition of Piaget's (1947) two complementary processes in the adaptive interaction between the child and his environment. These processes include (1) assimilation which is defined as inner organization or the pattern for later information processing and (2) accommodation, or outer adaptation, the coping with variations in the environment. He views the child's life as a "continuous

creation of increasingly complex forms and a progressive adaptation of these forms to the environment" and suggests that the greater the variety of situations to which the child must accommodate his behavioral structures, the more differentiated and mobile they become, the more rapid is his rate of intellectual development and the greater his range of interest in the novel and the new.

The wholeness of the learning situation is highlighted in his proposition that "all interaction with the environment involves both a structuring and a valuation . . . we cannot reason . . . without experiencing certain feelings and conversely, no affect can exist without a minimum of understanding or of discrimination." Impinging on the teaching-learning process, is Harlow's (1949) work relative to learning sets, his "learning to learn" and subsequent verification by Girardeau, Cantor (1959) and by Ellis and associates (1958) (1959) that mental retardates can form discrimination learning sets. From Harlow's experimentation are clear the possibilities of information processing to develop insights necessary for problem solving. Interpreted into classroom action can be his conclusion that techniques for gaining insights through developing learning sets require repetition of problem solving processes in a specified class of problems. To promote school learning, teachers focus on the child's being able to utilize and incorporate the familiar in developing new insights and to depend on previous behavior involving similar if not the same objects or persons. In each experience, however, reorganization of the situational elements is required.

In the experimental preschool program for young children diagnosed as mentally retarded, the action settings were established for implementation of the curriculum guide. Scheduled activities permitted each child to use well-established skills; through the activities, he was also introduced to new elements and variables, saw relationships, reorganized, sought information, experimented, solved problems and acted.

Among the settings provided by the teachers were discussion periods, handwork activities, story telling, music experiences, juice time, free play sessions, motor activities on the roof and in the gym, swimming, cooking, and trips. Each setting was developed in light of school readiness and focused on the cross-sectional considerations of concept development, work habits, attention, motivation, problem solving, language and speech and the effect on the child at home. Each setting was also viewed in terms of the teacher preparation of essential materials and equipment, the kinds of activities promoted and the nature of the children's participation.

The teachers' development of the guide sequences for the stated short range goals appeared as an insightful approach to the teacher-learning process. The teachers increased their ability to assess the child's status in the many areas, they recognized not only his standing at the moment but also the developmental level toward which to promote movement. Although the sequences require further analysis the teachers' conscious discovery of the goals and sequences required their detailed study of teaching sequence for child advancement in proficiency and understanding. Teachers sought reasons for their selection and use of classroom techniques and teaching resources.

The on-going classroom curriculum was centered around group cohesion and socialization. Group activities included all children and emphasized the interaction of child with child through the variety of experiences and discussions of past and future events. Prior to the initiation of free play activities, teachers confirmed the child's prerequisite learning for available free play activities to assure correct response and promote successful interaction. Manipulative skills were used as an active adjunct to projected and past experiences in and out of the classroom. Concerted effort was made to assure maximum meaningful action within the framework of the school program. Each activity was designed to promote development toward as many short range goals as possible. Most concepts were introduced through channels and generally, a variety of experiences with REAL objects preceded the introduction of use of symbols. House and Zeaman (1960) have raised the question concerning attention and learning since mentally retarded subjects showed a deficit in directing and maintaining attention rather than in learning per se.

Although emphasis was on the child's activity which was his response and on child centered projects, as suggested by Dewey (1902), the teachers required the course of study to enable them to determine the environment of the child, and thus by indirection, to direct. Thus, class activity was not interpreted as equivalent to incidental or opportunistic practice. It was, rather, the result of response to the two sets of the directions: those of the teacher, the Project's long range goals, and the child's operational patterns of time, subject matter, conceptualization and interpersonal relationship as they appeared and reappeared in the action settings.

Frandsen (1957) in extracting generally accepted learning theory has identified eleven principles of teacher direction for effective classroom operation. Among those particularly applicable in the experi-

mental preschool program were: promoting the child's self-recitation, achieving an over-all view, assuring a meaningful approach, providing verbal explanations, making relevant features identifiable, balancing thoroughness with variability of attack, using appropriate crutches, finding the most efficient approach for each child, and offering systematic guidance of experiences for the child's own discovery.

Structure and Reenforcement

Deterrents to the teacher's assurance of consistency and direction in learning are noted in Skinner's (1954) assumption that in a classroom, conditions of reenforcement are accidental and not precise mainly because teachers cannot serve large groups of children at one time. In contrast to this point of view, counteracting the diffusion of teacher effort in a group situation by individualized instruction has gained increasing attention of educational researchers and practitioners. Most common practice in programs for young elementary school children has been the establishment of small subgroups based on ability and achievement; for those in preschool programs, formation of groups has been dependent, for the most part, upon children's interests and activities. Gallagher (1960) experimented with daily individual tutoring as a supplement to the regular half-day group schooling for brain injured mentally retarded children in a residential school. Among his educational objectives was the child's acquisition of a pattern of learning with the learning entree focused on the child's attacking the problem because it would please someone he liked. The positive effect of establishing satisfactory personal relationships as well as immediate and recognizable success was noted in the development of perceptual skills, attention and motivation to learn. Undoubtedly, the child under study was strengthening the habit of perceiving the personal element.

Reviewing experimental studies in mental retardation Dunn (1959) reports findings indicating that the verbal labels for stimuli facilitate the learning process and that verbal praise is effective motivation. From the experimentation, it is clear that learning curves of retarded subjects approximate those of the normal although the rate of learning is slower. In the procedures used in the program under review here, verbal attention to the child's and the teacher's actions and to the elements in a total situation was deemed particularly appropriate for eliciting increasingly complex self-function.

Strauss and Lehtinen (1947) in their education of

neurologically impaired children call for structure, with a maximum of twelve children in a group, by controlling the seating of the children as well as the number and kind of other classroom stimuli. Children experiencing major difficulty in self-direction and organization are removed to the group's periphery with a highlighting of specific foci and personal support in goal directed endeavors through which success is assured.

Applicable in teaching children with learning problems are the four factors deemed important and clearly described by Dollard and Miller (1950). These are: drive (motivation), cue (stimulus), response (action or thought) and reenforcement (reward). Highlighted in education for children with learning problems is need for the teacher's noting of a child's dominant drive which when channelized by a selected cue(s) yields the desired responses which, in turn, are reenforced by the teacher. Prompt and relevant reenforcement is deemed essential to avoid augmentation of the learning difficulties and random behavior which might have resulted from previous nonreenforced responses. It is from the child that the teacher takes his cue for selecting and presenting the stimuli or materials to which the child can and will respond and from which he can make new discoveries. In the preschool set-

tings, relevant reenforcement included supplying correct answers (solutions and procedures) as long as necessary for the child's mastery of the process.

To ensure attention to each child's learning, the items were analyzed during the Project's final year to determine the requisite child readiness for programming toward the next step in each developmental sequence. Readiness was estimated by observation of the child's predictable or internalized behavior which the teacher could anticipate and which no longer seemed to require a child's trial-and-error approach.

Based on observations, teachers' anecdotal records and confirmation in the classroom, sample activities through which movement through the developmental steps was promoted were identified (See Chapter II). These activities are samples of the many through which children were encouraged and their growth directed. Both the guide items and the programming, arranged according to areas of development, were literally guides and are designed to supplement a curriculum sequence, not to be the curriculum sequence. In the preschool classes, prearranged experiential settings determined the activities to be presented.

The following expanded guide item relative to coloring will serve to illustrate a programmed guide item.

E 3. COLORING

(a) The five levels of the curriculum item:

1 holding for use	2 scribbling	3 awareness of space	4 ability to stay within design	5 conformity to design

THE RATING BASE

(b) Definition - process of interest to the teacher

The manipulation of crayons, with attention to the eye-hand coordination involved in discerning a space and coloring within the lines bounding that space.

(c) Details of behavior observed at each level

Child picked up crayons, held them; watched others using them.	Child used crayon to make marks, scribbled at random; seemed unaware of design.	Child scribbled or marked over design, crossing outlines but staying in the general area.	Child stayed within area, usually well within.	Child colored design with fair accuracy. Crossing a boundary was accidental.

THE PROGRAMMING

(d) <u>Element of behavior common to activity at each level</u>

| holds crayon | makes marks | perceives space | limits own marks | limits marks with respect to boundaries |

(e) <u>Teaching procedures which utilize element (d) above and move toward behavior at next level.</u>

| Verbal attention to ways of holding crayon. Direct help in making marks with crayon. | Verbal attention to child's marks, their location, and child's movements. Direct help in staying near dotted line Cutout guides if indicated. | Discussion and comparison of drawings: verbal attention to areas covered, and to location of scribbles. Revisions. | Narrative coloring. Discussion of pictures on basis of points 1, 2, 3 and 4. | Retracing out after coloring. Discussion and evaluation by children. |

Frandsen (1957) proposes, as one way to assure freedom from emotional disturbance in learning, the returning of children to small groups to function at concrete and familiar levels when difficulties are encountered. Through the flexible grouping of the preschool group, teachers correspondingly promoted the child's reassurance, provided essential reenforcements based on previous learnings, and presented cues for identification of the elements inherent in future problem solving situations.

Structure as applied in a preschool classroom is related to Inhelder's (1957) definition of it as a system in which the properties of its elements depend wholly or in part on the laws of the total system. The processes of integration and orderly development are thought of as products of the interaction of the three factors: maturation, experience through exercise and experience through social interaction. Teaching focus is essentially on the presentation to any child of one new element at a time and on the realization that learning takes place in a total setting.

Holland (1960) has emphasized Skinner's (1958) precise control of behavior through selection and arrangement of educational content, a consistent scheme and an awareness of the results obtained, the accomplishment of educational objectives. As recommended for programmed learning, educators in classrooms also heed the following three elements: (1) the breakdown of content into small steps, (2) the prompting of successive steps in the lesson through the preceding items or by hints explicitly for that purpose and (3) the gradual disappearance of cues, demonstration, prompts and hints as the autonomy of the child becomes evident, as he learns to disregard the irrelevant and makes selective use of elements relevant to a correct response.

In conclusion, the process of curriculum development and the involvement of all concerned resulted in a comprehensive program for preschool retarded children in a group setting. Among the questions considered were: (1) What is the basis for such a program? (assumptions) (2) What are the barriers to program operation? (teacher-oriented goals) (3) What should be happening in the school program? (child-oriented goals) (4) how should it happen? (direction-curriculum guide) (5) What makes it happen? (methodology) (6) Why? (rationale) and (7) What did happen? (the effects).

Rationale for the Curriculum

Children referred as mentally retarded at four or five years of age have by their very identification at this age experienced considerable failure and, because of their failure to achieve according to adult expectations, need to establish a pattern for learning, a workable self concept and a recognition of their own achievement. Primarily consideration in the curriculum development was on a step by step progress guide for <u>teachers</u> and a structuring of action settings for <u>children</u> with clearly noted stimuli, of interest to <u>specific</u> children, to provoke action for immediate reenforcement by the teachers. In the total learning setting were many elements to which attention and study would be directed in the future.

Of prime importance in the experimental setting was the learning process, the provision of a means of learning, of seeing relationships and of problem solving. The teachers were directed by their curriculum guide but the introduction of stimuli was viewed not as an isolated process of increasing a number of known facts but rather as a provision of new information to lead to new discoveries for the child, to be differentiated by him, to be re-assembled and reorganized and then integrated for more effective patterns of behavior and readiness for other cues or teacher selected materials. The cues were seen as leading the child toward next developmental steps; readiness for new learnings was to be fostered continually and sought through observation of the child in the action setting. Readiness was to be worked toward and expected; it was not awaited.

The program was based also on the assumption that the more opportunity the child had for applying workable behavior structures in a variety of selec-ted situations the greater would be his ability to modify his actions and to cope with the environment in which he lived. Through establishing relation-ships between what he saw or experienced and what he did or how he responded, the child increased his store of usable symbols as additional vehicles for learning. He also set up patterns for processing the information he obtained so that it was available for use in problem solving.

Since behavior is based on previous experiences, the experimental curriculum presented here in-cludes sample programming used by the teachers. Recognition was given to necessary prerequisite learnings, internalized by the child and therefore to be assumed by the teacher prior to his proceed-ing to the next step which must involve experience with the same or similar objects in new contexts. Instruction was seen as tied closely to the moment of optimum attentiveness. Each new experience was to provide opportunity for varied application of simple generalizations made by the child and as-sured teacher guidance toward increasingly effec-tive self-directed approaches.

Imitation of adult behavior in a relaxed but structured environment as well as the child's awareness and verbalization of that structure were consciously promoted to highlight continuity, a sure-footed freedom of the child's operation within limits and the establishment of attitudes of inquiry and responsibility.

The curriculum was designed to provide for an increasingly complex learning setting. Early ex-periences were to be directed toward satisfaction of obvious basic drives and to assure satisfaction of needs; few alternative expectations were offered and cues for response were strongly linked with the child's previous performance and interests. Serious teacher involvement in problem solving, as well as her verbalization and interpretation of results in light of the child's expectation were deemed es-sential to shifting gradually toward the child's self-action and the greater movement of the

teacher's role toward verification of questions to be asked, actions to be taken and answers to be expected.

Important in the program was to be careful con-sideration by the child of specified elements in the total environment with numerous opportunities to compare and contrast various aspects of elements. Multisensory stimulations through handling groups of objects and using them in a variety of settings formed a major base for intellectual development and pre-academic activities.

Teacher orientation was toward recognition and appreciation of the child's changing behavior and ability to command an increasing number of ele-ments in situations. Important was progress in the small steps the teachers identified; they were not to view achievement in terms of perfected skills. Children were to be observed in all activi-ties; questions were to be raised concerning bar-riers and behavior was to be studied. When progress was deemed erratic or grossly deviant from that expected, teachers were to appraise both their im-mediate objectives for the child and their selection of stimuli in the form of materials and activities.

Children were to be provided an environment conducive to their learning physical control and social adaptation and, in the process to develop systematically and maintain a pattern of continuing over-all growth.

REFERENCES

Almy, Millie C. "Children's Experiences Prior to First Grade and Success in Beginning Read-ing." Teachers College Record, Vol. 51 (1950) 392-393.

Argyris, Chris. "Some Propositions About Human Behavior in Organization." Symposium on Preventive and Social Psychiatry, Washington, D.C., U.S. Government Printing Office, 1958

Back, Kurt, "Influence Through Social Communica-tion." Readings in Social Psychology. Guy Swanson, Theodore Newcomb and Eugene Hartley (Eds.). New York, Henry Holt & Co., 1952.

Bales, Robert. Interaction Process Analysis. Cambridge, Addison-Wesley Publishing Co., 1950

Berkowitz, Leonard. "Sharing Leadership in Small Decision-Making Groups." Hare, P., Borgatta, E. and Bales, R. (Eds.). Small Groups. New York, Alfred A. Knopf, 1955.

Bruner, Jerome S. The Process of Education. Cambridge, Mass., Harvard University Press, 1961.

Cleugh, M.F. The Slow Learner. New York, Philosophical Library, 1957.

Crowder, William W. A Study of Out of School Experiences of Selected Second Grade Children with Implications for Revision of the Social Studies Course of Study. Doctor's Thesis, Bloomington, Indiana University, 1958.

Descoeudres, Alice. The Education of Mentally Defective Children. (Translated by E.F. Trowe). New York, D. C. Heath Co., 1928.

Dewey, John. The Child and the Curriculum. Chicago, University of Chicago Press, 1902.

Dollard, John and Miller, Neal E. Personality and Psychotherapy. New York, McGraw-Hill Book Co., Inc., 1950.

Duncan, John. Education of the Ordinary Child. New York, Ronald Press, 1942.

Dunn, Lloyd and Capobianco, Rudolph. "Mental Retardation." Review of Educational Research, 29 (1959) 451-470.

Durrell, Donald D. "Learning Difficulties Among Children of Normal Intelligence." Elementary School Journal, Vol. 55 (1954) 201-208.

Ellis, N.R. "Object-Quality Discrimination Learning Sets in Mental Defectives." Journal of Comparative Physiological Psychology, 51 (1958) 79-81.

Ellis, N.R. and Sloan, W. "Oddity Learning as a Function of Mental Age." Journal of Comparative and Physiological Psychology, 52 (1959) 225-230.

Estrans, Frank and Estrans, Elizabeth. The Child's World: His Social Perception. New York, Putnam's Sons, 1959.

Festinger, Leon, Schacter, Stanley and Back, Kurt. Social Pressures in Informal Groups. New York, Harper and Brothers, 1950.

Frandsen, Arden N. How Children Learn - An Educational Psychology. New York, McGraw-Hill Book Co., 1957.

Fuller, Elizabeth Mechem. What Research Says to to the Teacher About Kindergarten. Washington, D.C., National Education Association, 1961.

Gallagher, James. The Tutoring of Brain-Injured Mentally Retarded Children. Springfield, Ill., Charles C. Thomas, Publisher, 1960.

Girardeau, F.L. and Cantor, G.N. "The Formation of Discrimination Learning Sets in Mongoloid and Normal Children." Journal of Comparative and Physiological Psychology, Vol. 52 (1959), 566-570.

Goldstein, Herbert and Kass, Corinne. "Incidental Learning of Mentally Retarded Children." Journal of American Association on Mental Deficiency, Vol. 66 (1961) 245-249.

Goodlad, John I. "Curriculum: The State of the Field." Review of Educational Research, Vol. 30 (1960) 185-198.

Goodlad, John I. and Anderson, Robert H. The Ungraded Elementary School. New York, Harcourt Brace & Co., 1959.

Harap, H. and Mapes, Charlotte E. "The Learning of Fundamentals in an Arithmetic Activity Program." Elementary School Journal, Vol. 34 (1934) 515-525.

Harlow, H.F. "The Formation of Learning Sets." Psychological Review, Vol. 56 (1949) 51-65.

Havland, C. "Human Learning and Retention." S.S. Stevens (Ed.) Handbook of Experimental Psychology, New York, John Wiley and Sons, Inc., 1951.

Hildreth, Gertrude, "Puzzle-Solving With and Without Understanding." Journal of Educational Psychology. Vol. 33 (1942) 595-604.

Hilgard, E.R. Theories of Learning. New York, Appleton-Century-Crofts, Inc., (2nd Edition) 1956.

Holland, James G. "Teaching Machines: An Application of Principles from the Laboratory." A.A. Lumsdaine and Robert Glaser (Eds.) Teaching Machines and Programmed Learning. Washington, D.C., National Education Association, 1960.

House, Betty J. and Zeaman, David. "Visual Discrimination Learning and Intelligence in Defectives of Low Mental Age." American Journal of Mental Deficiency, Vol. 65 (1960) 51-58.

Hunt, J. McV. Intelligence and Experience. New York, The Ronald Press, 1961.

Ingram, Christine P. Education of the Slow Learning Child. New York. The Ronald Press, 1953.

Inhelder, B. "Developmental Psychology." Annual Review of Psychology, P. Farnsworth and G. McNemar (Eds.) Palo Alto, California, Annual Reviews Inc., 1957.

Inskeep, Annie D. Teaching Dull and Retarded Children. New York, Macmillan Co., 1926.

Iscoe, Ira and Giller, Donald. "Areas of Concept Formation in the Mentally Retarded." American Journal of Mental Deficiency, Vol. 64 (1959) 112-116.

Jennings, Helen. "Leadership and Sociometric Choice." Swanson, G., Newcomb, T. and Hartley, E. (Eds.) Readings in Social Psychology, New York, Henry Holt & Co., 1952.

Kaya, Esin. "A Curricular Sequence Based on Psychological Processes." Exceptional Children, Vol. 27 (1961) 425-428; 435.

Kelley, Harold and Thibaut, John. "Experimental Studies of Group Problem Solving and Process." Gardner Lindsey (Ed.) Handbook of Social Psychology, Cambridge, Addison-Wesley Publishing Co., 1954.

Kirk, Samuel A. Early Education of the Mentally Retarded; An Experimental Study. Urbana, Illinois, University of Illinois Press, 1958.

Kirk, Samuel and Johnson, G.O. Educating the Retarded Child. Boston, Houghton-Mifflin Co., 1951.

Langford, Louise M. Guidance of the Young Child. New York, John Wiley and Sons, Inc., 1960.

Leavitt, Hazel M. Teaching the Kindergarten Child. New York, Harcourt, Brace and Co., 1958.

Lewin, Kurt and Grabbe, Paul. "Conduct, Knowledge and Acceptance of New Values." Journal of Social Issues, I (1945) 53-64.

Lloyd, Frances. Educating the Sub-Normal Child. New York, Philosophical Library, 1953.

Maritain, Jacques. Education At the Crossroads. New Haven, Yale University Press, 1957.

Martens, Elise H. Curriculum Adjustment for the Mentally Retarded. U.S. Office of Education Bulletin, Washington, D.C., Government Printing Office, 1950.

Mowrer, O. Hobart. Learning Theory and the Symbolic Process. New York, John Wiley and Sons, Inc., 1960.

Nissen, Henry W. and others. "Effects of Restricted Opportunity for Tactual, Kinesthetic and Manipulative Experience on the Behavior of a Chimpanzee." American Journal of Psychology, Vol. 64 (1951) 485-507.

Olmstead, Michael S. The Small Group. New York, Random House, 1959.

Padilla, S.G. "Further Studies on Delayed Pecking of Chicks." Journal of Comparative Psychology, Vol. 20 (1935) 413-443.

Piaget, Jean. Comments on Vygotsky's Critical Remarks Concerning the "Language and Thought of the Child" and " Judgment and Reasoning in the Child." Mass. Institute of Technology, The MIT Press, 1962.

Piaget, Jean. Psychology of Intelligence. (Translated by M. Piercy and D.E. Berlyne). London, Routledge & Kegan Paul, 1947.

Piaget, Jean. The Origin of Intelligence in Children. New York, International Universities Press, 1952.

Read, Katherine H. The Nursery School: A Human Relationships Laboratory. Philadelphia, W.B. Saunders Co., 1955.

Riesen, A.H. "The Development of Visual Perception in Man and Chimpanzee." Science, Vol. 106 (1947) 107-108.

Sharp, George. Curriculum Development as Re-education of the Teacher. New York, Bureau of Publications, Teachers College, Columbia University, 1951.

Sheehy, Emma D. The Fives and Sixes Go to School. New York, Henry Holt & Co., 1954.

Skinner, Burrhus F. Science and Human Behavior. New York, Macmillan Co., 1958.

Skinner, B.F. "The Science of Learning and the Art of Teaching." Harvard Educational Review, Vol. 24, (1954) 99-113.

Smith, B.O., Stanley, W.O. and Shores, J.H. Fundamentals of Curriculum Development. Yonkers-on-Hudson, N.Y., 1957.

Smith, Marion F. Teaching the Slow Learning Child. New York, Harper and Brothers, 1954.

Stevens, Godfrey. "An Analysis of Objectives for Education of Retarded Children." Journal of American Association on Mental Deficiency, Vol. 63 (1958) 225-235.

Stratemeyer, Florence B., Forkner, Hamden L., McKim, Margaret G., and Passow, A. Harry. Developing a Curriculum for Modern Living. New York, Bureau of Publications, Teachers College, Columbia University, 1957.

Strauss, Alfred A. and Lehtinen, Laura. Psycho-pathology and Education of the Brain Injured Child. Vol. I, New York, Grune and Stratton, 1947.

Wallin, J.E. Wallace. Education of Mentally Handicapped Children. New York, Harper and Brothers, 1955.

Weber, Max and Traeltsch, Ernst. The Theory of Social and Economic Organization. Talcot Parsons (Ed.) New York, Oxford University Press, 1947.

Wrightstone, J.W. "Evaluation of the Experiment with the Activity Program in the New York City Elementary Schools." Journal of Educational Research, Vol. 38 (1944) 252-257.

CHAPTER 2

THE CURRICULUM GUIDE AND ITS PROGRAMMING

INTRODUCTION

The Curriculum Guide developed for use in the experimental classes contained one hundred and ninety items, each with a five point descriptive scale. The scales referred to details of development in intellectual, creative and imaginative, social, emotional, manipulative, motor, and self-help areas. They constituted a set of short-range goals toward which the teachers worked in the mediating preschool experiences, and which contributed in turn to the attainment of long-range objectives. For the teachers of the experimental classes, the Guide served two purposes, a) for observing and rating the behavior of the preschool children, and b) for program planning and evaluation.

From their day to day use of the five point scale, the teachers were enabled to delineate gradations of behavior within each level of the Curriculum Guide. These intermediate steps were summarized in the Programming which is defined here as a series of readiness activities leading to continually more complex behavior. In addition, the original five-point descriptive scales were revised and augmented over the four years of experimental class work. The Guide would again be subject to revision for any extension of its use, since the items and the scale describing them would be responsive to changes in any of the four variables considered by the curriculum study group, i.e., the school setting, the available materials and experiences, the children in the classes, and the teachers.

This chapter includes descriptions of the plan and use of both the Curriculum Guide and the Programmed Guide, the text of the revised five-point Guide, and the text of the programming.

THE CURRICULUM GUIDE AS A RATING FORM

Although the Guide was changed with each year of teacher experience, the form first completed and ready for use early in the second year (1958-59) of the preschool was retained as the rating form until the end of experimental classwork in June, 1961. Thus it was possible to collect comparable second-year ratings of children completing the preschool work in 1959, 1960, and 1961, and first-year ratings for children comprising the younger groups in 1958-59 and 1959-60. The latter two groups became the older groups of 1960 and 1961. In Chapter VI of the present report, these composite teacher ratings are presented and discussed. The present section is devoted to a discussion of the rating form itself.

In working out the five-point scale, gradations of performance for the hundred and ninety items of the original guide were described on the basis of observed behavior of children enrolled in the first preschool groups (the younger and older classes of 1957-58). The resulting descriptive tool made it possible to mark the position of an individual child, with respect to any item, on a readiness scale which functioned as a set of intermediate goals. Thus, consideration was directed toward one of five acceptable levels of competence in the behaviors teachers thought might be developed in the preschool, rather than toward the usual dichotomous satisfactory-unsatisfactory base. The competence level commonly considered satisfactory for children of the same chronological age is represented by step five on the descriptive scale.

A sample is included here to illustrate the phrasing of the levels and to show the manner in which the scale facilitated recording. The preschool goal of this item was development of the eye-hand coordination involved in <u>coloring</u> within an outlined area.

The five levels of the curriculum item appeared as follows:

1	2	3	4	5
holding for use	scribbling	awareness of space	ability to stay within design	conformity to design

In this item, as in all others, the sequence indicated in levels 1, 2, 3 and 4 was seen to occur repeatedly in the pilot classes. That is, the child who scribbled held the crayon; the child who was aware of the space could also hold the crayon and scribble, and so on. It was the pattern observed in the subjects of the present study and provided a workable sequence for planning and for teaching.

The descriptive scales provided teachers with an objective measure of pupil performance and a breakdown of successive steps in the learning of a task. The child who was performing at any of the first four levels was doing something highly relevant to performance at level five. Though far from competent in conformity to design, e.g. coloring within the outlines of a pictured apple, he could do something and was ready for something more. In the five-point descriptions were clues to the nature of the "something more" and suggested situations which would facilitate performance one step nearer the eventual goal. The assessments, three each year, on the Guide ensured teacher use of the child's current status for curriculum planning.

Comparison of individual ratings with composite class ratings enabled the teachers to measure classroom efficiency and to identify program gaps. If a child's rating in an activity area remained constant over time, the teacher sought to identify the child's unsolved difficulty. However, if a similar lag was observed in the entire class, the problem might represent the teacher's problem in programming. Similarly, a marked acceleration of individual growth in one area was deemed idiosyncratic, whereas such a concentration of group gains would tend to indicate skewed programming.

THE CURRICULUM GUIDE AS BASE FOR PROGRAMMING

The five descriptive levels of the Curriculum Guide were used as the base of a second set of guidelines, the programmed curriculum items or the behavior range at each level. The revised Guide provided the skeleton for the expanded form, since the teachers wished to base the extension on the corrected and revised rating summary. Each expansion includes:

(a) the five levels of the Curriculum Guide item to which the item referred and on which the teacher focused;
(b) the definition of the item: behavior under observation;
(c) samples of behavior observed at each level
(d) the statement of the predictable or internalized behavior which seemed essential at each level;
(e) a summary of activities based on the element (d) which were helpful in establishing readiness for behavior at the next level;

It is suspected that the readiness activities (e), which are not at present arranged in any sequential order, might in their turn yield to an ordering process similar to that of the original five levels. They, too, are based on observations which would need checking on additional subjects. At present, the Programmed Guide is at the same stage of development as was the basic Curriculum Guide in early 1958.

The scheme of the programming is designed to help with specific planning for individual development and for group experiences. Behavior assessed or rated at any given level of a Guide item contains the element needed for the experiences shown in the same vertical column. With opportunity to try the experiences, children seemed to develop the competency indicated for the next level.

The item on coloring already described in connection with rating will serve to illustrate the amplified stages noted above. The five-point scale of the Guide item is presented first; (a); (b) and (c), the rating base, give information relative to assessment of the child; (d) and (e) are descriptive of the programming:

E 3. COLORING

(a) The five levels of the curriculum item:

1	2	3	4	5
holding for use	scribbling	awareness of space	ability to stay within design	conformity to design

THE RATING BASE

(b) <u>Definition - process of interest to the teacher</u>

The manipulation of crayons, with attention to the eye-hand coordination involved in discerning a space and coloring within the lines bounding that space.

(c) <u>Details of behavior observed at each level</u>

1	2	3	4	5
Child picked up crayons, held them; watched others using them.	Child used crayon to make marks, scribbled at random; seemed unaware of design.	Child scribbled or marked over design, crossing outlines but staying in the general area.	Child stayed within area, usually well within.	Child colored design with fair accuracy. Crossing a boundary was accidental..

THE PROGRAMMING

(d) <u>Element of behavior common to activity at each level</u>

holds crayon	makes marks	perceives space	limits own marks	limits marks with respect to boundaries

(e) <u>Teaching procedures which utilize element (d) and move toward behavior at next level.</u>

Verbal attention to ways of holding crayon. Direct help in making marks with crayon.	Verbal attention to child's marks, their location, and child's movements. Direct help in staying near dotted line. Cutout guides if indicated.	Discussion and comparison of drawings: verbal attention to areas covered, and to location of scribbles. Revisions.	Narrative coloring. Discussion of pictures on basis of points 1, 2, 3 and 4.	Retracing outline after coloring. Discussion and evaluation by children.

For this item, as for several other items in which teachers felt that the children needed to see an unbroken sequence, such as the process of coloring a picture, the teachers participated in the coloring, calling attention of individual children to helpful techniques. These were, for coloring an outline drawing: (1) choosing colors or kinds of crayons; (2) tracing the lines of the design with the crayon; (3) coloring with smooth, light, parallel strokes; and (4) calling attention to the result by <u>retracing</u> outlines. The teacher also performed step (2) tracing for children until they showed competence in staying within the outline. Tracing was viewed as a non-verbal way of calling attention to the outline.

(Note: The complete text of this item can be found in the Programmed Guide; it has been abbreviated here to show the vertical arrangement of the stages.)

In any programmed item, the child who learned to handle all parts of a column was ordinarily already functioning at the next level. For example, if he could manage the items in column one, he had internalized the behavior held essential for functioning at level two. The various activities appeared to enable the child to reassess the situation and to handle it in a more complex manner. From teacher observation and subsequent study, it was concluded that the elements of behavior were cumulative, but apparently <u>rearranged</u> at each level, not simply added together.

Here, again, it would seem necessary to check use of the programmed items with additional groups of children. Use of successive small steps which took advantage of successive readinesses was deemed to be one way of ensuring that a child need not be retained, either actually or in the teacher's perception, by needless repetition of behavior at any one level. It also served to prevent a rating of "unready" for activity with a consequent well-meaning restriction of opportunity. Children in the experimental classes had opportunities to try out many processes and were shown successions or groups of related processes. The one kind of activity which was restricted or redirected, as often as teachers were able to do it, was repetition of a thing already learned. The learned detail, if repeated, was made a contributing part of a more complex activity or situation.

The two curriculum adjuncts included in the present section, the Guide and its programmed form, arranged according to areas of development, were sources of information about the preschool children and literally guides to activity selection. Both are in analytical form, and are designed to supplement a curriculum sequence, not to serve as a curriculum sequence. In the preschool classes, prearranged experience settings determined the activities which were to be presented. Each setting was a composite of elements which would be mastered by individual children at individual rates of learning. The activities were natural composites or relationships mentioned in the preceding paragraph. Planned experiences cut across curriculum areas, furthering goals of several kinds for children at different stages of growth. Similarly, single goals, such as manipulation of crayons, could be pursued in a number of different experience settings.

In Chapter III, describing the action settings, interwoven and interdependent goals can be traced and the provisions to accommodate individual learnings noted. The curriculum design, with its child ratings, program planning and evaluation, and individualized motivation is complex only in the description. In fact, the experience or action setting which promoted pupil learnings at different levels also made possible assessments of situations and individuals. It would have been an endless task, to test children separately on each item of the guide, or even to present situations in which the items were considered singly. An experience setting, since it was a conceptual whole, was also a setting which enabled teachers to evaluate individual performances in several areas at once. The context of the situation made memory of details no problem. Coloring a picture of an apple was not an isolated exercise: it was a review or summary of a sequence which included a shopping trip, a party, conversation periods, three-dimensional representation with clay or papier mache, painting of the modeled apples, and a chalk-talk summary by a teacher. Ordinarily, an eye-hand project such as this one was reported in the text and illustrations of the weekly class newsletter; it could also be a larger "news item" picture for bulletin posting or for carrying home. The tinting of an apple, in this context, was thus a prereading and pre-writing experience with symbols. The teachers, for rating purposes of the illustrative item, had a visible record of performance levels. They also had ratings for other items in intellectual and social areas. The efficiency of the descriptive scale, the implied methodology, and the fact that the Project teachers found it possible to construct situations which produced any particular results they wanted, would seem to indicate that further study of this kind of planning and evaluation would be productive.

The Curriculum Guide and the Guide's Rating Base and Programming which constitute the larger part of this chapter are presented with the caution that they are keys to teacher planning and teacher procedures, but not in themselves a course of study. They summarize details which are the teacher's responsibility, not details arranged for children's learning.

THE CURRICULUM GUIDE

REVISED FORM

A. INTELLECTUAL DEVELOPMENT

	1	2	3	4	5
1. LISTENING TO ORAL LANGUAGE	Listens for directions	Pays attention to oral language with supportive action	Responds to simple oral direction	Responds to a series of familiar oral directions	Can remember and carry an oral message
2. USING BOOKS	Listening while story is read	Selecting story to be read	Repeats words with teacher	Selects words by sight	Ready for reading
3. HANDLING OF BOOKS	Not destroying	Exploration with manipulation	Interest in pictures	Turning pages in anticipation	Use of books as a resource
4. PARTICIPATION IN STRUCTURE OR GROUP	Unconcern	Shows evidence attention in some way	Generally joins group	Listening with participation	Listening with anticipation
a. music at piano					
b. records					
c. story with props					
d. story					
5. SINGING	Evidence of rhythm	Vocalization with rhythm	Vocalization with rhythm and tune	Rhythm, tune, and pitch	Sings song with rhythm, tune, and pitch
6. VISUAL DISCRIMINATION	Diffuse visual activity	Can focus on motion	Can focus on something still	Recognition of an object	Symbolic behavior
7. AUDITORY DISCRIMINATION	Awareness of sound	Focusing on certain sounds	Imitates sound	Identifies common sounds (without looking)	Responds to patterns of sound
8. TACTILE DISCRIMINATION	Interest in touching	Explores and manipulates dry solids	Explores and manipulates wet materials	Discriminates shapes, size and texture with supportive cues	Discriminates shapes, size and texture without supportive cues

A. INTELLECTUAL DEVELOPMENT (Cont.)

	1	2	3	4	5
9. TASTE DISCRIMINATION	Interest in taste	Awareness of gross difference in taste	Interest in experimenting with taste	Identifying taste with supportive cues	Identifying taste without supportive cues
10. SMELL DISCRIMINATION	Interest in smell	Awareness of gross difference in smell	Interest in experimenting with smell	Identifying smell with supportive cues	Identifying smell without supportive cues
11. COLOR RECOGNITION					
a. concept	Interest in color	Interest in one color	Matching	Selection for pattern	Appropriate selection for pattern
b. language	Association of language symbol with color	Matching	Selecting color on request	Naming primary color	Naming shades - pastels
12. MATCHING	Participation in activity	Recognition and awareness	Putting together	Selecting likes at random	Generalizing discrimination
a. shapes objects					
geometric shapes					
b. size: coins					
c. primary colors					
d. numbers 1 - 5					
pictured groups					
symbols					
13. QUANTITY					
a. numbers	One versus many	One versus two	Counting	Grouping	Regrouping

A. INTELLECTUAL DEVELOPMENT (Cont.)

	1	2	3	4	5
13. QUANTITY (Cont.)					
b. size	Little versus big	Gross assortment by size	Matching	Series	Patterns
c. time	Now	After while versus tomorrow	Activity schedule	Activity in relation to clock position	Awareness of telling time
14. TIME CONCEPT	Apparent lack of awareness	Evidence of focus	Association with cue	Ability to anticipate and wait	Can plan for future
15. NATURE STUDY					
a. plants	Exploration and interest	Awareness of effects	Interest in growth	Imitation in care	Empathy for
b. animals	Exploration and interest	Notice of reaction	Imitation in caring for	Empathy for	Independent, spontaneous care
c. weather	Exploration and interest	Differentiation and recognition of	Awareness of ef-	Question and discussion re weather	Association of experience
16. PROBLEM SOLVING	Sees problem and withdraws	Asks for help or attracts attention without trying	Random trial and error	Trial and error based on previous experiences	Assesses situation before moving and acting
17. SELF-CONCEPT OR AUTONOMY	Realization of external objects	Can go to get	Refuse to get	Can make a	Can assess
18. OBEYING RULES	Unaware that rules exist	Aware of given rules but non-conforming	Tries to conform; needs support	Conforming to usual rules	Acceptance and flexibility in conforming

B. IMAGINATION AND CREATIVE EXPRESSION

	1	2	3	4	5
	Interest at a distance	Touching & Exploration	Use of materials in imitation of simple pattern	Experimentation & elaboration	Imaginative & creative use of available materials
1. SAND PLAY					

B. IMAGINATION AND CREATIVE EXPRESSION (Cont.)

	1	2	3	4	5
	Interest at a distance	Exploration	Imitation	Enjoyment and ease in activity	Participates with originality
2. WATER PLAY					
a. water painting					
b. soap suds					
c. fishing					
d. swimming					
e. bubbles					
f. washing clothes, dishes, dolls					
3. DRAWING					
4. PAINTING					
5. FINGER PAINTING					
6. CLAY					
7. DRAMATIC EXPRESSION					
a. individual					
b. group dramatic play					
c. structured dramatic play					
d. puppetry					
8. CREATIVE RHYTHMS					
a. individual					
b. group					

B. IMAGINATION AND CREATIVE EXPRESSION (Cont.)

	1	2	3	4	5
8. CREATIVE RHYTHMS (Cont.)					
c. structured					
9. RHYTHM BAND					

C. SOCIAL DEVELOPMENT

	1	2	3	4	5
1. RELATEDNESS TO CHILDREN	Apparently not interested in others	Awareness and interest in others	Moving toward some individual	Establishment of a definite relationship	Give and take relationship with the group
2. RELATEDNESS TO ADULTS	Apparently not interested in adult(s)	Awareness and interest in adult(s)	Moving toward some adult(s)	Establishment of a definite relationship	At ease with most adults
3. SHARING	Passive release	Defending or resisting release	Release with adult encouragement	Releases voluntarily	Initiates or agrees to cooperative use
4. CONSIDERATION OF OTHERS	Pre-occupation with self	Consideration upon awareness of advantages	Empathizing with others	Consideration of friends	Consideration of people in general (justice)
5. RECEIVING HELP	Passivity	Resistance	Expression of need	Selecting optimum source	Successful method of obtaining
6. RESPECTING PROPERTY RIGHTS	Claims ownership indiscriminately. Unaware that rules exist	Identification of own possessions. Aware of given rules but non-conforming	Recognition of others' possessions. Tries to conform; needs support	Respects other's ownership with reminders. Conforming to routine rules	Respects own and other's property. Acceptance of explained changes in rules
7. EXPRESSIONS					
a. adults	Apparently unaware of formal expression	Apparently aware of formal expression	Prompted or imitative expression	Initiates expression in usual situations	Appropriate independent use of expression in a variety of situations
please					
thank you					

C. SOCIAL DEVELOPMENT (Cont.)

	1 Apparently unaware of formal expression	2 Apparently aware of formal expression	3 Prompted or imitative expression	4 Initiates expression in usual situations	5 Appropriate independent use of expression in a variety of situations
7. EXPRESSIONS (Cont.)					
a. adults (Cont.)					
you are welcome					
apology					
greeting					
offering					
b. children					
please					
thank you					
you are welcome					
apology					
greeting					
offering					
8. JUICE TIME					
a. attitude	Refuses to join in juice time	Will approach the table at juice time	Will sit in group with reminders	Will sit with the group	Anticipates, apparently enjoys; looks forward to juice time
b. participation	Helps in single tasks	Carries, passes solids in bowls	Pours	Suggests a way to help	Socially aware of processes (setting table, etc.)
9. PREPARING FOOD	One-step (instant drink)	One-step cooking (jello)	Simple multiple step process	Sandwiches	Preparation of menu and food for a simple meal

C. SOCIAL DEVELOPMENT (Cont.)

	1	2	3	4	5
10. GROUP GAMES	Does not participate	With adult	With adult and children	With one child	With children
11. TRIPS					
a. participation	Willingness to go	Conforms to routines with reminders	Conforms to routine	Accepts responsibility in routine child expects	Conforms to flexible schedule
b. traffic safety	Stopping at curb before crossing	Response to traffic light	Crossing street without light	Anticipation of cars turning corners	Assessing street situation and crossing safely
c. planning	Staying on sidewalk on the block	Interest in planning	Noting landmarks along planned route	Recalling and recognizing landmarks	Planning route, reaching destination and return

D. EMOTIONAL DEVELOPMENT

	1	2	3	4	5
	General unresponsiveness	Evidence of internal response	Evidence of open response	Expansion and experimentation with open response	Can express emotion appropriately
a. contentment					
b. pleasure					
c. joy					
d. love					
e. compassion					
f. grief					
g. displeasure					
h. anger					
i. hatred					

E. MANIPULATIVE DEVELOPMENT

	1	2	3	4	5
1. CUTTING	Two hands on scissors	One hand random snipping	One hand, series of related cutting	One hand, following line, more or less	Cutting out
a. teacher holding paper					
b. independent with paper					
2. DRAWING	Exploration	Designs	Representation	Imitating others	Imitating other's drawing
3. COLORING	Holding for use	Scribbling	Awareness of space	Ability to stay within design	Conformity to design
4. FINGER PAINTING	Willingness	Smearing (exploring boundaries of paper)	Trial and error in use of body	Trial and error design	Deliberate purposeful design
5. CLAY, DOUGH PLASTICENE	Lack of interest	Touching and exploring	Patting, rolling, squeezing	Imitative use of material	Participation with originality
6. PASTING	Willingness	Spreading randomly	Spreading one side only	Spreading and turning over to stick	Pasting on specific area
7. MANIPULATION OF PAPER	Interest at a distance	Exploration	Imitation	Enjoyment and ease in activity	Initiation for expressed purpose
a. folding					
b. rolling					
c. wrapping					
8. STRING, YARN, RIBBON					
a. winding					
b. rolling					
c. sewing					

E. MANIPULATIVE DEVELOPMENT (Cont.)

	1	2	3	4	5
9. HAMMERING	Exploration	Attention to hammer boards	Hitting pegs of hammer board	Inserting and hammering nails	Joining wood with nails
10. SAWING	Exploration	Holding saw directly: partial cut	Cutting: interest in random pieces	Cutting piece for use, with help	Cutting piece for use in construction
11. USING SCREW DRIVER	Exploration	Trial and error use of tool	Random screwing, unscrewing	Screwing, unscrewing with direction	Using to place screws
12. BEAD STRINGING	Large threaded beads	Large kindergarten beads, large needle	Small kindergarten beads, large needle	Commercial beads (1/4" - 1/2"), small needle	Beads on flexible wire
13. PEGS	Exploration	Random activity large pegs	Follows direction - large pegs	Follows direction - small pegs	Purposeful design
14. CARS, TRUCKS, TRAINS (toys)	Watching and carrying	Rolling and watching wheels	Making it go	Dramatic play	Dramatic play using other materials
15. TRAINS AND TRACKS	Exploration	Putting pieces of track together	Running train on straight track	Joining tracks for functional use	Dramatic play using other materials
16. BLOCK BUILDING	Handles, carries, piles in irregular masses	Beginning construction and simple designs	Further development of patterns, techniques of handling	Dramatic representation (house)	Attempts to reproduce actual structure, careful symmetry
17. TINKER TOYS	Exploration and interest	Random with success (manipulative)	Spontaneous design	Imitating purposeful design	Creative purposeful design
18. TOPS	Interest at a distance	Exploration	Trial and error use of top	Imitation	Enjoyment and ease in activity
19. PUZZLES	Exploration and interest	Physical trial and error	Following guide lines	Thoughtful trial and error	Pre-placement recognition
a. coordination board					

E. MANIPULATIVE DEVELOPMENT (Cont.)

19. PUZZLES (Cont.)	1 Exploration and interest	2 Physical trial and error	3 Following guide lines	4 Thoughtful trial and error	5 Pre-placement recognition
b. two piece					
c. three piece					
d. five piece or more					
e. non-insert					

F. MOTOR DEVELOPMENT

	1 Evidence of ability	2 Functional though awkward motion	3 Evidence of control	4 Sureness of movement	5 Purposeful and appropriate use of mode
1. WALKING					
2. RUNNING					
3. MARCHING					
4. JUMPING					
5. HOPPING					
6. SKIPPING					
7. DANCING					
8. STAIRS					
a. climbing	Going up with assistance, two feet per tread	Up holding rail, two feet per tread	Up without holding on, two feet per tread	Up with assistance or holding on, one foot per tread	Up without holding on, one foot per tread
b. descending	Going down with assistance, two feet per tread	Down holding rail, two feet per tread	Down with assistance, one foot per tread	Down holding rail, one foot per tread	Down without holding on, one foot per tread

F. MOTOR DEVELOPMENT

	1	2	3	4	5
9. JUMPING ROPE	Interest in	Attempts to jump	Jumps from standing position	Runs and jumps into moving rope	Jumps without concern about rope
10. SLIDING	Interest	Someone with child	Someone helping	Someone near	Independently
11. BALL PLAYING	Trapping	Stand still, hands ready for bounced ball	Moving, hands reach for ball bounced	Success catching ball on the fly	Catching undirected ball
a. catching large ball					
small ball					
b. throwing large ball	Release	Proximate release with direction	Distant release	Distant release with direction	Moving and throwing
small ball					
12. WAGON	Interest	Riding in while someone pulls	Pulls empty wagon	Pulls wagon and someone or something	Push wagon with one foot
13. TRICYCLE	Child's pushing	Child sitting on it	Someone pushing	Using his feet	Independently
14. TRACTOR					
15. SCOOTER	Interest	Willingness to try with support	Standing on while pushed	Success with making scooter go, one foot	Using scooter for ride with two feet
16. CARS, TRUCKS, TRAINS (carriers)	Watching in motion	Pushing	Getting on	Getting on and moving	Riding somewhere
17. MUSICAL INSTRUMENTS	Exploration for sound	Pounding (e.g. drum)	Shaking(e.g. bells)	Striking 2 hands together	Holding with 1 hand, striking with other
18. PIANO PLAYING	Banging	Differentiation of loud and soft	Singing while playing	Sings tune while playing	Piano and singing in tune and rhythm

G. SELF HELP

1. DRESSING	1 Dependence	2 Awareness, willingness, interest	3 Helping Adult	4 Independence with direction	5 Independence
a. buttoning					
unbuttoning					
b. snaps					
c. zipper up					
down					
starts jacket zipper					
d. knots tying					
untying					
e. bows tying					
untying					
f. hat on					
off					
g. boots on					
off					
h. shoes on					
off					

G. SELF HELP (Cont.)

1. DRESSING (Cont.)	1 Dependence	2 Awareness, willing-ness, interest	3 Helping Adult	4 Independence with direction	5 Independence
i. socks on					
off					
j. mittens on					
off					
k. gloves on					
off					
l. open-front garments on					
off					
m. slipover garments on					
off					
n. dress on					
off					
o. pants on					
off					
p. snowpants on					
off					

G. SELF HELP (Cont.)

	1	2	3	4	5
1. DRESSING (Cont.)	Dependence	Awareness, willingness, interest	Helping Adult	Independence with direction	Independence
q. scarf on					
off					
2. HAND WASHING	Exploration, dabbling	Helping adult	Washing palms	Washing whole hand	Consideration of clothing and independence
3. TOILET EDUCATION	Needs reminding	Knows when and asks for help	Knows when and partially independent	Knows when and does it	Comfortably conforming to group schedule
4. JUICE TIME	Dependence	Awareness, willingness, interest	Helping adult	Independence with direction	Independence
a. setting table					
b. pouring juice					
c. passing crackers					
d. helping self to more food					
e. cleaning table					
f. washing table					
g. washing dishes					
h. drying dishes					
i. putting dishes away					

G. SELF HELP (Cont.)

	1	2	3	4	5
5. SKILLS					
a. using spoon	Interest in self feeding	Finger feeding	semi-solid in spoon	Liquid in spoon	Solid in spoon
b. using fork	Interest in using fork	Using fork like a spoon	Using fork with ease	Cutting with fork	Using fork appropriately
c. using knife	Interest in using knife	Spreading with knife	Cutting with knife	Using knife and fork together	Using knife efficiently
d. drinking	Can drink with help	Can drink from cup with occasional spills	Drinks independently	Can eat and drink	Drinks, eats, talks
6. APPEARANCE					
a. combing hair	Dependence	Awareness, willingness, interest	Helping adult	Independence with direction	Independence
b. brushing teeth					
c. wiping nose					
7. CARE OF CLOTHING					
a. hanging up clothing	Dependence	Awareness, willingness, interest	Helping adult	Independence with direction	Independence
b. placing over-shoes					
8. HOUSEKEEPING ACTIVITIES					
a. putting toys away					
b. opening doors					
c. clean-up after activity					

G. SELF HELP (Cont.)

	1 Dependence	2 Awareness	3 Accepts and follows advice	4 Usually responsible	5 Responsible for own safety
9. SAFETY					
a. in classroom					
avoidance of sharp instruments					
with hot water					
on stairs					
holding on to bannisters					
protection of head from bumps					
b. on playground					
sliding					
swinging					
see-sawing					
climbing					
sandbox play					
wheel toys					
10. INDEPENDENT TRAVEL (building)	Across hall to washroom	Return to classroom	Building entrance to classroom	Classroom to known destination	Go and return

1.   LISTENING TO ORAL LANGUAGE
RATING

THE FIVE LEVELS OF THE CURRICULUM ITEM

1. listens for directions	2. pays attention to oral language with supportive action	3. responds to a simple oral direction	4. responds to a series of familiar oral directions	5. can remember and carry an oral message

DEFINITION OF THE TERM: BEHAVIOR UNDER OBSERVATION

The child's attention to oral language as indicated by his responses. The item includes, besides the response to direct instructions in a situation (e.g. one involving safety), attention, comprehension, and response to planning situations, conversation periods, and activity periods. The item does not rate obedience, which is discussed in another section. That is, a negative answer was a possible response, in this particular item.

DESCRIPTION OF BEHAVIOR OBSERVED AT EACH LEVEL

Child listened for directions; responded orally or with a smile, but did not act in accord with language he listened to, or give relevant oral response.	Child listened to directions; responded when shown or helped with the implied action. This included help with oral responses.	Child listened to, understood, and acted upon a single direction or suggestion, or answered a single question.	Child acted in accord with a language paragraph, dealing with known contexts (e.g. "It is time to clean up the room. As soon as you have put away your things, you may go to the bathroom and wash up, then come and help with tables for juice.")	Child remembered and delivered an oral message to another child or teacher, to the secretary in the office or to his mother at home.

PROGRAMMING

PREDICTABLE (INTERNALIZED) BEHAVIOR USED IN PROGRAMMING FOR NEXT LEVEL

Attends to spoken language.	Understands combination of oral and action language.	Understands language for a single idea, without action cues.	Understands language for several related ideas.	Remembers another's language and relays it to a third person.

TEACHING PROCEDURES TO ESTABLISH READINESS FOR NEXT LEVEL

Teacher use of language a) to give suggestions to group, b) to describe child's on-going activity, c) to review activities which had been planned and described according to a) and b). Teacher support of child in group situation (a,b). Teacher help with imitative language.	Verbal attention to steps in daily routine and choosing activities. Verbal emphasis in help given to child, (e.g. It is time to wash your hands. Come, I'll go with you and help you.) Gradual withdrawal of physical cues, (e.g. Can you go by yourself this time? I'll come along in a minute.)	Elaboration of simple familiar ideas to complex series. (e.g. "Can you wash by yourself? Be sure to use soap and to rinse your hands. Can you reach the towels? Wipe your hands carefully. Then come back and let me see your hands." ... "Mm, you did use soap. Your hands smell clean, and they are dried very nicely.") Group planning, discussion of familiar sequences.	Expansion of paragraph language to include planning of new activities. (e.g. We are going to make pictures of fire engines. Here are red trucks, firemen, bells and hoses. We'll paste the truck first, like this. Where do the firemen go?) Conversation, evaluation of direction-following. Individual help to child, followed by request that he help another. Using child as messenger in classroom, then to bathroom.	Extension of message idea to following areas: a) longer message in classroom, b) longer message to office, c) longer message home. Request for oral response. Telling child what response will probably be: a) one possibility, b) one of two possibilities, c) open-ended question.

2. USING BOOKS

RATING

THE FIVE LEVELS OF THE CURRICULUM ITEM

1. listening while story is read	2. selecting story to be read	3. repeats words after teacher	4. selects words by sight	5. ready for reading

DEFINITION OF THE TERM: BEHAVIOR UNDER OBSERVATION

The child's use of books as a language resource. Noted were responses of a child to stories read in a group or in one-to-one situations with a teacher. (This structure enabled a rating on story-response for children with whom the group structure was unproductive.)

DESCRIPTION OF BEHAVIOR OBSERVED AT EACH LEVEL

Child listened to story, looked at illustrations and helped turn pages.	Child chose book, asked teacher to read it for him.	Child repeated phrases and sentences, supplied ends of sentences, rhyming words, concluding sentence.	Child identified one or more words in a text; picked out alphabet forms.	Child matched page-turning to actual text. Asked teacher to write sentences, words, letters on board; tried to copy letters, words; identified printed words in meaningful and/or familiar contexts.

PROGRAMMING

PREDICTABLE (INTERNALIZED) BEHAVIOR USED IN PROGRAMMING FOR NEXT LEVEL

Watches while another uses book.	Designates book to be used (chooses content)	Notices and repeats spoken symbols.	Notices and points out visual symbols.	Uses verbal and visual symbols as routes to content.

TEACHING PROCEDURES TO ESTABLISH READINESS FOR NEXT LEVEL

Use of books here was directed toward selection for content. The indicated readiness-for-reading procedures are not drill work, but activity used unobtrusively. The teacher notes responses of the particular child or children who show evidence of readiness.

Choosing book: verbal attention to reasons for selection: size; illustrations; relatedness to other activities; content. Verbal attention to selections of children: "You like these big books with the real things in them." "You must like pictures of school children because you choose this book so often." "John likes the insect book. He is interested in knowing all about them."	Verbal attention to choices. Gradual emphasis on content — what the whole book is about, not limited to the separate pages or illustrations. Use of symbols: picture news about favorite books such as copying front cover on board, copying title of book. Supplementary news sentences and pictures.	Attention to word symbols. a) Pointing to a high-interest word, as sh-h-h, each time it occurs. b) Moving finger and pausing at each word in a high-interest sentence. c) Printing high-interest word or sentence on board and illustrating.	Same as 3, gradually enlarging the noticing vocabulary. Giving child opportunity to copy short word, sentence. (See item 12a3, REPRESENTATION) Providing experiences with alphabet blocks, cutout letters.	Individual work in story reading and music setting. Repetition of situation and related language, rather than drill on words.

3. HANDLING OF BOOKS

RATING

THE FIVE LEVELS OF THE CURRICULUM ITEM

1. not destroying	2. exploration with manipulation	3. interest in pictures	4. turning pages in anticipation	5. use of books as a resource

DEFINITION OF THE TERM: BEHAVIOR UNDER OBSERVATION

The child's physical use of the book. The item notes the relationship between a child's handling of pages and his interest in the book's symbolic contents.

Child showed little interest in looking at books, respected others' enjoyment; did not treat books as toys.	Child selected books from rack; opened them; turned pages at random; returned books to rack. Looked at several books in rapid succession, sometimes upside-down.	Child turned pages systematically inspecting pictures, commenting on them or asking for comment.	Child turned pages, commented or asked for comment on sequental story.	Child took appreciable time to "read" a book; chose books for free-play activity; at reading time, chose books with care.

PROGRAMMING

PREDICTABLE (INTERNALIZED) BEHAVIOR USED IN PROGRAMMING FOR NEXT LEVEL

Knows how to handle books; interests lie elsewhere.	Opens book, turns pages.	Attends to pictures in book.	Turns pages, following story sequence.	Chooses "reading" as an activity

TEACHING PROCEDURES TO ESTABLISH READINESS FOR NEXT LEVEL

The opening activity of looking at books and selected materials, which solved problems created by different arrival times, provided regular experiences with books.

Involving child physically in reading activity including passing out or collecting books, arranging books on rack. Observing child for useable motivation. Showing child book or picture in a book related to his interests. Providing experience based on books.	Using commercial books on topics of interest to child; having illustrations with clear and uncluttered pictures with story content. Using teacher-made books with sturdy pages; texts already familiar to child, songs, experiences. Individual reading situations, direct help with page-turning, when needed.	Class discussion of reading period, books, children's favorites. Verbal attention to story sequence in new books. Verbal focus on way of turning pages: "One at a time." "Look on the next page." "Turn the page and look at the next picture." Planned introduction of new books. a) "advance notice," b) general description of contents, c) page by page reading of book, d) placing book in rack "You can look at it later, if you have time.	Individual reading situations, with teacher asking child to tell contents from pictures. Class discussion of favorite books, child's own books, careful use of books brought from home. Gradual introduction of planning for use of books: turn-taking, free choice of schedules.	Introduction of lending library: a) use of library cards, b) library days, c) reports on use of books at home, d) care of borrowed books. Relationships to citizenship concepts, borrowing and returning; care of public property; awareness of time, etc.

4a. PARTICIPATION IN STRUCTURE OF GROUP: MUSIC AT PIANO

RATING

THE FIVE LEVELS OF THE CURRICULUM ITEM

1. unconcern	2. shows evidence of attention in some way	3. generally joins group	4. listening with participation	5. listening with anticipation

DEFINITION OF THE TERM: BEHAVIOR UNDER OBSERVATION

The child's participation in group singing, motor rhythms, and rhythm band activities with the piano was the source of the music cues.

DESCRIPTION OF BEHAVIOR OBSERVED AT EACH LEVEL

Child showed no interest or awareness: might stay with group near piano, but attention was on other things as he interrupted music to ask questions about toys, schedule, or left group for another activity.	Child sometimes stayed with group at piano and listened to music; left own activity to join group, from time to time; listened from site of own activity. Also, child interfered purposefully with group's activity, with apparent intent of ending it.	Child usually joined group, watched others, listened, followed children engaged in rhythm activities, but did not try movements. (e.g. walked while others skipped, sat and watched Flopsy Flora)	Child listened and joined singing, and rhythmic games. Watched others, chose partners, helped others.	Child asked for favorite music activities, showed pleasure at hearing introduction to favorite tune, or favorite action cue (e.g. "Skip one window, Tidey-o") brought a smile and body-set for chorus "Jingling." Child "conferred" secretly with classmate, to decide on a request.

PROGRAMMING

PREDICTABLE (INTERNALIZED) BEHAVIOR USED IN PROGRAMMING FOR NEXT LEVEL

(Unconcern for music) shows interest in other materials, activities, persons.	Attends to music and/or activities, materials, persons.	Joins physical structure of group.	Joins activity in physical structure.	Knows and anticipates group activities.

TEACHING PROCEDURES USED TO ESTABLISH READINESS FOR NEXT LEVEL

Observation to identify possible motivation. Use of variety of group activities: a) songs of various kinds, b) rhythm activities, c) props for activities (flags, balloons, crepe paper streamers), d) percussion instruments. Incorporating piano activity in an activity sequence (e.g. as part of story, imaginative play, news item). Observation of child to identify nature of his interest.	Repetition of motivating situation. Providing partner if interest is personal. Providing role in group for child (e.g. asking if he would like to hear, do something specified; asking him to get props, distribute materials). Turn taking as group leaders, in singing actions, rhythm band.	Serial planning of group activity (through choosing a song and acting it, etc.). Suggestion by teacher when child seems unable or not ready to request favorite. Serial planning of turn-taking as action or singing leader. Verbal attention to group performance and contribution of individuals.	Use of songbooks as group focus. Group planning, led by teacher: for songs; for leaders of each song. Verbal attention to song choices (You like that because___). Verbal attention to choosing partners. ("A___ wants you for his partner." "B___ needs you to help him. B___ can help you. You march well together.") Sub-group planning ("A___, what would you like to do? Choose (1 or 2) children to do it with you."	Verbal attentions to favorite reasons for liking songs. Group planning, initiated by children. Use of symbols for songs (picture, print forms). Use of symbols for leaders (picture, print forms). Use of lists for deferred activities. ....We won't have time for John the Rabbit. I'll make a note on the blackboard and we can have it tomorrow.

4b. PARTICIPATION IN STRUCTURE OR GROUP: RECORDS

RATING

THE FIVE LEVELS OF THE CURRICULUM ITEM

1. unconcern	2. shows evidence of attention in some way	3. generally joins group	4. listening with participation	5. listening with anticipation

DEFINITION OF THE TERM: BEHAVIOR UNDER OBSERVATION

The child's participation in group structure when records were the source of music. As with the piano structure, class group activity was relied on to arouse interest of a few inattentive children.

DESCRIPTION OF BEHAVIOR OBSERVED AT EACH LEVEL

Child's attention was on other materials, activities. Child came into group to ask about extraneous matters.	Child joined group to listen, participate briefly; attended from site of own activity.	Child usually participated in physical structure of the group; stayed near source of music; watched others, handled props.	Child participated in listening and action processes; showed enjoyment.	Child suggested or chose records; anticipated actions; suggested props.

PROGRAMMING

PREDICTABLE (INTERNALIZED) BEHAVIOR USED IN PROGRAMMING FOR NEXT LEVEL

Shows interest in other activities, materials, persons.	Attends to record-player, music, materials.	Joins physical structure of music group.	Participates in activity, in physical structure.	Knows and suggests possible activities.

TEACHING PROCEDURES USED TO ESTABLISH READINESS FOR NEXT LEVEL

Observation of child to note possible motivations in the following record playing situations: with a) fingerplay activities. b) motor action. c) props. d) attention getting melody or words, illustrated by cutouts, chalk-talks. e) story connotations. Observation for personal ties, attractions. Making records part of an inclusive situation. (e.g. getting ready for juice time).	Repetition of device or situation observed to be effective. Providing role for child (e.g. holding record envelope, looking at related book, choosing favorite record). Turn-taking, choosing records. Turn-taking demonstrating action or getting cutouts.	Serial planning of record period. Turn-taking in leading group activity. Preliminary verbal summary of story, song(s) on a record. Use of symbols. Commercial or teacher made books illustrating record.	Group planning for use of records. Verbal attention to child's choices, reason for choice. "You like that because___". Use of descriptive phrases for melodies, action songs. Use of books, expanded. Sub-grouping of children, on basis of favorite records.	Verbal attention to kinds of songs, **records**. Group planning: use of record player for other activities. Use of symbols (pictures, cutouts, print forms) for plans (record choice, leader choice, deferred activity).

4c. PARTICIPATION IN STRUCTURE OR GROUP: STORY WITH PROPS

RATING

THE FIVE LEVELS OF THE CURRICULUM ITEM

1. unconcern	2. shows evidence of attention in some way	3. generally joins group	4. listening with participation	5. listening with anticipation

DEFINITION OF THE TERM: BEHAVIOR UNDER OBSERVATION

The child's participation in story telling period, when, to illustrate the story, tangible items including miniatures of story characters and objects, illustrative toys, cutouts or clay figures made by teacher as she talked, chalk drawings, and full-size objects were passed from child to child for inspection. The child's participation observed in this kind of structure, included, in addition to listening and responding to the story, ability to receive, inspect, and hold or pass the items.

DESCRIPTION OF BEHAVIOR OBSERVED AT EACH LEVEL

Child was busy with other activities.	Child listened from site of own activity; came to look at props; made verbal responses; looked at book after story period was finished.	Child joined physical structure; participated in handling of props.	Child listened, made responses to questions; (e.g. And then— do you know what happened?) used props to pantomime words used by teacher.	Child asked for favorite stories, anticipated episodes, supplied parts of story; noted any omissions.

PROGRAMMING

PREDICTABLE (INTERNALIZED) BEHAVIOR USED IN PROGRAMMING FOR NEXT LEVEL

Shows interest in other activities, materials, persons.	Attends to story and/or props.	Joins physical structure of group; handles props.	Joins physical structure, attends and responds to language, uses props.	Knows language of several stories, anticipates incidents, gets out props for story.

TEACHING PROCEDURES TO ESTABLISH READINESS FOR NEXT LEVEL

Observation of child for discovering motivation area in varied story setting; a) stories with full-size props (bowls, spoons for Three Bears, fox fur for Gingerbread Boy,) stories with miniatures, stories with illustrations made as story is developed, cutouts, clay props, chalk drawings, stories with teacher dramatization. b) in plot content (animal, cowboy); c) imagined, factual, humorous.	Repetition of story or situation liked by child. Use of similar techniques in other stories or chalk talk. Giving child role to promote physical participation: "B___, you like to play cowboy. Will you come and show us how the toy pony gallops?" Verbal attention to child's interests and activities re story content.	Group selection of story from several named by teacher. Turn-taking, in choosing stories. Dramatization with props. Discussion of story and related knowledge (TV, films, songs). Verbal attention: synopsis of plot; discussion of characters.	Repetition of stories with cues, repeated phrases (e.g. Caps for Sale, Three Billy Goats Gruff.) Turn-taking in telling of familiar stories to group, with props. Handwork: making setting for stories, making duplicate props.	Use of symbols (See 4b MUSIC RECORDS). Dramatization of stories, with props. Selection of furniture, relevant to stories. Classification of stories as real or make-believe. Comparisons of different texts.

4d. PARTICIPATION IN STRUCTURE OR GROUP: STORY

RATING

THE FIVE LEVELS OF THE CURRICULUM ITEM

1. unconcern	2. shows evidence of attention in some way	3. generally joins group	4. listening with participation	5. listening with anticipation

DEFINITION OF THE TERM: BEHAVIOR UNDER OBSERVATION

The child's participation in the group story period as stories were read or told from a book with illustrations as attention-focusing media. The structure to which this item refers was a large group situation. The child's response to a story in one-to-one relation with the teacher was not considered, in rating this item.

DESCRIPTION OF BEHAVIOR OBSERVED AT EACH LEVEL

Child gave attention to other activities and materials.	Child approached group, listened, looked at book; listened from site of own activity; chose book for individual use at time other than story period.	Child joined group (might bring toy or other object with him); watched other children's responses.	Child joined group response to teacher's questions; joined in repeated phrases.	Child asked for favorite books, anticipation of story events evidenced either verbally or by action or pantomime.

PROGRAMMING

PREDICTABLE (INTERNALIZED) BEHAVIOR USED IN PROGRAMMING FOR NEXT LEVEL

Shows interest in other activities, materials, persons.	Attends to oral language or to book, itself.	Joins physical structure.	Responds to story in group structure.	Promotes group enjoyment by own participation.

TEACHING PROCEDURES USED TO ESTABLISH READINESS FOR NEXT LEVEL

Observation to determine child's possible motivations, using stories a) with a variety of characters (children, animals, "grownups"), b) with varied action sequences (imaginative, factual, repetitive), c) from varied book forms, d) making connections with other classroom activities, e) in varied styles.	Repetition of stories observed to attract child's attention. Addition of stories in same category (a to e, in 1). Verbal attention to child's favorites; invitation to join group; giving child role, as, getting book; turning pages for T; sitting on T's lap.	Turn-taking in selection of stories. Planning for responses: "When we come to the part where the monkey says 'Tsk-tsk,' see if you can say it." Use of symbols: listing story titles by picture or word. Verbal attention to child's oral participation.	Adding to supply of stories. Turn-taking in giving responses: "And then what did the peddler do? E____?" Turn-taking in telling story from book. Verbal notice of group response to child narrator.	Expanding opportunities for children to tell story. Dramatization with book as guide. Verbal focus on child's performance as narrator, actor, listener, spectator.

5. SINGING

RATING

THE FIVE LEVELS OF THE CURRICULUM ITEM

1. evidence of rhythm	2. vocalization with rhythm	3. vocalization with rhythm and tune	4. rhythm, tune and pitch	5. sings song with rhythm, tune, and pitch

DEFINITION OF THE TERM: BEHAVIOR UNDER OBSERVATION

Behavior under observation was the extent of the child's participation in song structures (rhythm, tune, pitch, words).

DESCRIPTION OF BEHAVIOR OBSERVED AT EACH LEVEL

Child imitated clapping, body movement, finger play, with minimal accuracy.	Child spoke or sang refrain of a song, in unison with others, (e.g. Fire! "Here I (Am"). Speech might be approximate only, vocalized, hummed all or parts of songs.	Child used singing tone; approximated the melody; kept time with group.	Child sang in pitch, set by piano, record, or teacher.	Child used words of song, gave approximately correct musical accent.

PROGRAMMING

PREDICTABLE (INTERNALIZED) BEHAVIOR USED IN PROGRAMMING FOR NEXT LEVEL

Shows awareness of rhythm.	Uses voice, gives rhythmic accent.	Approximates tune, rhythm, with voice.	Matches own tune to that of others.	Knows words, tunes, rhythms of several songs.

TEACHING PROCEDURES USED TO ESTABLISH READINESS FOR NEXT LEVEL

Selection of group music a) for rhythmic activity (e.g. finger plays, song-dance combinations) (Row, Row; Let Everyone Clap Hands Like Me) b) for refrain (e.g. Old McDonald, Did you Go To My Barnee; Where is Thumbkin? c) for repetition of words (e.g. People on the Bus. Monkey See and Monkey Do.)	Selection of group music a) for simple melodic refrain, with rhythm (Where is Thumbkin? Two by Two, Here We are Together, All Around the Kitchen. b) for simple repetitious melody (Row, Row, Row, Here's a Ball for Baby, Davy Crockett, Jingle Bells.) Teacher hums, then names tunes.	Selection of group music for simple melody, varying stages. Turn-taking in leading group with familiar songs: physical leadership, then vocal. Program planning: getting suggestions from children; asking for sample of tune. Enlisting help of children in "remembering" a tune. Emphasis on listening, identifying familiar songs.	Selection of group music for language content: Johnny Appleseed, People on the Bus, John the Rabbit, Take Me Out to the Ball Game. Program planning: a) using descriptive phrases for songs, suggested by children (e.g. a slow song, a lively march, a soft song) b) discussion of children's preferences. Listening practice. Music cues without verbal cues, and singing. Pitch differences, tempo cues—variations in tempo: march, waltz.	Expansion of song repertoire. Listening practice. Beginning use of "scale" songs. Attention to autoharp, piano, xylophone as resources for child. Verbal attention to songs with similar melody, different rhythmic pattern.

6. VISUAL DISCRIMINATION

RATING

THE FIVE LEVELS OF THE CURRICULUM ITEM

1. diffuse visual activity	2. can focus on motion	3. can focus on something still	4. recognition of an object	5. symbolic behavior

DEFINITION OF THE TERM: BEHAVIOR UNDER OBSERVATION

The child's visual attention to activities, persons, objects and symbols. This particular item was used to rate simple use of vision; behavior at level 5 is expanded in other items in this section and in the section on manipulative development.

DESCRIPTION OF BEHAVIOR OBSERVED AT EACH LEVEL

Child watched activities in line of vision; did not fixate or make purposeful observation; fleeting responses to many stimuli.	Child followed activities of other children, visually and sometimes physically. Child's own choice of activities was often in motor area, but occasionally restricted to sitting still, and watching others.	Child used materials, inspected, arranged, matched, fitted together. Child handled books.	Child named objects, colors; asked for toys he noticed on cupboard shelves; used names of teacher, child or children.	Child recognized one or more kinds of symbols: miniatures, facsimiles, pictures, outline drawings, alphabet forms, numerals, maps.

PROGRAMMING

PREDICTABLE (INTERNALIZED) BEHAVIOR USED IN PROGRAMMING FOR NEXT LEVEL

Responds to visual stimuli, moves eyes.	Matches eye movements to moving stimulus.	Inhibits movements of eyes.	Identifies objects by sight.	Identifies abstractions of objects.

TEACHING PROCEDURES TO ESTABLISH READINESS FOR NEXT LEVEL

Continued visual behavior at levels 1 or 2 merits medical evaluation of vision Observation of child to find useful motivations. Observation of child to note consistency of visual behavior. Individual work at action level, getting child to identify own activity. Group activity, to provide opportunity for matching of actions.	Verbal attention to child's interest in movements; suggestions for participation, initiation. Introduction of activities involving objects a) holding and pushing, pulling, carrying, holding, putting away, going to get, b) release in rolling, throwing, passing, giving, trading, losing, c) looking for, getting from known place, finding in unaccustomed place.	Continued inspection and manipulation behavior raises further question of visual acuity. Activity with objects, color-toys in a) inspecting and manipulating, b) choosing, c) arranging, d) picking up in response to teacher's verbal cue.	Expansion of object "vocabulary" in various categories: a) functions, b) sizes, c) quantities, numbers, d) arrangements, (e.g. graduated sizes), e) colors. Handwork: making facsimiles, outlines from various materials. Symbols: matching objects to facsimiles and drawings; using objects for dramatic play.	Expansion of symbolic vocabulary for categories a) to e) in 4. (Leading to print forms, space concepts.)

7. AUDITORY DISCRIMINATION

RATING

THE FIVE LEVELS OF THE CURRICULUM ITEM

1. awareness of sound	2. focusing on certain sounds	3. initiates sound	4. identifies common sounds (without looking)	5. responds to patterns of sound

DEFINITION OF THE TERM: BEHAVIOR UNDER OBSERVATION

The child's response to sounds and patterns of sound. Levels 4 and 5 also imply child's interpretation of meaningful sounds and sound patterns. Symbolic behavior with respect to auditory stimuli is, as with visual behavior, expanded in other items in this section and in the sections on social and self-help development.

DESCRIPTION OF BEHAVIOR OBSERVED AT EACH LEVEL

Child responded to sound in some way; startled response; verbal response; movement; visual attention; or stiffening; obvious ignoring.	Child noted specific sounds, habitually: (e.g. responded to auditory stimuli related to own interests.)	Child initiated noises vocally, or reproduced them mechanically (e.g. door-slam, creak of hinges); imitated words, musical notes, animal sounds.	Child could identify "without looking" but often looked and acted in response. Identified and interpreted sounds related to class routine (footsteps; door sounds; sounds of materials used by others; voices in hall or observation booth; musical instruments)	Responded to sentences, directions, stories, etc.: musical tunes; series of noises associated with various activities.

PROGRAMMING

PREDICTABLE (INTERNALIZED) BEHAVIOR USED IN PROGRAMMING FOR NEXT LEVEL

Hears sound(s).	Attends to selected sound(s).	Reproduces sound(s).	Identifies sound with source.	Regulates own actions in accord with auditory perception.

TEACHING PROCEDURES TO ESTABLISH READINESS FOR NEXT LEVEL

Auditory response continued at this level merits medical evaluation of hearing.			Continuation at this level suggests possibility of some impairment.	Study of experiences for related auditory symbols: music, oral language, word, sentence, paragraph meanings, other academic experience areas.
Observation of child to determine sounds which attract attention. Incorporation of sounds into activities. Verbal attention to sounds: repetition; comments on kind of sound and its use. Group experience in producing sounds. (clapping, tapping, moving chairs, ringing bells.)	Verbal attention to sounds noted by child. Group experience in imitation of sounds: a) mechanically-produced sounds. b) vocalizations: animal sounds, exclamations, expressions of greeting, etc. (musical notes.)	Expansion of experiences of sounds. Verbal identification and description of familiar sounds. Searching for sources of unfamiliar sounds.	Verbal attention to child's responses to routine and unfamiliar sounds. Developing kinds of response, orderly attention, verbal comment, action response, inquiry.	

8. TACTILE DISCRIMINATION

RATING

THE FIVE LEVELS OF THE CURRICULUM ITEM

1. interest in touching	2. explores and ma-nipulates dry solids	3. explores and ma-nipulates wet materials	4. discriminates shapes, size and texture with sup-portive cues.	5. discriminates shapes, size and texture without supportive cues.

DEFINITION OF THE TERM: BEHAVIOR UNDER OBSERVATION

The child's use of hands and fingers to explore qualities of objects. Behavior at level 5, as in items on visual and auditory discrimination, is elaborated in various items of the section Manipulative Development, and in other items in this section (shape, discrimination).

DESCRIPTION OF BEHAVIOR OBSERVED AT EACH LEVEL

Child touched, picked up, held objects which interested him.	Child explored shape, density, texture, etc. of objects by smooth-ing, rubbing, pinching, sucking, licking, scratching, hefting, dropping, banging against other objects, pulling apart, taking apart, breaking or try-ing to break.	Child explored den-sity, resistance, tex-ture of clay, soap-suds, dough, finger-paint by squeezing, molding, smoothing; added water or other ingredients to clay, to change consistency.	Child used vision, verbal descriptions, kinesthetic cues to select blocks of various sizes; to choose dressup cloth-ing; to play object games.	Child used touch to select or correct his choice of blocks; to sort toys when putting them away; to insert puzzle pieces, to choose crackers at juice time. Played "blindfold" game identifying toys by touch.

PROGRAMMING

PREDICTABLE (INTERNALIZED) BEHAVIOR USED IN PROGRAMMING FOR NEXT LEVEL

Touches objects.	Handles objects which maintain shape, texture.	Handles objects which change shape when touched.	Compares shapes and other qualities by touch plus another sense.	Compares shapes, by touch alone.

TEACHING PROCEDURES TO ESTABLISH READINESS FOR NEXT LEVEL

Providing for inspec-tion of objects the child will be interested in handling. Using ob-jects relevant to expe-rience activities (e.g. foods of all kinds, seasonal items - pump-kin, feathers, pine branches, holly, cloth-ing items, toys). Ver-bal focus on object and its use, with qualities kept in appropriate modifying position (e.g. "Lift this pumpkin -it's heavy. Feel how smooth it is. It's round. Let's see if it will roll. Thump it - hear that sound.")	Verbal attention to ob-jects alike in various ways. a) size and/or shape, b) relative weight, c) hardness, density, d) texture, e) consistency. Plan-ning selection of ob-jects for activities on basis of attributes (e.g. a soft blanket for the little baby, a smooth board for a swing seat, thick soap for cake frosting). Gradual attention to materials as strong board, soft, easy to change.	Attention to change in texture when: adding water to clay, dough, soap; adding flour to sticky dough; cooking various foods. Testing by touch, over period of time (e.g. clay ob-jects in process of hardening; grapes and apples drying; leaves and flowers wilting; ice melting). Work in reproducing clay shapes, shapes of others. Verbal atten-tion to problem of locating own product by sight and touch.	Group discussion of resemblances and differences in items made by children. Selecting blocks for various activities by sight, checking by touch. Categorizing blocks, other ma-terials by shape, size, texture, in activity setting, as putting blocks, dressup ma-terial, other material away, according to size, shape, texture. Gradual introduction of situations for touch alone (e.g. checking consistency of clay, feeling on high shelf for ob-ject, handing child block while his atten-tion is on block tower).	Expansion of touch recognition. Use of blindfold games (e.g. identifying objects passed around table, finding a specific object in a bag or basket containing several objects). Finding familiar objects from verbal description. Finding unfamiliar objects.

9. TASTE DISCRIMINATION

RATING

THE FIVE LEVELS OF THE CURRICULUM ITEM

1. interest in taste	2. awareness of gross difference in taste	3. interest in experimenting with taste	4. identifying taste with supportive cues	5. identifying taste without supportive cues

DEFINITION OF THE TERM: BEHAVIOR UNDER OBSERVATION

The child's use of his sense of taste in various practical ways associated with the preschool activities.

DESCRIPTION OF BEHAVIOR OBSERVED AT EACH LEVEL

Child touched object with tongue; noticed, commented on "the taste" of a food item, did not qualify a taste, but used word in verb sense. "I tasted it. Let me taste it."	Child noted, commented on, responded to tastes in broad categories, good, not good, sweet, sour, hot (spicy).	Child tasted new foods; asked or expected teacher to comment on taste (qualifying word); reacted and supplied own qualifying term: "That (coconut milk) tastes ugly."	Child identified foods, such as sugar, chocolate, oranges, cinnamon, when he had seen box, wrapper, basket of fruit.	Child identified flavors in candy and other foods; dominant fruit juice in a mixture; chocolate in a hot drink. (Children often identified these things by brand names, e.g. Cocomalt, Nestle's, Bosco).

PROGRAMMING

PREDICTABLE (INTERNALIZED) BEHAVIOR USED IN PROGRAMMING FOR NEXT LEVEL

Tastes food(s) (knows tongue as organ of taste).	Knows tastes of several foods. Taste word is usually connected with one or two foods, only. (e.g. Candy is sweet, lemons are sour, pepper is hot.)	Tries new foods.	Distinguishes foods by sense of taste plus vision and/or smell.	Names foods from taste, generalizes flavors.

TEACHING PROCEDURES TO ESTABLISH READINESS FOR NEXT LEVEL

Use of foods as conversation items: Passing pumpkin around for inspection, manipulation; tasting outside shell; then cutting into, smelling and tasting pieces of pumpkin. Establishing an experiential base of tastes in conversation, activity periods; juice and cooking experiences.	Group discussion of similarities and differences in tastes of foods (e.g. "This tastes like real orange juice." "This is too hot - it is like pepper.") Gradual addition of new food flavors in juice period. Use of "surprises" in food items.	Continued introduction of new foods. Attention to changes in flavor by mixing foods. (e.g. adding cinnamon stick to hot orange punch; mixing onion dip; combining fruit juice flavors.) Turn-taking in choosing foods, juice. Verbal attention to flavors, "I like it because it is sweet."	Critical mixing of flavors (e.g. Is there enough sugar in this? More orange?) Planning mixtures, preparing, then checking taste with flavors or containers. Gradual use of "mystery" flavors, getting children to taste thoughtfully.	Expansion of taste experiences. Symbolic records. Conversation about items. (e.g. It tastes good, but what makes it taste that way?) Discussion periods: a) Discrimination about what is to be tasted (e.g. "B____ tasted some paste. I wonder what it tastes like. Oh, like toothpaste and it is salty. I prefer peppermint candy; or pretzels.) b) Favorites, c) menu planning.

10. SMELL DISCRIMINATION

RATING

THE FIVE LEVELS OF THE CURRICULUM ITEM

1. interest in smell	2. awareness of gross differences in smell	3. interest in experimenting with smell	4. identifying smell with supportive cues	5. identifying smell without supportive cues

DEFINITION OF THE TERM: BEHAVIOR UNDER OBSERVATION

The child's use of his sense of smell in various practical ways associated with the preschool activities.

DESCRIPTION OF BEHAVIOR OBSERVED AT EACH LEVEL

Child lifted items to nose, sniffed. Used verb, "I can smell it." "Smell the flower," but not a qualifying term.	Child noticed pleasant and unpleasant odors; pungent odors; odor of favorite food if it was distinctive. Following odor cues detected by children or teacher to discover a language in fragrances such as perfume, hair oil.	Child sniffed at foods, other things offered by teacher or classmate; child brought flowers, foods to school for group experience.	Child noted odor of popcorn, soup or hot punch when he had helped with preparation; matched odors with taste of foods; stated likes, dislikes, used odor names. (good, sweet, "like cinnamon," "terrible," "like cake baking."	Child noted and commented on odors in hall and sometimes traced them to source; identified foods by odors usually used as a way of determining rejection. Child named odors.

PROGRAMMING

PREDICTABLE (INTERNALIZED) BEHAVIOR USED IN PROGRAMMING FOR NEXT LEVEL

Smells or sniffs objects.	Relates several odors to sources.	Tests unfamiliar foods, etc. for odors.	Relates odor to sight and taste cues.	Recognizes odor, looks for source.

TEACHING PROCEDURES TO ESTABLISH READINESS FOR NEXT LEVEL

Providing experiences with objects having a variety of odors: flowers, raw vegetables, soap, toothpaste. Focus on activity and an object, giving attention to smell as a qualifying thing. Conversation to develop vocabulary beyond verb-use. "I smell____." "It has a good smell."	Verbal focus on words in ordinary use to describe odors such as sweet, good, peculiar, strange, clean, unpleasant. Following odor cues detected by children or teacher to discover a language incident (e.g. odor of mint gum. "I smell peppermint. Where does the smell come from? Who has been eating peppermint? A____ Oh! you have peppermint gum," or "Did you wash with soap? Let me smell your hands. That is a good clean smell.")	Conversation about new odors; comparison with familiar odors.("That smells like something else. Sniff it. It is almost the same as the smell of toothpaste.") Attention to changing the odor of something: washing hands with soap to replace onion smell; lotion or cream on hands; tonic on hair. Relating smell to taste: "Paste smells like candy, but tastes like salt." "Hot punch smells like cinnamon, but tastes sweet."	Planning and recalling cooking experiences; talking about odors to be expected, effect on others. Expansion of experiences: smelling, tasting, looking at various foods. Using paint of various kinds; quick-drying ink. Discussing odors noted in hallways.	Reversing process of 4: tracking to source odors such as paint, perfume, popcorn, onions, spice drinks. Blindfold guessing games, "Smell this. What is it? Can you guess?" Describing odors of pictured objects. Related to uses of soap, toothpaste, mouth wash, air fresheners, wax.

11a. COLOR RECOGNITION: CONCEPT

RATING

THE FIVE LEVELS OF THE CURRICULUM ITEM

1. interest in color	2. interest in one color	3. matching	4. selection for pattern	5. appropriate selection for pattern

DEFINITION OF THE TERM: BEHAVIOR UNDER OBSERVATION

The child's selection and use of various colored materials including tangible and play apparatus as well as the usual colored handwork items.

DESCRIPTION OF BEHAVIOR OBSERVED AT EACH LEVEL

Child chose colored materials for work or play; watched others using materials.	Child showed preference for a specific color, in a situation such as brown cookies, red paint, purple crayon, black paper.	Child chose one color consistently, for handwork. Imitated teacher or another child in selecting a crayon for use. Asked for toy, cookie, paint, etc. "like the one A has." and verified correctness of color given him.	Child chose crayons, and other colored items for handwork, etc. Used one or more crayons for a picture, repeating a procedure of putting one down and selecting another or the same one.	Child chose realistic colors for an illustration (picture or 3-D replica). Chose colors with apparent attempt to give a color effect, not necessarily realistic. Child gave a reason for a color choice.

PROGRAMMING

PREDICTABLE (INTERNALIZED) BEHAVIOR USED IN PROGRAMMING FOR NEXT LEVEL

Chooses colored materials.	Chooses one color.	Matches a designated color.	Chooses several colors, or chooses one, rejects several.	Matches colors to correspond to a model or an idea.

TEACHING PROCEDURES TO ESTABLISH READINESS FOR NEXT LEVEL

Providing a variety of colored materials. Observing child's preferences, or building a situation in which child will want to express a preference (e.g. letting child's friend choose first; mixing attractive pastel shade). Calling attention to color and child's preference.	Verbal attention to child's choice as "the same as ___'s color," or "different from everyone else." Providing two or three colors of lollipops, cookies or paint for child to choose from. Giving child "One like ___'s." Showing children how to mix shades of a primary color by adding white, to get a desired color.	Use of self-regulating color sets. Providing several colors, as before, but omitting a favorite color, making a second choice or focus necessary. Providing one or more choices (e.g. red and yellow jelly beans). Providing combinations ("You have blue, would you like some orange, too? That goes well with blue.") Verbal attention to child's clothing - matching or harmonizing colors. Drawing child's portrait and coloring with several colors.	Experiences with colored objects (e.g. fruits and vegetables) and follow-up handwork experiences. Alternate choices: white, red radishes; red, yellow apples; red, green peppers. Handwork and construction in connection with stories: alternate choices for clothing, furniture. Verbal attention to reasons for colors, color choice.	Expanded experiences in choice of colors, materials. Direct matching of colored paper, crayons. Selecting crayons to make a set.

11b. COLOR RECOGNITION: LANGUAGE

RATING

THE FIVE LEVELS OF THE CURRICULUM ITEM

1. association of language symbol with color	2. matching	3. selecting color on request	4. naming primary color	5. naming shades - pastels

DEFINITION OF THE TERM: BEHAVIOR UNDER OBSERVATION

The child's receptive and expressive use of color names in meaningful situations.

DESCRIPTION OF BEHAVIOR OBSERVED AT EACH LEVEL

Child uses one or more color names. (Not necessarily correctly, but to apply to color situations. e.g. might call all colors red.)	Child chose crayon lollipop or paper; to match one held up and named by teacher or another child.	Child chose color named but not pointed out by teacher. e.g. "Why don't you use green. We saw the grass in the park yesterday, and it was green, or I'd color blue, if I were doing it."	Child named color pointed out by teacher: "What color are these flowers? ... Can you make your picture yellow, too?"	Child named one or more blends or common pastels: light blue, pink, reddish-brown.

PROGRAMMING

PREDICTABLE (INTERNALIZED) BEHAVIOR USED IN PROGRAMMING FOR NEXT LEVEL

Knows that colors have names.	Matches color, listens to color name.	Correctly interprets one with color names.	Correctly uses one with color names.	Notices and knows name of one (plus) shades

TEACHING PROCEDURES TO ESTABLISH READINESS FOR NEXT LEVEL

Use of colored and coloring materials in a variety of situations. Observing child to locate favored color or favored object with a color property. Focusing child's attention on the favored color or color of favored object.	Repetition of color-plus-name experiences.	Expansion of speech experiences: naming crayons, paint colors, toy colors, spectrum. Use of color rhymes. Use of color names in sentences, phrases, and alone. "Reverse" naming: asking child to name color at random; giving him object of color named; helping him check correctness. (Teacher does not test by giving color other than one designated.)	Expansion of color experiences to include the following strong colors in natural situations primary: red, yellow, blue; secondary: orange, green, purple, brown; extremes: white, black. Through steps 1-3 mixing of white with one or more of above colors.	Expansion of experiences of shades, in meaningful situations: pink, gray, lavender, light blue, dark blue, light green, later, reddish brown, yellowish green. Use of paints, finger paints, and chalk for blending mixing.

12a, 1 & 2. MATCHING SHAPES: OBJECTS
(Including)   GEOMETRIC SHAPES

RATING

THE FIVE LEVELS OF THE CURRICULUM ITEM

1. participation in activity	2. recognition and awareness	3. putting together	4. selecting likes at random	5. generalizing dis- crimination

DEFINITION OF THE TERM: BEHAVIOR UNDER OBSERVATION

The child's selection of matching objects, in his use of play materials and tangible apparatus. The item, thus, encom-passed all materials provided in duplicate or which comprised natural pairs. Matching ranged from finding a pair of shoes for dress-up through getting another car for a playmate to pasting a cutout triangle on an outline drawing of a triangle. The activity was considered as a means to an end, rather than an end in itself. A separate rating was provided for one category of objects, geometric shapes, in assessing reading readiness.

DESCRIPTION OF BEHAVIOR OBSERVED AT EACH LEVEL

Child used materials including dressup clothing, blocks, pegs, doll materials, formboards.	Child looked for spe-cific items such as the second shoe, glove of a pair; another hat for a friend; duplicate blocks to finish a house; an inset for a formboard; another fork.	Child used pairs of shoes; assembled trains and barges; stacked paper cups; arranged matching toys for use.	Child showed pref-erences (e.g. strung cubes, beads, or spheres); used one shape of block exclu-sively; played with tangible materials which varied in color but not in shape: Easter eggs, alphabet blocks.	Child named or com-bined for use objects of same shape, different colors, sizes (e.g. blocks, balls, tops, pipes, boxes.)

PROGRAMMING

PREDICTABLE (INTERNALIZED) RESPONSE USED IN PROGRAMMING FOR NEXT LEVEL

Manipulates ma-terials.	Chooses matching objects.	Combines match-ing objects (2) for use.	Combines matching objects (more than 2) for use.	Combines matching shapes for use.

TEACHING PROCEDURES TO ESTABLISH READINESS FOR NEXT LEVEL

Incorporation of matched tangible materials (dress-up clothing; dishes in two or more sizes, block sets; crayons; scissors, etc., self-regulating sets of materials, including geometric form board) in day's activities. Action and fingerplay songs a) for matching movements, b) for pantomimed shapes.	Verbal attention to children's clothing, such as shoes, boots, mittens, gloves, stockings and to miss-ing items; tangible materials—beads, towers. Attention to shapes of separate parts in block play, Tinker-toy construc-tion. Handwork: dup-licating simple shapes in clay, dough, draw-ing around blocks. Individual attention to children using self-regulating sets.	Attention to larger sets of materials in sorting cutlery to put away or stacking dishes. Block play: attention to putting blocks away. Tinker toys: finding blocks needed to make dup-licate constructions. Handwork: Using stamp sets with inked pads. Using cookie cutters with play dough, real dough. Individual at-tention to children with self-regulating sets.	Group attention to self-regulating sets: colored boxes con-taining duplicate small toys; color towers; triangle par-quetry boards; nested blocks, dolls, eggs. Selection of beads for stringing, blocks for towers, drawing, stringing small bead neck-laces. Using sticks or toothpicks, to make shapes. Matching symbols.	Providing experience with symbols: match-ing 3-D alphabet shapes; 2-D cutouts; pictures to outline drawings (e.g. trees of various kinds, sizes). Rhymes with shape connotation. Here's a Ball; Here's a Ball for Baby; Eensie Weensie Spider; Chalk talks.

12, a3. REPRESENTATION

RATING

THE FIVE LEVELS OF THE CURRICULUM ITEM

1. vertical	2. horizontal	3. curve	4. diagonal	5. combination

DEFINITION OF THE TERM: BEHAVIOR UNDER OBSERVATION

The child's ability to produce and reproduce (with pencil, crayon, chalk or paintbrush) directional lines.

DESCRIPTION OF BEHAVIOR OBSERVED AT EACH LEVEL

Child made lines that were roughly perpendicular to lower edge of paper or blackboard used by child.	Child made lines that were roughly parallel to lower edge of paper or blackboard.	Child moved pencil, etc., in an arc to produce a curved line.	Child drew lines from left to right (or right to left) and down (or up) with respect to lower edge of paper.	Child combined directional lines in various forms.

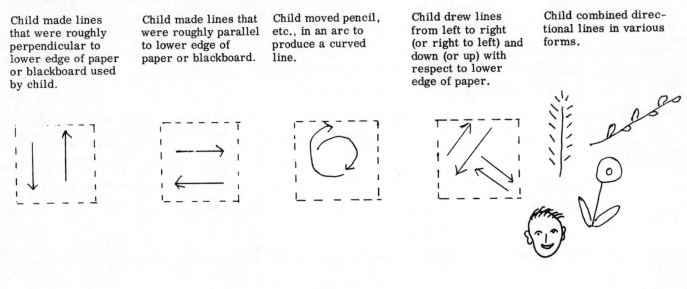

PROGRAMMING

PREDICTABLE (INTERNALIZED) BEHAVIOR USED IN PROGRAMMING FOR NEXT LEVEL

Moves hand toward and away from self or in head-to-waist line, (standing at board or easel).	Moves hand laterally, with respect to body.	Moves hand in circular direction.	Moves hand at a slant (2 directions combined).	Marks, stops, changes directions of hand.

TEACHING PROCEDURES TO ESTABLISH READINESS FOR NEXT LEVEL

NOTE: Order of levels arranged on basis of first groups, may not be generally applicable: later classes did not consistently follow this order, e.g. children made and imitated a curve before producing horizontal or vertical lines. Direct teaching of a circle was found to be successful, quite early; work on vertical and horizontal lines was effective later.

Teaching procedures for each form were the same, and children acquired the different directional skills one by one as they showed readiness.

Teacher use of the directional line in illustrative drawings, chalk talks.	Providing opportunities for noting, copying lines in imaginative contexts, especially repetitive drawings such as bars on a cage, fence posts, birthday candles, ladders.	Providing samples of alphabet forms (manuscript) composed of directional lines.	Giving direct help through guiding child's hand.	Tracing around objects including hands, feet, animal silhouettes, boxes, clamshells.

12b. MATCHING SIZE: COINS

RATING

THE FIVE STEPS OF THE CURRICULUM ITEM

1. participates in activity	2. recognition and awareness	3. putting together	4. selecting likes at random	5. generalizing discrimination

DEFINITION OF THE TERM: BEHAVIOR UNDER OBSERVATION

The child's ability (a) to match coins and (b) to distinguish one coin from another. Any combination of United States coins (penny, nickel, dime, quarter, half-dollar) was possible: selection and number of different coins depended upon the experiences of the particular group. For example, the number of coins at level 5 might range from two to five. This item deals with only two: penny and nickel. Work encompassed in the item was regarded as readiness for a more definitive study of the value of money. Coins were considered but one set of the materials to be compared for size.

DESCRIPTION OF BEHAVIOR OBSERVED AT EACH LEVEL

Child played with toy money, handled and recognized "real" money.	Child used name of one coin consistently.	Child collected, stacked pennies; used penny for purchase of 1 cent item.	Child was responsible for own money as he held on to it or put it away in purse or on a shelf; Child showed more concern for nickel and dime, than for a penny.	Child named and distinguished pennies, nickels, dimes, quarters, half-dollars.

PROGRAMMING

PREDICTABLE (INTERNALIZED) RESPONSE USED IN PROGRAMMING FOR NEXT LEVEL

Recognizes coin shape.	Identifies one coin.	"Collects" coins of one kind (penny) recognizes another (nickel).	Makes selective use of coins (penny, nickel).	Distinguishes, uses two coins (penny, nickel).

TEACHING PROCEDURES TO ESTABLISH READINESS FOR NEXT LEVEL

Attention to coins brought to school by children; naming of coin. Providing toy money for use in dramatic play. Counting coins brought by children. Saving coin, if child has brought it for that purpose.	Other coins added and developed through levels 2, 3, 4, 5, according to group activities.			
	Discussion of use for penny. Candy and gum machines; purchase of candy at store. Tracing around pennies, coloring them. Rubbing pencil across paper held firmly over coin. Songs: Christmas Is Coming. Nursery rhymes.	Counting pennies saved by individual children. Later, counting pennies brought for various projects. Discussion of uses for nickels. Shopping at grocery store for 5 cent items. Drawing or tracing and coloring penny, nickel. Rubbing pencil across paper, over coin.	Using both pennies and nickels for shopping. Counting and stacking nickels, pennies. Shopping: children having either a nickel or 5 pennies, for purchase.	Readiness or Experiences for money study. Expanding number of coins, to include all. Use of subway token. Use of coin bank. Use of symbols, picture, numeral, cent.

12c. MATCHING: PRIMARY COLORS

RATING

THE FIVE LEVELS OF THE CURRICULUM ITEM

1. participation in activity	2. recognition and awareness	3. putting together	4. selecting likes at random	5. generalizing discrimination

DEFINITION OF THE TERM: BEHAVIOR UNDER OBSERVATION

The child's handling and matching of toys and materials which were painted, colored or dyed in the primary colors. The secondary colors and black and white were ordinarily included very early, in color experience. This item did not consider the child's recognition of or oral use of the color names.

DESCRIPTION OF BEHAVIOR OBSERVED AT EACH LEVEL

Child used crayons and paints, handled colored papers; used tangible materials including matched sets.	Child accepted crayon offered to him as a match to one used by teacher; chose a crayon from a tray of similar crayons.	Child puts together two objects of same color including orange crayon to mark on orange paper; held own crayon or toy against one held by another child.	Child experimented with matching pegs in pegboard. Child chose one crayon or one color of paint consistently; showed preference for special colors; rejected certain colors.	Child made rows of matched pegs in pegboard. Child strung beads of one color; sorted sets correctly; made solid color squares with parquetry triangles.

PROGRAMMING

PREDICTABLE (INTERNALIZED) BEHAVIOR USED IN PROGRAMMING FOR NEXT LEVEL

Uses colored materials.	Accepts or selects objects with color as one criterion.	Juxtaposes two objects of same color.	Selects objects of preferred color or colors.	Sorts objects according to color.

TEACHING PROCEDURES TO ESTABLISH READINESS FOR NEXT LEVEL

Handwork: providing activities, materials which focus on one color at a time such as in food units, cutting apples from red paper; painting papier mache carrots; or even gathering elm leaves and cutout replicas to make a big tree. Action fingerplay experiences: Two Little Apples, John the Rabbit, Stories: Red Light, Green Light, Little Black Sambo, Tar Baby, The Little Fir Tree.	Turn taking in distribution of colored materials: carrying and passing out tray of blue crayons, basket of pink cookies, red punch, Offering choices such as red paper for apples or cherries; red mittens, blue mittens for pasting activity. Color rhymes, stories.	Expanded handwork activities for arranging one-color sequences: candles on soap-suds cake, frosting on play-dough cup cakes, pasted pictures. Verbal attention to suitable color choices. Verbal attention to children's preferences. Offering choices: pink or white cookies, red or yellow candy.	Expanded activities with one-color sequences; choice of sequences of candle colors, paint for toy furniture, dishes and Christmas tree decorations, Verbal attention to color preferences. Attention to sets of crayons in boxes.	Distribution of personal boxes of new crayons Providing for independent choice and mixing of paints. Verbal attention to color names. Focus on appropriate color choices.

12d1. MATCHING: NUMBERS, 1-5

RATING

THE FIVE LEVELS OF THE CURRICULUM ITEM

1. participation in activity.	2. recognition and awareness	3. putting together.	4. selecting likes at random.	5. generalizing discrimination.

DEFINITION OF THE TERM: BEHAVIOR UNDER OBSERVATION

The child's matching of groups of one to five objects. As in other matching items, materials used were the objects in everyday use in the classroom. The child's own fingers for instance were effective and natural number materials.

DESCRIPTION OF BEHAVIOR OBSERVED AT EACH LEVEL

Child joined number activities such as finger paly, songs, coin-manipulating, setting of tables, inspection of fingers and gloves.	Child accepted 1, 2 or more food items. Paid attention to oral description of numbers.	Child compared his 2 items with another's 2 items. Child chose 2 matching samples shown by teacher. Child distributed 2 items to classmates.	Child specified number of nuts, candles, pretzels he wanted; checked other's totals against his.	Child could check correctly and/or match groups to five (e.g. five pretzels apiece, enough chairs for five children.)

PROGRAMMING

PREDICTABLE (INTERNALIZED) BEHAVIOR USED IN PROGRAMMING FOR NEXT LEVEL

Joins number activities.	Notices group(s).	Compares or duplicates a group of two.	Chooses a number group and checks it.	Knows groups to 5.

TEACHING PROCEDURES TO ESTABLISH READINESS FOR NEXT LEVEL

Concepts of quantity Experience: random groups to five. Use of tangible materials with grouping elements, shell number game, dominoes, number pegboards, stepbuilding, tower building, train assembly. Verbal focus on number elements of familiar stories. Handwork projects, reproducing tangible models such as eggs in nest, cups on table. Random numbers.	Focus on group of two, using handwork projects as at level 1: (e.g. Two eggs in a nest, 2 cups on a table, etc.) Sharing one piece of candy for each child. Sharing: (2 x number of children) two tiny pieces of candy for each.	Imitative grouping, 3, 4, 5. Using crackers: breaking in 2 pieces, then 4. Using flowers, fish, minature figures, making bouquets of 3, 4, 5; bowls with 3, 4, 5 fish; fields, pens with 3, 4, 5 animals. Sharing (3 x number of children) tiny pieces of candy; also 4, 5. Verbal attention to groups of 1 to 5. Verbal attention to 1 to 5 fingers.	Experiences in choosing random numbers, all kinds of materials (e.g. "How many jelly beans do you want?" "How many pages would you like for your book?" "How old is your baby?" "How many candles do you want?") Grouping objects in sequence, in . .. . horizontal and vertical arrangements.	Use of symbols: a) pictures, b) outlines or space for placements, c) numerals. Expansion of experience with the variety of available materials. Verbal attention to diminishing group as candy is eaten piece by piece.

12d2. MATCHING NUMBERS: PICTURES OF GROUPS

RATING

THE FIVE LEVELS OF THE CURRICULUM ITEM

1. participation in activity.	2. recognition and awareness.	3. putting together.	4. selecting likes at random.	5. generalizing discrimination.

DEFINITION OF THE TERM: BEHAVIOR UNDER OBSERVATION

The child's matching of pictured groups to five. This use of symbols followed experiences in matching real objects, and symbolic groups were formulated from the tangible materials. Pasted groups, composed with shapes cut from construction paper, line drawings with felt-tip pen. crayon drawings and/or chalk drawings formed the series of pictures used; much of the child's observed activity was actual handwork.

DESCRIPTION OF BEHAVIOR OBSERVED AT EACH LEVEL

Child participated in cutting, pasting. Needed help to get correct groups and to set objects on representative drawings.	Child noted differences in pictured groups. Could set objects on representative drawings.	Child reproduced pictured groups pasting, drawing, correct number.	Child matched pictured groups, choosing favorite materials and favored quantity. Teacher made pictures for child, following child's direction.	Child matched correctly at request picture groups to 3.

PROGRAMMING

PREDICTABLE (INTERNALIZED) BEHAVIOR USED IN PROGRAMMING FOR NEXT LEVEL.

Uses handwork materials.	Relates pictured group to tangibles.	Reproduces or matches one group.	Selects random groups for representation.	Matches pictured groups to 5.

TEACHING PROCEDURES TO ESTABLISH READINESS FOR NEXT LEVEL

Experiences with number components, and related handwork in following sequence.	This process extending over period of time needed for individual children.			
	Experiences (as at level 1) focus on group of 2. e.g. Jack O'Lantern. a) Hallowe'en pumpkin, b) carving 2 eyes, 1 nose, 1 mouth, c) clay, papier-mache, etc. replica, d) pasted picture, e) drawing. Discussion of 2 eyes, 1 nose, 1 mouth at each level. Repetition with other experiences, teacher made books. Comparison of products, for number content.	Symbol series, keeping numbers to 5 in correct order: song and rhyme series: This Old Man, Here's a Ball, The Mystic Number, 1, 2, Buckle My Shoe, 1, 2, 3, 4, 5 I Caught. Teacher made books using children's experiences: Trick-or-Treat; Pigeons in the Park; Squirrel Hiding Nuts; Seeds Sprouting	Repetition of process for numbers 3, 4, 5. Reversal of process: a) Children chose handwork theme, designate numbers of objects, b) teacher arranged materials, c) children checked and completed 3-D or 2-D symbol.	Vicarious experiences a) provided by teacher Puppies coming from a doghouse, Rabbits eating clover, Man cathing fish, How many do you want? b) Invented by children. Readiness for understanding of numerals.

12d3. NUMBERS: SYMBOLS

RATING

THE FIVE LEVELS OF THE CURRICULUM ITEM

1. participation in activity.	2. recognition and awareness.	3. putting together.	4. selecting likes at random.	5. generalizing discrimination.

DEFINITION OF THE TERM: BEHAVIOR UNDER OBSERVATION

The child's matching of the numerals 1 to 5 as part of the readiness activities leading toward comprehension and reading of the printed symbols.

DESCRIPTION OF BEHAVIOR OBSERVED AT EACH LEVEL.

Symbols were, as much as possible, used in meaningful contexts. The teacher rated the child's matching of symbols within those contexts.

Child handled cut numerals (plastic, bakelite, or alphabet blocks); noticed calendar numerals; noted numbers in books, on cash register and food containers, on elevator shaft in building.	Child used generic term "numbers" to designate numerals.	Child picked out similar numerals, noticed them on calendar; repeated floor numbers in elevator.	Child remembered, asked for and watched for certain floors in elevator; looked for numerals in books; practiced ringing up amounts on cash register.	Child matched numerals to 5.

PROGRAMMING

PREDICTABLE (INTERNALIZED) BEHAVIOR USED IN PROGRAMMING FOR NEXT LEVEL

Uses materials showing symbols.	Applies general term to symbols.	Matches pair of like symbols.	Selects symbols for repetition.	Matches symbols 1 to 5.

TEACHING PROCEDURES TO ESTABLISH READINESS FOR NEXT LEVEL.

Providing visual, tactile and speech experiences with symbols of various kinds: a) Plastic cut-out symbols, b) Print symbols on calendar, news charts, cash-register, books, elevators, street numbers. c) Use of symbols for numbers above 5, for special events (e.g. birthdays, trip dates). Verbal attention to symbols.	Use of songs, rhymes using numbers in sequence (rote counting in sequence and interrupted sequence, e.g. 1, 2, 3, 4, 5.-1,2, Buckle My Shoe, Ten Little Indians, This Old Man). Counting while marching, 1, 2, 1, 2. Counting calendar days. Arranging, rearranging numerals in sequence. Focus on 1 or on other numeral important to child. For the preschool groups 6 or 7 was often matched first, because of birthdays.	Matching duplicate numerals. Verbal attention to numeral 1) whenever it appeared in various activities. Writing practice - making 1's. Expansion of activities to other numerals, keeping rote sequence but focusing attention on number being considered.	Attention to selected numerals taken out of rote sequence. Use in news charts, books, newspapers, handwork and construction projects, etc.	Formal matching activity (1 - 1 , 2 - 2) Focus on relation of symbols to quantity. Focus on copying of numerals in meaningful situations.

13a. CONCEPTS OF QUANTITY: NUMBERS

RATING

THE FIVE LEVELS OF THE CURRICULUM ITEM

1. one versus many	2. one versus two	3. counting	4. grouping	5. regrouping

DEFINITION OF THE TERM: BEHAVIOR UNDER OBSERVATION

The child's practical use of number concepts in daily classroom experiences. Imitative speaking of numbers and number phrases, rote counting and use of number rhymes and songs were considered as pertinent language, speech, music. Also observed was the way in which the child's actions were regulated by understanding of numbers.

DESCRIPTION OF BEHAVIOR OBSERVED AT EACH LEVEL

Child followed directions to take one cracker from a bowl of crackers, to choose one classmate as partner, to put one toy set away before getting out another.	Child used one and the other in language. Child followed directions to take two pieces of candy, to share one of a pair of toys with a classmate. Looked for both shoes of a pair, showed awareness of two hands.	Child counted four fingers and thumb. Counting objects, touched or moved them one at a time. Chose as co-workers 1, 2, 3 or 4 children. Took 1, 2, 3, or 4 pieces of candy. Checked by counting the number of crackers, candles, given by teacher.	Child was aware of absentees. Child noted missing parts of toys, wheels of vehicles, crayons in box. Child set juice table for 1, 2, 3 or 4: moved chairs and got dishes to make room for a fifth.	Child kept track of his own wraps; counted the group, orally or by action; knew when group was complete; could rearrange groups at tables, choose different sets of coworkers, divide toy sets fairly evenly; was aware of own and animal's anatomy including toes, legs, feet, chair legs, vehicle wheels.

PROGRAMMING

PREDICTABLE (INTERNALIZED) BEHAVIOR USED IN PROGRAMMING FOR NEXT LEVEL

Plus

Chooses one handful.	Chooses one, two.	Chooses or designates 1, 2, 3, 4.	Recognizes natural group of 2+, constructs 2+.	Changes groups of 2+.

Minus

Knows "B___ did not get one." "Lost mine, etc.	Knows "lost one mitten, both mittens." and "need one more."	Knows missing parts of 3+.	Knows too few cups, chairs, crackers, etc.	Knows absentees, missing wraps, other personal belongings.

TEACHING PROCEDURES TO ESTABLISH READINESS FOR NEXT LEVEL

Actions, songs and finger plays, "Where is Thumbkin? Two Little Blackbirds. See-saw, Up on the mountain, Stories: Caps for Sale, Gingerbread Boy. Teacher breaks crackers and cookies, passing these to children. "I broke these in half, take two pieces to have a whole one" or "take one of each kind if you like. Call attention to a lost glove mitten, etc.	Actions and finger plays This Old Man, Old McDonald, Three Little Pigs, Huckleberry Hound Builds a House. Passing small candies, pretzels: "Take two, two more." Breaking graham crackers in sections, along lines. Cutting apples in thirds, fourths, Teacher planning. Arranging children at small tables, for juice.	Action work and related handwork: juice time and pasting juice table picture; using wheel toys, making pasted pictures. Drawing around one hand. Choosing companions for juice table. Action and finger plays which form, then dissolve a group: Farmer in the dell, In and out the window, This old man.	Comparing sets, groups: things with two legs, four legs, four wheels; table setting birthday candles; room and walls. Setting small tables for 1, 2, 3, 4. Choosing several helpers for singing, reciting. Construction toys and road work: making cars, planes, etc. Verbal attention to number aspects of groups.	Actions and finger-plays. Counting out games, London Bridge. Building floors and elevator indicator. Use of symbols: pictures and miniatures, print numerals. Broken, divided crackers, apples. Use of money: penny, nickel, dollar.

13b. CONCEPTS OF QUANTITY: SIZE

RATING

THE FIVE LEVELS OF THE CURRICULUM ITEM

1. little versus big	2. gross assortment by size	3. matching	4. series	5. patterns

DEFINITION OF THE TERM: BEHAVIOR UNDER OBSERVATION

The child's practical use of the concept of size in daily classroom activities. Use of the oral language (big, bigger, biggest, little, long, etc.) was not measured by the item: focus was on the child's understanding of relative size, as evidenced by his choices and his use of manipulative activities.

DESCRIPTION OF BEHAVIOR OBSERVED AT EACH LEVEL

Child chose little or big items, according to his intended use of them, e.g. a larger piece of a favorite food, a smaller piece of something less well liked, paper for painting. Child compared self and his clothing with others and their clothing.	Child sorted blocks for putting away, noted big, little things such as clothing items.	Child matched while using: pairs of overshoes, knives, cups, blocks; functional pairs: big cup, big spoon; little bear, little bowl. Symbol-object (large ball and its picture.)	Child combined things of same size; strung large or small beads, sorted large, small cubes; made roads of matching blocks; set table with big cups and spoons.	Child imitated or originated patterns of materials of different sizes; alternating sizes bead strings, graduated sizes and towers.

PROGRAMMING

PREDICTABLE (INTERNALIZED) BEHAVIOR USED IN PROGRAMMING FOR NEXT LEVEL

Chooses big (little)	Generalizes big (little)	Matches two of a kind	Sorts a number of objects, according to size.	Perceives sizes in recurring patterns.

TEACHING PROCEDURES TO ESTABLISH READINESS FOR NEXT LEVEL.

Stories with big, little components: The Three Bears, Three Little Pigs, Three Billy Goats Gruff.

Providing materials of various sizes, relating them to activities large sheets of paper for painting, charts, coloring; small sheets for drawing, folding; lengths of wrapping paper for murals, large-sized chalk for drawing heavy lines and small for fine lines. Verbal attention to relative sizes of chairs, tables, clothing and people.	Verbal attention to child's choice of materials, when choice seems to be based on a size preference. Sorting activities: straightening boots in coat corner, arranging chairs at tables, putting away dishes, dolls, block sets. Handwork: pasting, clay, drawing activities.	Focus on pairs, sizes of pairs: shoes, gloves, stockings, feet, hands. Formal matching of cutouts - extremes of size. Experience with size-series: big, middle-sized, little applied to men's, women's.	Manipulation activities: sorting and arranging beads, blocks, pegs: one size - large, medium, small; two sizes - all large, all small; patterns - large, small alternated. Dividing food: large pieces, small pieces; equalizing portions.	Experiences leading to concepts of growth, conservation. Expansion of experience with progressive sizes: getting larger, getting smaller. Verbal attention to growth, decimation (e.g. people, animals, plants, ice water, food supplies, etc.)

13c. CONCEPTS OF QUANTITY: TIME

RATING

THE FIVE LEVELS OF THE CURRICULUM ITEM

1. now	2. after a while versus tomorrow	3. activity schedule	4. activity in relation to clock position	5. awareness of telling time

DEFINITION OF THE TERM: BEHAVIOR UNDER OBSERVATION

The child's utilization of the daily activity structure. The time unit here was the school day; observed was child's ability to plan his own activities in accord with orderly allotments of time.

DESCRIPTION OF BEHAVIOR OBSERVED AT EACH LEVEL

Child followed plans for now; acted in accord with materials and resources immediately available. (e.g. used paper, crayons, and table space for a drawing activity). Child did not defer activities on own initiative.	Child put away materials in anticipation of another activity; or continued with an occupation on hearing that another activity would be ready next, soon, afterwhile.	Child acted according to "adjacent" activities (e.g. music was followed by work period; free play was followed by clean-up, then juice; juice was followed by roof play, or projects.	Child noticed clock hands in conjunction with an activity; attended to clock position, for activity transitions.	Child used clock as clue for change in activity.

PROGRAMMING

PREDICTABLE (INTERNALIZED) BEHAVIOR USED IN PROGRAMMING FOR NEXT LEVEL

Acts on immediate clues.	Defers on changes in activity.	Know two plus consecutive activities: handles transition.	Includes clock symbol in activity.	Undertakes an activity because of clock symbol.

TEACHING PROCEDURES TO ESTABLISH READINESS FOR NEXT LEVEL

Planning activities: a) teacher planning tangible: setting out, showing materials for immediate and next activity, treating sequence as a double activity. Verbal: setting out materials for immediate activity and describing next activity. b) child planning asking child to choose next activity while he completes first activity or asking him to choose next activity, before he begins the first one.	Verbal attention to transitions. a) "Warning signal" "In ___ minutes we must get ready for juice." b) Teacher planning "You can start putting these things away, as we want to have juice and go to the playground." Conversational reviews of schedules (e.g. "We have had music and finished our handwork. Now it is time for free play.")	Verbal focus on a) Planning activities: arrangement of whole day's schedule. b) review on summary of day's activities. (e.g. "When your mother asks you what you did today, what will you tell her?") c) symbols: picture or print charts. Verbal attention to clock at transitions. ("Look at that clock! We must get ready to ___").	Use of play clock, setting hands in correct position for a major group movement (e.g. time to go to roof). Gradual increase in clock symbol references: "The clock says it is time for handwork." "The little hand is pointing to 10. That means get ready for the roof."	Verbal attention to limits. There is not enough time to get out the blocks. Handwork: making clocks with moveable hands. Verbal attention to numerals and little hand. Review of daily schedule, with related clock times. Leading to beginning time-telling.

14. TIME CONCEPT

RATING

THE FIVE LEVELS OF THE CURRICULUM ITEM

1. apparent lack of awareness	2. evidence of focus	3. association with cue	4. ability to antici- pate and wait	5. can plan for future

DEFINITION OF THE TERM: BEHAVIOR UNDER OBSERVATION

The child's utilization of the caldendar-time structure. The time unit was for this item, the day and the week; observed was child's ability to plan his own activities in accord with weekly plans. The item merges with the preceding one on the day's schedule and with later one on weather.

DESCRIPTION OF BEHAVIOR OBSERVED AT EACH LEVEL

Child engaged in activities according to the tangible materials which were available; did not pay attention to or remember announcements of future events; past events.	Child recounted past events, in response to stimuli which reminded him of similar things. Child listened to planning activities.	Child interpreted tangible or visible cues: (e.g. Putting on coats meant going someplace now; carrying home a permission form meant going on a trip later).	Child adjusted own plans to the class program; interpreted tomorrow, another day, next time, as not this time, not today.	Child helped to plan for 1 to 5 day blocks of time; knew recurring events (e.g. "Thursday we go swimming.")

PROGRAMMING

PREDICTABLE (INTERNALIZED) BEHAVIOR TO BE USED IN PROGRAMMING FOR NEXT LEVEL

Responds to immediate external stimulation.	Attends to planning activity; recalls past events including responses to internal stimuli such as wanting to repeat a past experience and showing inability to wait.	Associates stimuli with an event in the immediate future.	Associates verbal stimuli; defers activity for a while (operates within a days unit).	Operates within a time pattern.

TEACHING PROCEDURES TO ESTABLISH READINESS FOR NEXT LEVEL

Providing tangible stimuli for successive activities, as in previous item. Providing tangible stimuli for a two-day unit. Verbal attention to child's activity; suggesting repetitions on another day; letting child conclude activity - not breaking into it.	Verbal attention to sequence. Providing verbal links with past activities. (e.g."B___, you had a good time. with the grocery store yesterday. Do you want to play there again today? You can do that at free-play time." Extending use of verbal links; (e.g. "B___, you played in the store yesterday and again today. Are you going to play store again tomorrow at free-play time?" Use of picture symbols for group playing. Arrangement of well-defined play areas for reinforcing space cues.	Providing tangible plus verbal cues: Setting out as cues, materials for several activities. Listing plans for use of materials. a) for immediate use. b) for use later in the day. Gradual emphasis of verbal cues; omission of tangible cues. Group planning. Group recall.	Group discussion of recurrent activities. Group planning. Use of calendar symbol through introduction of a calendar large and sturdy enough to hold tangible records of events (24" x 30" minimum.)	Use of calendar with picture and print symbols. (Calendar large enough for legible sentences, clear pictures 24" x 30" minimum.) Calendar, time songs, work for days of week.

15a. NATURE STUDY: PLANTS

RATING

THE FIVE LEVELS OF THE CURRICULUM ITEM

1. exploration and interest	2. awareness of difference	3. interest in growth	4. imitation in care	5. empathy for

DEFINITION OF THE TERM: BEHAVIOR UNDER OBSERVATION

The child's participation in activities involving plant life. Plant materials used in the classroom were:

Cut branches, leaves, branches, cut flowers, pink branches (from plants observed in park or from child's home), acorns, grass.	Tops of carrots, potatoes, onions.	Onion sets, beans, seeds of various kinds (pumpkin, orange, carrot).	Foliage plants, bulbs, flowering plants.	

DESCRIPTION OF BEHAVIOR OBSERVED AT EACH LEVEL

Child showed interest in leaves, cut flowers, plants. Child was attentive to stories about planting seeds, tending to plants.	Child noticed differences in appearance: leaf shape, stalk, seeds.	Child watched for seedlings to come up; noted growth in plants.	Child brought seeds and carrot tops to plant; watered plants.	Child tried to keep soil properly moist; touched plants carefully; watched blossoms on flower open.

PROGRAMMING

PREDICTABLE (INTERNALIZED) BEHAVIOR USED IN PROGRAMMING FOR NEXT LEVEL

Notices growing things and/or items brought to classroom.	Notices variations in leaf shapes, flowers.	Notices changes in size, watches care.	Helps with care of plants.	Relates care to growth of plants.

TEACHING PROCEDURES TO ESTABLISH READINESS FOR NEXT LEVEL

Trips to park, a) to pick up leaves, acorns, sticks; b) to observe grass, flowers, and to bring back clump of grass, etc. Conversations about flowers and branches brought by teacher or children. Planning use of carrot tops, onion sets.	Use of window garden: Observation of plants, conversation about watering; watching for first leaf or shoot on carrot, onion, potato. Attention to seeds: Planting seeds from Hallow'een pumpkin. Looking for and planting seeds from oranges, apples. Related stories, songs: The Carrot Seed, John the Rabbit, Johnny Appleseed.	Use of window garden: Observation of vegetables. Watching for seedlings to come up. Use of symbols. Experience books, newspaper items, songbooks. Conversation about care of plants, different kinds of plants.	Use of window garden: (Vegetables, continued). Flower, foliage plants. Bulbs. Turn-taking in care of plants. Use of symbols as in (3). Attention to trees: fruit trees, plants. Vicarious experience accounts, anecdotes by teacher, other children.	Use of symbols: Pictures and models of gardens and farms. Experience with real garden, project.

15b. NATURE STUDY: ANIMALS

RATING

THE FIVE LEVELS OF THE CURRICULUM ITEM

1. exploration and interest	2. notice of reaction	3. imitation in care	4. empathy for	5. independent, spontaneous care

DEFINITION OF THE TERM: BEHAVIOR UNDER OBSERVATION

The child's attention to animals available in the classroom. These included at various times hamsters, white mice, turtles, frogs, and fish; dogs belonging to staff personnel, and "traveling zoo" animals brought to the classroom.

DESCRIPTION OF BEHAVIOR OBSERVED AT EACH LEVEL

Child watched or touched animals, asked questions about them.	Child touched, talked to, held animals; fed them, commented on movements and sounds of animals.	Child helped with feeding and care; imitated teacher's way of watching and handling.	Child handled animals gently without needing reminder; showed interest in supplying animal's favorite food.	Child brought food for animals; noticed when water or food was needed; saved juice-time food for mice, caught flies for turtle.

PROGRAMMING

PREDICTABLE (INTERNALIZED) BEHAVIOR USED IN PROGRAMMING FOR NEXT LEVEL

Notices animals and their movements.	Notices animal's responses to own or other children's actions.	Helps to get desirable responses.	Relates care to well being of animal.	Knows how to care for animal.

TEACHING PROCEDURES TO ESTABLISH READINESS FOR NEXT LEVEL
(ATTENTION TO REACTIONS, FOOD NEEDS: CARE OF ZOO ANIMALS, ON VISITS TO ZOO OR WHEN BROUGHT TO CLASS.)

Preparation for appearance of animals in class using photographs, relevant stories both fantasy and factual; inspection of cage, bowl, box. Discussion of child's probable role. Observation of children's behavior. Discussion of behavior, alternative behavior.	Planning for care of animal: food, shelter, handling. Experiences in finding, buying food. Use of symbols. Experience books. Related handwork.	Turn-taking in feeding. Experiences in handling animals: patting, stroking, holding, watching. Vicarious experiences. Teacher anecdotes, children's comments and anecdotes.	Continued observation of animal for appearance and behavior: condition of fur, way of moving, appetite as signs of good health. Verbal attention to children remembering about feeding care: planning for assumption of responsibility.	Extension of experiences; personal and vicarious with tame and wild animals. Use of symbols (toys, photos, experience records, books). Use of mechanical toys for movements. Readiness work for use of texts, geographical concepts.

15c. NATURE STUDY: WEATHER

RATING

THE FIVE LEVELS OF THE CURRICULUM ITEM

1. exploration and interest	2. differentiation and recognition of	3. awareness of effect	4. question and discussion re weather	5. association of experience

DEFINITION OF THE TERM: BEHAVIOR UNDER OBSERVATION

The child's attention to weather phenomena, and his behavioral adjustment to weather.

DESCRIPTION OF BEHAVIOR OBSERVED AT EACH LEVEL

Child noticed major phenomena; sun, rain, wind, sleet, snow, cold, heat. Child reacted emotionally (e.g. showed uneasiness at thunder, pleasure at snow).	Child commented on weather phenomena; used several terms correctly.	Child noted personal responses: cold hands, wet feet; possibility of snow play; reaction to thunder.	Child discussed activities related to weather: snow play, clothing choice, effect of sun, rain on plants, birds.	Child remembered previous experiences such as affect of snow on travel; uses of wind, weather re outdoor play. Child helped to make plans contingent on weather.

PROGRAMMING

PREDICTABLE (INTERNALIZED) BEHAVIOR USED IN PROGRAMMING FOR NEXT LEVEL

Notices weather phenomena.	Distinguishes common variations.	Associates weather with own activity.	Associates weather with other persons, things.	Combines weather and time factors.

TEACHING PROCEDURES TO ESTABLISH READINESS FOR NEXT LEVEL

Verbal attention to weather phenomena. Flexible recreation schedule, choosing activities appropriate to weather, as: snow-play; indoor play (gym) in bad weather; trips to park on fair days. Observation of children to note any pronounced reactions. Use of fingerplays, stories, with weather connotations. Eensie-weensie Spider, Carrot Seed, Caps For Sale.	Experiences continued: Verbal attention to adjustment to weather conditions including fastening coats before going out in cold weather; using raincoats, umbrellas; using mittens for snowplay; bending head against wind. Handwork: pasted pictures of sun, rain, snow scenes, miniature landscapes, clothing assemblies such as pasting cap, coat on child for snow scene.	Verbal attention to class's and child's adjustment to weather, and to other people's adjustment. Observation of animals. Use of symbols, using morning newspaper accounts and radio forecasts of unusual weather experienced by child that morning. Planning for trip home. Relating weather to daily calendar.	Verbal attention to adjustment to previous day's weather. a) the child's, b) the parents', c) the teacher's, d) other individuals', e) animals through use of newspaper accounts. Relating weather to season of year. Planning special activities. a) Open plans for a fine day, a rainy day, a cold day. b) Plans for a designated day, contingent on weather and with an alternate plan.	Verbal focus on activities for rainy days. Recall and planning. Vicarious experiences children's, teacher's, newspapers accounts). Review of school year events, vacation activities.

16. PROBLEM SOLVING

RATING

THE FIVE LEVELS OF THE CURRICULUM ITEM

1. sees problems and withdraws	2. asks for help or attracts attention	3. random trial and error	4. trial and error based on previous experience	5. assesses situation before moving and acting

DEFINITION OF THE TERM: BEHAVIOR UNDER OBSERVATION

The child's method of achieving goals in all areas of development. Although the child tended to use variations of one of the five approaches noted here, he might show strength in one or two special areas. The rating given was for the child's usual approach to problems. The descriptions given below are drawn from observations of a self-help activity, putting on a coat.

DESCRIPTION OF BEHAVIOR OBSERVED AT EACH LEVEL

Child, unable to get coat on, left garment and turned to another activity.	a) Child brough coat to teacher or to another child; asked for help. b) Child stood near coat on hook or held coat and waited for help but did not ask for it.	Child tried various ways of getting into coat, succeeded by chance or attracted attention and help by his self-help efforts.	Child remembered part of process: recognized a chance repetition of a successful movement; recognized and avoided some incorrect movements.	Child arranged coat correctly before trying to put it on; followed effective sequence of movements.

PROGRAMMING

PREDICTABLE (INTERNALIZED) BEHAVIOR USED IN PROGRAMMING FOR NEXT LEVEL

Moves away from problem.	Refers problem to another person.	Assumes responsibility for trying.	Assumes responsibility for partial solution.	Assumes responsibility for solution.

TEACHING PROCEDURES TO ESTABLISH READINESS FOR NEXT LEVEL

Effective problem solving, considered as an aspect of situations, is dependent upon, first, the child's mastery of whatever facts are essential to a solution and, second, his comprehension of the idea of his responsibility for using the facts. The following procedure for calling attention to the responsiblity presumes that the child possesses the relevant facts. Again the example is from the physical problem of putting on a coat.

Calling attention of child to his role: suggesting that he bring his coat to the teacher for help, or ask another child for help.	Calling child's attention to possibility of trying: giving a plan of action ("Can you put this arm in this sleeve? The other arm in the other sleeve? Now smooth your coat over your shoulder. Can you do it again?")	Helping child to recall a previous successful attempt ("I remember that you held the coat right here by the collar, with this hand, and then put the other hand in the sleeve. Can you do it again?")	Helping child to recall the whole process (first sleeve, second sleeve, shoulder and collar smoothing) and to repeat it.	Extending idea of child's assumption of responsibility to other self-help items, and to items in other areas.

17. SELF-CONCEPT
or
AUTONOMY

RATING

THE FIVE LEVELS OF THE CURRICULUM ITEM

1. realization of external objects	2. can go to get	3. refuse to get	4. can make a choice	5. can assess

DEFINITION OF THE TERM: BEHAVIOR UNDER OBSERVATION

The child's behavior with respect to materials and activities available to him in the preschool program. The five levels indicate an expanding field for exercise of self-direction and a corresponding self-control. (Discussion of this item deals with theory only, with the understanding that autonomy, like the problem-solving, is exercised with respect to sets of relevant facts.)

DESCRIPTION OF BEHAVIOR OBSERVED AT EACH LEVEL

Child accepted materials offered, participated in activities suggested to him.	Child obtained materials, participated in activities without direct suggestion.	Child refused materials, refused to participate, chose not to participate.	Child chose between two possibilities, compliance-refusal.	Child surveyed situation, made choice on basis of past experinece, future plans.

PROGRAMMING

PREDICTABLE (INTERNALIZED) BEHAVIOR USED IN PROGRAMMING FOR NEXT LEVEL

Accepts material on activity.	Moves to get material and joins activity.	Moves to get alternatives.	Chooses from alternatives (remembers)	Remembers and plans.
Controls things.	Controls space.	Controls people.	Controls past time.	Controls future time on basis of past experience with things, space, people.

TEACHING PROCEDURES TO ESTABLISH READINESS FOR NEXT LEVEL.

Enrichment of experiences. Observation of child to find interests providing materials in direction of individual child's growth.	Providing opportunities for refusal. Verbal attention to child's preferences, likes, dislikes.	Providing opportunities for refusal and further choice. Verbal attention to personal relationships.	Providing opportunities for choice. Attention to reasons for choice. Recall of other choices, results. Provision for planning.	Expansion of opportunities for planning: (remembering, making choices on basis of past experiences: "predicting").

18. OBEYING RULES

RATING

THE FIVE LEVELS OF THE CURRICULUM ITEM

1. unaware that rules exist	2. aware of given rules but non-conforming	3. tries to conform, needs support	4. conforming to usual rules	5. acceptance and flexibility in conforming

DEFINITION OF THE TERM: BEHAVIOR UNDER OBSERVATION

The child's obedience to regulations regarding the general routine of the school day. The rules governed several broad conduct and safety areas.

DESCRIPTION OF BEHAVIOR OBSERVED AT EACH LEVEL

Child acted on impulse; showed no awareness of group behavior, paid no attention to suggestions plans.	Child acted on impulse; ignored suggestions; refused verbally to follow suggestions or "did the opposite."	Child listened to reminders about rules, yielded to impulse without support or supervision.	Child regulated behavior in routine situations, by rules.	Child accepted temporary changes in rules, listened to reasons; could suggest changes.

PROGRAMMING

PREDICTABLE (INTERNALIZED) BEHAVIOR USED IN PROGRAMMING TOWARD NEXT LEVEL

Obeys personal rules.	Notices but rejects other (new) rules.	Obeys school rules with help.	Notes transgression of rules: chooses conformity to new rules.	Applies new rules to changing situations.

TEACHING PROCEDURES TO ESTABLISH READINESS FOR NEXT LEVEL

a) Providing opportunities for child to apply his own rules: observation of child to note special activity and toy interests (e.g. affinity for a certain car); providing for favored activities and for use of favored toys (e.g. assigning car to child). b) Verbal attention to acceptable behavior in above situations (e.g. "B___ likes that car. He has one just like it at home.") c) Observing child's behavior in non-tailor-made situations (necessary routines). Verbal attention to conflicting interests. Description to child of rules he apparently follows: ("You wanted the car. You took it." and providing acceptable substitutes: "Ask A___ if you may have it next.")	Continued provisions for child's use of own rules, but with inclusion of a school rule: (e.g. "A likes this car. He may have the first turn with it. Then B will have a turn next.") Verbal attention to acceptance of school rules. Providing materials for group experience in child's favored activity. (e.g. "A likes the big car. Others like it. So I have set out these cars for everybody." "You can paste these to make a picture to take home") Verbal attention to group participation.	Planning: Setting up turn-taking procedures. Setting up schedules to give child's preferences in turn with other children's and teacher's preferences. Verbal attention to performances: Recall of former behavior. (e.g. "A___ used to get very angry when he wanted that car. Today he had a turn and B___ and C___ had turns, too."). Variation in order of turns.	Group planning: Teacher points out her responsibility for maintaining several rules. Children assume responsibility for ordinary give-and-take in class. Verbal attention to child's behavior, when he tried to maintain a general rule; noted and corrected another's misbehavior. Gradual shift of responsibility for all of his own behavior to child. Verbal attention to reasons.	Group planning for trips: Discussion of situations to be encountered and of applicable rules. (e.g. "We will take our own toys to the playground, so we have cars and shovels to use in the sand-box.") Use of symbols. Picture-book records of trips. Picture plus print forms. Simple lists of rules. Verbal attention to reasons for rules. (Citizenship factors.)

1. SAND PLAY

RATING

THE FIVE LEVELS OF THE CURRICULUM ITEM

1. Interest at a distance	2. touching and exploration	3. use of other material in imitation of simple pattern	4. experimentation and elaboration	5. imaginative and creative use of available materials

DEFINITION OF THE TERM: BEHAVIOR UNDER OBSERVATION

The use of sand as a creative or expressive medium. Sand play as it pertains to safe cooperative use of the material is discussed in SELF HELP (G: 9b, 5). Creative use was within this safety framework.

DESCRIPTION OF BEHAVIOR OBSERVED AT EACH LEVEL

Child watched sand play; did not touch sand or attempt to play.	Child joined group in box, to watch, or child played in box when no other children were using it. Child handled and explored containers, tools, small toys.	Child filled cups, pails, etc. using spoons or shovels, funnels, poured sand from one container to another; carried water to sand box; ran toy cars in sand.	Child filled containers, identified product, called them e.g. soup, meatloaf, muffins. Child used containers as molds for damp sand, and called attention to products. Child made patterns with sive, funnels.	Child played games with continuity; e.g. fixed materials for a party; ran a dump-truck, a tug boat; molded and shaped damp sand with hands.

PROGRAMMING

PREDICTABLE (INTERNALIZED) BEHAVIOR USED IN PROGRAMMING FOR NEXT LEVEL

Watches sand play	Explores sand	Imitates play of others	Uses sand equipment in various ways	Plans for, carries out game and work sequence

TEACHING PROCEDURES TO ESTABLISH READINESS FOR NEXT LEVEL

Teacher participation in group at sandbox, handling of materials. Invitation to child to join. Showing new equipment in class, letting child carry it when class went to roof. When necessary, using other toys to redirect other children, and leave sandbox empty.	Teacher participation using sand, equipment in various ways to show possibilities of the materials. Participation in and initiation of impromptu imaginative episodes, e.g., tasting soup, blowing out candles on a birthday cake, making roads. Verbal attention to sand play experiences.	Encouragement of imaginative uses, dramatic episodes. Elaboration of play ideas, episodes, into sequences. Introduction of chance materials as equipment, e.g. bottle caps, juice cans, small sticks. Teacher participation in imaginative sequences. Recall of roof experiences, beach experiences.	Continued elaboration of sequences. Attention to qualities of dry sand and wet sand, and comparison of uses: pouring, molding, hauling. Planning of activities before going to roof. Exploration of large sand area at playground. Recall of experiences. Realistic behavior: uses of equipment to restore loose sand to box.	Teacher participation using instances of spontaneous modeling of wet sand to begin use as a plastic material: constructing terrains and molding objects.

2a. WATER PLAY. WATER PAINTING

RATING

THE FIVE LEVELS OF THE CURRICULUM ITEM

1. Interest at a distance	2. touching and exploring	3. use of other material in imitation of simple pattern	4. experimentation and elaboration	5. imaginative and creative use of available materials

DEFINITION OF THE TERM: BEHAVIOR UNDER OBSERVATION

Use of paint brushes, sponges, mops and brooms, with water, as materials for painting. Waterpainting, done casually in clean-up situations or purposefully with flat brush and small pail or mop and large pail was closely associated with cleaning activity. The child's interest in the appearance and disappearance of wet areas on various surfaces was the element which distinguished the imaginative aspect considered in the present item.

DEFINITION OF BEHAVIOR OBSERVED AT EACH LEVEL

Child watched others but did not explore use of water as a play material.	Child experimented with wet sponge on flat surface; watched effect of his work.	Child experimented with sponge on table and wall slate, or with brush on paper and easel. Chile used flat brushes, brooms and mops on roof, spreading water on brick pavement.	Child made purposeful swathes on slate, table or roof pavement. Child used pail and flat brush to paint bricks of pavement and protective wall. Experimented with squeezing, re-soaking sponge on table.	Child played out drama-tic ideas with paint brush and pail, used ladder or board scaffold. Child ex-perimented with design on slate.

PROGRAMMING

PREDICTABLE (INTERNALIZED) BEHAVIOR USED IN PROGRAMMING FOR NEXT LEVEL

Watches play	Tries materials or helps with clean-up	Uses brush	Tries out various activities	Anticipates and plans for activity

TEACHING PROCEDURES TO ESTABLISH READINESS FOR NEXT LEVEL

Teacher participation in clean-up activities: sponge on blackboard, sponge, paper towels on table surfaces, wet mop on floor. Verbal attention to dark trail left on surface by damp sponge. Enlisting help of child in get-ting equipment. Enlisting help in clean-up.	Situations for cooper-ative clean-up of tables, wall slate, easel. Group obser-vation of use of large mop, toy mop. Teach-er participation in clean-up groups (showing different movements). Verbal attention to patterns, evaporation.	Use of wet brush or sponge on paper, as a preliminary to finger painting. Exploration of results in using brush dipped in water, at easel. Verbal at-tention to wet foot prints, finger and hand prints. Use of flat brushes, pails of water for random painting.	Planning for use of paint brushes, mops, on roof, and sponges, brushes in classroom: a) blocking out units. e.g. paint one brick, one section of wall, one board. b) taking turns with brushes, sponges. c) coopera-ting in covering a surface. Suggesting various dramatic play situations (e.g. making ladders, scaffolds).	Verbal attention to re-sults from clean-up se-quences. Verbal attention to process of evaporation. Discussion of uses of water painting, scrubbing, Exploration of other re-sults, e.g. chalk on a wet board, thick paint on wet paper. (Direct preparation for science.)

2b. WATER PLAY: SOAPSUDS
2e.   BUBBLES

RATING

THE FIVE LEVELS OF THE CURRICULUM ITEM

1. interest at a distance	2. touching and exploring	3. use of other materials in imitation of a simple pattern	4. experimentation and elaboration	5. imaginative and creative use of available materials

DEFINITION OF THE TERM: BEHAVIOR UNDER OBSERVATION

Use of soapsuds as an expressive medium. Types of activity were determined by consistency of mixtures and ranged from exploration of foamy suds to spreading and molding of a plastic mixture. For a related preparatory experience see hand washing (Self-help, section G). Bubble-blowing (e) was one aspect of soap-suds play. Steps (1) and (2) were common to items (b) and (e).

DESCRIPTION OF BEHAVIOR OBSERVED AT EACH LEVEL

(b, e) Child watched play of others, did not join activity.	(b, e) Child stirred soapsuds in bowl, touched and experimented with suds.	(b, e) Child used beater to mix suds, straw for blowing. Child poured suds from one container to another.	(b) Child made patterns with suds having the consistency of whipped egg-whites. Explored results from adding color to mixture; explored soapsuds patterns in clean-up activities using sponge. (e) Child attempted various bubble effect, used pipe, fingers.	(b) Child created items for use in other activities: plastic mixture for modeling, making play-foods. (e) Child explored various patterns, strings of bubles, large bubbles and tried to float bubbles in air.

PROGRAMMING

PREDICTABLE (INTERNALIZED) BEHAVIOR USED IN PROGRAMMING FOR NEXT LEVEL

Watches others	Handles	Tries processes	Notices results	Plans process needed to accomplish purpose

TEACHING PROCEDURES TO ESTABLISH READINESS FOR NEXT LEVEL

Planning activity as a special occasion, announcement of prospective activity immediately preceding it, or an hour, day, several days ahead, depending on class composition. Teacher participation in mixing of suds, initial exploration. Verbal attention to mixing and play activities.	Announcement of activity in advance. Recall of previous experiences. Verbal attention to a) materials used b) consistency of mixture c) use of equipment such as rotary beaters, egg whips, spoons, straws.	Development of two kinds of activity. Verbal attention to processes and results. b) exploration of suds - transferring, spreading. e) exploration of bubbles including some children's learning to blow through a straw. Blowing bowl, full of bubbles, watching bubbles spill over edge of bowl.	b) situations for use of thick mixture in spreading with a knife, molding in hands, leaving overnight to "jell", adding colored material. e) situations for use of straw, bubblepipe, or loop made by thumb and finger, for blowing single bubbles, strings of bubbles, floating bubble.	b) Planning activities. Production of frosted cakes, cookies for houseplay. Production of modeled objects. e) Planning activities. Blowing bubbles of var-sizes. Verbal attention to floating, reflection of light, color traces. (Introduction of science).

2c. WATER PLAY: FISHING

RATING

THE FIVE LEVELS OF THE CURRICULUM ITEM

1. interest at a distance	2. touching and exploring	3. use of other materials in imitation of simple pattern	4. experimentation and elaboration	5. imaginative and creative use of available materials

DEFINITION OF THE TERM: BEHAVIOR UNDER OBSERVATION

Use of toy fishing rods, hooks, and fish for expressive play. Materials in order of sequential use included a) plastic fish, with holes for hooking, poles with string line, and plastic hooks; b) plastic fish with bit of metal at mouth, metal fish, and poles with string line and magnet. c) rods with reels, cord lines, and hooks or magnets. d) poles with string lines and snap clothespins as hooks. e) sea shells, frogs, other beach and water items.

DESCRIPTION OF BEHAVIOR OBSERVED AT EACH LEVEL

Child watched others using equipment.	Child handled fish, rods, hooks.	Child tried processes: attaching and detaching fish, winding and unwinding line on reel.	Child "fished", made comments on fish or other objects caught.	Child played out a game sequence, alone or with others.

PROGRAMMING

PREDICTABLE (INTERNALIZED) BEHAVIOR USED IN PROGRAMMING FOR NEXT LEVEL

Watches others	Handles materials	Tries processes	Notices, calls attention to results.	Plans and reports on activity.

TEACHING PROCEDURES TO ESTABLISH READINESS FOR NEXT LEVEL

Providing equipment for use in free-play situation. Verbal attention to "fishing" concept. Help with manipulative process with hooks and lines presented first.	Provision for turn-taking. Supplying materials for a group of three or four children. Verbal attention to "catching" fish, to colors, kinds of fish.	Providing additional materials such as magnetic hooks, clothespin hooks. Planning free-play activities, provision for choosing fishing equipment. Verbal attention to manipulative and imaginative aspects.	Providing additional materials. Discussion of "real" fishing. Planning imaginative sequences. Reporting on activity, as number of fish caught, what happened to fish, use of reel.	Teacher participation to provide additional sequences such as cooking. Verbal focus on equipment. Discussion of water activities, ocean, lake, boats, fishing, fish. Preparation for science, recreation.

2d. WATER PLAY: SWIMMING

RATING

THE FIVE LEVELS OF THE CURRICULUM ITEM

1. interest at a distance	2. touching and exploring	3. use of other materials in imitation of simple pattern	4. experimentation and elaboration	5. imaginative and creative use of available materials

DEFINITION OF THE TERM: BEHAVIOR UNDER OBSERVATION

Participation in the swimming program. Observed was development of familiarity with the water, use of play equipment, and ways of playing in and near a swimming pool within the framework of safety rules generally applicable in swimming situations.

DESCRIPTION OF BEHAVIOR OBSERVED AT EACH LEVEL

Child watched activity of others; might not change to swimming suit, on first experience in pool area.	Child dressed for swimming; sat on edge of pool or on steps leading into water; dabbled fingers, toes in water; entered pool; let adult carry him in pool.	Child moved around edge of pool, holding rail; held to wooden float or plastic raft, pulled by adult, played with beach ball.	Child put face in water, blew bubbles; held nose and ducked head; kicked with feet; walked around pool holding to float; played game of ball.	Child tried prone float; jumped into pool from edge; experimented with arm, leg movements; swam holding to float or swam a few free strokes.

PROGRAMMING

PREDICTABLE (INTERNALIZED) BEHAVIOR USED IN PROGRAMMING FOR NEXT LEVEL

Watches activity	Touches water, toys	Tries activities in water	Uses water-play processes	Plans for swimming activity; reports

TEACHING PROCEDURES TO ESTABLISH READINESS FOR NEXT LEVEL

Teacher participation in activity. Verbal notice of individual children. Use of activity of enthusiastic children to get interest of apprehensive children. Use of floats, ball games with children sitting on steps.	Classroom planning of pool activities. Discussion of toys, floats, balls. Taking water toys (e.g. one or two boats) to pool. Discussion and review of activity of individual children.	Classroom planning for use of floats, balls, toys. Review of activities. Classroom discussion of bubble-blowing, ducking heads, kicking. Use of side rails. Extension of use of floats for towing, swimming. Use of balls as buoys. Group games.	Classroom planning, review of pre-swimming activities; bubble blowing, floating, holding nose, jumping. Discussion of individual performances. Planning and reporting on pre-swimming, post-swimming sequence.	Refinement of physical processes. Planned practice in bubbling prone float. Discussion of instances of actual swimming. Discussion of safe behavior in and near water.

2f. WATER PLAY: WASHING CLOTHES, DISHES, DOLLS

RATING

THE FIVE LEVELS OF THE CURRICULUM ITEM

1. Interest at a distance	2. touching and exploring	3. use of other materials in imitation of simple pattern	4. experimentation and elaboration	5. imaginative and creative use of available materials

DEFINITION OF THE TERM: BEHAVIOR UNDER OBSERVATION

Washing of toy equipment such as dolls, doll clothes, doll dishes and dressing materials in imaginative play, during free-play periods.

DESCRIPTION OF BEHAVIOR OBSERVED AT EACH LEVEL

Child watched play of others, washing dishes, using kitchen equipment.	Child joined play of others, or explored materials by self.	Child used toy sink or real sink for dish-washing or clothes-washing; used sponge and soap to bathe dolls.	Child included dishwashing, etc. in simple dramatic sequence, alone or with group.	Child utilized various materials (e.g. dish-rack, teakettle, towels) in elaborate sequences. Child might or might not assess results.

PROGRAMMING

PREDICTABLE (INTERNALIZED) BEHAVIOR USED IN PROGRAMMING FOR NEXT LEVEL

Watches others	Touches materials; joins activity	Tries out equipment	Uses equipment for a purpose	Plans and reports on activities

TEACHING PROCEDURES TO ESTABLISH READINESS FOR NEXT LEVEL

Supplying materials for house and doll play. Verbal attention to materials, activities of children. Observation of individuals, to note area of interest.	Verbal attention to ongoing use of materials, equipment. Review of free-play activities; notice of individual's roles.	Verbal attention to ongoing activities. Promotion of cooperative situations. Planning activity; discussion and review of play sequences.	Supplying additional materials; use of clothesline, clothespins on roof. Teacher participation in dramatic play, suggestions aimed at establishing cooperative groups. Verbal attention to sequences discussion of similar home activities.	Continued opportunity for free-play experience. Verbal focus on efficient process, results. (Leading to related trip to laundromat.)

3. DRAWING

RATING

THE FIVE LEVELS OF THE CURRICULUM ITEM

1. interest at a distance	2. touching and exploring	3. use of other materials in imitation of simple pattern	4. experimentation and elaboration	5. imaginative and creative use of available materials

DEFINITION OF THE TERM: BEHAVIOR UNDER OBSERVATION

Drawing, in the Curriculum Guide, was rated in two ways, as a creative process and as an aspect of manipulative development. In both cases, behavior under observation was use of pencil, crayon and chalk to make marks on paper or chalk board. In rating the expressive aspects, decisive factors were as follows: a) The child called his activity "drawing." b) He also identified his product as a specific object or called it "a picture" or "something I made (or drew)." Observed here was the extent to which drawing was an expressive medium, not the quality of the products which ranged from scribbles to representative drawings. Choice of drawing as a free-play activity is included in ratings at levels 4 and 5.

DESCRIPTION OF BEHAVIOR OBSERVED AT EACH LEVEL

Child watched others use materials. Child might sit at table, holding pencil, and with paper in front of him, but did not mark paper.	Child examined and tried out pencil, chalk; made marks on paper, scribbled, or attempted outline drawings; called attention to results.	Child used various materials for making marks or drawings; tried to imitate or copy single forms; tried drawing around toys, objects.	Child chose drawing as a free-play activity. Child used combinations of lines or outlines, tried to express ideas (e.g. drew objects connected with a situation). Child tried combinations of color.	Child used pencil and crayons in combinations, drew recognizable forms expressing an idea or assigned a meaning to an unidentifiable combination of lines. Child often chose drawing as a free-play activity.

PROGRAMMING

PREDICTABLE (INTERNALIZED) BEHAVIOR IN PROGRAMMING FOR NEXT LEVEL

Watches others, stays with group using pencils, crayons.	Holds pencil, marks.	Makes purposeful marks; aware of idea of reproducing marks.	Makes purposeful marks; produces various forms at will.	Uses drawing as a way of expressing an idea.

TEACHING PROCEDURES TO ESTABLISH READINESS FOR NEXT LEVEL

Verbal focus on manipulation: things that can be done with materials, per se. Teacher participation: in drawing period, in various ways to express ideas. a) formalized symbols: curved sweeps for wind, undulating lines for water, straight lines for boundaries. b) representative drawings. c) process-based lines (directional scribbling, shading, dots, broken lines).	Continued attention to process in finger, hand and arm movements which produce various effects. Verbal attention to ideas behind drawings; teacher use of line drawings to illustrate news items, weather phenomena. Attention to drawing of experiences, teacher illustration of class experiences through chalk-talks or drawings for bulletin board. Child's imitative drawing of settings or objects.	Gradual decrease in attention to known processes. Verbal attention to novel processes tried by individual children. Focus on use of various materials for recording experiences; introducing variant uses of materials such as white chalk on black or blue paper, paint on murals.	Continued focus on recording of experiences. Careful structuring of experiences to highlight tactile and kinesthetic elements. Recall of tactile elements for drawing purposes.	Continued structuring of experiences. Continued use of drawing to express personal particpation in experiences. Attention to vicarious experiences (e.g. "B___ was there, too. What was he doing?") Discussion periods: evaluation and interpretation of children's drawings.

4. PAINTING

RATING

THE FIVE LEVELS OF THE CURRICULUM ITEM

1. interest at a distance	2. touching and exploring	3. use of other materials in imitation of simple pattern	4. experimentation and elaboration	5. imaginative and creative use of available materials

DEFINITION OF THE TERM: BEHAVIOR UNDER OBSERVATION

Use of painting materials, at easel, tables, or on floor, for expressive painting. Children maintained interest in the process (as distinguished from representative and drawing aspects) throughout the two years of attendance. Elements which seemed pertinent to this interest were the shapes including straight and curved lines, solid color areas, dots, dashes, and the combinations of flat primary colors and pastels, mixed, mingled, shaded, and overlaid.

DESCRIPTION OF BEHAVIOR OBSERVED AT EACH LEVEL

Child watched others painting; inspected easel; looked at completed painting; did not use materials.	Interest in process; child put on smock; tried out materials; experimented with stirring paint, making marks. Child imitated movements of others.	Interest in effects: child made marks, filled in areas or entire paper; repeated own marks; imitated others including asking for same color as another child.	Child mixed and combined colors; noted and experimented with various consistencies and color or line effects. Child named color(s) he wanted; chose work area; asked to paint or to continue painting when activity was scheduled.	Child asked about schedule; chose painting as a free-play activity; stayed at activity for long period. Showed selectivity for colors, patterns, paint consistency. Talked about finished painting.

PROGRAMMING

PREDICTABLE (INTERNALIZED) BEHAVIOR USED IN PROGRAMMING FOR NEXT LEVEL

Watches other children.	Handles paint, brushes, paper.	Imitates movements.	Helps make preparations; notices results.	Anticipates and arranges for painting; uses painting as a preferred activity.

TEACHING PROCEDURES TO ESTABLISH READINESS FOR NEXT LEVEL

Providing opportunities to watch: scheduling painting as a turn-taking activity, providing a well defined painting area as easel area, or painting table. Verbal attention to prepared materials excluding smock, paint, brushes, paper. Verbal attention to ongoing activity rather than to results. Planning for future turns at painting. Offering opportunities to child.	Continued painting as a turn-taking activity. Involving child in preparations, choosing and mixing color, managing jar and brushes. Verbal attention to effects produced by varied use of brushes. Discussion of completed paintings.	Verbal attention to: effects achieved by various children, cooperation, such as buttoning smocks, and clean-up. Experience with an alternate work area. Planning experience: choosing colors and work area; forming a group. Offering painting as a work-period choice.	Continued comments, comparisons of effects. Comments on preparation, clean-up. Planning expanded to include child's responsibility for cooperative preparation and clean-up. Gradual withdrawal of direct supervision of painters. Offering painting as a free-play activity.	Continued comments. Conversation involving children in discussion of pictures (e.g. "A___ made the colors run together. I like the way it looks.") Connection between handling of materials and effects. Child named connection between picture and what he meant to paint.

5. FINGER PAINTING

RATING

THE FIVE LEVELS OF THE CURRICULUM ITEM

1. interest at a distance	2. touching and exploring	3. use of other materials in imitation of simple pattern	4. experimentation and elaboration	5. imaginative and creative use of available materials

DEFINITION OF THE TERM: BEHAVIOR UNDER OBSERVATION

Use of fingerpaint as an expressive medium.

DESCRIPTION OF BEHAVIOR OBSERVED AT EACH LEVEL

Child watched other children and teacher using materials; did not participate in activity.	Child accepted paper and paint offered by teacher; chose a color. Child poked at paint, drew with one finger; spread paint with finger tips ordinarily using only one hand. Child often initiated clean-up.	Child used fingers, palms, side of hand, tongue depressor to achieve different effects; tried both hands; usually asked for different colors for each painting; printed alphabet forms or tried outline drawings in paint.	Child initiated paper preparation and paint distribution. Chose colors, tried mixtures. Two or more colors were rarely left partly mixed as child smoothed and mixed until colors blended. Child chose finger-painting as activity.	Child chose finger-painting as a free-play activity; mixed several colors, showing mingled and shaded effects. Completed pictures might contain representative drawings.

PROGRAMMING

PREDICTABLE (INTERNALIZED) BEHAVIOR USED IN PROGRAMMING FOR NEXT LEVEL

Watches others.	Explores materials.	Imitates processes.	Copies, notices results.	Anticipates, prepares for, and carries out activity; shows results.

TEACHING PROCEDURES TO ESTABLISH READINESS FOR NEXT LEVEL

Providing opportunities to watch by presenting fingerpainting as a group activity; later, by setting up a painting area for a subgroup. Verbal attention to preparation of paper, spooning paint, children's hand and finger movements, hanging paintings to dry.	Involving child in preparation of table, paper, paint. Verbal attention to on-going activity. Teacher participation: spreading paint, then making patterns in wet paint. Focus on results of activity such as color and line effects.	Verbal attention to ways of achieving effects. Comparison of children's movements. Comparison of completed paintings. Planned activity; getting out materials, choosing colors. Offering fingerpaint as a work activity.	Planning activity continued. Gradual withdrawal of direct supervision. Verbal attention to child's successful preparation, painting, co-operative clean-up. Including finger-painting in list of free-play activities.	Planning continued. Conversation: involving children in discussion of paintings, (This is pretty. How did you get the paint that way? What colors did you use here?) Leading to color mixing, line effects.

6. CLAY

RATING

THE FIVE LEVELS OF THE CURRICULUM ITEM

1. interest at a distance	2. touching and exploring	3. use of other materials in imitation of simple pattern	4. experimentation and elaboration	5. imaginative and creative use of available materials

DEFINITION OF THE TERM: BEHAVIOR UNDER OBSERVATION

Use of modeling clay as an expressive medium. Observed also were use of related plastic materials which were products of other activities including playdough, plastic soap mixture and papier-mache which were shaped by finger and hand pressure.

DESCRIPTION OF BEHAVIOR OBSERVED AT EACH LEVEL

Child watched others using the material.	Child poked, patted, rolled material, pinched off pieces of clay, etc., usually saying he was making some object, as, cookies, money.	Child imitated rolling and patting clay on table surface or between palms; repeated a process to make several similar objects, as, snakes, balls, cookies; imitated others' motions, products; used flat sticks, or knives to cut clay.	Child combined separate pieces to make a larger shape; often named the shape after noting a chance resemblance to an object. Child might recognize identifiable shapes.	Child chose clay as free-play activity. Made objects which fitted into an imaginative context (e.g. story illustrations, as Tarbaby; birthday cake).

PROGRAMMING

PREDICTABLE (INTERNALIZED) BEHAVIOR USED IN PROGRAMMING FOR NEXT LEVEL

Watches activity.	Explores material.	Imitates manipulative processes.	Produces shapes.	Anticipates, plans for, and carries out activity.

TEACHING PROCEDURES TO ESTABLISH READINESS FOR NEXT LEVEL.

Provision of opportunities for matching. Teacher participation in group activity. Verbal attention to manipulation processes. Presentation of materials as part of various imaginative sequences.	Teacher participation in group activity. Verbal attention to manipulation and shapes produced (e.g. patting to make cookies, rolling to make snakes, shaping with fingers to make a bowl). Comparing products, suggesting imitation.	Verbal attention to shapes' similarities and differences. Provision for sub-group activity: offering as work-period choice. Provision of auxiliary material, sticks, knives for clay; cookie-cutters for dough. Planning activity; getting out, putting away materials.	Planning continued. Scheduled clay work to follow a story period and planned illustrations for story. Conversation about products - ideas suggested by shapes. Including clay in list of free-play activities.	Planning, continued. Focus on ideas suggested by products. Verbal attention to action figures ("What is the boy doing?").

7a. DRAMATIC EXPRESSION: INDIVIDUAL

RATING

THE FIVE LEVELS OF THE CURRICULUM ITEM

1. interest at a distance	2. exploration	3. imitation	4. enjoyment and ease in activity	5. participates with originality

DEFINITION OF THE TERM: BEHAVIOR UNDER OBSERVATION

The child's individual imaginative play. Focus was on his make believe alone, with or without materials (props) but needing no interaction with other children or adults. Behavior was observed not only during free-play periods when play materials were available, but in music, reading, and handwork activities.

DESCRIPTION OF BEHAVIOR OBSERVED AT EACH LEVEL

Child watched play of other children; observed performance in music, handwork. Did not participate. Ordinarily, work with manipulative materials served as vantage point from which to observe dramatic play of others.	Child moved into a play area vacated by others; handled materials, books left by others; walked back and forth watching children; looked over boxes of materials; carried one or more props (often objects he brought from home) about the room.	Child moved into unoccupied area or took out materials and imitated activities he had watched. Also, child carried a book to a quiet corner and turned pages, telling, singing, or acting out a story for himself or for and with a puppet. Child might terminate play if anyone approached or commented.	Child showed behavior of (3), but was not disturbed by nearness of others. Looked up, smiled or nodded at comment from others. Child might repeat performance in a turn-taking situation.	Child acted out structured sequences such as complete stories, songs, cowboy play, house play. Ordinarily participated with enjoyment in a birthday party or music program.

PROGRAMMING

PREDICTABLE (INTERNALIZED) BEHAVIOR USED IN PROGRAMMING FOR NEXT LEVEL

Watches play of others.	Moves toward play area, handles materials.	Imitates imaginative episodes.	Maintains activity in presence of other stimuli.	Plans for and carries out dramatic activity.

TEACHING PROCEDURES TO ESTABLISH READINESS FOR NEXT LEVEL.

Provision of a variety of materials for house-play, "occupations" play, recreation fantasy. Provision of areas for use of songs and stories containing easily developed dramatic ideas. Use of turn-taking sequences in various music periods. Verbal attention to dramatic play of individuals. Verbal attention to small items brought from home.	Provision of variety of materials, duplicate sets of materials; observation from a distance, of individual child, to locate area of interest. Manipulation of situations to leave materials in reach of child. Verbal attention to child's interest in specific items. Verbal attention to play routines. Turn-taking continued.	Provision of materials in play areas continued. Careful observation of child's activity, manipulation of situation to foster development of ideas (e.g. bringing additional props to child; altering schedule to give child time to finish his play). Conversation about various activities: suggesting that child might allow others "some time."	Continued provision of materials, play areas. (Additions to supplies were within frameworks, to expand ideas rather than amounts of materials.) Planning for programs, music periods ("Who would like to do a marching or a magician act? Take Me Out to the Ball Game?" with teacher suggesting ideas). Verbal focus on special abilities.	Continued expansion of materials. Planning by children. Conversation about individual performances. Verbal attention to movement from real to make believe and back to real, in class activity.

7b. DRAMATIC EXPRESSION: GROUP DRAMATIC PLAY

RATING

THE FIVE LEVELS OF THE CURRICULUM ITEM

1. interest at a distance	2. exploration	3. imitation	4. enjoyment and ease in activity	5. participates with originality

DEFINITION OF THE TERM: BEHAVIOR UNDER OBSERVATION

The child's imaginative dramatic play with at least one other child. The theme or idea might be spontaneous, suggested by materials used, or remembered from story or music situations in which group and individual dramatic play were often interwoven.

DESCRIPTION OF BEHAVIOR OBSERVED AT EACH LEVEL

Child watched play of other children, from sidelines, from place at a worktable, or from own play position (Child interrupted own activity to watch group.)	Child moved into group. (e.g. he might knock on door, enter kitchen where a tea party was in progress; find milk carrier and deliver milk, bring a chair and join the party, or enter, smile, leave again.) Child occupied area after group left.	Child moved into play area and got out props in advance of or with children usually in group; helped with building of situation. Child joined group, conformed to imaginative structure.	Child was part of group, contributed to development of the dramatic sequence, conformed to familiar structure.	Child initiated group dramatic sequences; suggested ideas; brought variations or new elements to familiar sequences.

PROGRAMMING

PREDICTABLE (INTERNALIZED) BEHAVIOR USED IN PROGRAMMING FOR NEXT LEVEL

Watches dramatic play of other	Joins group.	Fits own actions to group structure.	Follows group dramatic idea, contributes to group dramatic play.	Plans dramatic play: adds details.

TEACHING PROCEDURES TO ESTABLISH READINESS FOR THE NEXT LEVEL.

Provision of a variety of materials for group play. Provision of areas as settings. Use of music periods, story periods with props to promote teacher-originated participation. Verbal attention to possibilities of materials (e.g. New objects were presented in conversation periods).	Planning activity to promote forming of groups, enlargement of groups. Teacher participation in on-going play. Discussion of various group activities as, comments on "good" ideas, ways in which individual children participated. Observation of child's interests. Offering additional material to establish child in parrallel play. Suggesting ways in which child might join group.	Discussion periods, with focus on connected ideas (structures) of group dramatic sequences. Planning for repetition of play sequences: "Tomorrow, you could play house again and B___ could be a neighbor coming in for coffee."	Discussion of roles played by individual children "You made a good father, D___, I liked the way you fed the baby and talked to your daughter." Verbal attention to new ideas, variations. Attention to materials for play: getting cooperation of children in increasing supplies (e.g. groceries for store).	Planning by children: materials, group to be involved and dramatic idea. Verbal attention to movement from real to make-believe and back to real: "and now the people who live here have to clean everything up and get ready for some real juice."

7c. DRAMATIC EXPRESSION: STRUCTURED DRAMATIC PLAY

RATING

THE FIVE LEVELS OF THE CURRICULUM ITEM

1. interest at a distance	2. exploration	3. imitation	4. enjoyment and ease in activity	5. participates with originality

DEFINITION OF THE TERM: BEHAVIOR UNDER OBSERVATION

"Structured dramatic play" was the dramatization of episodes or sequences from external sources. Structure, present in both individual and group dramatic play, was provided by the child's experience or his understanding of the use of the immediately-present materials. The structured play was based on vicarious experience of some kind (through books, teacher's stories, narrative songs, and music). Although children could alter sequences and improvise freely in their own group play, dramatization considered here was confined to a specified framework. Actual dialogue and ways of performing the sequence were spontaneous, however, and rating was on child's participation with the non-personal structure.

DESCRIPTION OF BEHAVIOR OBSERVED AT EACH LEVEL

Child watched performance of others.	Child joined in action sequences, or explored roles alone. (e.g. a Goldilocks curled up in each of several imaginary beds several Baby Bears crying.)	Child participated, imitating action and words of others.	Child played out a role with fair accuracy and verbalization. Performance was usually imitative. Essentially stayed in character, did not switch roles.	Child played a role accurately, either spontaneously or with additions of variations of others' dramatization. Child helped to keep story moving in right direction.

PROGRAMMING

PREDICTABLE (INTERNALIZED) BEHAVIOR USED IN PROGRAMMING FOR NEXT LEVEL

Watches performance of others.	Performs actions associated with one or more roles.	Imitates actions and speech.	Knows action and speech for one or more roles.	Knows total structure of dramatic episode or sequence; plans.

TEACHING PROCEDURES TO ESTABLISH READINESS FOR NEXT LEVEL.

Repetition of story or song, which provides structures for dramatic play. Teacher dramatization of story using movements, intonations to distinguish characters. Story with props. Action-reading of familiar stories by pausing for child(ren) to supply movement for a phrase as fingers to the lips for "Shh" in Quiet Little Indian, shaking finger at monkeys in Caps for Sale.	Response reading of stories: waiting for children to supply words and expressions, as "This is too hot!" in The Three Bears. Verbal attention to children's speech.	Cooperative telling of story; waiting for children to supply words and action for episodes and scenes. Verbal attention to children's voice tones and actions. Attention to illustrations as guides to story sequence.	Providing for children's "reading" of stories and action songs; gradual withdrawal of teacher from role of narrator. Planning for structured performance.	Expansion of dramatization activity to include stories of various kinds: a) folk tales b) vicarious real-life stories as, The Rabbit and Teacher's Appletree. c) Legends and stories from history. d) Familiar daily schedules of children.

7d. DRAMATIC EXPRESSION: PUPPETRY

RATING

THE FIVE LEVELS OF THE CURRICULUM ITEM

1. interest at a distance	2. exploration	3. imitation	4. enjoyment and ease in activity	5. participates with originality

DEFINITION OF THE TERM: BEHAVIOR UNDER OBSERVATION

The child's use of hand puppets for dramatic play. Patterns of puppet play observed included: a) handling a puppet and carrying on a conversation with it; b) holding a puppet and talking through it to other children with puppets; c) using two or more puppets and working out a dramatic sequence.

DESCRIPTION OF BEHAVIOR OBSERVED AT EACH LEVEL

Child watched use of puppets by others.	Child handled puppets, inserted hand, tried to move puppet's hands, head.	Child imitated simple movements making puppet bow, dance, clap hands, shake head. Child spoke for puppet, using simple expressions, such as, Hello, Bye-bye, No.	Child handled both movements and speech, carrying on a conversation of one of the three types mentioned.	Child manipulated puppet easily, fitted words and motions into a structure developed by him and/or other children; child helped others to develop themes.

PROGRAMMING

PREDICTABLE (INTERNALIZED) BEHAVIOR USED IN PROGRAMMING FOR NEXT LEVEL

Watches puppets and/or dramatic process.	Handles puppets.	Uses verbalization.	Handles verbalization, action at same time.	Constructs or contributes to a sequence.

TEACHING PROCEDURES TO ESTABLISH READINESS FOR THE NEXT LEVEL

Teacher participation: use of puppet to address group; use of two puppets for question-answer conversation routines; use of two or more puppets as teacher and one or more children, for group conversation. Attention to puppet's movements as clapping, waving, bowing, shaking or nodding head, turning, sitting. Providing puppets for use during free-play period.	Teacher participation as before, with attention to verbalization in greetings, "Yes" and "No" answers, "thank you." Offering puppets to child in situation where he might develop an idea (e.g. child looking at a book might be interested in reading to a puppet.) Offering rubber animals for zoo building and animal sounds.	Teacher use of sets of puppets, enacting an episode of actions and words. Providing sets of materials matched to stories and experiences familiar to children (toy dolls, toy farms, to supplement puppets). Verbal attention to group and individual dramatizations.	Verbal attention to dramatization of several sequences such as, Father going to work; Children going to school; Mother caring for baby; Three Bears, and Gingerbread Boy. Focus on structure and continuing theme. Planning, carrying out a puppet program.	Continued provision for dramatizations of various kinds, as in group dramatic play and structured dramatic play; Folk tales and other stories, historical episodes, legends, real happenings of children. Leading to further clarification of concepts real, make-believe, concepts of time, distance.

8a. CREATIVE RHYTHMS: INDIVIDUAL

RATING

THE FIVE LEVELS OF THE CURRICULUM ITEM

1. interest at a distance	2. exploration	3. imitation	4. enjoyment and ease in activity	5. participation with originality

DEFINITION OF THE TERM: BEHAVIOR UNDER OBSERVATION

The child's individual rhythmic expression. Responses to rhythms, like dramatic expression, was considered under three aspects: individual, group, and structured. Thus, the rhythmic expression rated on the present item was in the same category as individual dramatic expression — it was the child's personal response to music. For developing individual rhythmic expression, the most effective teaching processes were in group situations. Programming of this item, then, is included in the programming for the following item (b).

DESCRIPTION OF BEHAVIOR OBSERVED AT EACH LEVEL

Child watched rhythm activity but did not participate.	Child asked for a particular song or record, or looked pleased when another child requested one he liked. (He still might not join in the activity, however.) Child experimented with movements suggested by tune or words of song.	Child imitated movements of others, e.g. marching, running, twirling. There was usually a lag of several seconds in this phase, i. e., child watched others briefly, then imitated.	Child responded to the music, not waiting for cues from others. Child requested favorite tunes, recognized tunes.	Child improvised, sometimes led the group; usually began to show rhythmic controls in his expressive movements.

PROGRAMMING

PREDICTABLE (INTERNALIZED) BEHAVIOR USED IN PROGRAMMING FOR NEXT LEVEL

Watches activity of other children; seems to listen to music.	Performs; shows interest in one or more action tunes.	Observes and matches movement of others.	Supplies movement to familiar tunes.	Uses repertoire of movements; experiments with various combinations.

TEACHING PROCEDURES TO DEVELOP READINESS FOR NEXT LEVEL.

Building group action vocabulary, Record periods, listening to story records in which songs or words suggest actions (e.g. Train to the Zoo; Little Gray Ponies; Where, oh Where is Pretty Little Susie?) Action Songs: Here We Are Together; Rockabye Baby; Mary had a Little Lamb. Music clues: marching, tip-toeing, jumping, whirling. Activities built up gradually, over a period of several weeks.	"Serial" planning, asking for suggestions, one by one, during period: "Who can think of a good song?" "Is there a record which someone specially wants to hear?" "I'd like to play some marching music. Would you like to march today?" Use of animal movements: Gallop like a horse. Presenting songs as action setting. "Listen, I'm going to play some dancing music. Can you dance?" Asking various children to lead group movements. Leader imitates teacher.	Continued Serial planning. Tunes and activities supplied by children and noted by teacher. Discussion of repetitions. Elaboration of context. Use of props such as harness bells for Little Gray Ponies, crepe paper streamers for dancing. Fingers dancing at tables, on floor.	Verbal attention to individual activities in group: improvisations, new motions. Turn-taking as leaders; children who make improvisations as leaders. Work on recognition of music cues: a) Teacher names actions in same order in which she will play them, gives serial cues. b) Teacher names actions, changing order slightly in playing. c) Teacher plays music, without preliminary naming.	Use of music plus narrative: a) children interpreting story b) children utilizing music cues. Expanded use of props; experimenting with use of various kinds of handclaps, pats on table, small "noises". Verbal attention to individual activities. Use of individualized materials, teacher-made personalized books: Judy Dances, Jimmy Marches, A Book for Jackie, Take Me Out To the Ball Game, Barbara's Pussy-willow Song. Use of commercial books-children selecting songs. Leading to awareness of preferences; awareness of individual contributions to group; symbolic records of individual activity and group activity.

8b. CREATIVE RHYTHMS: GROUP

RATING

THE FIVE LEVELS OF THE CURRICULUM ITEM

1. interest at a distance	2. exploration	3. imitation	4. enjoyment and ease in activity	5. participation with originality

DEFINITION OF THE TERM: BEHAVIOR UNDER OBSERVATION

The child's participation in group rhythm experiences such as marching, skipping, tiptoeing where each child governed his own response to various rhythms. In the corresponding aspect of dramatic expression, this item dealt with group improvisations; rhythmic accuracy was not essential in the rating though it was observed as the child moved to easy participation.

DESCRIPTION OF BEHAVIOR OBSERVED AT EACH LEVEL

Child watched group, listened to music, did not participate.	Child moved with group, or stayed at edge of group, trying various movements. Child requested records or tunes, but might not participate in activity after requesting song.	Child imitated others, ordinarily with a lag in performance.	Child requested tunes, records; might use actions to ask for tune; joined expressive movement of the group; recognized tunes.	Child made up variations for rhythmic activities; identified various tunes; usually showed some rhythmic patterning.

PROGRAMMING

PREDICTABLE (INTERNALIZED) BEHAVIOR USED IN PROGRAMMING FOR NEXT LEVEL

Watches activity of other children; seems to listen to music.	Performs; shows interest in one or more action tunes.	Observes and matches movement of others.	Supplies movements to familiar tunes.	Uses repertoire of movements; experiments with various combinations.

TEACHING PROCEDURES TO DEVELOP READINESS FOR NEXT LEVEL

Building group-action vocabulary. Record periods, listening to story records in which songs or words suggest actions (e.g. Train to the Zoo; Little Gray Ponies; Where, oh Where is Pretty Little Susie?) Action Songs: Here We are Together; Rockabye Baby; Mary had a Little Lamb. Music clues: marching, tip-toeing, jumping, whirling. Activities built up gradually over a period of several weeks.	"Serial" planning - asking for suggestions, one by one, during period: "Who can think of a good song?" "Is there a record which someone specially wants to hear?" "I'd like to play some marching music. Would you like to march today?" Use of animal movements. Gallop like a horse. Presenting songs as action setting. "Listen, I'm going to play some dancing music. Can you dance? Asking various children to lead group movements. Leader imitates teacher.	Continued Serial planning. Tunes and activities supplied by children and noted by teacher. Discussion of repetitions. Elaboration of context. Use of props such as harness bells for Little Gray Ponies, crepe paper streamers for dancing. Finger dancing at tables, on floor.	Verbal attention to individual activities in group: improvisations, new motions. Turn-taking as leaders; children who make improvisations as leaders. Work on recognition of music cues: a) Teacher names actions in same order in which she will play them, gives serial cues. b) Teacher names actions, changes order slightly in playing. c) Teacher plays music, without preliminary naming.	Use of music plus narrative: a) children interpreting story b) children utilizing music cues. Extended use of props; experimenting with use of various kinds of handclaps, pats on table, small "noises". Verbal attention to individual activities. Use of individualized materials teacher made personalized books: Judy Dances; Jimmy Marches, A Book for Jackie, Take Me out To the Ball Game, Barbara's Pussy-willow Song. Use of commercial books - children selecting songs. Leading to awareness of preferences; awareness of individual contributions to group; symbolic records of individual activity and group activity.

8c. CREATIVE RHYTHMS: STRUCTURED

RATING

THE FIVE LEVELS OF THE CURRICULUM ITEM

1. interest at a distance	2. exploration	3. imitation	4. enjoyment and ease in activity	5. participates with originality

DEFINITION OF THE TERM: BEHAVIOR UNDER OBSERVATION

The child's rhythmic response in structured situations. In group creative rhythms (item immediately preceding) activity was actually structured by the nature of the music, and performance within that structure was individual and free, i.e. the child marched or danced or tiptoed as he chose. The same music and activities could be used for structured rhythms by specifying the manner of response. Other structures were provided by finger-play songs, fixed narrative sequences, and action songs including folk dances and singing games.

DESCRIPTION OF BEHAVIOR OBSERVED AT EACH LEVEL.

Child watched finger-play, dances. Did not participate.	Child sat or moved with group, listened participated from time to time; usually tried concluding part of an activity. Child might request a particular tune or dance.	Child imitated as much of the structure as he could; might lag slightly behind group rhythm, in responses.	Child synchronized own movements with group rhythms; took turns as leader of group.	Child suggested tunes; new details for familiar rhythmic patterns; made new combinations of movements for new songs.

PROGRAMMING

PREDICTABLE (INTERNALIZED) BEHAVIOR USED IN PROGRAMMING FOR NEXT LEVEL

Watches structured rhythms.	Participates in physical structure; tries rhythmic movements.	Imitates sequence of movements.	Knows and enjoys one or more sequences.	Combines movements in new structures.

TEACHING PROCEDURES TO ESTABLISH READINESS FOR NEXT LEVEL.

(Teacher participation at all levels)

Providing single structures to watch. a) Records, songs in which listening alternates with period of extended activity. (e.g. Train to the Zoo; Rainy Day) b) Songs with momentary repeated structures (Clap, Clap Your Hands). Refrain songs: Old McDonald, Fire). c) Songs with continuous simple structure (Row-row-row, The King of France). d) Inhibition release structures (Little Gray Ponies, Jack in the Box, Tidey O, Here We Are Together.) Verbal attention to children's participation.	Use of song structures which provide adequate reaction time: Here's a Ball for Baby, Put Your Fingers in the Air, I Point to Myself. Dance structure: Mulberry Bush. Use of song structure with quicker tempo, more complicated repeat movements: Where Is Thumbkin, This Old Man, People on the Bus, Here We Are Together. Use of group motor activities: march, tiptoe, run in sequence, with changes marked verbally and by forte accent on first bars of each new change. Verbal attention to children's responses. Planning of sequence.	Use of complicated song structures: Here's a Ball, Open Shut Them, Way up in an Apple Tree, Here We Are Together. Use of dance structure: Flopsy Flora, Clap Dance, Shoemaker's Dance. Group motor and song activities, piano cues; marching (fast, slow, quietly); Row-row (fast, slow, hard). Planning of sequences, following printed list. Review: check-off the list. Providing turns at leading.	Planning of sequences. Planning turn-taking as leader. Discussion and evaluation of activity. Use of books to structure familiar songs. Verbal introduction to new activities through musical dramatization of story. Birthday programs, serialized planning with structure provided by program, free rhythms in individual performance.	Birthday programs: Pre-planning of total program. Expansion of song vocabulary. Use of: John the Rabbit, Up in a Balloon, Up on the Housetop. Leading to work on symbols.

8d. CREATIVE RHYTHMS: RHYTHM BAND

RATING

THE FIVE LEVELS OF THE CURRICULUM ITEM

1. interest at a distance	2. exploration	3. imitation	4. enjoyment and ease in activity	5. participation with originality

DEFINITION OF THE TERM: BEHAVIOR UNDER OBSERVATION

The child's use of percussion instruments in a group situation. The rhythm band provided a structured activity within which individual expressive use of instruments was possible. The discussion of manipulation of rhythm instruments, in another section, presents in greater detail the introduction of various instruments.

DESCRIPTION OF BEHAVIOR OBSERVED AT EACH LEVEL

Child watched and listened to instruments used by others.	Child examined, tried out instruments in group situation and after group had finished activity.	Child held instrument, imitated movements of others; might not follow rhythm of group.	Child manipulated instrument with ease; kept rhythm pattern with group.	Child gave major attention to rhythm and group activity; handled instrument purposefully; introduced variations.

PROGRAMMING

PREDICTABLE (INTERNALIZED) BEHAVIOR USED IN PROGRAMMING FOR NEXT LEVEL

Watches and listens.	Produces sounds with instrument.	Imitates movements in group situation.	Controls production of sounds.	Uses sounds for expression in group context.

TEACHING PROCEDURES TO ESTABLISH READINESS FOR NEXT LEVEL

Introduction of different instruments in connection with other music activities. Observation of child to determine preferences. Verbal attention to preference and to action involved. Planning for use with, "We are going to sing Jingle Bells - We ought to try the bells," or, starting activity and getting out rhythm instruments later.	Continued use of instruments in general activities. Same kind of instrument for each child: stick bells for Jingle Bells, Frere Jacques; harness bells for Little Gray Ponies, Jingle Bells; cymbals for marching. Verbal attention to child's use of instrument, in group. Experimentation with different rhythmic patterns.	Use of instruments in structured situation for motion and inhibition. a) Song structure: Tidey-o, Frere Jacques, King of France. b) Story structure: Quiet Little Indian, Little Gray Ponies, record of Circus Parade. c) Tune structure of familiar dance or song. Dance, waltz, march of Flopsy Flora, Where is Thumbkin. Verbal attention to rhythm of group and of individual as part of group.	Use of various combinations of instruments. Use of instruments, bands for sound effects in marching, tiptoeing, galloping, skipping. Patterns of alternate playing, inhibition. Introduction of patterned activity and instruments, as march, with drums; halt, drums quiet. Verbal attention to patterns of silence and sound. Turn-taking as leaders, leading to section bands and individual performances.	Turn-taking, assigning leadership to children trying new patterns. Two-group rhythm bands, a) group playing together using two different instruments; b) groups playing alternately using two different instruments; c) "solo" performances by individuals. Beginning use of symbols in chart for use of bells.

1. RELATEDNESS TO CHILDREN

RATING

THE FIVE LEVELS OF THE CURRICULUM ITEM

1. apparently indifferent to others	2. awareness and interest in others	3. moving toward some individual(s)	4. establishment of a definite relationship	5. give and take relationship with the group

DEFINITION OF THE TERM: BEHAVIOR UNDER OBSERVATION

Child's relationship with other children in the group. Withdrawal, contact, cooperation, aggression of various kinds, verbal comment (including tattling and complaints) were considered evidence of a relationship. Teaching processes were aimed at guiding children toward constructive relationships.

DESCRIPTION OF BEHAVIOR OBSERVED AT EACH LEVEL

Showed interest in objects, materials. Had play-pattern with materials. Showed interest in teachers' use of objects.	Gave attention to classmate because of toys: wanted to exchange toys, or simply to take them. Noticed classmates way of using toys particularly those with which child had had no previous experience.	Child tried one pattern of relating: a) cooperative b) competitive or c) aggressive	Child set up a play relationship, or personal tie with another child; formed a communication relationship with teachers or other adult.	Individual and sub-group relationships. Child had workable relationship with one or more children was part of a sub-group in a favorite activity.

PROGRAMMING

PREDICTABLE (INTERNALIZED) BEHAVIOR USED IN PROGRAMMING FOR NEXT LEVEL

Notices and uses objects and materials	Notices activities of individuals	Tries a pattern of relating such as: a) cooperation b) competition c) aggression	Forms a relationship	Forms practical individual and sub-group relationships

TEACHING PROCEDURES TO ESTABLISH READINESS FOR NEXT LEVEL

Providing duplicate or similar toys. Provision for group activities with multiple supplies. Comparison of ways of play. Comparison (likenesses) of handwork products.	Providing ample group supplies. Provision of duplicate toys used in a shared setting. Verbal attention to variant uses. Comparison (likenesses and differences) of products. Provision for helping another child.	a. Providing materials for shared work, play. b. Provisions for turn-taking. c. Provisions for helping, leadership. Verbal attention to shared toys, materials, supplies. Class planning sharing of responsibilities.	Provisions for setting up more groups for interactions. Class planning, sharing of responsibilities.	Providing opportunities for exploring roles in sub-groups formed for work or play purposes.

2. RELATEDNESS TO ADULTS

RATING

THE FIVE LEVELS OF THE CURRICULUM ITEM

1. apparently indif- ferent to adults	2. awareness and in- terest in adults	3. moving toward some adult(s)	4. establishment of a definite relationship	5. at ease with most adults

DEFINITION OF THE TERM: BEHAVIOR UNDER OBSERVATION

Child's relationship to adults. Patterns resembling those observed in the child's relatedness to children were often observed in seeking contact with adults; the child withdrawing from adults ordinarily set up early working relationships with one or more children. Teaching procedures did not attempt to deal with sources of preferences, but used existing behavior as the basis for serviceable in-school relationships.

DESCRIPTION OF BEHAVIOR OBSERVED AT EACH LEVEL

Child's interest was in toys, materials, room setting.	Child watched adults, played near adult, withdrew from or re- jected attention of adults.	Child began to use name of adult(s), Asked for mater- ials, asked for help, stayed near adult. Child tried to con- trol adult's attention, time.	Child worked with adult, showed pro- ducts, reported news items; reported phy- sical discomfort; sought attention of one or more adults; consistently tried to control.	Child had a working re- lationship with most adults; cooperated Shared tasks. Child had some idea of roles of different adults and regulated own behavior in accord with situation.

PROGRAMMING

PREDICTABLE (INTERNALIZED) BEHAVIOR USED IN PROGRAMMING FOR NEXT LEVEL

Shows interest in toys, interest in children.	Shows interest in adult's activity.	Refers problems, questions, etc. to particular adult(s); chooses adult as partner.	Shares practical re- lationship with an adult.	Relates to various adults.

TEACHING PROCEDURES TO ESTABISH READINESS FOR NEXT LEVEL.

Providing mater- ials liked by child. Commenting on child's work, play. Using formalized greetings. Comment- ing on group and sub-group activities.	Providing mater- ials. Setting up ac- tivity groups with preferred adult. Giving physical help.	Continuing provision of materials, physical support, activity di- rections. Guiding ag- gressive interest. Setting up activities involving additional adults. Verbal atten- tion to other adults introducing, enlist- ing aid. Planning ac- tivities.	Utilization of child's pattern in group ac- tivity. Substitutions of adults in various group roles. Provid- ing opportunities to transfer relation- ships to other adults.	Verbal attention to relationships recall, review, planning.

3. SHARING

RATING

THE FIVE LEVELS OF THE CURRICULUM ITEM

1. passive release	2. defending or re-sisting release	3. release with adult encouragement	4. releases voluntarily	5. initiates or agrees to cooperative use

DEFINITION OF THE TERM: BEHAVIOR UNDER OBSERVATION

Sharing of toys and materials in the group situation. Teachers' use of existing behavior, in this item, resembled and kept pace with readiness work in several other social development items.

DESCRIPTION OF BEHAVIOR OBSERVED AT EACH LEVEL

Child let others take materials he was using with no reaction.	Child held on to toys, blocked others from area; repossessed toys taken, if possible. Tantrum behavior at necessary teacher interference.	Child made behavior fit into necessary turn-taking, sharing situations with adult supervision, agreed to brief or longer term trades.	Child shared, took turns in familiar situations, as, turns on tricycle. use of puzzles. traded for own advantage.	Child helped plan for turns, offered materials to children waiting for them. traded for material benefits.

PROGRAMMING

PREDICTABLE (INTERNALIZED) BEHAVIOR USED IN PROGRAMMING FOR NEXT LEVEL

Interest in an object.	Defends possessions.	With help, chooses to give up possessions.	Experience in suggesting, arranging, turn-taking. Experience in cooperation. Shares, with attention on thing shared.	Experience in sharing with different class-mates. Shares with attention on other person.

TEACHING PROCEDURES TO ESTABLISH READINESS FOR NEXT LEVEL

Return of toys and plan for later re-lease. Verbal attention to child's ability to retain toy. Use of duplicate toys.	Use of duplicate toys in shared situations. Use of different toys in shared situations. Brief exchange of toys. Verbal attention to exchanges. Use of group activities. with comparison of toys used, products of handwork.	Planning for use of various toys, e.g., "What are you going to do on the roof?" "Then, you and A and B all want turns with the tricycle. Whose turn is it to be first?" Verbal attention to personal cooperation: planning cooperative uses, as "A could ride the tri-cycle and B could run the gas station this time."	Providing opportunities for sharing toys with various children in group.	Planning for cooperative activities as distin-guished from use of toys.

4. CONSIDERATION OF OTHERS

RATING

THE FIVE LEVELS OF THE CURRICULUM ITEM

1. preoccupation with self	2. consideration upon awareness of advantage	3. empathizing with others	4. consideration of friends	5. consideration of people in general - justice

DEFINITION OF THE TERM: BEHAVIOR UNDER OBSERVATION

Child's consideration of comfort and feelings of others in playing and carrying out his own activities.

DESCRIPTION OF BEHAVIOR OBSERVED AT EACH LEVEL

Child asked for or chose things for self: was concerned with his own comfort, preferences, activities. Used expressions, "It's mine." "But I need it."	Child asked for or chose things for another child (or children) when his own activity involved the other(s). Also offered service, sympathy, materials to others and enjoyed attention given to his sharing. "You can play with this if you'll give me that."	Offered service, sympathy, materials to another; took apparent pleasure in other's use of material, response to service. Used expressions, "You take this to play with." "B ___ wants one, too."	Offered service, etc. to close friends in class; enjoyed responses of friends. Used expressions, "Is there one for A ___ ?" "I'll save this for A ___."	Offered services to others besides friends, presented non-personal reasons to classmates, adults when asking for materials for self and others. Used expressions such as, "We should save one for S ___." "B ___ has not had a turn yet."

PROGRAMMING

PREDICTABLE (INTERNALIZED) BEHAVIOR USED IN PROGRAMMING FOR NEXT LEVEL

Has preferences, favorite activities.	"Trades" with attention to objects or activities.	"Trades" with attention to person; or helps with intent to give pleasure.	Plans activities to benefit special friends.	Plans on basis of an abstract idea.

TEACHING PROCEDURES TO ESTABLISH READINESS FOR NEXT LEVEL

Providing duplicate materials, activities. Providing opportunities for including others in child's favorite activities. Verbal comparison of use of materials, way of acting.	Verbal notice of reaction of children helped. Supporting child's attempt to help another. "Setting stage" for offers of help.	Verbal notice of helper's feelings, recipient's feeling. Guiding children to choose activities favoring cooperation. Guiding children toward choice of helping role. Utilizing friendships existing in class. (Natural pairs, groups.)	Providing activities for small groups. Working other children into natural pairs or groups for shorter or longer projects. Verbal attention to common likes, dislikes, wants.	Enlarging number and kind of situations. Verbal attention to common likes, dislikes, wants. Planning on whole-group basis.

5. RECEIVING HELP

RATING

THE FIVE LEVELS OF THE CURRICULUM ITEM

1. passivity	2. resistance	3. expression of need	4. selecting optimum source	5. successful method of obtaining help

DEFINITION OF THE TERM: BEHAVIOR UNDER OBSERVATION

Method of obtaining help in any of the school activities. Need for "help" did not always reflect inability of child to complete the activity: exploration of personal relationships seemed to be the basis of some requests for help.

DESCRIPTION OF BEHAVIOR OBSERVED AT EACH LEVEL

Child let adult or another child help him in dressing, eating, other self-help activities, without apparent concern.	Child objected to help, either because he wanted to try or because he did not want task completed.	Child asked for help in activity.	Child asked aid of person most likely to be able to give it.	Child enlisted aid of adults and/or children for various processes.

PROGRAMMING

PREDICTABLE (INTERNALIZED) BEHAVIOR USED IN PROGRAMMING FOR NEXT LEVEL

Permits help.	Refuses help.	Recognizes need for help.	Recognizes competence in others.	Gets help in various situations.

TEACHING PROCEDURES TO ESTABLISH READINESS FOR NEXT LEVEL

Verbal attention to process. Verbal attention to person helping. Verbal attention to child's ability to perform part of an activity, as, placing a picture on the bulletin board, after teacher had helped with the hard work.	a) Verbal attention to independence of child. Direct teaching of process involved. b) Verbal attention to purpose of activity. Help in completing activity (same kind of help given to passive child.)	Verbal attention to process; physical help where needed. Discussion of result: identifying child's part, helper's share of result. Verbal attention to reason for giving help. "I will button your sweater because I want to show you how to do it." "I'd like to button this pink sweater."	Recognition of helper and verbal attention to kind of help given, e.g., "I am glad Dorothy tied your shoes for you. She ties good firm bows." Suggesting ways of returning favors. "Now you could help Mary Ann with her boots."	Attention to skills of different adults, children. Attention to weak areas of various adults, children. Providing situations in which services might be exchanged.

6. RESPECTING PROPERTY RIGHTS

RATING

THE FIVE LEVELS OF THE CURRICULUM ITEM

1. claiming owner-ship	2. identification of own possessions	3. recognition of others' pos-session	4. respects other's property with reminders	5. respects own and others property

DEFINITION OF THE TERM: BEHAVIOR UNDER OBSERVATION

Care of own and others' property.

DESCRIPTION OF BEHAVIOR OBSERVED AT EACH LEVEL

Child claimed toys he liked and wanted, toys similar to some he had at home. Sometimes child wanted to take (or took) school toys home.	Child recognized objects he had brought to school or wraps worn to school.	Child named owner of object he had or wanted, but did not necessarily return it to owner.	Child accepted teachers reminder to return property to owners and to put away school toys.	Child identified own and others' property. Gathered up own belongings to take home, returned other objects to owners or stored school things in cupboards.

PROGRAMMING

PREDICTABLE (INTERNALIZED) BEHAVIOR USED IN PROGRAMMING FOR NEXT LEVEL

Chooses toys for use.	Cares for own possessions.	Watches others care for their posessions.	Returns other's possessions.	Gets permission for handling objects.

TEACHING PROCEDURES TO ESTABLISH READINESS FOR NEXT LEVEL

Verbal attention to toys chosen. Conversation about personal toys at home. Discussion of school toys. Planning for use in school: putting away at end of activity or at end of session.	Verbal attention to child's possessions. Designating shelf for safe storage. Focus on toys brought to school, ownership by various children. Providing opportunity for child to permit others to inspect and return personal items. Playing games at close of school: "Whose coat is this?" "Who brought this _____ to school?"	Continued provision of opportunities for inspecting personal toys, returning toys to owners, storing toys on "checking" shelf. Continued assembling of possessions at end of each session, returning to owners.	Provision for inspecting, borrowing, returning, putting away things belonging to various individuals. Teacher "loans" of various items. Teacher gifts of various items.	Activities looking toward citizenship. Circulating library activities. Joint projects (e.g., bringing materials for grocery store; cooking activities). Caring for, cleaning, and repairing materials for group use.

7a1. EXPRESSIONS: PLEASE
b1.

RATING

THE FIVE LEVELS OF THE CURRICULUM ITEM

1. apparently una-ware of formal expression	2. apparently aware of formal expression	3. prompted or imitative expression	4. initiates expression in usual situations	5. appropriate independent use of expression in a variety of situations

DEFINITION OF THE TERM: BEHAVIOR UNDER OBSERVATION

Use of the expression, "please" in asking for tangible items, help, or favors.

DESCRIPTION OF BEHAVIOR OBSERVED AT EACH LEVEL

Child asked for objects, did not use customary request form.	When asked, "What do you say?" or "How do you ask ____ for the (toy)?" child smiled or indicated in some way awareness of expression.	Child repeated "Please" at Teacher's suggestion or in response to questions as in 2.	Child ordinarily used "Please" in asking for objects.	Child used "Please" when asking for objects and for help with tasks.

PROGRAMMING

PREDICTABLE (INTERNALIZED) BEHAVIOR USED IN PROGRAMMING FOR NEXT LEVEL

Attends to objects, (toys, materials, crackers and juice at snack time.)	Recognizes term.	Imitates word.	Uses in learned situations.	Uses with idea of courtesy.

TEACHING PROCEDURES TO ESTABLISH READINESS FOR NEXT LEVEL

Teacher use of expression when making legitimate requests for things. Comment on use of expression by various children in group. e.g., "Oh, B, would you say that again so the others can hear it?", "You said please so nicely," (clearly, etc.) or "B says please very well.	Experience with taking turns with favorite toys. Experience in juice-time routine: passing refreshments, pouring juice, asking for more food. Verbal attention to ways of asking for things.	Continued opportunity to share, plan for sharing, receive, plan for asking. Verbal attention to situations appropriate for use of please. Verbal attention to giver's responses, as, giving up or exchanging a toy to please another child.	Continued situations for sharing, asking, receiving. Verbal focus on appropriate affirmative, negative responses. Verbal focus on inappropriate responses. Verbal attention to inappropriate use of "please."	Continued situations for sharing. Evaluation of individual uses of expression and of individual responses to expression. Use of variant expressions "If you please?" "If you will . . ." "I'd appreciate it if . . ." "Could you . . .?"

7a2. EXPRESSIONS: THANK YOU
b2.

RATING

THE FIVE LEVELS OF THE CURRICULUM ITEM

1. apparently unaware of formal expression	2. apparently aware of formal expression	3. prompted or imitative expression	4. initiates expression in usual situations	5. appropriate independent use of expression in a variety of situations

DEFINITION OF THE TERM: BEHAVIOR UNDER OBSERVATION

Use of expression "thank you," "thanks," when receiving tangible things (gifts, portions, or loans) and favors of various kinds.

DESCRIPTION OF BEHAVIOR OBSERVED AT EACH LEVEL

Child did not use expression when receiving tangible objects. Smile or gesture was credited when child did not have speech.	Child smiled, nodded, or otherwise showed awareness when reminded about saying "Thank you."	Child used expression when reminded "What should you say?" "Can you say 'Thank you'?", "Can you thank _____?" "You should say 'thank you' when ___ gives you that."	Child usually said, "Thank you" for objects, direct help.	Child used "Thank you" in accepting gifts, loans, crackers at juice time, and in response to compliments.

PROGRAMMING

PREDICTABLE (INTERNALIZED) BEHAVIOR USED IN PROGRAMMING FOR NEXT LEVEL

Attends to objects.	Recognizes expression	Tries to use expression. Imitates expression.	Uses expression in learned situation.	Uses expression with idea of courtesy.

TEACHING PROCEDURES TO ESTABLISH READINESS FOR EACH LEVEL

Teacher's use of expression. Experience in distributing and accepting treats, juice time refreshments. Experience in exchanging toys. Verbal attention to use of "thank you." Child who seems unaware of expression to be given extra chances to distribute, chance to receive the "thank you's."	Teacher's continued use of expression. Continued experience in distributing and accepting various objects, treats. Verbal attention to children's use of expression.	Continued experiences with reminder and expectation that child use expression. Verbal attention to instances of sharing. Verbal attention to use by various children. Variations in expression. Planning a sequence: "B will you pass his candy. You will all say 'Thank you,' and C will say 'You are welcome.'"	Continued experiences as before. Verbal focus on intentions in sharing and on appropriate uses of "thank you," "you are welcome."	Continued experiences, with increased attention to the good will, thoughtfulness of children arranging treats, distributing refreshments, loaning toys. Use of equivalent expressions, "Thank you very much." "That is kind of you." "I appreciate it."

7a3. EXPRESSIONS: YOU ARE WELCOME
b3.

RATING

THE FIVE LEVELS OF THE CURRICULUM ITEM

1. apparently una-ware of formal expression	2. apparently aware of formal expression	3. prompted or imitative response	4. initiates expressions in usual situations	5. appropriate independent use of expression in a variety of situations

DEFINITION OF THE TERM: BEHAVIOR UNDER OBSERVATION

Use of "You are welcome," "You're welcome," in response to expressed thanks.

DESCRIPTION OF BEHAVIOR OBSERVED AT EACH LEVEL

Child showed no awareness or recognitions of expressions.	Child looked at teacher, when teacher suggested use of expressions, might smile or nod.	Child repeated expression after teacher, or in response to question "What could you say?"	Child usually used expression when another said, "Thank you."	Child habitually used expression.

PROGRAMMING

PREDICTABLE (INTERNALIZED) BEHAVIOR USED IN PROGRAMMING FOR NEXT LEVEL

Attends to objects.	Notices expression.	Imitates words.	Uses word in some situations.	Uses word with idea of courtesy.

TEACHING PROCEDURES TO ESTABLISH READINESS FOR NEXT LEVEL

Teacher used expression. Use of expression by other children in situations where passing of materials or special treats is part of sequence. Emphasis on expression in "Thank you" and "You are welcome" exchange.	Verbal attention to expression as used by others in class situation. Visits to stores using the "Thank you" - "You are welcome" exchange. Turn-taking in passing materials, with practice in use of expression.	Attention to child's successful use of expression. Verbal attention to activities in which expression is useful. (Passing cookies, materials, giving help, spontaneous sharing)	Verbal attention to child's voluntary use of expression. Summary and discussion of several expressions: "Will you have one?"; "Thank you"; "You are welcome"; "I'll help you"; "Thank you."	Expansion of use in intangible situations. Attention to idea of giving pleasure. Alternate expressions: "That is all right"; "I'm glad you like it."

7a4. EXPRESSIONS: APOLOGY
b4.

RATING

THE FIVE LEVELS OF THE CURRICULUM ITEM

1. apparently unaware of formal expression	2. apparently aware of formal expression	3. prompted or imitative expression	4. initiates expression in usual situation	5. appropriate independent use of expression in a variety of situations

DEFINITION OF THE TERM: BEHAVIOR UNDER OBSERVATION

Use of an apology form such as "Oh!", "Sorry," "I'm sorry," "I didn't mean to," for physical offense against another person. Physical offense included such intentional or unintentional actions as bumping, pushing, knocking objects from another's hand, taking objects in use by another, hitting.

DESCRIPTION OF BEHAVIOR OBSERVED AT EACH LEVEL

Child did not express regret for physical offense: seemed unaware he had hurt another, or looked puzzled when other person reacted with tears, etc.	Child's expression showed doubt; he might use smile when teacher made peace.	Child repeated "I'm sorry" after teacher; apologized when asked "What do you tell ____?"	Child usually said, "I'm sorry" for physical offense.	Child apologized for offense without being prompted; apologized for hurting feelings.

PROGRAMMING

PREDICTABLE (INTERNALIZED) BEHAVIOR USED IN PROGRAMMING FOR NEXT LEVEL

Interest in other children, teacher, objects.	Recognizes expression and situations.	Imitates expression.	Uses expression in situations.	Uses expression with idea of courtesy.

TEACHING PROCEDURES TO ESTABLISH READINESS FOR NEXT LEVEL

Use of apology by teacher, e.g., for accidental bumping. Teacher attention to accidents, with suggested apology. Attention to ways of doing things to avoid physical hurts.	Continued use by teacher. Attention to incidents, with prompted apology. Attention to ways of making things right.	Verbal focus on apology situations: ways of accepting apology and restitution. Attention to effective, acceptable ways of accomplishing children's aims. Situations of doing things for others.	Verbal attention to apology situations. Practice of "avoidance" skills. Practice in motor control. Focus on cooperative relationships.	Continued practice in cooperative relationships, motor control, attention to legitimate use of apology; forethought, realization of consequences. Attention to avoiding repetition of offenses. Use of variants: "I'm sorry." "I apologize."

7a5. EXPRESSIONS: GREETING
b5.

RATING

THE FIVE LEVELS OF THE CURRICULUM ITEM

1. apparent lack of knowledge of formal response	2. awareness of formal response	3. prompted or imitative response	4. initiates expression in usual situations	5. appropriate independent use of expression in a variety of situations

DEFINITION OF THE TERM: BEHAVIOR UNDER OBSERVATION

Use of a salutation, when meeting adults and children. Expressions used most frequently were Hi, Hello, Good morning, Good afternoon. Use of names to salute children and/or teachers (by children who developed speech after entrance) was recorded as use of greeting form. Use of Good-bye, Bye-bye, See you tomorrow.

DESCRIPTION OF BEHAVIOR OBSERVED AT EACH LEVEL

Child did not use or respond to greeting by word, look, or action.	Child smiled, nodded at greeting of others. Also child turned away, moved away from speaker (indicating either shyness or refusal to respond).	Child said, "Hello," "Hi," "Good-bye," to another, when prompted, or in imitation of other children or teacher.	Child responded to another's greeting, and used greeting in routine arrival, leave-taking.	Child used "Hello," "Good-bye," a) on arrival at school; on leaving school; b) to greet other arrivals; to take leave of someone leaving the group; c) to greet acquaintances in hall.

PROGRAMMING

PREDICTABLE (INTERNALIZED) BEHAVIOR USED IN PROGRAMMING FOR NEXT LEVEL

Fact of arrival, departure.	Recognizes expressions "Hello," "Hi," "Good-bye."	Imitates expressions.	Responds to and uses in routine situations.	Uses expression with idea of courtesy, satisfaction, pleasure.

TEACHING PROCEDURES TO ESTABLISH READINESS FOR NEXT LEVEL

Consistent personalized use of expression by teacher. Verbal attention to children present, absent. Use of greeting songs which emphasize physical presence, absence. Here We Are Together. Oh, Where; Good Morning.	Continued use of expression, songs, attention to individual children. Verbal attention to greetings used by various children.	Continued use of expressions. Opportunities to exchange greetings: e.g., Good morning sung to a child returning after absence. Practice in shaking hands while saying "How do you do." Continued prompting for children ready for it.	Continued opportunities for noting absentees, children present, singing about group, etc. Asking children to greet newcomers, guests. Prompting greeting in new situations, as excursions to offices, resource rooms, stores. Formal roll-call by teacher.	Expanded opportunities. Roll call by children. News items about absentees, returnees. Introductions. Sending children on errands after rehearsing conversation (prepared for by arranging with persons children will meet).

7a6. EXPRESSIONS: OFFERING
b6.

RATING

THE FIVE LEVELS OF THE CURRICULUM ITEM

1. apparent lack of knowledge of formal response	2. awareness of formal response	3. prompted or imitative response	4. initiates expression in usual situations	5. appropriate independent use of expression in a variety of situations.

DEFINITION OF THE TERM: BEHAVIOR UNDER OBSERVATION

Use of an expression to indicate offering. "Have one," "Here," "For you," "Do you want ____?" For teaching processes, however, it was necessary to observe behavior underlying the use of a verbal offer, that is, ways of sharing and receiving.

DESCRIPTION OF BEHAVIOR OBSERVED AT EACH LEVEL

Child did not use verbal offer. Child usually did not offer items to others.	Child offered objects to others, using a touch, vocalization, to attract attention. Child smiled and complied, or shook head in refusal, when asked to offer objects to others.	Child passed materials, food, using rehearsed or imitative "For you," "Would you like ____?"	Child used expression "For you," "There's one for everyone," when he had a special treat for group.	Child used an expression to accompany process of passing, sharing, offering.

PROGRAMMING

PREDICTABLE (INTERNALIZED) BEHAVIOR USED IN PROGRAMMING FOR NEXT LEVEL

Receives, accepts.	Notices and recognizes expression.	Imitates.	Uses expression in familiar situation.	Uses expression spontaneously, with idea of courtesy.

TEACHING PROCEDURES TO ESTABLISH READINESS FOR NEXT LEVEL

Use of expressions by teacher in passing, dividing, offering objects. Personal offering, "For you" to attract attention to concepts of giving, receiving. Situations, for this level, were ones in which supplies were the same for all: passing crayons, paper; passing crackers, cookies; distributing "surprises," treats.	Continued use of "enough for all" situations, with accompanying use of expression. Use of situations in which child could do the distributing, and teacher the talking. Verbal notice of actions of offering and expressions used by various children.	Building situations in which child could plan for use of "For you." Special notice to treats brought by class members. Situations in which one item such as a big apple or a piece of cake is divided.	Continued situations as before. Offering to guests. Introduction of choice situations. Initially for group of 15, 7 of one thing, 8 of another, where the variable is color or flavor or sex appropriateness. Later, choice of 3 or 4 kinds. Final choice from 15 different things.	Appropriate refusal situations. Expansion of experiences. Variables of size, in situations for choosing. Messenger situations with rehearsed offering phrases. Attention to criteria for choice. Acceptance, refusal on basis of appropriateness, health aspects, friendship. Use of variants: "Would you like ____?" "What kind would you like?" "Would you like to try ____?"

8a. JUICE TIME: ATTITUDE

RATING

THE FIVE LEVELS OF THE CURRICULUM ITEM

1. will come at juice time	2. will sit with reminder	3. will sit in group	4. will participate	5. interest

DEFINITION OF THE TERM: BEHAVIOR UNDER OBSERVATION

Willingness to join the class group for juice and crackers.

DESCRIPTION OF BEHAVIOR OBSERVED AT EACH LEVEL

Child came to juice table, took a chair, sat with group. Might not remain at first.	Child joined group at table and remained with reminder that this was expected of him. Child might not accept food.	Child stayed with group without reminder: might or might not accept snack.	Active participation so far as self was concerned: accepted juice, crackers; drank; ate.	Child was interested in process: might anticipate, inquire about schedule, help remind others.

PROGRAMMING

PREDICTABLE (INTERNALIZED) BEHAVIOR USED IN PROGRAMMING FOR NEXT LEVEL

Comes into group.	Stays, or returns after leaving group.	Stays at table voluntarily.	Shares in food.	Shares in group concerns.

TEACHING PROCEDURES TO ESTABLISH READINESS FOR NEXT LEVEL

Teacher moved at quick pace in serving juice, crackers, and in starting to eat; excused reluctant children after they have had a chance to note activity. Opportunities to help with pouring or serving.	Attention to purpose of group; comments on food, serving process. Giving opportunities to serve; comments on turns for all. Excusing children who find sitting difficult. Giving a clean-up duty, if possible.	Beginning conversation: questions about foods to elicit responses. Planning clean-up. Planning after-juice activity. Excusing children who showed restlessness to undertake a clean-up task and/or to get ready for next activity.	Conversation about food. Recall of past experiences. Planning for future snacks. When appreciable number of children have reached this stage it is profitable to use a weekly list of helpers or a plan for turn-taking.	Conversation about objects other than food, moving toward social interchange. Processes relating to juice, as menu, serving, clean-up, made secondary in importance.

8b. JUICE TIME: PARTICIPATING

RATING

THE FIVE LEVELS OF THE CURRICULUM ITEM

1. assign to help another	2. carrying, passing solids in bowl	3. pouring	4. suggests a way to help	5. socially aware of processes (setting table, etc.)

DEFINITION OF THE TERM: BEHAVIOR UNDER OBSERVATION

Participation in various motor and manipulative aspects of the group juice period, including: (a) carrying bowls of food, pitchers of juice, paper cup supplies, to tables, (b) putting napkins or towels at places, or passing them to seated children, (c) passing bowls of food, (d) pouring juice for self or for group, (e) clearing tables, etc. (See SELF-HELP (A), clean-up activities.)

DESCRIPTION OF BEHAVIOR OBSERVED AT EACH LEVEL

At teacher's request, child performed a service for another child or for Teacher, e.g., brought a chair for a classmate; made room beside self; got a cup or towel; spread a towel; passed the cracker bowl; poured juice.	Child carried bowl around table, offering food to others; or, when seated at table, received bowl from child beside him, helped self, then passed bowl on to child on other side.	Child poured juice for all children at his table, passing filled cups one by one along table, indicating verbally or by gesture, "This is for ____." Child checked to make sure no one was missed.	Child asked if he could pass napkins, pour, or help with any other tasks of preparation or clean-up.	Child remembered different processes: got supplies for table(s), set places for group, commented on completeness or incompleteness of preparations. Was aware of necessary correspondence between number of children and quantities, though he might not be able to count or estimate correct amount.

PROGRAMMING

PREDICTABLE (INTERNALIZED) BEHAVIOR USED IN PROGRAMMING FOR NEXT LEVEL

Helps a definite child.	Notices all children, while passing food.	Notices all children while pouring juice.	Chooses from available tasks.	Remembers general sequence of processes.

TEACHING PROCEDURES TO ESTABLISH READINESS FOR NEXT LEVEL

Opportunities to help various children. Opportunities to help two or three selected children. Verbal attention to helping behavior. Thanking children for services.	Experiences in grouping, individualizing, regrouping by naming, pointing out omissions. Verbal attention to individuals: "You passed the crackers to A and B and C. Did D get a cracker?"	Verbal review of processes (pouring, passing, separating cups to help child who poured, refilling pitchers. Discussion of "turns."	Verbal reviews of processes; summaries. Planning. Discussion of efficient methods. Fair sharing of turns; fair sharing of food. (Inclusion of special "treats," with one item for everybody. "We will have to save this one for E because he is absent.")	Regrouping of children on various bases, planning for groups of three or four. E.g., "A and B are upstairs with Mrs. C. We will fix places at this little table and they can have juice here when they come back." Then, "F, will you fix a table for A and B so they can have something to eat when they get back?" Finally, "G, would you like to choose three children to sit with you at this table? You can set the table and pour and serve." (Subordinating process to purpose.)

9. PREPARING FOOD

RATING

THE FIVE LEVELS OF THE CURRICULUM ITEM

1. one-step (instant drink)	2. one-step cooking (jello)	3. simple multiple-step process	4. sandwiches	5. preparation of menu and food for simple meal

DEFINITION OF THE TERM: BEHAVIOR UNDER OBSERVATION

Behavior under observation was the child's participation in "cooking activities" of various kinds. Readiness for cooking activities at levels 3, 4, and 5 was built up by manipulation of utensils in other activities, and by experiences in self-help items, such as washing. Curriculum items pertinent to preparing food are: dough-play, soapsuds play, clay manipulation, house play, sand play, hand washing, table clearing, washing, and participation in group activities of other kinds: use of knife, fork, spoon.

DESCRIPTION OF BEHAVIOR OBSERVED AT EACH LEVEL

Child stirred dry powder, sugar, etc. in own cup of water.	Child shared class process of stirring or beating with rotary beater.	Child helped with one or more parts of process (mixing, stirring, washing, vegetables, cutting, peeling, watching heat source).	Child helped with mixing and spreading of butter, dips, jelly, etc. and with arranging serving dishes.	Child helped with fruit, vegetables, spread own bread; fixed own milk.

PROGRAMMING

PREDICTABLE (INTERNALIZED) BEHAVIOR USED IN PROGRAMMING FOR NEXT LEVEL

Uses spoon for stirring, drinks immediately.	Uses rotary egg beater; waits for food to set, cool.	Uses knife, nut-cracker, hammer, is careful of heat source; waits for food to be ready later, or on following day.	Uses knife; fork for mixing; handles bread slices; waits till all are ready before eating.	Attends to preparation of two or more items.

TEACHING PROCEDURES TO ESTABLISH READINESS FOR NEXT LEVEL. (Cooking and manipulative experiences.)

Mixing drink requiring sugar and dry power. Mixing dry powder with hot milk or water, blowing to cool. Mixing hot drink, setting aside to cool. Soapsuds play for use of beater.	Cracking and eating nuts. Shelling peanuts. Shelling popcorn. Peeling oranges, bananas. Cutting cake. Peeling carrots. Washing celery, peppers. Mixing play dough. Spreading paste, soapsuds frosting.	Looking at food pictures, choosing sandwich and snack items. Reading recipes (especially recipes sent by parents). Using spoon with jelly, peanut-butter. Using knife with cheese, butter. Using cookie cutters on soft bread.	Looking at food pictures, choosing lunch items. Combining: soup with bread; soup with crackers; hot punch with cookies or cake; milk with sandwiches.	Expansion of menus in class situations or for special picnics. Planning discussion of good foods, healthful lunches, pleasing flavor combinations.

EXAMPLES OF FOOD PREPARED AT EACH LEVEL

Milk, chocolate milk, fruit ades, instant broth.	Jello, instant pudding, sour cream dip, etc. Easter eggs (dyeing only) toasting marshmellows.	Cornbread, cake, tossed salad, applesauce, nut fudge, sugar cookies, popcorn (shelling and popping) Easter eggs (boiling), hot spiced punch.	Open-faced sandwiches, double sandwiches, crackers and wafers with spreads.	Soup, bread and butter milk, salad, bread and butter, milk, fresh fruit, bread and butter.

10. GROUP GAMES

RATING

THE FIVE LEVELS OF THE CURRICULUM ITEM

1. alone	2. with adult	3. with adult and children	4. with one child	5. with children

DEFINITION OF THE TERM: BEHAVIOR UNDER OBSERVATION

Participation in organized games. Solitary play took the form of rehearsal of what child had learned from watching class group. If the latter was the case, teachers interpreted the child's performance as a cue to introduce the game.

DESCRIPTION OF BEHAVIOR OBSERVED AT EACH LEVEL

Child played alone with table game materials (e.g., Bingo) and/or pantomimed motor games (Ring-around-a-Rosy) alone. Did not join group.	Child played table games and/or motor games with an adult. Did not join child group.	Child played table games and/or motor games when game was led by an adult.	Child played table and/or motor games with one child, usually with close friend.	Child played table and/or motor games with children without direct teacher supervision.

PROGRAMMING

PREDICTABLE (INTERNALIZED) BEHAVIOR USED IN PROGRAMMING FOR NEXT LEVEL

Uses game materials.	Plays with person who takes responsibility for rules.	Plays with group; conforms to rules.	Remembers game rules, sequence.	Conforms to game rules, playing correctly with group.

TEACHING PROCEDURES TO ESTABLISH READINESS FOR NEXT LEVEL

For new game: comment on newness, discussion of materials. For familiar game: invitations for child to join group.	Continued playing with child and asking another adult or one child to join game. Asking another adult to take first adult's place. Asking a child to substitute.	Encouraging children to lead games by calling, as picture lotto cards, bingo numbers. Asking children to help with motor games by remembering song texts, procedures, as in Farmer in the Dell.	Enlarging group for brief periods, "Why don't you ask A to play, too?" Verbal attention to group playing game. "Two are playing ____." "Three make a good game." "There are cards enough for four children."	Enlarging number of games. Discussion of favorites.

11a. TRIPS: PARTICIPATION

RATING

THE FIVE LEVELS OF THE CURRICULUM ITEM

1. interest in going	2. going with reminder	3. conforming to routine	4. accepting responsibility in routine child expects	5. conforming to flexible schedule

DEFINITION OF THE TERM: BEHAVIOR UNDER OBSERVATION

Child's acceptance of responsibility for his own behavior in trips away from schoolroom. "Standing rules" for trips included:

(a) Formation of group. Child stayed with partner. Child and partner stayed with class group. Child was responsible for own belongings.

(b) Citizenship processes: Appropriate use of common facilities, sidewalk playground equipment, subway seats, etc. Care about littering. Consideration of strangers using same facilities.

(c) Safety processes. Stopping at curbs, noting signal lights, signs, obeying rules in parks, zoos. Assessing situation and regulating activity in accord with possible dangers in zoo, on ferry, at airport, on subway.

DESCRIPTION OF BEHAVIOR OBSERVED AT EACH LEVEL

Child wanted to go; might help with plans; agreed to suggestions for desirable behavior.	Child needed reminders during trip: usually a) about staying with partner and group, b) observing citizenship rules, c) observing safety rules.	Child in familiar place stayed with group, observed citizenship rules, observed safety rules.	Child followed familiar pattern of behavior in trips to unfamiliar places.	Child adjusted behavior to new places, new routines, unexpected changes in routines.

PROGRAMMING

PREDICTABLE (INTERNALIZED) BEHAVIOR USED IN PROGRAMMING FOR NEXT LEVEL

Understands plans	Follows plans, with help.	Follows familiar plans.	Remembers plans and directs own movements.	Adjusts to change.

TEACHING PROCEDURES TO ESTABLISH READINESS FOR NEXT LEVEL

Experience in choosing and being chosen partner. Experience in following teacher's directions in class. Consideration of classmates in use of classroom facilities.	Verbal review of in-school trips. Verbal review of desirable behavior. Meeting visitors. Planning for trips away from building: talking of routes. Recall of trips with parents and in own neighborhood.	Reviewing routes, experiences of in-school and off-campus trips. Planning trips with attention to: projected route or means, goal, behavior, getting permission from parents, reporting to parents.	Reviewing personal interactions with guide, at fire station, clerks, cashiers, staff and faculty members in college. Recalling routes followed, individual problems, group and partner cooperation. Consciously retracing routes.	Reviewing and planning trips. Listing rules. Changing plans to solve an unexpected problem. Reviewing and recording trips, "map" making. Reviewing processes in the following situations: going from store to store looking for certain items; exploring park facilities; traveling through school building.

VERBAL REVIEW OF BEHAVIOR ON TRIPS

Daily trips to and from car, bathroom, water fountain, elevator, roof, gym. Persons involved limited to class group.	To and from office, stores, around block, apartments of teachers, park, playground. Contact with persons outside of class group.	Trips to firehouse, laundromat, park (for picnic), college facilities - (snackbar, laboratory kitchen) neighborhood facilities. Interaction with strangers.	Trips on subway, to zoo, to department stores, on ferry, to airport. Controlling interaction with strangers; consideration of others; use of public facilities.	

11b. TRIPS: TRAFFIC SAFETY

RATING

THE FIVE LEVELS OF THE CURRICULUM ITEM

1. stopping at curb before crossing	2. reaction to street-light	3. crossing street without light	4. anticipation of cars turning corners	5. assessing street situation and crossing safely

DEFINITION OF THE TERM: BEHAVIOR UNDER OBSERVATION

Child's attention to and interpretation of traffic lights, stop signs, vehicle movement and pedestrian movement. Behavior recorded was in actual situations, on various off-campus errands, trips and visits.

Both first and second year children had experiences in group travel, and attention was called to various safety precautions observed by teachers. Second year children were given opportunities to observe lights, etc. for the group; to interpret signals, and to serve as monitors and guides.

DESCRIPTION OF BEHAVIOR OBSERVED AT EACH LEVEL

Child stopped at curb, looked at light, watched traffic.	Child identified stop signals (red) go signals (green) watched light changes.	Child gauged crossing on street with stop sign; followed adult directions at unguarded crossing.	Child watched for cars turning corner at intersections.	Child gauged traffic to cross safely: watched light, or noted stop sign; looked for directions for traffic; watched while crossing; crossed promptly (but did not run).

PROGRAMMING

PREDICTABLE (INTERNALIZED) BEHAVIOR USED IN PROGRAMMING FOR NEXT LEVEL

Imitates adult movement.	Notices light, interprets.	Interprets stop signs, cross walk lines, traffic on one street.	Interprets traffic on cross street.	Crosses with light and takes precautions for traffic.

TEACHING PROCEDURES TO ESTABLISH READINESS FOR NEXT LEVEL

Noticing traffic light; verbal comment on color of light, light change. Review, recall.	Noting absence of light, at some crossings; stop signs at others. Pausing, checking traffic. Response to stop signs. Review, recall.	Noting traffic at intersection, turning of cars. Waiting for cars to turn corner. Review, recall.	Noticing negotiations of traffic. Reviewing trip incidents, etc.	Planning trip, selecting place to cross streets.

11c. TRIPS: PLANNING

RATING

THE FIVE LEVELS OF THE CURRICULUM ITEM

1. staying in block on sidewalk	2. interest in planning	3. noting landmarks along planned route	4. recalling and recognizing landmarks	5. planning route reaching destination, and return

DEFINITION OF THE TERM: BEHAVIOR UNDER OBSERVATION

Child's attention to and memory for travel details including use of sidewalk and elevator, and recognition of buildings, crossings and other landmarks as clues to route.

DESCRIPTION OF BEHAVIOR OBSERVED AT EACH LEVEL

Child followed sidewalk, noted buildings, in block, incline of sidewalk.	Child listened to plans, showed interest in destination; helped decide where to go.	Child looked at, commented on and/or listened to descriptions of distinctive landmarks.	Child noted landmarks on return trip; remembered them on subsequent trips.	Child used recall of landmarks in planning; checked landmarks on trip return. Child could act as guide for group.

PROGRAMMING

PREDICTABLE (INTERNALIZED) BEHAVIOR USED IN PROGRAMMING FOR NEXT LEVEL

Follows sidewalk.	Shares planning.	Notes details of route.	Recognizes details, on passing them.	Remembers details and incorporates them in planning.

TEACHING PROCEDURES TO ESTABLISH READINESS FOR NEXT LEVEL

Repeated experience on sidewalk, as in going to corner to mail a letter, walking to end of block to look at buildings, walking around block to see display windows, for exercise, to learn general arrangement of school building. Noticing "across the street" goals for later trips, stores apartment buildings, street leading to park. Verbal attention to purpose of a sidewalk.	Verbal review of activities at destination after return to classroom. Experiences in planning, with following elements: a) nearness to familiar places; b) landmarks to look for; c) approximate distance.	Use of symbols. Verbal review of return trip; buildings; terrain. Elevation. Drawings of buildings. Planning for going and returning on a familiar trip. Asking children (partners) to guide group back to school.	Use of symbols. Verbal review of going, coming. Drawings of buildings, etc. in elevation, sidewalks in plan. Verbal attention to finding way to destination; letting two children act as guides.	Expansion of trips, routes, ways of getting to park. Handwork, tracing footprints on long sheet of paper. Using small footprints in drawings.

D. EMOTIONAL DEVELOPMENT

THE FIVE LEVELS OF THE CURRICULUM ITEM

1. general unrespon-siveness	2. evidence of internal response	3. evidence of open response	4. expansion and experimentation with open response	5. can express emotion appropriately

DEFINITION OF THE CURRICULUM ITEMS: BEHAVIOR UNDER OBSERVATION

The degree and manner of the child's emotional responses. The teachers were interested in behavior indicative of the following nine affectional responses: joy, contentment, pleasure, anger, displeasure, grief, love, compassion, hatred.

Problems were inherent in observing and interpreting the child's actions, facial expressions and words, and the connotations of the terms selected for the Guide. The word hatred, for example, was used by some to express dislike, impatience, boredom, or a temporary suspension of friendship. For others, the word meant a strong, enduring emotion with moral significance. Meanings of all the words had similar personal and sometimes regional variations in connotation. Practicable solutions to the observation problems will be noted in the following discussion. The theoretical base helped although it could not obviate the problem of word meanings. In observation and interpretation of the child's ability to express emotions, teachers, by using successive ratings, noted the direction of the child's movement, his growth in ability to express. Individual teachers used the definition most comfortable for them as the basis of their successive ratings. Note was made of the changes in behaviors, rather than emotionality per se. The change, or difference, was observable and recorded as an evaluation of the child. Any single rating was, however, very likely to be a reflection of the teacher's emotional status or attitude complex. Ratings on these items, and their interpretation, require caution and reservation.

BEHAVIOR UNDER OBSERVATION

For rating a child on the nine items, teachers had two resources. These were, a) the child's facial or bodily or verbal expression of response to activities, persons and things, and b) observation of the child's movement toward or avoidance of activities, persons and things. The second of these appeared to be more effective in early ratings of new pupils. The extent to which a child entered and remained in an activity, the fact of participation or avoidance, was a gauge of his contentment, pleasure, displeasure, in that activity or some element of it. Similarly, the child's seeking out or staying with or avoiding a particular person was indicative of an emotional modification of some kind. The periodic ratings noted the changes in this behavior and the expansion of the child's ability to give appropriate expression to his feelings.

Verbal, facial and bodily expressions seemed to be inconsistent at the initial ratings. For a few pupils, surface indications and overt actions had to be accepted with reservations for appreciable periods of time since these children apparently had not acquired customary expressions and gestures of pleasure, anger or other emotions. They sometimes used conventional "signs" of one emotion to express another meaning, as laughing when in pain; gave no surface indications of emotional response; or used a stereotyped response to all activities. The facts of a child's participation and interpersonal relationships were used as clues to anomalous expressions or for development of some mobility in expression.

PROGRAMMING

The form for presenting programming for these items has been altered slightly to permit expanded discussion. In the sections which follow, two items, ANGER and PLEASURE, are discussed. The observed behavior at each level, and the programmings for the next level are given in parallel columns for purpose of comparison. It will be noted that the aim of the programming was the same for any emotion. Teachers encouraged the child to a) recognize his response, b) relate it to the cause, c) express it in socially acceptable ways, d) verbalize it, and e) plan appropriate responses.

DESCRIPTION OF BEHAVIOR OBSERVED AT LEVEL 1

Apparent general unresponsiveness. The child did not show recognizable signs of anger or pleasure in situations which would ordinarily elicit such responses from children. He drifted away from situations or rejected activities, or seemed not to be aware of agression or frustrating circumstances. This lack of response was consistent in a variety of situations.

DESCRIPTION OF BEHAVIOR OBSERVED AT LEVEL 2

Evidence of internal response. The child, otherwise apparently unresponsive, made unobtrusive movements and showed slight changes in expression. Teachers were alert for such responses in situations into which they had intentionally introduced unaccustomed elements.

Sample behavior of children rated at level 2 included:

Anger

Eye expression (widening or narrowing eyelids); facial expression (smiling); leaving a situation, then imitating the aggression in interaction with another child; locating, visually, the individual connected with a previous incident, before initiating an activity which has been interrupted. (For some children, apparent inward anger and inward fear produced similar behavior. By handling the interaction, it was possible to help the children with either problem.) Asking about a child who had been part of a disagreement on a previous day.

Pleasure

Looking momentarily at an activity or object, then looking away; consistently looking away from an activity; moving to sit near or play near a child engaged in an activity; looking at related materials; accepting souvenirs such as handwork items; commenting on an activity, a day or so after it took place; smiling briefly; making a slight move to join.

The clue the teachers sought was a change in the child's ordinary mode of response. Again, for this level, close observation of children who seemed unfamiliar with open responses was necessary.

TEACHING PROCEDURES AT LEVEL 2 TO ESTABLISH READINESS FOR LEVEL 3

The slight inner response was a fact upon which to build. It was usually possible to discover elements which produced pleasure or to detect bothersome elements, once a child manifested some response. Teachers continued to use techniques from the preceding level.

Anger

Anticipating repetitions of a situation and arranging probable solutions. (e.g., "Yesterday, John did not like it when Billy took his green paper. Today, we'll let John choose the color he wants. Next, Billy can look and see if he wants the same color. Now John and Billy can sit here and work together. Maybe they can make their pictures alike. They do not have to get angry.") Verbalizing the cause of conflict whenever possible, and suggesting ways of expressing feeling. (e.g., "Billy, give John his green paper. Come and get some for yourself. And, John, tell Billy, 'No. This is my paper. There is more paper on that table.'") Calling attention to disagreements, their causes and outcomes. Noticing situations in which a child substituted verbal expression of anger for physical attack. "Matching" responses of two children, and calling attention to solutions of similar problems.

Pleasure

Repeating the pleasure-giving situation to assure desired response; using effective elements in a variety of situations (e.g., if a child seemed to enjoy a situation because he was sharing it with a particular classmate, the personal relationship was made an element of a different situation: sitting together in the sand box, to sitting together at music time.) Repeating for imitation and encouragement the child's pleasure-response and trying to elicit more open response, as, imitative verbal expression or a hand-clap. "Matching" responses of child to those of others: "Both you and John like to play with the Tinker toys. Would you like to take them to that table and make something together." "You like the color red, don't you? So does John. Both of you choose red nearly every day."

DESCRIPTION OF BEHAVIOR OBSERVED AT LEVEL 3

Evidence of child's open response. The child responded openly to an identified stimulus. Behavior at Level 3 included:

Anger

Using voice or action expressions of anger: crying, screaming, jumping up and down, throwing materials; using aggression against

Pleasure

Using verbal expressions of pleasure; facial responses: smiling, laughing; and body responses: clapping, nodding; asking for a

another — pushing, hitting; using verbal language (e.g., "No!" "Go away." "I don't like you."); disrupting activity of others; recalling the emotion, after a situation was past, by directing verbal protests toward the offenders.

repetition of an activity or another turn with a toy; asking for a variant of the activity or toy; getting another child to share an activity; describing an activity, with recall of pleasurable elements, a day or more after its occurrence. Misdirected responses needing teacher help, for this item were: running away from an activity which a classmate wished to share; pushing away a child who wished to look or share; using responses such as: "Oh, no!" "Again!" with apparent lack of appreciation of the nature of the response.

Conventionally understood responses were ordinarily accepted at face value. The less desirable or not as conventionally understood responses were considered as evidence that some element other than the focal one was affecting the child's behavior. Some children, for example, seemed to take pleasure not in a toy but in monopolizing it; or in saying "Oh, no!" in imitation of a favorite classmate who really meant "no."

TEACHING PROCEDURES AT LEVEL 3 TO ESTABLISH READINESS FOR LEVEL 4

Anger

Verbal attention to the child's expressions of anger; suggesting additional expressions (e.g., "I do not like that. That was unkind. It makes me feel cross, unhappy, angry."): planning to avoid unnecessary use of anger as a solution to problems through sharing, exchanging, helping, planning turns; comparing responses and expressions of anger, in different situations; calling attention to the cause-reaction-outcome series, in various situations; noting instances of turn-taking, respect for others, respect for ownership, and instances in which there was violation of those or other rights. Calling attention to ways of handling violations (e.g., "Tell John that that is your car and he must ask you if he may use it.")

Pleasure

Verbal attention to the children's responses to situations, people, things; suggesting additional verbal expressions (e.g., "I like that." "We had fun." "This is my favorite toy." "I'd rather color today."); planning for pleasure in experiences by planning how to show enjoyment; comparing favorite activities; attempting to redirect inadequate responses by calling verbal attention to matters of ownership; providing for turn-taking in work and play sequences enjoyed by all; providing for turn-taking with school toys; calling attention to the right to reserve personal possessions; suggesting and requiring conventional assertions of ownership and respect for ownership; suggesting trading or sharing, as solutions to problems caused by a child's attaching pleasure to activities other than the ones to which it belongs; discussing, evaluating and appreciating the ironic response.

So far as possible, programming avoided repetition of situations known to produce irregular responses, in favor of those known to elicit a conventional response. An attempt to correct, after the reaction had appeared seemed to provide a reenforcing practice of the undesired response and a focus of attention which promoted its reappearance. Therefore, teacher direction was toward providing situations where comfortable relationship would receive the repetition and extra practice. Legitimate anger or displeasure and legitimate defense of property had their place. Irrelevant aggression was referred to its cause, not accepted as a response in a situation where it was inappropriate.

DESCRIPTION OF BEHAVIOR OBSERVED AT LEVEL 4

Expansion and experimentation with open response. The child was able to some extent to refer his responses to the correct stimuli. The relationship between overt response and less obvious affect, and between both of these and the classroom stimulus were increasingly apparent. Children's expansion and experimentation with open response included:

Anger

Greater variety of verbal expressions of anger; fewer overt actions; more frequent use of socially acceptable solutions; increased awareness of ways of avoiding conflict; use of language, comparing reactions,

Pleasure

Variety of facial and verbal expressions; use of interpretable expressions; participation in planning for group and individual activities; use of language describing parallels between personal responses and responses of others extension to vicarious situations. (e.g., "The peddler wants his caps. He was so angry that he jumped up and down like this. That is how I did when I wanted Billy's car.)

(e.g., "Patty and I want to do that." "Could I take one to Mary, too, so we can both have one?" "My mother knows that song and she sang it for me."); seemingly negativistic responses which dramatized a situation. For example, the "Oh! no!" mentioned in 3 might be elaborated and burlesqued.

TEACHING PROCEDURES AT LEVEL 4 TO ESTABLISH READINESS FOR LEVEL 5

Anger

Encouraging verbal description of reactions (child's own, others'); noting causes of anger (child's own behavior which caused anger of others, others' behavior causing anger), or situation which produced expression; verbal attention to rights and duties, in various situations (e.g., the right to have a turn and the need to respect turns of others, or the right to control a personal possession, with the corresponding obligation to respect ownership of other individuals).

Pleasure

Encouraging verbal description and discussion of pleasurable activities; noting elements of situations which are sources of pleasure; planning activities for group pleasure of parents, siblings, others. (e.g., Christmas gifts, valentines, plans to help with work at home; choosing between alternate responses, for example, moving from tangible to intangible, from choosing a gift to choosing how to answer a suggestion or request.)

DESCRIPTION OF BEHAVIOR OBSERVED AT LEVEL 5

Can express emotion appropriately. Observed in relation to child's age and also in relation to teacher's concept of appropriateness.

Anger

Ability to express anger in an understood and acceptable way; ability to recognize just cause for anger; ability to accept limitations on unjust anger (e.g., teacher intervention when anger used to gain a personal point, in violation of rights of another, or at expense of group); ability to assess situations and recognize own feeling; ability to choose alternative behavior.

Pleasure

Ability to express how he felt in some conventionally-understood way; ability to relate his feelings to the stimulus; ability to choose an appropriate response in a situation; ability to plan consciously for and to elicit a desired response from another person.

TEACHING PROCEDURES AT LEVEL 5 TO ESTABLISH READINESS AT NEXT LEVEL

Programming at this level included situations which would provide opportunity for the child to strengthen his grasp of the behavior patterns described and to apply them in increasingly complex situations.

From observations of the children over a period of time teachers concluded that apparent unresponsiveness for anger and pleasure might be an indication of a variety of elements at work.

Anger

(Apparent) inability to feel anger; (apparent) inability to show anger; failing to respond in a way which teachers were able to interpret as anger; use of a response which teachers might interpret as unresponsiveness; lack of awareness of the element which might produce anger; response to another element (e.g., the child who ignored pushing or hitting when intent on getting possession of materials and the child who did not react when materials were taken from him by another); or unresponsiveness in a new situation.

Pleasure

(Apparent) inability to feel pleasure; (apparent) inability to show pleasure; lack of comprehension of the situation; lack of experience in responding in a way which the teachers were able to interpret as pleasure; use of a response, as immobility, which teachers might ordinarily interpret as unresponsiveness; lack of awareness of the focal situation — concentration on an element of it, with a response appropriately based on a previous experience with the element; or unresponsiveness in a new situation.

Unresponsiveness in a new situation occurred so often, with new children during the first week or weeks in school that it seemed to be referrable to a habitual response to strange adults, strange children, and strange surroundings. Teachers made initial ratings of children after the children's responses began to show differentiation.

TEACHING PROCEDURES AT LEVEL 1 TO ESTABLISH READINESS FOR LEVEL 2

Anger

Notice of interactions of the kind mentioned above, and discussing the situation with the children concerned. (e.g., "You took the beads away from Bobby. You do not have to do that. There are other beads on the shelf." "You did not like it when John took the beads. Why don't you show him where you got the beads.") Verbal attention to instances of anger-based behavior, to draw attention to legitimate resentment and ways of expressing it. (e.g., "Billy took Mary's beads. Mary was angry. She said, 'Those are my beads. Go get some from the shelf, Billy.'") Arranging materials and situations where there might be occasion for anger so that the feelings and a solution can be brought to attention and verbalized. Teacher participation: showing legitimate anger and verbalizing the feeling, its cause, and its solution. Emphasizing the pattern of stimulus - honest response - appropriate expression of response.

Pleasure

Simple activities, with attention to and emphasis on the focal point of the activity such as: a) talking about the kind of cracker which would be served as a snack; showing the cracker container; letting child pass the crackers to other children (for a child withdrawing from the juice-time activity but particularly fond of crackers), b) noticing a new or different item of apparel worn by the child; getting other children to notice it; finding pictures to illustrate; giving the child an oral comment to relay to his mother. The purpose of such individualized "feelers" was to locate an element or aspect of a situation which did motivate the child. Effective cues appeared to be in the area of interpersonal relationships; the teachers often elicited desired responses by touching upon such a connection. (e.g., passing the crackers and carrying the compliment on a new shirt home to mother, were the probable successful probes, in the examples cited. Verbal attention to responses of other children in the group, assuring clear definition of the stimulus and response: "John likes these little round crackers. They are crisp and buttery. He likes to bite them." "John has a new T-shirt, too. His has green and brown stripes. He likes the long sleeves for cold weather." Verbal focus on the expected effect of planned activities: "We are going to the park to play today. It will be fun because there is an enormous sand box. We'll take all the sand toys because there will be room enough for everyone to play." Teacher participation: showing pleasure in appropriate situations and with customary signs of pleasure: a smile, an excited movement, a pat or a hug as appropriate traditional signs for small children, thus setting a pattern of stimulus - honest response appropriate expression of response, for child imitation.

1a. CUTTING: TEACHER HOLDING PAPER
1b.   INDEPENDENT WITH PAPER

RATING

THE FIVE LEVELS OF THE CURRICULUM ITEM

1. two hands on scissors	2. one-hand random snipping	3. one-hand series of related cutting straight through page	4. one-hand, following line, more or less	5. cutting out

DEFINITION OF THE TERM: BEHAVIOR UNDER OBSERVATION

Child's manipulation of metal scissors. The strong interest of the preschool pupils in cutting and (with the younger ones) an apparent lack of experience with scissors made it advisable to construct a double scale for this item.

DESCRIPTION OF BEHAVIOR OBSERVED AT EACH LEVEL

1a. (teacher holding paper)

Child held one handle with each hand, cut by moving hands toward and away from each other; scissors were ordinarily held in horizontal plane.	Child held scissors in one hand, moved thumb and fingers to make short cuts along edge of a paper (fringing)	Child kept scissors going, to cut a strip from a sheet of paper.	Child cut across a sheet of paper, on or near a guide line; child cut on or near a circle drawn on the paper.	Child cut out simple shapes drawn on paper (circle, square, triangle).

1b. (independent with paper)
Child held one scissor handle with each hand, cut by moving hands toward and away from each other. Child laid paper on table, held it between knees, weighted it

Other levels same as in 1a.

PROGRAMMING

PREDICTABLE (INTERNALIZED) BEHAVIOR USED IN PROGRAMMING FOR NEXT LEVEL

Brings scissors blades together and separates them.	Operates blades with one hand, makes single cuts.	Operates blades and moves hand forward.	Cuts and moves hand forward along a perceived line.	Cuts, stops, and changes direction.

TEACHING PROCEDURES TO ESTABLISH READINESS FOR NEXT LEVEL
(Procedures were the same for both stages, teachers gave direct help at either stage by holding paper, if necessary, so child could focus on scissors manipulation.)

Teacher participation; to provide observation experience of one-hand cutting in connection with stories, records, calendar facts. "Fringing" grass, hair and beards, decorative fringe for children's use in pasting. Helping child find best way of holding scissors in one hand.	Verbal attention to children's snipping. Expansion of fringing activities (e.g."Can you make some long grass?" "This is a girl. She could have longer hair." "Make a long beard for your mask." Gradual increase in length of cut (2,3,4 snips in same direction).	Verbal attention to use of strips: (paper chains, stems for flowers, long shapes for pasted designs, etc.) Focus on drawn lines; pasting activities, cut strips placed along drawn lines and between pairs of lines. Teacher participation: cutting along heavy lines to make strips, regular shapes.	Verbal attention to use of cutout shapes (including free-hand shapes) for making pictures. Cutting around firm shapes: objects such as fruit, eggs, bottles cut from corrugated cardboard, covered by child with colored paper, cardboard serving as guide for scissors.	Expansion of cutting to include familiar objects, etc. Free hand cutting demonstrated by teacher.

2. DRAWING

RATING

THE FIVE LEVELS OF THE CURRICULUM ITEM

1. exploration	2. designs	3. representation a. vertical b. horizontal	4. imitating others	5. imitating other's drawings

DEFINITION OF THE TERM: BEHAVIOR OBSERVED AT EACH LEVEL

Child's use of pencil, chalk, brush, or crayon for drawing. Rating was on the use of materials to make, repeat, and imitate combinations of lines and forms. Drawings might or might not be recognizable symbols of object named by child.

DESCRIPTION OF BEHAVIOR OBSERVED AT EACH LEVEL

Child experimented with pencil or other implement, scribbling, making directional lines of various kinds and intensities.	Child combined connected lines to make forms, including lines, crosses, rows of circles and line drawings of people or things.	Child used vertical and/or horizontal lines to depict parts of experiences (e.g. tooth-paste box, ladder).	Child imitated hand and arm movements, e.g. round and round, up and down, back and forth; responded to the the reinforcement of verbal description.	Child looked at drawings of others, imitated from the visual pattern.

PROGRAMMING

PREDICTABLE (INTERNALIZED) BEHAVIOR USED IN PROGRAMMING FOR NEXT LEVEL

Uses implement to make marks on paper.	Connects varied lines in a whole.	Makes vertical and horizontal lines at will.	Interprets movement in terms of lines.	Sees and reproduces the lines composing a drawing.

TEACHING PROCEDURES TO ESTABLISH READINESS FOR NEXT LEVEL

Verbal attention to child's exploratory drawings: naming actions of hand and arm, noticing combinations of lines. Teacher participation: imitating and naming movement of child: repeating scribbled lines; drawing connecting lines between scribbles drawing circles to enclose several scribbles. Demonstrating and naming simple actions and forms (e.g. "I go around like this and put a line down and there's a lollipop.")	Verbal attention to child's carefully made and duplicated forms. Copying child's forms. Suggesting additional details. Calling child's attention to chance resemblances in his designs. (e.g. "That looks just like a duck. That is the duck's bill and there are the feet and there's the tail.") Teacher participation: "framing" papers by drawing lines just inside edges of paper to make a rectangle; combining forms to make a picture (e.g. a snowman in the park, a long, long train.)	Verbal focus on using vertical and horizontal lines for "framing". Matching kinesthetic images to line drawings of boxes, tables, chairs, pencils. (e.g. running fingers or hand along edges of box, drawing lines to match.) Narrative drawings with objects (e.g. "Here is a table...a chair on this side...a chair on the other side... and here are two plates, etc. Now we can have breakfast.") Asking child's help with part of drawing, above.	Expansion of action-imitation idea: combinations and variations of circular, up-and-down, back-and-forth motions. Verbal attention to relationships between child's movements, lines. (e.g. "This is a good line. How did you make it? Can someone else do the same thing?") Teacher participation. Verbalizing actions. (e.g. "I'm drawing two lines this way, and two lines down. Now I'll make two round wheels and this is a car. Now I'll make another. Now you make one.")	Verbal attention to successful imitation of drawing. Planning pictures to be drawn. Recalling and illustrating experiences. Labeling recognizable drawings. Use of symbols and expressive drawing.

3. COLORING

RATING

THE FIVE LEVELS OF THE CURRICULUM ITEM

1. holding for use	2. scribbling	3. awareness of space	4. ability to stay within design	5. conformity to design

DEFINITION OF THE TERM: BEHAVIOR UNDER OBSERVATION

Use of crayons for coloring space enclosed by lines. The manipulative aspect of interest here was the eye-hand coordination involved in recognizing a space and staying within the lines bounding that space.

DESCRIPTION OF BEHAVIOR OBSERVED AT EACH LEVEL

Child picked up crayons; held them; watched others using them.	Child used crayon to mark on paper; scribbled at random; seemed unaware of any design on the paper.	Child scribbled or marked a cross design, crossing outlines but staying in general area.	Child stayed within outline (often well within, leaving an uncolored band between crayoning and outline.) Child might make one or two marks only, within form.	Child colored design, fairly accurately, with an occasional accidental crossing of boundary lines.

PROGRAMMING

CHILD'S PREDICTABLE (INTERNALIZED) BEHAVIOR USED IN PROGRAMMING FOR NEXT LEVEL

Holds crayons for use.	Marks marks on paper.	Colors in area containing perceived design.	Colors within perceived boundary.	Colors space delimited by lines of design.

TEACHING PROCEDURES TO ESTABLISH READINESS FOR NEXT LEVEL

Direct help for child wanting to use crayon: teacher covers child's hand, guides marking or scribbling. Verbal attention to best way of holding crayon.	Verbal attention to marks made by child; to location of marks; to movements, suggestion and help in staying near design.	Discussion and comparison of all drawings for: location of coloring, area cover covered. Suggestions for revision (sometimes supplying another design for child to color).	Four-step narrative for coloring: (e.g. "We need a red crayon for this picture. We follow the lines, first, then we color inside the lines. Then we look at it and see whether it is finished.") Discussion of child's picture on four points.	Retracing outline, after coloring. Discussion: criteria for color choices. Planning. Evaluation of coloring. strokes, accuracy. Labeling of pictures. (Beginning use of symbols).

TEACHER PARTICIPATION IN COLORING ACTIVITY, USING FOLLOWING SEQUENCE:
a) Choosing colors; b) Tracing lines of design; c) Coloring design with smooth parallel strokes;
d) Calling attention to movements and results.

Directing child's attention to (a), above.	Directing child's attention to (c).	Directing child's attention to (d).	Directing child's attention to (b).	Directing child's attention to sequence (a-d).

4. FINGER PAINTING

RATING

THE FIVE LEVELS OF THE CURRICULUM ITEM

1. willingness	2. smearing (exploring boundaries of paper).	3. trial and error in use of body	4. trial and error	5. deliberate purposeful design

DESCRIPTION OF THE TERM: BEHAVIOR UNDER OBSERVATION

Child's manipulation of finger paint. Focus was on the use of finger, hand and arm muscles.

DESCRIPTION OF BEHAVIOR OBSERVED AT EACH LEVEL

Child accepted paper. paint: poked at paint with fingers, used finger as brush to make lines.	Child used fingertips to spread paint down or across paper; gradually used flat of fingers, then hand for spreading over paper.	Child used two hands, moved trunk forward and back to make vertical patterns; turned shoulders right and left to make horizontal arcs.	Child experimented with spreading movements of hand (circular, vertical, horizontal, diagonal) and/or synchronized "mirror" movements with two hands. Used fingers to trace patterns in paint surface.	Child spread paint, then worked out pattern, made drawings in paint surface, or used paint as a writing medium.

PROGRAMMING

PREDICTABLE (INTERNALIZED) BEHAVIOR USED IN PROGRAMMING FOR NEXT LEVEL

Uses fingertip(s) for trial lines.	Uses flattened fingers, hands to cover paper.	Uses body movement in conjunction with hand movement.	Uses combinations of movements, notes results.	Knows and repeats movements to get desired effect.

TEACHING PROCEDURES USED TO DEVELOP READINESS FOR NEXT LEVEL.
At all levels, teacher marks child's name on paper by printing in wet paint surface.
See levels 4, 5 for special use of this process.

Opportunity to choose one of two or three colors. Verbal attention to results of finger-drawing. Direct help to children wanting it. Display of pictures. Teacher participation: preparation of paper (dipping or moistening with hand) distributing paint directly on to paper, spreading paint with fingers, palm. Calling attention to result.	Verbal attention to successful spreading of paint. Display of pictures. Opportunity to prepare paper. Teacher participation: Showing motor aspect in narrative painting: (e.g. "I smooth the paper and wet it just wet enough. Next, the paint. I think blue would be a good color. Now, I want to make blue water with waves like this. And here is the sky, smooth and blue.)" Providing ample space for movement.	Opportunity to dip out paint. Verbal attention to child's activity in spreading; comment on directional patterns. Discussion of paintings, (e.g. "How did you get this nice swirl? That looks like a mountain. How did you do it?)" Display of paintings. Teacher participation. Use of finger(s) to pick out designs from wet paint background.	Opportunity to use two colors. Verbal attention to experimental designs. Planning for use of color. Display of painting. Teacher participation: narrative painting, while producing a cohesive picture. "Framing" paper with hand stroke. Providing central focus for children at smoothing level, by printing name in large letters in the wet paint	Free access to several colors. Planning and evaluation discussion. Verbal attention to child's movements and results. Attention to paintings with center of interest, duplicated designs, etc. Teacher participation: printing child's name in small letters, on margins ("So it won't interfere with the picture"); printing title at bottom.

5. CLAY, DOUGH, PLASTICENE

RATING

THE FIVE LEVELS OF THE CURRICULUM ITEM

1. lack of interest	2. touching and exploration	3. patting, rolling, squeezing	4. imitative use of material	5. participation with originality

DEFINITION OF THE TERM: BEHAVIOR UNDER OBSERVATION

Child's manipulation of plastic media. Creative and expressive use of these was discussed in another section. Of interest here was the child's use of fingers, hands and arms in exploration of the materials.

DESCRIPTION OF BEHAVIOR OBSERVED AT EACH LEVEL

Child preferred other activities.	Child picked up and put down lump of clay; pinched off and inspected small pieces; scratched with fingernail, made holes with finger or stick.	Child used whole lump of clay, patting, dropping to flatten, squeezing. Child pulled off small lumps and rolled, patted.	Child imitated teacher or others, rolling to make cookies, balls, snakes, bowls.	Child combined simple forms to produce integrated complex forms; e.g. balls to make snowman; long rolls and flat pieces to make a tree; pinched off bits to make abstract forms or objects and characters from stories.

PROGRAMMING

PREDICTABLE (INTERNALIZED) BEHAVIOR USED IN PROGRAMMING FOR NEXT LEVEL

Shows interest in other children and/or imaginative contexts created by teacher.	Handles material, experiments with finger movements.	Uses fingers, hands and body pressures to produce shapes.	Imitates others' movements, to produce copies.	Uses two or more manipulations in original combinations.

TEACHING PROCEDURES USED TO DEVELOP READINESS FOR NEXT LEVEL.

Supplementing initial medium, modeling clay: Introducing several plastic media via other activities: play dough (cooking), papier mache (pasting) plasticene (shopping). Teacher participation: using exploratory activities, commenting on results; developing manipulative vocabulary (poke, roll, pound, pat, cut, mark, pinch off). Verbal attention to child's preference, interest.	Verbal attention while child works with material: description of actions as in (1); comments on results. Enlisting child in clean-up: encouraging him to collect the clay lumps and squeeze them together. Displaying interesting exploratory items. Teacher participation: focus on two or three manipulative processes (rolling, patting, pulling apart).	Teacher participation: imitating child's different manipulative techniques; having other children imitate. Verbal attention: planning what to make, discussing possible ways of making it, displaying simple forms.	Teacher participation: circular imitation, started by teachers. Verbal attention to similar movements, similar results. Verbal attention to child's attempts to combine forms, or, experimental combinations by teacher "If I make a big ball, a middle-sized ball and a little one, I'll have a snowman.	Teacher participation: Combining forms used by children to produce new ideas. Making illustrative clay figures while telling story. Planning how to illustrate a story. Evaluation of forms in terms of effective manipulation.

6. PASTING

RATING

THE FIVE LEVELS OF THE CURRICULUM ITEM

1. willingness	2. spreading randomly	3. spreading one side only	4. spreading and turning over to stick	5. pasting on specific areas

DEFINITION OF THE TERM: BEHAVIOR UNDER OBSERVATION

Child's manipulation of materials in pasting activities. Movements involved were use of fingers to spread paste, and of fingers, hand and arm for handling paper, etc. Eye-hand coordination was of particular importance at level 5.

DESCRIPTION OF BEHAVIOR OBSERVED AT EACH LEVEL

Child wanted to paste; accepted materials; and accepted help or suggestions of teacher in initial experiences.	Child spread paste on part(s) of material to be pasted; some children applied thick layers of paste, others applied one or more lumps and did not spread.	Child applied paste to one side of paper or material. Child needed help in choosing side for spreading and in turning over to stick.	Child spread paste on back of picture (he might still need help in determining the back), turned paper and patted it to make the bond. (A few children applied a second layer of paste over the picture and mounting.)	Child applied paste to picture, turned it, and affixed it to one of the following: a) mounting sheet; b) matching outline; c) appropriate place in a composite picture (e.g., wheels on a car).

PROGRAMMING

PREDICTABLE (INTERNALIZED) BEHAVIOR USED IN PROGRAMMING FOR NEXT LEVEL

Touches paste; tries process.	Spreads paste with fingers or brush.	Confines paste to designated side of paper.	Spreads paste on one side, turns pasted item to affix it.	Pastes item in designated or appropriate area.

TEACHING PROCEDURES TO ESTABLISH READINESS FOR NEXT LEVEL

Providing small-area pasting, so child can use fingertip spreading (e.g. dishes on a table, flowers in a flower box). Using collage-type pasting: feathers on a bird outline, petals on flower-stems, candy hearts, sequins, pussywillow catkins along drawn lines, fringed grass along a base line. Discussion of process required to make object stick. Using large-area pasting as part of another activity (e.g. cutout pictures on cardboard, for later use as jigsaw puzzles).	Providing 3-D shapes for large-area pasting, with the shapes providing a tangible limit for spreading (e.g. paste on sides of box to be decorated with colored paper; milk cartons or light bulb maraccas; partially finished papier-mache items). Making class murals with cutout shapes to be pasted. Planning and recall discussions. How to spread paste. Examination of surplus paste, after drying period.	Pasting colored paper on cardboard shapes for cutting. Making torn-paper collages on sheet of construction paper. "Framing" sheet of paper; framing picture pasted on mounting sheet. Teacher participation; narrative pasting. a) applying paste. b) turning shape or picture over, c) pounding or patting it firmly in place. Verbal attention to child's finished work. Display of pictures.	Making posters illustrative of children's experiences with progressive narrowing of area in which an item is to be pasted: a) pasting children's heads in bus windows. b) setting table as in (1), but setting two plates at ends of table, c) pasting bell, hose, firemen, on a firetruck, etc. d) pasting food pictures on paper plates e) pasting picture on spot of paste placed by teacher. Verbal attention to good placement.	Pasting double figures together (e.g. joining upper parts of two cutout dogs, to make a standup toy; making suitcases, cages): leading to recognition of shape similarities; and matching of symbols.

7a. MANIPULATION OF PAPER: FOLDING

RATING

THE FIVE LEVELS OF THE CURRICULUM ITEM

1. interest at a distance	2. exploration	3. imitation	4. enjoyment and ease in activity	5. initiation for expressed purpose

DEFINITION OF THE TERM: BEHAVIOR UNDER OBSERVATION

Child's manipulation of paper in various classroom activities. Motor processes were doubling a sheet of paper over on itself, and running fingers or hand along the fold to make a crease. Eye-hand coordination involved was the matching of edges, before creasing. Folding of towels, doll linens, and scarves included in the rating of this item.

DEFINITION OF BEHAVIOR OBSERVED AT EACH LEVEL

Child watched others fold paper.	Child unfolded and refolded letters, newspapers, handkerchiefs.	Child doubled paper. using two hands or one; and/or ran hands or finger along doubled edge.	Child doubled paper and made a firm crease; tried to match edges.	Child selected folding as free activity: made books, birthday folders, fans.

PROGRAMMING

PREDICTABLE (INTERNALIZED) BEHAVIOR USED IN PROGRAMMING FOR NEXT LEVEL

Watches process.	Handles paper.	Imitates gross movement.	Uses finer manipulation, eye-hand coordination.	Subordinates process to purpose.

TEACHING PROCEDURES TO ESTABLISH READINESS FOR NEXT LEVEL

Folding paper for child: letter to insert in envelope; folder for birthday card; fan for play, etc. Verbal attention to result; to crease mark in paper.	Providing materials for various purposes. Pre-folding items, opening them out (for child to refold). Verbal attention to crease, matched edges. Physical help to child in making a fold in sheet of firm paper.	Verbal emphasis on process ("You fold it over this way then smooth it with your hand.") Discussion of birthday folders, book pages produced by folding. Discussion of matched edges.	Experiences in folding clothes items (scarves). Expansion of activity to fit into experiences. (e.g. birthday party plans; trip to laundromat; making room decorations, making double standing figures.) Verbal discussion of quality of handwork.	Providing materials for free activity; paper towels, clothing. Attention to folding neatly. matching edges.

7b. MANIPULATION OF PAPER: ROLLING

RATING

THE FIVE LEVELS OF THE CURRICULUM ITEM

1. interest at a distance	2. exploration	3. imitation	4. enjoyment and ease in activity	5. initiation for expressed purpose

DEFINITION OF THE TERM: BEHAVIOR UNDER OBSERVATION

Child's skill in rolling sheets of paper for various purposes. The manipulative process was a two-hand one, with child rolling the paper with or without help of flat surface (e.g. the table, child's lap).

DESCRIPTION OF BEHAVIOR OBSERVED AT EACH LEVEL

Child watched others, handled rolled paper.	Child unrolled paper, tried to re-roll.	Child used gross motor approach, imitating the two-hand movement; and usually produced a loose single roll.	Child coordinated two hands to make a fairly tight roll.	Child rolled up paintings to take home, murals for storing, made tubes for use as telescope.

PROGRAMMING

PREDICTABLE (INTERNALIZED) BEHAVIOR USED IN PROGRAMMING FOR NEXT LEVEL

Watches process.	Examines rolled paper, notes curls.	Uses approximate movements.	Manipulates paper effectively.	Subordinates rolling to purpose.

TEACHING PROCEDURES TO ESTABLISH READINESS FOR NEXT LEVEL

Provisions for purposeful rolling at all levels: rolling drawings, paintings to take home; making handwork items: tubes for telescopes, megaphones; movie-strips on cardboard tubing; cornucopias, Maybaskets, Christmas tree ornaments, and corrugated-paper flower pots, Christmas tree tubs.

Teacher participation: a) rolling paper for child, having him hold it while Teacher secures roll with rubber or string; b) rolling paper, letting child carry it without tying.	Pre-rolling paper for a) child's use in rolling. b) for child to smooth out for drawing. Teacher participation: continued help with string or rubber band for tying.	Verbal attention to child's movements (e.g. rolling on table surface, rolling against stomach while standing) tightness of roll, evenness of ends. Rolling, re-rolling to get thinner tube.	Attention to sizes of of tubes for various purposes. Attention to fastening: teacher holding rolled paper while child ties or pastes. Planning handwork items.	Broadening experiences. Use of symbols, pictures print forms. Expanding meaning: rolling down hill, rolling paper around arm.

7c. MANIPULATION OF PAPER: WRAPPING

RATING

THE FIVE LEVELS OF THE CURRICULUM ITEM

1. interest at a distance	2. exploration	3. imitation	4. enjoyment and ease in activity	5. initiation for expressed purpose

DESCRIPTION OF THE TERM: BEHAVIOR UNDER OBSERVATION

Child's hand and eye-hand coordination in wrapping small packages. Various materials were used - foil, thin manila wrapping paper, and tissue paper. Handling of fastening (tape, string, staples, pins) was not included in rating of the item.

DESCRIPTION OF BEHAVIOR OBSERVED AT EACH LEVEL

Child watched others wrap package; enlisted services of teacher for own package, held it while teacher fastened or tied it.	Child inspected package, often unwrapped it; tried folding paper over article to be wrapped.	Child set article on paper, folded paper over top, turned article and paper together.	Child wrapped article; creased ends in some way; might try tying.	Child wrapped article quickly; was interested primarily in destination of package.

PROGRAMMING

PREDICTABLE (INTERNALIZED) BEHAVIOR USED IN PROGRAMMING FOR NEXT LEVEL

Watches process.	Tries to wrap; unwraps; tries to re-wrap.	Gets paper around article.	Folds paper, all sides.	Subordinates wrapping to purpose. (Does not unwrap.)

TEACHING PROCEDURES TO ESTABLISH READINESS FOR NEXT LEVEL
Provision for purposeful wrapping, at all levels. Small items (as extra clothing) in bags. Gifts for parents, others. Packages to mail.

Teacher participation: Teacher wraps package for child, child holds while teacher ties or tapes. Providing wrapped packages of various kinds, for children to open (starting with paper bags, rolled at top).	Providing materials for wrapping: a) paper bags with tops to be folded down; b) long sheets, article to be folded into paper c) large sheets to be folded around article, four folds; d) foil (to be folded to conform to contour of article). Teacher participation: tying; setting article squarely on sheet of paper; guiding child's hands, in turning article.	Verbal attention to successful wrapping: (article covered) Attention to handling extra ends, folding, waiting for tying. Use of symbols: cutout "package" with string tied around it, drawings. Teacher participation: help with folding ends neatly.	Verbal attention to neat package, leaving wrapping on a well-done package. Choosing wrapping paper, tags, etc. Use of symbols. Name or phrase on tags (for B___). Addressing package to mail.	Verbal attention to attractive paper. "Designing" paper. Use of symbols, address labels, gift tags; wrapping appropriate to occasion. (Leading to additional holiday units, postal service).

8a. MANIPULATION OF STRING AND YARN: WINDING

RATING

THE FIVE LEVELS OF THE CURRICULUM ITEM

1. interest at a distance	2. exploration	3. imitation	4. enjoyment and ease in activity	5. initiation for expressed purpose

DEFINITION OF THE TERM: BEHAVIOR UNDER OBSERVATION

Child's two-hand and eye-hand coordination in winding yarn, thread, or string on spools, paper spills, etc.

DESCRIPTION OF BEHAVIOR OBSERVED AT EACH LEVEL

Child watched others.	Child handled lengths of string, unwound, tried to wind. (Usually a wide two-arm movement permitting string to slide off spool.)	Child wound string held one hand more or less steady and wound with the other. Teacher secured end of string and started winding.	Child wound lengths of thread on spools; Needed no help in starting.	Child wound string on yarn for use in sewing. (e.g. chose and matched colors) wound several short lengths on one spool.

PROGRAMMING

PREDICTABLE (INTERNALIZED) BEHAVIOR USED IN PROGRAMMING FOR NEXT LEVEL

Shows interest in string or process.	Handles materials, moves both hands.	Holds with one hand, winds with other hand.	Manages string and process.	Subordinates process to purpose.

TEACHING PROCEDURES TO ESTABLISH READINESS FOR NEXT LEVEL

Provision of experiences in which string and yarn are needed.

Teacher participation. Taking lengths of yarn from large ball or spool for use in activity. Verbal comment on spool: having child hold spool, while teacher pulls string. Having child rewind a short end of the string.	Direct help with re-winding, when child indicates readiness. Verbal attention to smaller lengths of string - to unwinding, rewinding.	Distribution of paper spills, three-foot lengths of yarn for winding. Verbal attention to appearance of balls. Direct help in breaking off length of yarn from spool.	Preparing string for group activity: collecting short lengths on one spill; saving lengths of string or cord. Verbal attention to neat winding, color-matching.	Expansion of activities: coiling swing ropes; jumping ropes; coiling extension cord.

8b. MANIPULATION OF RIBBON: ROLLING

RATING

THE FIVE LEVELS OF THE CURRICULUM ITEM

1. interest at a distance	2. exploration	3. imitation	4. enjoyment and ease in activity	5. initiation for expressed purpose

DEFINITION OF THE TERM: BEHAVIOR UNDER OBSERVATION

Child's manipulative control in rolling ribbons, crepe paper streamers. Both fine finger manipulation and eye-hand coordination were involved in the process.

DESCRIPTION OF BEHAVIOR OBSERVED AT EACH LEVEL

Child watched others using materials.	Child took ribbons from dress-up stores; unwound them; tried to wind ribbons, played with and tried to rewind serpentine.	Child wound ribbon around palm; rolled wide crepe paper streamers and wide ribbon, after teacher started process. (i.e., started a roll to serve as center).	Child rolled ribbon, crepe paper and serpentine (checked evenness of roll).	Child rolled ribbon to put away; other material for play purposes.

PROGRAMMING

PREDICTABLE (INTERNALIZED) BEHAVIOR USED IN PROGRAMMING FOR NEXT LEVEL

Matches process.	Handles materials; tries winding around palm.	Rolls with fingers, palm (wide ribbon).	Rolls with attention to.	Subordinates process to purpose.

TEACHING PROCEDURES TO ESTABLISH READINESS FOR NEXT LEVEL

Provision for experiences in which ribbon, paper strips, crepe-paper streamers and serpentine were used.

Teacher activity. Calling attention to rolled ribbons, crepe paper, etc. Unwinding it, rewinding, while helping with clean-up. Showing winding on palm. Providing streamers for parties.	Individual help to children showing readiness. Providing streamers for exploration of wind activity. Verbal attention to rolling strips to take home. Rolling ribbons to put away.	Individual help with use of fingertips (hand curved while rolling). Verbal attention: a) to keeping edges of ribbon even; b) to different ways of rolling (palm and fingers).	Verbal attention to "party" favors; streamers and ribbons for New Year's party, birthday, May-day, outdoor play. Use of symbols: pictures, including snapshots, drawing action pictures. Planning for clean-up.	Planning continued. Extension of calendar ideas, handwork (use of strips for papier mache work), play. Verbal attention to bandages, first aid.

8c. MANIPULATION OF STRING, AND YARN: SEWING

RATING

THE FIVE LEVELS OF THE CURRICULUM ITEM

1. interest at a distance	2. exploration	3. imitation	4. enjoyment and ease in activity	5. initiation for expressed purpose

DEFINITION OF THE TERM: BEHAVIOR UNDER OBSERVATION

Child's eye-hand coordination and fine muscle control in use of needle and thread. Materials considered in this item included: a) fiber board sewing cards with long-tipped laces; b) cardboard sewing cards with (short tipped yarn laces, crewel needles); c) nylon net with wire stemmed artificial flowers; d) construction paper with crewel needles, narrow ribbon; and e) coarse-weave material on hoop with sharp needle, yarn. The process observed was the running or basting stich (front-to-back threading through a hole or marked spot on the material). Sewing on cloth was included in the activities of children who had shown interest in stringing tiny beads (ordinarily, second year).

DESCRIPTION OF BEHAVIOR OBSERVED AT EACH LEVEL

Child watched others sew with materials; used sewing boards and tipped laces in other activities.	Child ordinarily worked with large boards, making random stitches. Tried other materials.	Child "sewed": pushed needle (lace-tip) through board, turned board over, again pushed needle through.	Child used various materials; did not tangle stitches; tried to make stitches of uniform length.	Child sewed for a purpose; making small card picture, making valentines, birthday cards. Making initialed towels or handkerchiefs.

PROGRAMMING

PREDICTABLE (INTERNALIZED) BEHAVIOR USED IN PROGRAMMING FOR NEXT LEVEL

Watches process; uses materials for other activities	Makes single stitches.	Makes consecutive stitches.	Follows single line or pattern.	Subordinates process to purpose.

TEACHING PROCEDURES TO ESTABLISH READINESS FOR NEXT LEVEL

Use of allied materials, pegboards, beads. Provision of heavy sewing cards. Verbal attention to work with fiber-board and laces. Use of paper punch to make holes.	Individual help where indicated, a) in catching needle or tip as it comes through material for next stitch. b) in turning material for next stitch. Handwork projects as, decorating greeting cards with ribbon lacing. Verbal attention to process.	Individual help where indicated. Verbal attention to process, a) planning, b) inspection, c) comparing guidelines. Handwork, running stitch around edge of card.	Expansion of choice of materials (reconstructing from 1 to 3, for each kind of material, when necessary). Verbal attention to finished product, quality of work, purpose of work.	Verbal attention. "Useful" sewing (e.g. buttons, torn garments). Leading to study of family roles, personal appearance.

9. HAMMERING

RATING

THE FIVE LEVELS OF THE CURRICULUM ITEM

1. exploration	2. directing to hammer board	3. hitting pegs of hammer board	4. inserting and hammering nails	5. joining wood with nails

DEFINITION OF THE TERM: BEHAVIOR UNDER OBSERVATION

Child's manipulation of hammers. Finger and hand coordination for holding the hammer; arm control for pounding; and eye-hand coordination for hitting board, nail or peg were the factors taken into account in rating the child.

DESCRIPTION OF BEHAVIOR OBSERVED AT EACH LEVEL.

Child watched others; handled hammer; tried pounding movement.	Child pounded, made contact with some part of hammer board.	Child pounded pegs of hammer board, and pounded them through to other side.	Child put nail in started hole, hammered it into wood.	Child drove nail through two pieces of wood, used nail as axle to attach wheel to board (made things).

PROGRAMMING

PREDICTABLE (INTERNALIZED) BEHAVIOR USED IN PROGRAMMING FOR NEXT LEVEL

Holds hammer, knows use.	Controls approximate direction of hammer.	Controls direction with fair precision.	Coordinates eyes and hands to strike nail head.	Uses process for a purpose.

TEACHING PROCEDURES TO ESTABLISH READINESS FOR NEXT LEVEL

Providing opportunity for use of hammer board (planning, turn-taking). Teacher participation to demonstrate use, if necessary. Discussion of process: pounding pegs level, turning board.	Teacher participation: discussion of child's work; asking child to aim at peg indicated by teacher. Verbal attention to specific aiming and results. (e.g. You pounded this one, then this one, "You hit at the side, that time." "You hit it exactly. Pound it again.")	Introduction of additional materials (rubber hammer, nails corrugated boxes, hammer, nails and threaded shapes or beads; hammer, thumb tacks or nails, and wall board). Verbal attention to child's designs. Teacher participation: demonstrating construction. Planning for turns with various hammering of materials.	Introduction of additional materials, soft wood (e.g. fruit crate, ends) wire nails, light weight hammer (8 oz.). Teacher participation: starting nail-holes when necessary. Showing process with wood. Use of symbolic records. (e.g. pictures of nail-board patterns, woodwork).	Use of records and stories about building. Symbolic records, work action-sketch. Leading to use of patterns, interpretation of sketches.

10. SAWING

RATING

THE FIVE LEVELS OF THE CURRICULUM ITEM

1. exploration	2. holding saw: partial cut	3. cutting interest in random pieces	4. cutting piece for use, with help	5. cutting piece for use in construction

DEFINITION OF THE TERM: BEHAVIOR UNDER OBSERVATION

Child's handling and use of one of the shopwork tools, a 16 inch crosscut saw. Skills observed in effective use were a) firm grip; b) coordinated back-to-front arm movement; c) control of arm pressures; and d) eye-hand coordination for making a planned cut (level 5).

DESCRIPTION OF BEHAVIOR OBSERVED AT EACH LEVEL

Child handled saw; tried various ways of holding wood; made nicks along edge of board but lacked firm grip.	Child held saw firmly; cut in groove started by teacher; used short erratic strokes.	Child cut in groove started by teacher; used firmer strokes; cut off random shapes.	Child cut a piece of desired shape, with teacher help.	Child (with minimum starting help when necessary) cut pieces for car bodies, boat-hulls, wood bases for toys, drum-sticks.

PROGRAMMING

PREDICTABLE (INTERNALIZED) BEHAVIOR USED IN PROGRAMMING FOR NEXT LEVEL

------------------Interest in manipulation-------------------- ------------Interest in product--------------

Holds materials, imitates arm movements.	Holds firmly, imitates arm movements.	Holds firmly, coordinates arm movements.	Holds, guides saw with help.	Holds and guides saw.

TEACHING PROCEDURES TO ESTABLISH READINESS FOR NEXT LEVEL

Construction activities involving use of tools: Verbal attention placed on things to be made. The context gave scope for the child interested in process and the child interested in results. Additional pieces of lumber were available for exploration.

Project (individual) Making corncob pipes. Making sticks for rhythm band (from 1/4" dowels). Making wood blocks: 2" x 3" or 1" x 3" soft pine. Verbal attention to length of sticks, process of sawing. Use of sandpaper on cut ends.	Project (group) Making standard for tree (1" x 3" soft pine) or long tree branch; trimming ends of long pieces to make even: cutting short pieces for base. Verbal attention to straight cuts and to small pieces cut from ends.	Project (group) Sawing pegboards. Making swing boards (cutting lengths of 1" x 4" pine; cutting triangle notches in ends of board). Verbal attention to pencil line guides; triangle and space it came from; smoothness of board. Use of sandpaper for smoothing cut ends.	Project (individual) Making cars or wagons using ready made wheels. Making wheels (sawing disk from broomstick). Making boats. Verbal attention to smooth surfaces, symmetry, drawing lines for guides.	Planning (group and individual). Use of straight edge a) Substantial board (1" x 3"), b) metal square, c) ruler. Use of supplementary materials: plastic items, toy figures. Independent use of vise.

11. USING SCREWDRIVER

RATING

THE FIVE LEVELS OF THE CURRICULUM ITEM

1. exploration	2. trial and error use of tool	3. random screwing unscrewing	4. screwing, unscrewing with direction	5. using to place screws

DEFINITION OF THE TERM: BEHAVIOR UNDER OBSERVATION

Child's purposeful use of screwdrivers. Skills involved were eye-hand coordination, two-hand coordination, control of fingers for turning screwdriver, and control of pressure. Included in this item was use of gimlets for starting screw holes.

DESCRIPTION OF BEHAVIOR OBSERVED AT EACH LEVEL

	Holes for screws already made			
Child experimented with screwdriver, tried fitting it to head of various screws and nails in classroom. Child used toy rubber screw driver in same way.	Child used steel screwdriver and fingers on metal screws, experimented with turning. Child used gimlet, in holes made by teacher or another child.	Child used screwdriver to remove screws from board and to replace. Child placed rubber screws in holes pierced in corrugated box.	Child used screwdriver to place or remove screws as requested by teacher. Child used gimlet to make holes started by teacher.	Child inserted screws in partly finished holes, screwed them into wood. Child made holes with gimlet, or spot marked by pencil dot.

PROGRAMMMING

PREDICTABLE (INTERNALIZED) BEHAVIOR USED IN PROGRAMMING FOR NEXT LEVEL

Holds tool; matches blade to screwheads and nailheads.	Holds tool firmly; turns.	Uses tool with screws, (not nails).	Makes purposeful use of tool, holds firmly, turns effectively.	Uses pressure to fix screws in wood.

TEACHING PROCEDURES TO ESTABLISH READINESS FOR NEXT LEVEL

Providing materials for unscrewing and replacing screws: a) rubber tools, screws, nails and corrugated box with holes; b) rubber tools, bolts and nuts, and cardboard strips with holes; c) steel screwdriver and board with easily removed screws; d) gimlet and board with ready-made holes.

Free play activity through five steps; purposeful use of screwdriver in 4, 5.

Dramatic play. Carpentry; repairing. Use of tangible toys: constructo set; screwboard; nuts and bolts. Verbal attention to fitting screws in holes; turning movement. Use of gimlet.	Dramatic play continued. Individual help with placing screwdriver in groove of screw. Verbal attention to difference between nails, screws and to straightness of screw, gimlet.	Dramatic play continued. Individual help: exchanging screws, gimlet, in boards. Verbal attention to making holes with gimlet; pressure, firm grip.	Verbal attention to screws in furniture: tightening loose screws; replacing lost ones. Planning and making pegboards, cars.	Use of symbols: pictures of tools, nails. matching tool to thing indicating its use. Verbal attention to correct choice of tools, fastenings.

12. BEAD STRINGING

RATING

THE FIVE LEVELS OF THE CURRICULUM ITEM

1. large threaded beads	2. large kindergarten beads, large needle	3. small kindergarten beads, small needle	4. commercial beads 1/4-1/2", small needle	5. beads on flexible wire

DEFINITION OF THE TERM: BEHAVIOR UNDER OBSERVATION

Child's handling of various bead-type materials. The five levels of the item refer to progressively smaller materials, requiring increasingly precise movements of hands and fingers, and more exact visuo-motor coordination. The item noted only coordination factors, not arrangement of patterning of beads.

DESCRIPTION OF BEHAVIOR OBSERVED AT EACH LEVEL

(In each case the needle, rod, or threading device is longer than the block or bead to be strung. Steel needles were converted to crewel needles by snipping off ends with cutting pliers)

Child removed and/or replaced threaded disks on pegs (e.g. color-tower). threaded cylinders, cubes, spheres on 3/4 inch wooden rods.	Child strung 1-1/2 inch or larger beads on cord with strong threading device.	Child strung 1/2 to 3/4 inch beads on heavy cord with threading device (e.g. crewel needle or bodkin).	Child strung beads with small needle, sewing elastic or thread.	Child strung small beads on flexible steel wire, pipe cleaners.

PROGRAMMING

PREDICTABLE (INTERNALIZED) BEHAVIOR USED IN PROGRAMMING FOR NEXT LEVEL

Uses palm grasp for putting large shapes on rods.	Holds needle with fingers, thumb, bead with palm or finger-thumb grasp.	Holds both bead and needle with finger-thumb grasp.	Uses finger-thumb grasp with fair co-ordination, on small materials.	Uses finger-thumb grasp with precision, on fine materials; uses sharp needle.

TEACHING PROCEDURES TO ESTABLISH READINESS FOR NEXT LEVEL

Providing blocks, dowels of various sizes. Using tinker toy dowels with large wooden beads. Using peg sets (pegs plus beads, shaped to fit on pegs). Verbal attention to completed towers, blocks on dowels.	Providing various kinds of needles (steel, plastic tipped laces, cords stiffened with lacquer.) Providing 1/8" dowels for use with small kindergarten beads.	Providing varied needles (steel, plastic, lacquered) smaller than those in step 2. Providing fine steel needles, flexible covered wire (telephone cable, bell wire). Beginning use of picture symbols, news stories.	Planning and discussion periods. Symbolic records of child's work. Gift-making (necklaces for mother, sister, self). Use of pipe cleaners for threading (flower stem arrangements).	Expansion of materials and their use; a) matching beads from cut paper, plastic straws, macaroni, b) stringing with sharp steel needle: cut paper, pumpkin seeds, crepe paper leis, sea shells, c) sewing cards, d) felt and plastic toys to be stuffed.

13. PEGS

RATING

THE FIVE LEVELS OF THE CURRICULUM ITEM

1. exploration	2. random activity large pegs	3. direction - large	4. direction - small	5. purposeful design

DEFINITION OF THE TERM: BEHAVIOR UNDER OBSERVATION

Child's insertion of pegs in pegboards of several kinds. Fitting pegs required manipulative control, eye-hand co-ordination in matching peg to hole, and ability (after the first levels) to use directional placement. Pegboards were considered a variant of beadstringing, with a stable board replacing the threaded blocks or beads.

DESCRIPTION OF BEHAVIOR OBSERVED AT EACH LEVEL

Child examined materials, tried fitting pegs.	Child fitted 1/2 x 3" pegs in large board, random placement.	Child filled 1/2" board; later, child made rows of pegs.	Variants included in rating were putting birthday candles in holders, candles in cake, flat pegs in grooves. 3/16" pegs. Child filled board; made rows; framed board.	Child made and named arrangements: "fence," "birthday cake," "road." Might add color as a design factor.

PROGRAMMING

PREDICTABLE (INTERNALIZED) BEHAVIOR USED IN PROGRAMMING FOR NEXT LEVEL

Knows relationship of peg to hole.	Fits large pegs.	Fits large pegs, controlling direction of placement.	Fits small pegs, controlling direction.	Produces a pattern.

TEACHING PROCEDURES USED TO ESTABLISH READINESS FOR NEXT LEVEL
Including commercial pegboards and class-made "birthday cakes" in free-choice materials.

| Providing boards and pegs of various sizes. Using turn-taking procedures. | Individual attention Suggesting filling the board, making a row of pegs, etc. Verbal attention to child's finished work. | Planning, discussing use of pegboards. Using pegboard sets as props for story telling. Providing related materials such as cars, animals. | Planning, discussing use of pegboard sets. Making symbolic records of child's work (pictures). Mixing peg sets, for size discrimination. Making flower pot with pipe cleaner plants. | Verbal attention to color elements. Hand-work: use of gimlet, brace and bit to make pegboards. Use of symbols: pictures, size-records, print forms. |

14. MINIATURE CARS, TRUCKS, TRAINS

RATING

THE FIVE LEVELS OF THE CURRICULUM ITEM

1. watching and carrying	2. rolling and watching wheels	3. making it go	4. dramatic play	5. dramatic play using other materials

DEFINITION OF THE TERM: BEHAVIOR UNDER OBSERVATION

Child's use of small and/or miniature wheeltoys. Skills observed included use of hand and finger muscles, and eye-hand coordination in guiding cars, trucks and trains.

DESCRIPTION OF BEHAVIOR OBSERVED AT EACH LEVEL

Child watched others play. Child carried car about the room or held car while watching others.	Child kept car in hand and rolled it back and forth. Favorite sites were the blackboard tray or table, where child could bring eyes to level of car wheels.	Child pushed car, letting go of it, across floor or under or on table. Child fastened train cars together.	Child played traffic games with others; imitated sounds of siren, horn and motor. Experimented with speeds.	Child loaded truck with blocks, cards; used cars in block play, pushing them under or across bridges, and on roadway; used miniature cars on pegboards or on traffic and roadmaps.

PROGRAMMING

PREDICTABLE (INTERNALIZED) BEHAVIOR USED IN PROGRAMMING FOR NEXT LEVEL

Handles cars, watches play of others.	Pushes cars, knows how they work.	Releases car purposefully.	Rehearses familiar process, associated with cars.	Uses car as part of a more inclusive concept.

TEACHING PROCEDURES TO ESTABLISH READINESS FOR NEXT LEVEL
(Cars, trucks and trains, in separate supplies and in story-context sets, were included with free-choice material).

Providing vehicles of various kinds and sizes (1 inch to 15 inch).	Experience records of various kinds: class projects to provide records of bus, subway, boat trips.			
	Verbal attention to construction of cars (kind, size, number of wheels; train hook-ups) and way of operation. Related handwork (pasted cars, fire-trucks, buses, trains).	Verbal attention to "traffic" rules. Suggestions for play: help with vocal play. Attention to print symbols for car sounds.	Planning for, and discussion of use of cars. Providing other materials (traffic layout, pegboard roads, "maps"). Suggesting uses for blocks.	Woodwork: making simple cars. Symbols: picture-maps, directional arrow, duplicating block structures. Related items: transportation, vacation travel, traffic safety.

15. TRAINS AND TRACKS

RATING

THE FIVE LEVELS OF THE CURRICULUM ITEM

1. exploration	2. putting pieces of track together	3. running train on straight track	4. joining tracks for function	5. dramatic play using other materials.

DEFINITION OF THE TERM: BEHAVIOR UNDER OBSERVATION

Child's manipulation of put-together wooden tracks and train cars. Details observed included: finger and hand strength; eye-hand coordination in joining tongued track sections; and constructing a functional track. Performance on this item was related to child's familiarity with miniature train systems, an aspect not rated.

DESCRIPTION OF BEHAVIOR OBSERVED AT EACH LEVEL

Child played with train cars; watched others; pulled pieces of joined track apart.	Child laid tracks in a line; experimented with joint; achieved partial or firm joint.	Child ran engine, car(s) along 2 or 3 section track; child might also simulate track with long building blocks.	Child constructed long straight track, curved track, Y-switch. (A few achieved a circular or oval track).	Child used blocks and boards to construct bridges and tunnels; loaded and unloaded cars, switched cars.

PROGRAMMING

PREDICTABLE (INTERNALIZED) BEHAVIOR USED IN PROGRAMMING FOR NEXT LEVEL

Explores tracks, cars, tries joints, couplings, wheels.	Manipulates track sections.	Uses tracks, train in correct relationship.	Constructs usable track arrangement.	Uses material as part of more inclusive concept.

TEACHING PROCEDURES TO ESTABLISH READINESS FOR NEXT LEVEL
Including train-sets in free choice materials.

Verbal attention to child's interest, and attempts to manipulate. Help in joining track sections; help in disconnecting.	Help with fitting sections to make a straight track. Planning for, discussion of use of materials. Use of related books. e.g. Big Book of Real Trains.	Attention to child's running of cars. Vocabulary (back, go ahead, switch).	Verbal attention to dramatic possibilities: suggestions re blocks, small dolls; offering materials; giving verbal suggestions when necessary.	Symbolic records of play: pictures, handwork, map, symbols. Woodwork: repairing couplings; making trains, as records of real experiences.

16. BLOCK BUILDING

RATING

THE FIVE LEVELS OF THE CURRICULUM ITEM

1. handles, carries piles in irregular manner.	2. beginning construction and simple designs	3. further development of patterns; techniques of handling.	4. dramatic repretation (house)	5. attempts to reproduce actual structure, careful symmetry.

DEFINITION OF THE TERM: BEHAVIOR UNDER OBSERVATION

Child's manipulation of blocks. The item refers principally to maple kindergarten blocks, including numerous architectural shapes, but also refers to use of 2-inch and 1-inch cubes. Skills observed ranged from palm grasp to eye-hand coordination in making steady representative structures.

DESCRIPTION OF BEHAVIOR OBSERVED AT EACH LEVEL

Child carried or hauled blocks; piled them at random. Built to knock down. Knocked down others' structures, for noise.	Child made towers, roads, simple bridges. Built to knock down. Knocked down others structures, as way of relating.	Individual and cooperative. Child placed blocks carefully: towers were steady, roads and floors straight. Child put away blocks with some care; constructed facade, called it a house.	Increasing incidence of cooperative building. Child built a 3D structure, with walks to make an enclosure; built steps.	Cooperative building. Child built recognizable structures (zoo, bridge, school, subway). Also built symmetrical arrangements, called attention to them.

PROGRAMMING

PREDICTABLE (INTERNALIZED) BEHAVIOR USED IN PROGRAMMING FOR NEXT LEVEL

Holds, stacks blocks (hand-grasp plus motor behavior).	Builds line structures, (eye-hand coordination, plus some motor behavior).	Builds carefully with eye for symmetry, (straightness).	Builds in three dimensions.	Builds as part of a concept.

TEACHING PROCEDURES TO ESTABLISH READINESS FOR NEXT LEVEL

Verbal attention to ongoing activity. Verbal descriptions of structures. Guidance in restoring, rebuilding towers.	Verbal attention to qualities of structures (e.g. height, straightness, duplicates). Guidance in cooperative building.	Verbal attention to ways of building blocks, matching edges. Picture symbols, to illustrate structures made by child(ren).	Planning discussions Symbolic record picture or pictures of child's structure. Use of child's structure for dramatic play (providing or drawing attention to props).	Planning discussions. Symbolic records. Handwork: pasting blockouts to make walls, bridges. Making toys for use with structures. Use of blocks to illustrate experiences.

TEACHER PARTICIPATION WHEN NECESSARY FOR SHOWING NEW USES FOR BLOCKS; BUILDING OF DEMONSTRATION STRUCTURES AS PART OF A STORY OR CONCEPTUAL SETTING.

Making samples for child to imitate, suggesting cooperative building (roads, tall towers) helping to store blocks.	Laying bridge across duplicate towers, laying "floor" of rectangle blocks, showing uses for arches cylinders, and other shapes.	Laying out an enclosure, room, etc. Building a solid wall, walls.	Building stairways, adding chimneys, roofs to houses. Constructing doors, windows.	Copying a drawing of a structure (interpretation of symbols).

17. TINKER TOYS

RATING

THE FIVE LEVELS OF THE CURRICULUM ITEM

1. exploration and interest	2. random with success (manipulative)	3. spontaneous design	4. imitating purposeful design	5. creative purposeful design

DEFINITION OF THE TERM: BEHAVIOR UNDER OBSERVATION

Child's use of tinker toys or similar toys. Eye-hand coordination needed for this was the same as for pegboard manipulations; also necessary was finger and hand strength, since with this toy, dowels fit snugly in holes. Attention to design, in the item, was not for the purpose of evaluating the child's structures, but for estimating his ability to manipulate a number of dowels and joints.

DESCRIPTION OF BEHAVIOR OBSERVED AT EACH LEVEL

Child tried to insert dowels in joint sockets; watched and imitated others; asked others to make designs for him; pulled pieces apart.	Child inserted dowels in joint sockets; strung pieces together at random; pulled pieces apart.	Child joined pieces at various angles; named his structure (which might or might not be recognizable) after it was made.	Child imitated others' structures; repeated his own designs.	Child made representative designs or interesting "abstract" combinations, (e.g. steam shovel, road grader, or abstractions with pivoting parts). Child used supplementary materials (dolls, figures, spools, e.g. for abacus, rifle).

PROGRAMMING

PREDICTABLE (INTERNALIZED) BEHAVIOR USED IN PROGRAMMING FOR NEXT LEVEL

Tries to manipulate pieces.	Fits pieces together.	Fits pieces; evaluates (names) work.	Puts pieces together in accordance with a plan.	Construction subsidiary to another activity.

TEACHING PROCEDURES TO ESTABLISH READINESS FOR NEXT LEVEL
(Tinker toys available as free-choice material. Teacher participation when necessary, to show different uses of materials.)

Verbal attention to child's on-going activity. Description of making lollipops, drumsticks, dumbbells. Making sets of wheels.	Attention to child's products. Use of products for group activities (e.g. drumsticks with cardboard and metal containers) Making cars, moveable slides on dowels (using spools)	Conversation about child's products. Use of picture symbols. Displaying child's work for a day or two. Making levers, pivots of various kinds, cannon, ferris wheels.	Picture-symbol record of products. Use of products for small group play. Duplication of patterns (e.g. asking child to make a second car for another child; suggesting that he copy another's item). Making more complex items (steam, shovel, sewing machine, abacus.)	Picture-symbol records used for duplication of child's products. Beginning use of patterns for new combinations (interpretation of symbols).

18. TOPS

RATING

THE FIVE LEVELS OF THE CURRICULUM ITEM

1. interest at a distance	2. exploration	3. trial and error use of top	4. imitation	5. enjoyment and ease in activity

DEFINITION OF THE TERM: BEHAVIOR UNDER OBSERVATION

Child's skill in spinning tops by finger action. Manipulative processes included the child's coordination of fingers and thumb, and his eye-hand coordination as evidenced by the release of the top on table surface or floor. Tops were variants of a single form, a disc or other shape on a stem.

DESCRIPTION OF BEHAVIOR OBSERVED AT EACH LEVEL

Child watched others spin tops.	Child handled top, tried to set it upright; tried turning it (slow motion).	Child twirled top with fingers, usually released it at oblique angle.	Child twirled top, released it at right angle to surface part of the time; listened to suggestions and watched others carefully.	Child spun top effectively; tried to keep two or more tops spinning at once; spun other objects; played cooperatively using tops.

PROGRAMMING

PREDICTABLE (INTERNALIZED) BEHAVIOR USED IN PROGRAMMING FOR NEXT LEVEL

Watches process.	Holds top with fingers.	Uses fingers effectively.	Uses fingers, releases top.	Subordinates manipulation to other purposes.

TEACHING PROCEDURES TO ESTABLISH READINESS FOR NEXT LEVEL

Spinning was an adjunct to matching, sorting, and categorizing of sets of tangible materials. Teaching activity was in the free-play setting and usually was individual or in small groups.

Including child in group using tops. Offering child sets containing additional tops.	Verbal attention to a) colors, sizes, composition of tops, b) child's manipulation. Individual help with spinning. Offering different sizes, shapes, to locate top most effective for learning.	Individual help with different tops to teach finger movement, release.	Verbal attention to movement of top across floor. Cooperative use of colors, sizes. Use of top in games: spinning within a designated area.	Making tops from cardboard, dowels, tinker-toys. Use of symbols: pictures, print forms, diagrams of movement.

19a   PUZZLES: COORDINATION BOARD
19b,c,d   INSERT PUZZLES

RATING

THE FIVE LEVELS OF THE CURRICULUM ITEM

1. exploration and interest	2. physical trial and error	3. following guide lines	4. thoughtful trial and error	5. pre-placement recognition

DEFINITION OF THE TERM: BEHAVIOR UNDER OBSERVATION

Child's use of form-board type puzzles. Manipulation factors observed included handling of the one-piece inserts, and eye-hand coordination needed for correct insertion. The coordination board contained colored pairs of circles, squares, triangles, rectangles.

DESCRIPTION OF BEHAVIOR OBSERVED AT EACH LEVEL

Child took puzzle for use, removed pieces, tried to replace. Some children's interest was solely in removal; they were fascinated by one set of insert puzzles which had dime-size holes for use in pushing out pieces.	Child tried one insert in all spaces on a board, or all inserts in one space.	Child seemed to match parts of outlines and/or general shape.	Child tried insert in spaces of same general shape, rotated pieces to try them.	Child selected insert to match space or space to match insert he had picked up. Child's glance moved from insert to space, before trial.

PROGRAMMING

PREDICTABLE (INTERNALIZED) BEHAVIOR USED IN PROGRAMMING FOR NEXT LEVEL

Removes inserts from puzzle board.	Tries to replace inserts.	Notices resemblances when inserts are next to spaces.	Uses vision and manipulation to place inserts.	Watches space and shape visually, then sets insert in correct space.

TEACHING PROCEDURES TO ESTABLISH READINESS FOR NEXT LEVEL.
(Puzzles introduced as a group experience, then included in free-play activities. Individual attention was given to the children wanting it. A number of children enjoyed working out processes without help, and asked for assistance only when puzzles had to be put away quickly.)

Attention to child's activity in taking puzzle apart. Providing help in replacing pieces. (Help ranging from replacing insert, having child pat it in firmly to pointing out, "The shoe goes in here, I think.") Varying process by getting child to remove an insert and replace it immediately if he does not do this himself.	Telling story to match figure, insert, puzzle. Individual attention and help continued: showing child how to trace contours of spaces with finger; calling attention to color cues; calling attention to duplicate shapes for coordination board; laying insert beside correct space, for child to slide into place.	Telling story about figure insert puzzles, describing actions of figures. (e.g. "This is the milkman bringing the milk. The cat comes running to get some milk. The dog comes running, but he is chasing the cat. The milkman is tall. His truck is big.") Asking child questions. (e.g. "Where do you think the big boy goes? Who is standing here by the truck?")	Individual attention to child's shape-matching. When process is obvious: helping child to interpret space (e.g. a wagon would have to go here - this boy is pulling his wagon.) Verbal attention to child's choice of puzzles for free-play. Conversation about his work with them. Inspection of puzzles to make correct placement.	Providing opportunity for child to tell story. Mixing pieces from two puzzles, (later from three) helping child sort pieces by story content. (Leading to understanding of language and relationships shown in puzzles.)

19 e. PUZZLES: NON-INSERT

RATING

THE FIVE LEVELS OF THE CURRICULUM ITEM

1. exploration and interest	2. physical trial and error	3. following guide lines	4. thoughtful trial and error	5. pre-placement recognition

DEFINITION OF THE TERM: BEHAVIOR UNDER OBSERVATION

Child's manipulation of cardboard puzzles with die marks in the recessed frame, as well as of wooden puzzles without such guides.

DESCRIPTION OF BEHAVIOR OBSERVED AT EACH LEVEL

Child examined puzzles, took pieces from frame.	Child tried pieces in various positions; usually placed a piece more or less accidentally.	Child placed pieces with "distinctive" contours around edge of puzzle (e.g. head of a pony).	Child placed pieces approximately, rotated pieces to try various placements.	Child looked at and matched contours.

PROGRAMMING

PREDICTABLE (INTERNALIZED) BEHAVIOR USED IN PROGRAMMING FOR NEXT LEVEL

Removes puzzle pieces from frame.	Tries pieces in various parts of frame.	Notices similar contours by juxtaposition of piece to space.	Recognizes contours, tries pieces (vision and manipulation).	Matches pieces to space before placement.

TEACHING PROCEDURES TO ESTABLISH READINESS FOR NEXT LEVEL.
(Puzzles of this type introduced as group activity, then included in free-choice activities. Individual attention for children wanting it.)

Handwork: using magazine illustrations to make 2, 3, 4-piece, etc. puzzles. Verbal attention to child's taking apart activity. a) Discussion of picture shown. b) Notice of pieces as they are taken out c) Help with replacing. d) Discussion of picture, repeated (recognition of it as being complete again). Construction of 3-D reproductions of puzzles using real objects, when possible.	Telling stories about puzzle. Construction of 2-D reproductions of puzzles (pasted, then cut apart). Showing child how to lift and replace individual pieces. Verbal recognition of child's work.	Use of tactile cues - running finger along contour of space. Help with recognition of puzzle parts (e.g. "Those are the pony's legs. Here is where the pony is standing, also. The pony is standing here. Can you find the pony's legs?)" Help with tactile matching of space-contour to piece-contour; visual check.	Help with rotation of piece, when child knows approximate placement. Discussion of ways of placing pieces. (e.g. "Slide the piece gently, and it will go in.")	Mixing pieces from 2, then 3 puzzles, then separating and solving. Giving child opportunity to tell story as he places pieces. (Leading to understanding of language relationships shown in puzzle.)

1. WALKING

RATING

THE FIVE LEVELS OF THE CURRICULUM ITEM

1. evidence of ability	2. functional through awkward motion	3. evidence of control	4. sureness of movement	5. purposeful and appropriate use of mode

DEFINITION OF THE TERM: BEHAVIOR UNDER OBSERVATION

Child's motor control in walking. The levels of the rating scale served as a check on how the child used this form of locomotion, since all children observed were able to walk. Level 1 was used to rate children who habitually ran rather than walked.

DESCRIPTION OF BEHAVIOR OBSERVED AT EACH LEVEL

Child was observed walking, but avoided doing so if he could get help.	Child walked to get places but showed poor coordination; stumbled over obstacles occasionally; "overshot" goal - e.g. bumping into it; moved trunk to keep balance.	Child walked with fair coordination; watched for obstacles; held trunk in more or less vertical line.	Child walked well, usually gracefully, no swaying of trunk. Child avoided obstacles automatically.	Child walked when that form of movement was efficient and expected. (e.g. moving through halls, about classroom).

PROGRAMMING

PREDICTABLE (INTERNALIZED) BEHAVIOR USED IN PROGRAMMING FOR NEXT LEVEL

Maintains balance at walking pace.	Uses mode for locomotion; controls legs.	Controls legs and trunk fairly well.	Has automatic control of legs and trunk.	Suits locomotion to situation.

TEACHING PROCEDURES TO ESTABLISH READINESS FOR NEXT LEVEL.

Providing running space. Walking with child in situations where it was necessary in halls or classroom. Providing materials, activities in which walking is an essential part. Focus on instances of appropriate use of running.	Providing walking space in classroom, in playground, etc. Providing partners. Using walking as a part of music activity. Dramatizations with walking featured.	Use of music and dramatization to develop ways of walking (like a bear, a dog, an elephant; tiptoeing). Focus on walking "nicely," "gracefully," quietly."	Verbal attention to ways of walking. Focus on correct choice of walking, in various situations. Planning how to go various places.	Class planning, discussion, etc. Beginning use of symbols (pictures, word). Beginning map-making.

2. RUNNING

RATING

THE FIVE LEVELS OF THE CURRICULUM ITEM

1. evidence of ability	2. functional through awkward motion	3. evidence of control	4. sureness of movement	5. purposeful and appropriate use of mode

DEFINITION OF THE TERM: BEHAVIOR UNDER OBSERVATION

Child's motor control in running. Level 1 was used to rate children who could not control both locomotion and balance. They were observed trying to run, but their rate of movement was only slightly faster than walking and more a matter of arm swinging and body angle than of speed.

DESCRIPTION OF BEHAVIOR OBSERVED AT EACH LEVEL

Child could quicken pace slightly; imitated body angle of runner.	Child could quicken pace; might hold shoulders back and stomach out, or stiffen knees and rock from side to side; did not avoid obstacles or stop efficiently.	Child quickened pace; showed easier shoulder carriage; used flexed arms for balance; rarely ran into obstacles.	Child ran quickly, easily; avoided obstacles; stopped gracefully.	Child ran for a purpose. (games, teacher's request). Did not run in inappropriate situations.

PROGRAMMING

PREDICTABLE (INTERNALIZED) BEHAVIOR USED IN PROGRAMMING FOR NEXT LEVEL.

Quickens pace slightly, adjusts balance.	Quickens pace, maintains balance.	Maintains balance in running, stopping.	Maintains balance, controls motor processes involved in running, stopping.	Suits locomotion to situation.

TEACHING PROCEDURES TO ESTABLISH READINESS FOR NEXT LEVEL

| Providing space for running on playground, in gym, in room for some activities. Providing situations (dramatic play, races). Running with children who need "feel" of speed. | Running with children who need support for balance. Verbal attention to running games on roof. Verbal attention to walking. Telling stories which involve running (e.g. Gingerbread Boy). | Use of music, dramatization: (running like a horse, a dog, a mouse; fast, slow, lightly). Verbal attention to child's way of running. | Verbal attention to various ways, appropriate times to use running. Focus on correct choice of running, in activities. | Broadened experiences; Races, tag, ball games. Attention to symbols, both pictures and word. |

3. MARCHING

RATING

THE FIVE LEVELS OF THE CURRICULUM ITEM

1. evidence of ability	2. functional through ackward motion	3. evidence of control	4. sureness of movement	5. purposeful and appropriate use of mode

DEFINITION OF THE TERM: BEHAVIOR UNDER OBSERVATION

Child's motor control in matching locomotion to 2/4 or 4/4 tempo. The levels of this item outlined the child's progress toward accented rhythmic motion.

DESCRIPTION OF BEHAVIOR OBSERVED AT EACH LEVEL

Child walked to march music, or stamped feet in irregular patterns.	Child moved with others, stamped feet fairly consistently (not necessarily on the beat) held self more or less straight.	Child stamped foot on accented beat, part of time; held body erect, sometimes stiff.	Child kept the tempo most of the time; held self erect easily (not stiff); noted the beat with less pronounced stamp.	Child helped others to keep time, could lead group; showed some other way of accenting beat (Verbal: Hup!, Left!, Pum! Action: swinging arm, waving flag.)

PROGRAMMING

PREDICTABLE (INTERNALIZED) BEHAVIOR USED IN PROGRAMMING FOR NEXT LEVEL

Shows awareness of music.	Controls legs to stamp feet while walking.	Tries to match stamping to accented chords.	Controls accent without concentrated attention.	Gives accent with two different movements.

TEACHING PROCEDURES TO ESTABLISH READINESS FOR NEXT LEVEL

Providing opportunity for marching. Selecting music with well-defined beat: especially a tune such as Davy Crocket or Johnny Appleseed, known to children in other situations. Using tapping with marching tunes.	Providing opportunity for marching in various ways: single file with partners in long line (The King of France). Verbal attention to beat of a tune.	Dramatization: "This is how (a soldier, a toy soldier, a bear) marches. Slow, fast marching. Verbal focus on foot stamp. Verbal attention to beat of a drum! Turn-taking with drum beating while standing by piano.	Dramatization of musical selections. Use of flags, stick-bells while marching. Control; marching, stopping, marching again. Turn-taking with drum, turns as leader. Verbal focus on tempo: PUM, pum.	Use of drum while marching (cymbals, tambourine). Focus on symbols (picture, word.)

4. JUMPING

RATING

THE FIVE LEVELS OF THE CURRICULUM ITEM

1. evidence of ability	2. functional through awkward motion	3. evidence of control	4. sureness of movement	5. purposeful and appropriate use of mode

DEFINITION OF THE TERM: BEHAVIOR UNDER OBSERVATION

Child's motor control in lifting both feet from the floor at the same time. Observed were jumping up into the air from a standing position on the floor and down from a standing position on a stair, step, chair, box.

DESCRIPTION OF BEHAVIOR OBSERVED AT EACH LEVEL

Child could shift feet on floor; jump slightly while supporting self with table, or with teacher's support. Or child prepared to jump, then stepped with one foot.	Child lifted self from floor, or jumped from single step, bottom step, or curb; usually, much swinging of arms, bending, ending with an awkward and small jump; child sometimes fell.	Child jumped from single step, with some swinging and "getting ready," could regain balance without falling; landed noisily.	Child jumped in several situations, landing was steady, usually light and quiet.	Child jumped lightly, well, in play and music activities. Usually, tried to jump rope, or jumped from second step, a chair. Used symbols.

PROGRAMMING

PREDICTABLE (INTERNALIZED) BEHAVIOR USED IN PROGRAMMING FOR NEXT LEVEL.

Tries; accepts support.	Lifts both feet at same time, without help.	Maintains balance, while jumping.	Jumps without special attention to balance.	Uses jumping as a means.

TEACHING PROCEDURES TO ESTABLISH READINESS FOR NEXT LEVEL

Helping child by holding two hands, one hand; direct teaching of jumping from a chair or a step. Providing play situations on roof (obstacle course).	Use of music, (quick chords); Jumping with a partner. Dramatic play: "jumping" on all fours to help with getting feet an inch or more off floor (frog, rabbit, dog jumping for bone.)	Jumping in song context, with partner (lightly, hard). Verbal attention to ways of jumping off steps, on to rug or circle marked on floor. (Table support when needed.)	Control: jumping, stopping, and jumping; number, context, (1 jump, 2 jumps). Finger play to music. Verbal focus on ways to jump. (backward, forward).	Conversation about animals, etc. Use of symbols (pictures, word).

5. HOPPING

RATING

THE FIVE LEVELS OF THE CURRICULUM ITEM

1. evidence of ability	2. functional through awkward motion	3. evidence of control	4. sureness of movement	5. purposeful and appropriate use of mode

DEFINITION OF THE TERM: BEHAVIOR UNDER OBSERVATION

Child's motor control in hopping on one foot. (Children showed a special interest in this activity; teacher procedures were partly based on their intent to learn).

DESCRIPTION OF BEHAVIOR OBSERVED AT EACH LEVEL

Child stood on one foot, shifted other foot slightly along the floor; supported self by table or piano.	Child lifted self an inch or so; did a hop-step sequence (stepped to regain balance after each hop).	Child took two or three hops in succession; regained balance with little trouble.	Child took several hops; was still interested mainly in accomplishment.	Child tried hopping games (to music and in play) sometimes tried to jump rope on one foot.

PROGRAMMING

PREDICTABLE (INTERNALIZED) BEHAVIOR USED IN PROGRAMMING FOR NEXT LEVEL

Considers hopping a desirable accomplishment

Maintains balance on one foot, standing.	Hops in place; recovers balance.	Maintains balance while hopping forward.	Maintains balance and hops without concentrating on process.	Uses skill in hopping as a means.

TEACHING PROCEDURES TO DEVELOP READINESS FOR NEXT LEVEL

Providing extra opportunities for practice. Direct teaching of ways to lift one foot, hop with support. Providing music for hopping. Teaching the child to raise his foot forward, instead of bending knee, was effective. (Hopping on alternate feet).	Dramatic play: hop like a rabbit (on all fours, then lifting one foot). Music structure for hopping (in circle, around room, to___)	Asking child who hopped well to help another child. Verbal attention to ways of hopping (lightly, fast).	Verbal focus on number of hops, hopping from one place to another. Verbal attention to foot used for hopping.	Use of hopping in game context, story context, story context. Use of symbols. Attention to process of skipping.

6. SKIPPING

RATING

THE FIVE LEVELS OF THE CURRICULUM ITEM

1. evidence of ability	2. functional through awkward movement	3. evidence of control	4. sureness of movement	5. purposeful and appropriate use of mode

DEFINITION OF THE TERM: BEHAVIOR UNDER OBSERVATION

Child's motor control in skipping. Teachers observed two stages in development of skipping. The first was imitating the rhythmic forward movement (substituting, for the skipping, a gallop, a trot, or a forward kick with one foot while hopping with the other foot); the second stage was mastering the sliding hop which distinguishes skipping from other forms of locomotion. The child was not rated for this item if he did not approximate the sliding hop.

DESCRIPTION OF BEHAVIOR OBSERVED AT EACH LEVEL

Child moved by hopping and shifting self forward (one or both feet)	Child took two or three sliding hops in succession; lifted foot, took an exaggerated raised position (one or both feet).	Child took two or three skips, with lifted foot and leg lightly flexed, swayed from side to side (one or both feet).	Child moved easily, held trunk and head erect; body stayed in perpendicular plane.	Child skipped smoothly to music; used mode in games like drip-the-handkerchief; had good balance. One foot skipped credited for young children. Two foot skipping for older.

PROGRAMMING

PREDICTABLE (INTERNALIZED) BEHAVIOR USED IN PROGRAMMING FOR NEXT LEVEL

Stands on one foot, hops "in place."	Stands on one foot, shifts forward (hops).	Maintains balance while repeating several skipping steps. (Two feet or one, i.e. skip and step)	Repeats smoothly; brushes sole of shoe along floor rather than lifting it. (one or two feet).	Subordinates skipping to activity (one foot skip rated here for 5 year old - two feet for older child).

TEACHING PROCEDURES TO ESTABLISH READINESS FOR NEXT LEVEL

General approach: Situations in which skipping would contribute to the experience (music and story activities); direct instruction when child showed readiness.

Situations: Goldilocks skipping through woods. Skipping to music (Going Down to Town) Teacher participation: skipping with children showing readiness.	Situations: dancing hop: raising free foot up and forward, marching: raising free foot up and forward. Jig step (Virginia Reel). Teacher participation as before.	Situations: start-and stop situations (Going Down to Town: Virginia Reel; medly of activities, using music cues) Verbal attention to hopping movement.	Situations: longer intervals of skipping in medley. Verbal attention to children's use of skipping. Use of symbols: silhouettes showing foot and body positions.	Broadened experiences: stories, music, game activities, (e.g. Drop the Handkerchief). Focus on symbols, pictures, outline drawings, words.

7. DANCING

RATING

THE FIVE LEVELS OF THE CURRICULUM ITEM

1. evidence of ability to	2. functional though awkward movement	3. evidence of control	4. sureness of movement	5. purposeful and appropriate use of mode

DEFINITION OF THE TERM: BEHAVIOR UNDER OBSERVATION

Child's motor control in moving to various kinds of music - from simple whirling to rock 'n roll, set routines of folk dances, and expressive dancing which have been discussed in the sections on Social Development and Imagination and Creative Activity.

DESCRIPTION OF BEHAVIOR OBSERVED AT EACH LEVEL

Child moved arm(s), leg(s), hand(s) and/or body in response to music; ordinarily used one response (e.g. jumping, bowing, turning); dancing usually did not fit music tempo.	Child still had a favorite mode, which showed some smoothness; imitated others movements.	Child could start, stop, start again his favorite motion and alternate it with other motions. (Followed tunes with verbal cue.)	Child used two or more motions, matching his dancing to the music. (Recognized a few simple tunes.)	Child used one or more patterns; recognized tunes and could match responses to music.

PROGRAMMING

PREDICTABLE (INTERNALIZED) BEHAVIOR USED IN PROGRAMMING FOR NEXT LEVEL

Moves in response to music stimulation.	Repeats a movement.	Controls one or more movements.	Combines and alternates movements.	Patterns movements according to music pattern.

TEACHING PROCEDURES TO ESTABLISH READINESS FOR NEXT LEVEL

Group dancing, free or imitative movement. Turn taking, in group situation. Listening to music, using finger-play, finger-dancing on table.	Turn-taking in group situation. Verbal attention to child's favored motion. One motion dance with partner (Row, Row, Row). Matching end of dance to end of tune. Listening to music, finger and hand play in which one movement was repeated as a refrain.	Verbal attention to several kinds of music. ("This is good for whirling - for dancing this way - for clapping.") Listening to vocal numbers, for cues to motion. Group dramatic dancing.	Simple structured group dancing (e.g. Danish Clap Dance) for combining, alternating steps. Structured dances with partners (picking up partner's motions). Verbal attention to patterns.	Broadening recognition base - two or more marches, waltzes (to be danced to, not named). Broadening pattern base - song-dances, popular dances. Attention to symbols.

8a. STAIRS - CLIMBING

RATING

THE FIVE LEVELS OF THE CURRICULUM ITEM

1. going up with assistance, two feet per tread	2. up holding rail, two feet per tread	3. up without holding rail, two feet per tread	4. up with assistance or holding rail, one foot per tread	5. up without holding on, one foot per tread

DEFINITION OF THE TERM: BEHAVIOR UNDER OBSERVATION

Child's motor control in stair climbing. Use of hand rail or bannister, discussed as a safety measure in the Self-help section, was observed for this item as an aspect of the child's motor coordination and maintenance of balance in climbing steps.

DESCRIPTION OF BEHAVIOR OBSERVED AT EACH LEVEL

Child held hand of teacher; went up slowly. Teacher assistance sometimes included pulling or lifting, to help child shift weight to higher step.	Child used handrail to pull self from one step to next, or to maintain balance.	Child climbed slowly, usually in center of step; moved arms as balances, or held arms stiff at side.	Child alternated feet in climbing; held teacher's hand, or held rail to maintain balance. Usually climbed rapidly.	Child climbed efficiently, alternating feet, with no assistance.

PROGRAMMING

PREDICTABLE (INTERNALIZED) BEHAVIOR USED IN PROGRAMMING FOR NEXT LEVEL

Controls muscles of one leg.	Lifts self on one leg and maintains balance by means of banister.	Lifts self (one leg) and maintains balance, without support.	Controls muscles of both legs when given support.	Maintains balance and control of both legs.

TEACHING PROCEDURES TO ESTABLISH READINESS FOR NEXT LEVEL

Holding child's hand as long as necessary. Letting child hold banister with other hand. Withdrawing support on last step of stairway. Gradually withdrawing support, letting child shift weight to banister.	Arranging partners for stair climbing (a skilled climber with a less skilled one). Use of steps on slide. Encouraging child to release hold on banister on last step. Using steps with no rails (parks, Columbia student walk).	Direct teaching: Renewing support; suggesting that child try other foot for stepping up. Practice in hopping, stamping, dancing with both favored and less favored legs.	Verbal attention to use of either foot in climbing. Helping child to go up steps rapidly. Verbal attention to quick climbing. Using steps with no rails.	Continued opportunity for practice on steps without rails. Verbal focus on safety factor. Holding rail when there is one. Walking, not running; helping others. Planning trips where stairs, escalators will be encountered. Use of picture symbols, beginning map-making.

8b. STAIRS: DESCENDING

RATING

THE FIVE LEVELS OF THE CURRICULUM ITEM

1. going down with assistance, two feet per tread	2. down holding rail, two feet per tread	3. down with assistance one foot per tread	4. down holding rail, one foot per tread	5. down without holding on, one foot per tread

DEFINITION OF THE TERM: BEHAVIOR UNDER OBSERVATION

Motor control in descending stairs. As in climbing, two skills were involved, control of leg muscles and ability to maintain balance.

DESCRIPTION OF BEHAVIOR OBSERVED AT EACH LEVEL

Child regained balance at each tread. Child held teacher's hand; descended slightly in advance of teacher letting teacher support weight, or one step behind teacher, who helped with balance.	Child regained balance on each tread. Child held rail to maintain balance, or leaned on rail to support weight and maintain balance.	Child, with support, maintained balance for several steps, alternating legs.	Child supported self with rail; alternated legs for several steps.	Child controlled leg muscles of both legs, maintained balance without support.

PROGRAMMING

PREDICTABLE (INTERNALIZED) BEHAVIOR USED IN PROGRAMMING FOR NEXT LEVEL

controls one leg, for descending.	controls one leg, and maintains own balance, using rail.	controls both legs, for descending.	controls both legs; maintains balance with help of rail.	maintains balance, uses both legs.

TEACHING PROCEDURES TO DEVELOP READINESS FOR NEXT LEVEL

Teacher-help as long as necessary: help given first in way child seems to prefer (teacher on step above or below child) then changed to other mode. Teaching use of banister. Gradual transfer of support to banister.	Teacher-support, with direct teaching of use of alternate feet. Assigning partners, letting skilled child take teacher's place with child learning. Verbal attention to stepping down with alternate feet (e.g., counting steps) asking child to do last 2,3, 4 treads holding rail.	Verbal attention to use of legs, alternately counting steps. Teacher support in use of playground ladders and slide, alternating feet on rungs or steps.	Conversation about ways of going up and down steps. Review and planning; safety factors. Teacher support if needed in use of stairways in park, whenever rail is absent.	Conversation: safety factors, planning trips where stairway will be encountered; experience on escalators. Use of picture symbols; beginning map-making.

9. JUMPING ROPE

RATING

THE FIVE LEVELS OF THE CURRICULUM ITEM

1. interest in	2. attempts to jump	3. jumps from standing position	4. runs and jumps into moving rope	5. jumps without concern about rope

DEFINITION OF THE TERM: BEHAVIOR UNDER OBSERVATION

Child's motor control in jumping rope. Children had the opportunity to try jumping with individual ropes and with ropes turned by teachers. Rating was only on jumping in a rope held by skillful turners. Rope-turning might profitably be included as a separate item: it had to be taught and was learned by a number of children.

DESCRIPTION OF BEHAVIOR OBSERVED AT EACH LEVEL

Child watched rope jumping; picked up and played with ropes not being used; helped teacher turn for others.	Child asked for turn; stood at center of rope; jumped erratically; jumped or stepped over rope held motionless on ground; often stopped jumping when rope was turned so that rope contacted feet.	Child jumped so that his feet cleared the swinging rope; usually a few successful jumps at first; later, rhythmic jumping.	Child stood at side, followed descending rope to get to position for jumping (usually termed "front door" in jumping vocabulary). Jumped with varying success.	Child jumped rhythmically, several times before missing.

PROGRAMMING

PREDICTABLE (INTERNALIZED) BEHAVIOR USED IN PROGRAMMING FOR NEXT LEVEL

watches activity.	tries motor ability in rope situation.	regulates jump according to movement of rope.	controls running and jumping to fit movement of rope.	jumps without direct attention to rope factor.

TEACHING PROCEDURES USED TO DEVELOP READINESS FOR NEXT LEVEL

Providing individual ropes for child's experimentation. Using patterned jumping in other contexts: music and dancing activities, jumping over rope, board. Including child in jumping group (e.g., help with turning rope). Verbal attention to children jumping (e.g., counting jumps).	Verbal reference to rules for turn-taking. Giving child regular turn at jumping. Verbal attention to elements of success (e.g., "Just as the rope went over, you got ready to jump," "You jumped high that time.") Practice in rhythmic jumping for children interested.	Verbal focus on jumping rhythm. Use of traditional rhymes. Practice in various speeds. Attention to traditional rules governing turns. Jumping and turning for others. Notice given children able to run and jump; practice entry and jump in other contexts.	Conversation about jumping; planning for roof activity. Increasing use of rhythms, counting, etc. Direct teaching for children interested, running in and out.	Adding to combinations of movements (e.g., run in, jump once, run out, jump twice, turning while jumping, jumping with partner, etc.) Emphasis on cooperative game. Beginning use of symbols.

10. SLIDING

RATING

THE FIVE LEVELS OF THE CURRICULUM ITEM

1. interest	2. someone with child	3. someone helping	4. someone near	5. independently

DEFINITION OF THE TERM: BEHAVIOR UNDER OBSERVATION

Child's motor control in coming down a variety of metal playground slides. Observation was on four different size slides; a five-foot slide (too small except for introduction to sliding); an eight foot slide on which to master safety rules; a ten foot slide to help children make the transition to the higher apparatus in the nearby playground. Use of the sliding board required a combination of motor coordination and balance control in addition to a lack of fear.

DESCRIPTION OF BEHAVIOR OBSERVED AT EACH LEVEL

Child stayed near slide, watched others, climbed steps to top, but backed down steps rather than slide; let adult lift him to slide (at point where it levels cff) and guide him to end of slide.	Child climbed steps and went down slide with adult or other child sitting behind him (i.e., balance was supplied by adult).	Child climbed steps, sat down first with help, then without help, went down with adult (on ground) holding hand to help with balance, or with adult to catch him at bottom.	Child used slide when adult was near; frequently called to adult "Watch me," evidently getting support from adult's attention. Later, "Watch me" called attention to child's pride in achievement.	Child used slide without physical or visual support, observing safety rules. Child began to use variant ways of sliding.

PROGRAMMING

PREDICTABLE (INTERNALIZED) BEHAVIOR USED IN PROGRAMMING FOR NEXT LEVEL

watches process.	tries slide.	maintains or helps to maintain balance.	maintains balance, controls movements, with verbal or visual support.	maintains balance in simple sliding, without attention to process.

TEACHING PROCEDURES USED TO ESTABLISH READINESS FOR NEXT LEVEL

Including child in group of children sliding: letting him help (taking hand of another child at end of a slide to help him to his feet). Reference to hand rails for climbing, side of slide for holding to, in sliding.	Use of turn-taking context. Teacher help: lifting child to top of slide and guiding him down; sliding with child. Conversation (recall and planning) surface, effect of rain; ways of coming down slide.	Help given as long as necessary. Gradual withdrawal of physical support. Verbal emphasis of safety rules. Having child sit momentarily at top of slide, survey view, before sliding.	Introduction of two variations: coming down prone, feet first (expression applied "Like a crab"); and prone, head first ("Like a fish").	Verbal focus on safety. Recall and planning. Supervised climbing of sliding surface; testing slipperiness of an unfamiliar slide; safe use of sides of slide as brakes. Running hand on side.

11a.1 BALL PLAYING: CATCHING LARGE BALL

RATING

THE FIVE LEVELS OF THE CURRICULUM ITEM

1. trapping	2. stand still, hand ready for bounced ball	3. moving, hands ready for ball bounced	4. success in fly ball	5. catching undirected ball

DEFINITION OF THE TERM: BEHAVIOR UNDER OBSERVATION

Child's motor control in catching a large ball. Children used the two-hand catch with consideration of position of the child's hands for catching: underhand, palms upward, and overhand, palms vertical or downward. Both methods, past level 2, implied coordination of motor processes and visual estimate of direction and position of the ball.

DESCRIPTION OF BEHAVIOR OBSERVED AT EACH LEVEL

a) Underhand. Child held hands palms up, trapped ball tossed to him between hands or against chest. b) overhand. Child closed hands over ball tossed into lap. Child closed hands over ball rebounding from floor and hitting palms.	Child caught ball bounced to him, in upturned palms. Child closed hands over ball bounced by himself or by another person.	Child moved toward ball, to bring hands under it as it started downward arc. Child moved toward ball, caught it on upward bounce.	Child moved to bring hands under a high-tossed ball. Child moved, reached up for a high ball.	Child estimated direction, moved to get hands in position. Child estimated direction, moved and reached up to catch ball.

PROGRAMMING

PREDICTABLE (INTERNALIZED) BEHAVIOR USED IN PROGRAMMING FOR NEXT LEVEL

holds hands ready and closes hands over a stopped ball.	stops ball with hands.	Adjusts to slight change in direction of ball.	assesses direction of ball in air (general direction already anticipated).	gauges direction of a ball and moves toward it.

TEACHING PROCEDURES TO ESTABLISH READINESS FOR NEXT LEVEL
Teacher participation at first four levels, when accuracy in throwing is necessary.

| Sending ball to child in various ways: rolling, bouncing, tossing, throwing gently (aiming directly at child's hands to promote his closing hands over ball). Group play: rolling, tossing, bouncing from one child to another. Verbalization for each child (e.g., "I will toss the ball to M. M, are your hands ready? Here it comes.") | Providing opportunity to practice stopping ball coming at various speeds though not too fast. Accompanying process of bouncing and catching with verbalization. Conversation about different kinds of balls, leading to use of basketball "dribbling." Counting action song, Bounce, Bounce, Ball. | Variations of bouncing and catching, tossing and catching. Gradual increase of height of toss, to provide experience in seeing the ball against the wall or sky. (Previous catching had the floor as the stable reference point.) | Playing games of "catch" with large ball. Verbal attention to turning, reaching, jumping, etc. to catch. Verbal attention to watching ball, tossing ball up in the air, watching it as it falls. Tossing beanbags, toy parachutes. | Varying ball size, using beanbags. Verbal attention to reaching for a ball and stopping its progress with one hand, bouncing with one hand, catching with one hand. Use of symbols. |

11a.2 BALL PLAYING: CATCHING SMALL BALL

RATING

THE FIVE LEVELS OF THE CURRICULUM ITEM

1. trapping	2. stand still, hands ready for bounced ball	3. moving, hands ready for ball bounced	4. success in fly ball	5. catching undirected ball

DEFINITION OF THE TERM: BEHAVIOR UNDER OBSERVATION

Child's motor control in catching a small ball. As in large ball play, coordination of movements and vision became increasingly important in levels 3, 4 and 5. At levels 1 and 2, the process was ordinarily a two-hand catch. Children who progressed to levels 3, 4 and 5 were usually experimenting with a one-hand catch. The ball playing item as a whole seems applicable to children beyond the preschool level.

DESCRIPTION OF BEHAVIOR OBSERVED AT EACH LEVEL

a) underhand Child trapped ball between hands.	Child held hands cupped to receive ball.	Child held cupped hand(s) in line of ball's fall.	Child moved to bring cupped hand(s) under ball in line of fall.	Child assessed direction of ball, moved to catch it in cupped hand(s).
b) overhand Child closed hands over ball tossed into lap, or stopped by chest, etc.	Child reached hands out to get ball.	Child moved toward and caught ball on upward bounce.	Child moved and reached to intercept ball in line of fall.	Child assessed direction, moved and reached for ball.

PROGRAMMING

PREDICTABLE (INTERNALIZED) BEHAVIOR USED IN PROGRAMMING FOR NEXT LEVEL

holds hands ready and closes hands over a stopped ball.	stops ball with hands.	adjusts to slight change in direction of ball.	assesses direction of ball in air (general direction already anticipated).	gauges direction of a ball and moves toward it.

TEACHING PROCEDURES TO ESTABLISH READINESS FOR NEXT LEVEL
Teacher participation at first four levels, when accuracy in <u>throwing</u> is necessary.

Sending ball to child in various ways: rolling, bouncing, tossing, throwing gently (aiming directly at child's hands to enable him to close hands over ball). Group play: rolling, tossing, bouncing from one child to another. Verbalization for each child (e.g., "<u>I</u> will toss the ball to <u>M. M,</u> are your hands ready? Here it comes.")	Providing opportunity to practice stopping ball coming at various speeds though not too fast. Accompanying process of bouncing and catching with verbalization. Conversation about different kinds of balls, leading to use of basketball "dribbling." Counting action song, <u>Bounce, Bounce, Ball.</u>	Variations of bouncing and catching, tossing and catching. Gradual increase of height of toss, to provide experience in seeing the ball against the wall or sky. (Previous catching had the floor as the stable reference point.)	Playing games of "catch" with small ball. Verbal attention to turning, reaching, jumping to catch. Verbal attention to watching ball, tossing ball up in the air, watching it as it falls. Tossing beanbags, toy parachutes.	Varying ball size, using beanbags. Verbal attention to reaching for a ball and stopping its progress with one hand, bouncing with one hand, catching with one hand. Use of symbols.

11b.1 BALL PLAYING: THROWING LARGE BALL
11b.2   THROWING SMALL BALL

RATING

THE FIVE LEVELS OF THE CURRICULUM ITEM

1. release	2. proximate release with direction	3. distant release	4. distant release with direction	5. moving and throwing

DEFINITION OF THE TERM: BEHAVIOR UNDER OBSERVATION

Child's motor control in throwing a large ball. Two ways of release were rated separately — the underhand <u>toss</u> and the overhand <u>throw</u>, since each process had identifiable stages. However, the elements of child behavior used for programming procedures were similar for both tossing and throwing as well as for large and small balls.

DESCRIPTION OF BEHAVIOR OBSERVED AT EACH LEVEL

a) underhand

Child tossed ball with one or two hands, moved arms and sometimes body in line of toss.	Child tossed ball to another person, or into a basket, box. Ball went high at first.	Child tossed ball high in air at first; later, shifted hands to side of ball to get horizontal distance.	Child tossed ball to another child or over a barrier.	Child ran or walked and tossed ball in selected direction.

b) overhand

Child half-threw ball, pushed ball, throwing to another person; bounced ball on floor.	Child threw ball in direction of another person - did not always adapt force to distance. Child bounced ball to another person.	Child threw or bounced ball with force enough to carry it some distance.	Child threw ball to another child, at a wall, or along the ground in direction he had selected.	Child ran or walked and threw ball in selected direction.

PROGRAMMING

PREDICTABLE (INTERNALIZED) BEHAVIOR USED IN PROGRAMMING FOR NEXT LEVEL

gives some impetus to released ball.	gives some direction and some impetus to released ball.	releases ball with force.	gives direction and force to ball.	adjusts direction and force to own line of movement.

TEACHING PROCEDURES TO ESTABLISH READINESS FOR NEXT LEVEL

Teacher participation as catcher, as long as necessary, to ensure that the child throwing the ball observed its catching by another person.

Using game situation: tossing or throwing ball into basket, box, etc.: rolling ball along floor; rolling, tossing, bouncing ball toward various objects or to another person. Visual and verbal attention to course of moving ball.	Using game situations; gradually increasing distance to target or person receiving ball. Verbal attention to motor process in throwing.	Experimental throwing and game situations, in larger settings: rolling and tossing ball down slopes and flat areas in park. Use of beanbags, toy parachutes for distance throwing. Visual, verbal attention to line of flight of object. Focus on interaction aspect of throwing, catching.	Broadening game experience. Conversation about games of various kinds; use of various kinds of balls. Experimental running, stopping and throwing, and running and throwing (in gym, park).	Verbal focus on games. Beginning study of rules. Use of symbols, pictures, maps.

12. WAGON

RATING

THE FIVE LEVELS OF THE CURRICULUM ITEM

1. interest	2. riding while someone pulls	3. pulls empty wagon	4. pulls wagon and someone or something	5. pushes wagon with one foot

DEFINITION OF THE TERM: BEHAVIOR UNDER OBSERVATION

Child's control in using a wagon for various kinds of play on the roof. The levels of the curriculum item represent three kinds of motor ability.

DESCRIPTION OF BEHAVIOR OBSERVED AT EACH LEVEL

Child watched others with wagon, followed wagon about the roof, examined it when opportunity arose.	Child maintained balance in moving wagon.	Child pulled wagon, first as a muscle experience, later experimenting with routes (pulling around pieces of equipment and through narrow spaces).	Child pulled wagon, loaded lightly or heavily (actual loads observed ranged from a small toy or broom to three classmates).	Child knelt in wagon with one leg, propelled wagon with other leg; guided wagon with its tongue.

PROGRAMMING

PREDICTABLE (INTERNALIZED) BEHAVIOR USED IN PROGRAMMING FOR NEXT LEVEL

watches play.	uses wagon in one way.	pulls wagon.	exerts force in pulling wagon.	coordinates different motor processes (movement of one leg, inhibition of other, visuomotor coordination to control direction of wagon).

TEACHING PROCEDURES USED TO ESTABLISH READINESS FOR NEXT LEVEL

Verbal notice of child's interest in wagon. Providing opportunity for child to examine wagon, helping him explore if necessary. Arranging for turn with wagon, offering ride, with teacher pulling. Arranging for ride with a child who liked pulling wagon.	Verbal notice of child's riding. Arranging for turns in riding. Suggesting that child return favor and pull others.	Noticing activity, ways of pulling. Attention to empty wagon. Suggesting ways of using wagon (e.g., for putting away blocks).	Verbal attention to interchange of favors. Notice of usefulness of wagon, wheelbarrow, other toys adapted to hold materials. Incorporation of wagon in traffic games, by teaching pushing with one foot.	Expansion of use of wagon, i.e., construction of roads, ramps. Preparatory to traffic study, occupation exploration.

13. TRICYCLES

RATING

THE FIVE LEVELS OF THE CURRICULUM ITEM

1. child's pushing	2. child sitting on it	3. someone pushing	4. using his feet	5. independently

DEFINITION OF THE TERM: BEHAVIOR UNDER OBSERVATION

Child's motor control in use of two different size tricycles. The levels of this item involved several different motor skills, combined in independent tricycle riding.

DESCRIPTION OF BEHAVIOR OBSERVED AT EACH LEVEL

Child walked beside or behind tricycle, holding handle bars and pushing or pushing against saddle. Child sometimes held handle bars, placed one foot on rear platform or bar, and pushed with other foot.	Child sat on tricycle, sometimes held handle bars, watched others playing.	Child sat on seat, held handle bars, let someone push or pull him. Usually he held his feet up, or out at each side, away from pedals.	Child walked straddling and guiding tricycle. Child put feet on pedals while someone pulled or pushed him, guided tricycle. Also, child pedaled, relied on someone else to guide tricycle.	Child pedalled and guided tricycle.

PROGRAMMING

PREDICTABLE (INTERNALIZED) BEHAVIOR USED IN PROGRAMMING FOR NEXT LEVEL

moves tricycles, not riding.	maintains balance on non-moving tricycle.	maintains balance on moving tricycle.	guides tricycle, associates pedaling with movement.	maintains balance, guides tricycle and pedals at same time.

TEACHING PROCEDURES TO ESTABLISH READINESS FOR NEXT LEVEL

Providing for turn-taking with tricycle (opportunity for learner to experiment and to assure child's use of both sizes). Teacher helped children who wanted to mount tricycle.	Verbal attention to child's use of tricycle. Offering to pull child on tricycle, then offering to push.	Examination of tricycle: turning it on side and turning wheels, pedals. Verbal attention to movement of pedals, as tricycle moves. Showing child how to move tricycle back and forth, by pushing pedals alternately. Helping child hold feet on pedals, and pulling or pushing him.	Verbal attention to child's successful pedaling, steering. Including child in small traffic sequence. Scheduling turns on tricycle before going to roof; focus on pedaling.	Verbal focus on movement of wheel toys on roof; traffic routes, safe use, speed. Preparatory to traffic study.

14. TRACTOR

RATING

THE FIVE LEVELS OF THE CURRICULUM ITEM

1. child's pushing	2. child sitting in it	3. someone pushing	4. using his feet	5. independently

DEFINITION OF THE TERM: BEHAVIOR UNDER OBSERVATION

Child's motor control in riding a push-pedal tractor, including his maintenance of balance while climbing in, visuo-motor coordination in steering, and thrust of legs on the pedals as three distinguishing processes in this activity.

DESCRIPTION OF BEHAVIOR OBSERVED AT EACH LEVEL

Child pushed tractor, tried to control direction.	Child climbed in, sat in tractor turning wheel and putting feet against pedals.	Child sat in tractor while someone pushed. He might hold feet on pedals, might move feet as if riding a kiddie-car.	Child propelled tractor by pedaling, or by pushing with feet. Child might or might not steer.	Child steered and pedalled tractor.

PROGRAMMING

PREDICTABLE (INTERNALIZED) BEHAVIOR USED IN PROGRAMMING FOR NEXT LEVEL

moves tractor by pushing.	climbs into car, manipulates steering wheel.	tries to pedal, turns steering wheel.	propels car, manages pedals.	steers and pedals tractor.

TEACHING PROCEDURES TO ESTABLISH READINESS FOR NEXT LEVEL

Providing for turn-taking with tractor. Verbal notice of child's interest in and use of tractor. Helping child to get in car, showing operation of pedals, steering wheel.	Verbal attention to child's sitting in car. Involving child in traffic game, offering to push car, arranging turns so child sees another moving in car.	Pushing child, getting others to push. Helping child to reach pedals and follow pedal movement with feet. Verbal attention to child's efforts to move.	Verbal attention to pedaling. Help in steering if necessary. Involving child in traffic situation. Planning for use of tractor, before going to roof.	Expansion of traffic play. Attention to lines of traffic, direction of traffic, signals, leading to safety rules. Beginning use of symbols, maps.

15. SCOOTER

RATING

THE FIVE LEVELS OF THE CURRICULUM ITEM

1. interest	2. willingness to try with support	3. standing on while pushed	4. success with making scooter go, one foot	5. using scooter for ride with one foot

DEFINITION OF THE TERM: BEHAVIOR UNDER OBSERVATION

Child's motor control in play with a scooter. After the first year, the scooter was replaced with an Irish Mail, selected to give opportunity for development of upper trunk movements. Motor skills observed in operating the scooter, included guiding, balancing on single wheels, with one and two feet and propelling with one foot (a movement similar to one described in the item on wagon play).

DESCRIPTION OF BEHAVIOR OBSERVED AT EACH LEVEL

Child watched others with scooter; examined scooter; held it upright and pushed, pulled, or dragged it across the roof pavement.	Child stood with one or both feet on scooter held upright by another person, usually teacher.	Child stood with both feet on scooter while teacher pushed; child at times touched ground with one foot, in imitation of propelling movement.	Child held steering bar, stood on scooter with one foot, pushed with the other, varying distances.	Child gained momentum by pushing with one foot, then coasted for short distance.

PROGRAMMING

PREDICTABLE (INTERNALIZED) BEHAVIOR USED IN PROGRAMMING FOR NEXT LEVEL

pushes scooter correctly.	tries balancing with support.	maintains balance and steers, while moving (two feet, one foot).	balances, steers, and moves self. (One foot.)	balances on two feet and steers.

TEACHING PROCEDURES TO ESTABLISH READINESS FOR NEXT LEVEL

Providing for turn-taking to allow for examination, exploration. Verbal attention to child's interest in scooter. Offers of help in standing on scooter.	Verbal attention to child's interest in standing on scooter. Offers of help in pushing, helping to guide.	Providing for turn-taking in rides. Enlisting cooperation of other child(ren) in pushing learners. Verbal attention to way of pushing scooter. Help with balancing on one foot.	Verbal attention; planning ahead for use of scooter. Recall of incidents in play, including child with scooter in traffic games. Help in learning to coast when indicated.	Discussion of use of scooter in traffic games, safety factors. Beginning use of symbols (pictures, road-maps, teacher-made books: The Roof Book, Toys for a Boy, How Many Wheels?)

16. CARS, TRUCKS, TRAINS

RATING

THE FIVE LEVELS OF THE CURRICULUM ITEM

1. watching it in motion	2. pushing it	3. getting on it	4. getting on it and moving it	5. riding somewhere

DEFINITION OF THE TERM: BEHAVIOR UNDER OBSERVATION

Child's motor control in riding small carrier toys on the roof and in the classroom, including various wooden and metal trucks and engines and a wooden tractor-trailer combination. Maintaining balance while getting on and riding, and use of legs to propel and steer the cars were the two motor factors observed. (Leg movement was the same as that used with kiddie cars and Taylor Tots.)

DESCRIPTION OF BEHAVIOR OBSERVED AT EACH LEVEL

Child watched another riding, followed car or repeatedly ran in front and watched car approach him.	Child pushed carrier – either bending down and pushing or crawling alongside the car.	Child got on car, sat on it and examined parts, sat on it and watched activities of other children.	Child got on, propelled car varying distances, backward and forward.	Child used car as means of transportation; used it in imaginative games.

PROGRAMMING

PREDICTABLE (INTERNALIZED) BEHAVIOR USED IN PROGRAMMING FOR NEXT LEVEL

watches, follows.	moves carrier.	gets on, balances self on carrier.	gets on, maintains balance, propels carrier.	rides and guides carrier.

TEACHING PROCEDURES TO ESTABLISH READINESS FOR NEXT LEVEL

Observation of child to identify individual preference; providing for turn-taking. Verbal attention to child's interest and activity: following, looking at, watching, playing with.	Verbal attention to child's play with carrier: noticing motion of wheels. Offering child help in getting on.	Verbal attention to child's preference: conversation about riding. Attention to imaginative elements. Suggesting errands using carrier.	Verbal attention: conversation about imaginative games with carrier, including planning for use of carrier, in free-play and roof activities.	Safety factors. Comparison of various toys (where one sits, how the wheels work). Use of symbols, pictures, "maps."

17. MUSICAL INSTRUMENTS

RATING

THE FIVE LEVELS OF THE CURRICULUM ITEM

1. exploration for sound	2. pounding (e.g. drums)	3. shaking (e.g. bells)	4. striking two hands together	5. holding with one hand, striking with other.

DEFINITION OF THE TERM: BEHAVIOR UNDER OBSERVATION

Child's motor control in use of percussion band instruments. Skills observed included use of hand and arm muscles and coordinated movements of two hands and arms. (Use of the instruments in a rhythm structure is discussed in the section on Imagination and Creative Expression).

DESCRIPTION OF BEHAVIOR OBSERVED AT EACH LEVEL

Child tried out instruments in various ways: picked up, tapped, shook, pounded, struck against another surface.	Child used palm of hand on drumhead or tambourine; used stick or sticks on drum.	Child held in hand and shook stick-bells, wrist-bells, harness-bells, brass India bells.	Child held pairs of cymbals, sand blocks, and moved both hands to strike pieces together. Child used similar method with tambourine.	Child held block, or triangle, or drum in one hand, moved other hand to strike.

PROGRAMMING

PREDICTABLE (INTERNALIZED) BEHAVIOR USED IN PROGRAMMING FOR NEXT LEVEL

associates instruments with production of sounds.	child's two hands execute same movement. Repeats movement needed with drum.	repeats hand movement of shaking.	child's hands execute same movement, but in opposite directions.	moves one hand and inhibits movement of other hand.

TEACHING PROCEDURES TO ESTABLISH READINESS FOR NEXT LEVEL

After preliminary exploration of various percussion instruments, use of each kind of instrument was taught to the class group: that is, all children learned two-hand movements, opposite movements, different motion for each hand. Handwork projects were used to augment the supply of instruments, as indicated below.

Observation of child's interest to locate best starting place. (Usually the drum.) Making drums and sticks from juice cans and dowels; making bongo drums from cartons.	Expansion of use of various kinds of drums. Use of march music to develop control in pounding. Making harness bells, wrist and hand bells from strap sleigh bells. Making maracas from milk cartons and light bulbs.	Expansion of use of bells, maraccas. Use of structuring music to develop inhibition of movement. Making cymbals, block type instruments (small aluminum baking dishes, blocks sawed from boards.)	Expansion of use of blocks, cymbals. Use of music to structure movement; making blocks and sticks from building blocks and dowels. Making tambourines from pie plates.	Expansion of use of blocks and sticks. Use of music to develop inhibition. Beginning activity leading to rhythm band. (Two groups alternating, two groups combining.) Beginning use of symbols.

18. PIANO PLAYING

RATING

THE FIVE LEVELS OF THE CURRICULUM ITEM

1. banging	2. differentiation of loud and soft	3. singing while playing	4. sings tune while playing	5. piano and singing match in tune and rhythm

DEFINITION OF THE TERM: BEHAVIOR UNDER OBSERVATION

Child's motor skill in piano playing. The five levels showed a gradual refinement of control as the child learned to fit his gross arm-hand movements to music structures.

DESCRIPTION OF BEHAVIOR OBSERVED AT EACH LEVEL

Child used forearm movement; struck keys with all four fingers; tried all parts of keyboard; listened to sounds. Sometimes tried side of fist on keys.	Child regulated movement to produce softer tones; could play series of loud and soft tones or an irregular pattern of loud and soft tones.	Child sang or hummed while striking keys; interest was chiefly in sound from piano.	Child sang a familiar song while playing. Piano notes became an accompaniment; rhythm of piano keys might match rhythm of song.	Child struck keys rhythmically, matching accented beats of song. Child moved hands up and down keyboard, matching note sequence of song (not necessarily on pitch).

PROGRAMMING

PREDICTABLE (INTERNALIZED) BEHAVIOR USED IN PROGRAMMING FOR NEXT LEVEL

uses hands to produce sound.	controls force of movements.	notices correspondence between piano notes and vocal music.	subordinates motor activity to musical pattern.	matches motor activity to rhythm and tune criteria.

TEACHING PROCEDURES TO ESTABLISH READINESS FOR NEXT LEVEL

Developing listening and singing processes with records, piano, autoharp. Using piano with activities; soft, loud cues to walking, marching, singing.	Verbal attention to loud and soft music, fast and slow music. Expansion of one activity, as "Row, Row, Row", at normal rate then "fast," "slow," "gently," "hard". "You are rowing your boat in a storm."	Planning: Encouraging children to request song (used in 2) and specify way it should be played. Musical narratives: high notes for birds, mice squeaking; low notes for growls, muttering. Verbal attention to child's use of piano. Suggestions for finding notes.	Singing at piano: single note tunes picked out by teacher and called to children's attention. For children interested: teaching use of black keys. Teaching how to go up and down the keyboard.	Verbal attention to approximation achieved by child. Exploration of other scaled instruments; toy xylophone, toy flute, matched bells, mouthharp. Exploration of bazooka type instruments; tissue paper comb, toy bazooka.

1a1. DRESSING - BUTTONING

RATING

THE FIVE LEVELS OF THE CURRICULUM ITEM

1. dependence	2. awareness, will-ingness, interest	3. helping adult	4. independence with direction	5. independence

DEFINITION OF THE TERM: BEHAVIOR UNDER OBSERVATION

Child's self-reliance in handling buttons on his own garments. Although dress-up materials offered opportunity for manipulation practice, rating on the item was for the child's handling of his own garments in day-to-day situations.

DESCRIPTION OF BEHAVIOR OBSERVED AT EACH LEVEL

Child did not button coat, sweater. Child paid no attention to buttons; started for home with coat open if left to own devices.	Child fingered buttons, buttonholes. Child watched teacher and watched classmates fasten coats. Child asked for help with his own coat.	Child pulled two sides of garment together; tried to fit buttons to buttonholes. "Hold still," held chin out of way for teacher to fasten garment; watched teacher and classmates; tried to help classmate. Child performed half of process.	Child buttoned own coat with starting help from teacher; needed reminders to continue. Child might need assistance with difficult buttons, buttonholes.	Child buttoned coat, sweater, when necessary in routine activities. Child needed no reminders about buttons, although he might need help in mastering new fastenings or buttons on stiff garments.

PROGRAMMING

PREDICTABLE (INTERNALIZED) BEHAVIOR USED IN PROGRAMMING FOR NEXT LEVEL

shows interest in a contingent activity	touches, looks at buttons, buttonholes.	brings button and buttonhole together, or facilitates action by teacher	inserts button in buttonhole, pulls it through	is responsible for process and for remembering to do it

TEACHING PROCEDURES TO ESTABLISH READINESS FOR NEXT LEVEL

(Stories: Gingerbread Boy, Little Snowman. Activities: dress-up, handwork, cooking, snow-play.)

Observation of child to note activity which will be useful as motivation (going to roof, park, etc.; dressing after swimming, to be ready for juice). Teacher participation: buttoning garment for child, efficiently and at moderate speed. Verbal attention to motivating activity.. Verbal attention to kinds, colors, sizes of buttons.	Observation of child: noting and building on any movement useful for process. Teacher participation: responding to the child's request for help; responding to comments on buttons. Verbal attention to settling garment on shoulders, straightening edges of garment-closing; bringing button, hole together.	Observation of child: noting and using any approximation of buttoning. Teacher participation: sharing the task (e.g. "You push the button part way through and I'll catch it and pull it the rest of the way." and "Here! I've pushed the button through. See if you can pull it the rest of the way."); buttoning garment except for one button in easiest location and suggesting that child "finish."	Observation to note point at which child needs help: giving verbal encouragement or physical assistance. Verbal focus o. performance of child. Discussion of s. ing in buttoning task; exchange c services. Comparison of kinds and sizes ... buttons. Use of symbols: pictures, picture stories, number pictures.	Extension to other areas: weather aspects - when coats should be buttoned, when they can be left open. Self-care: noting condition of buttons (e.g. loose, lost), planning for replacing. Appearance: correct buttoning; color contrast or match.

1a2. DRESSING: UNBUTTONING

RATING

THE FIVE LEVELS OF THE CURRICULUM ITEM

1. dependence	2. awareness, willingness, interest	3. helping adult	4. independence with direction	5. independence

DEFINITION OF THE TERM: BEHAVIOR UNDER OBSERVATION

Child's self reliance in unbuttoning his own coat, sweater, or other garment. Dress-up materials provided extra experience in this as in other dressing items, but rating was done on the child's performance with his own clothing.

DESCRIPTION OF BEHAVIOR OBSERVED AT EACH LEVEL

Child made no move to unfasten garment buttons (e.g. on arrival at school, child entered into activity without unbuttoning or removing coat; or child tried to pull off garment without unbuttoning it.)	Child watched others; child fingered buttons; pulled at coat opening; pulled coat open (sometimes breaking threads holding button); asked teacher for help with buttons.	Child helped by, a) holding self quiet while teacher worked, b) pointing out button and holding garment for teacher, c) pushing at button, d) unfastening one or more buttons, with teacher doing the rest. Child might help classmates.	Child unbuttoned garment, pushing or maneuvering buttons through hole, not pulling garment open. Child might need help with button in difficult position, as at throat; might need verbal encouragement for some time after mastering process. Child could be relied on to help others.	Child unbuttoned own garments in ordinary situations and routines; did not need or wait for reminders.

PROGRAMMING

PREDICTABLE (INTERNALIZED) BEHAVIOR USED IN PROGRAMMING FOR NEXT LEVEL

shows interest in activity contingent on getting garment unbuttoned	touches buttons; watches process	assists in process	manages process with verbal assistance	is responsible for process in appropriate situations

TEACHING PROCEDURES TO ESTABLISH READINESS FOR NEXT LEVEL

(Stories: Gingerbread Boy, Little Snowman, with related handwork, dress-up, and cooking activities.)

Observation of child to note activity useful for motivation. Teacher participation: unbuttoning garment for child, efficiently and at moderate speed. Verbal attention to necessity of unbuttoning garments for removal (restoring a sweater to original condition when child has tried to pull it over head, and unbuttoning correctly).	Observation of child: using for teaching process any effective movement (especially finger-thumb coordination mentioned). Teacher participation: responding to child's request for help with buttons. Verbal attention to getting garment in position, with room for finger manipulation.	Observation of child, noting and utilizing effective movements. Teacher participation: sharing the task (e.g. "I'll do this button at the top and this one. Now you do the next one. Now I'll do the last one.") Gradual reduction of amount of physical assistance, increase of verbal encouragement.	Helping child with details when necessary. Verbal focus on performance of child. Discussion of exchange of service in unbuttoning: comparison of kinds and sizes of buttons. Use of symbols: pictures, picture stories.	Extension to other areas: weather aspects — "Your coat is buttoned all the way, today. Can you unbutton it? It is cold out, and you needed to be warm." Self-care: noting buttons loosened or broken off by pulling at garment; planning for replacement.

1b. DRESSING: SNAPS

RATING

THE FIVE LEVELS OF THE CURRICULUM ITEM

1. dependence	2. awareness, will-ingness, interest	3. helping adult	4. independence with direction	5. independence.

DEFINITION OF THE TERM: BEHAVIOR UNDER OBSERVATION

The child's self reliance in fastening snaps on his own clothing. (Unfastening presented little or no problem.)

DESCRIPTION OF BEHAVIOR OBSERVED AT EACH LEVEL

Child did not attempt to fasten snaps; seemed unaware of problem.	Child asked for help with the snap; paid attention to process.	Child held chin up for teacher to fasten helmet; straightened strap; held waist-band together for teacher to fasten jeans, etc.	Child felt for two halves of snap, brought halves to-gether, and fas-tened them, with verbal direction.	Child fastened snaps on own garments.

PROGRAMMING

PREDICTABLE (INTERNALIZED) BEHAVIOR USED IN PROGRAMMING FOR NEXT LEVEL

shows interest in contingent activity.	watches process.	tries part of pro-cess.	does with help	knows and uses process appropriately.

TEACHING PROCEDURES TO ESTABLISH READINESS FOR NEXT LEVEL

Teacher assistance with fastening provided as long as necessary. Use of dress-up clothing with easily-fastened, prominent snaps.

Verbal attention to snap halves, to loca-tion on garment. Description of pro-cess, while teacher does the fastening.	Attention to snap it-self: asking child to find both halves. Guidance of one of child's hands, by teacher. Attention to child's posture (holding chin up, holding body straight.)	Asking child to get garment ready for fastening. Asking child to complete fastening.	Verbal help with en-tire process. Phys-ical help if needed. Attention to steps in process. Verbal attention to success-ful dressing.	Asking child to help others. Review of fastenings of various kinds.

                                    1c1.   FASTENING
                                    1c2.   DRESSING: ZIPPER   OPENING
                                    1c3.   STARTING

                                            RATING

THE FIVE LEVELS OF THE CURRICULUM ITEM

1. dependence	2. awareness, will-ingness, interest	3. helping adult	4. independence with direction	5. independence.

DEFINITION OF THE TERMS: BEHAVIOR UNDER OBSERVATION

Item c1.   Child's self-reliance in closing a zipper with one closed end, or an open zipper on a jacket after teacher had started the slide for him.

Item c2.   Child's self-reliance in opening a zipper fastening, with teacher help if necessary for starting the process.

Item c3.   Child's self-reliance in starting an open-end zipper, as on a jacket or sweater.

Observed for rating was the child's handling of his own clothing. The item was not rated on the basis of play activity with practice material or dress-up clothing.

DESCRIPTION OF BEHAVIOR OBSERVED AT EACH LEVEL

1) Child seemed un-aware that zipper needed fastening.	Child asked for help with zipper. Child matched edges of jacket and inspected slide.	Child put hand on teacher's while she operated zipper; completed process begun by teacher.	Child fastened zip-per with verbal di-rection.	Child was responsible for meshing zipper.
2) Child seemed un-aware of problem - might try to remove garment without at-tempting zipper.	Child asked for help. Child might pull at slide, attempt to work it. Child watched T manipu-late slide.	Child put hand on teacher's; completed task started by teacher.	Child opened zipper with verbal direc-tion.	Child was responsible for opening zipper on own garments.
3) Child showed no awareness of prob-lem; might move slide without joining two sides of fasten-ing.	Child held out two ends of zipper to ask for help. Child watched T engage ends of zipper.	Child held own hands over teacher's; watched closely; dis-engaged ends with-out help.	Child followed di-rections to engage two ends of zipper. Child at these levels helped other children.	Child engaged ends of zipper and closed jacket.

                                            PROGRAMMING

PREDICTABLE (INTERNALIZED) BEHAVIOR USED IN PROGRAMMING FOR NEXT LEVEL

Shows interest in clothing (own or others'), interest in contingent activity.	watches process; moves zipper slide.	holds self, garment, to facilitate dressing or undressing; moves slide effectively.	opens, closes and/or starts zipper with verbal prompting.	opens, closes, starts zipper as part of an activity.

<pre>
1c1.   FASTENING
1c2. DRESSING: ZIPPER OPENING
1c3.   STARTING
</pre>

RATING
(Continued)

TEACHING PROCEDURES TO ESTABLISH READINESS FOR NEXT LEVEL

d,1 plus d,3

Teacher participation continued as long as necessary, with teacher performing complete sequence to give child comprehension of whole process and purpose: a) settling jacket on shoulders or pants around hips; b) straightening sides of opening; c) engaging ends of zipper (on open jacket); d) pulling slide along track smoothly, holding garment straight; e) locking zipper slide (or patting it, if it does not lock) when entire zipper is closed.

Verbal attention to purpose of dressing (outdoor play, adjusting clothing after toileting).	Verbal attention to process (a e, above): describing each movement as it occurs. Asking child to adjust garment for zipping.	Verbal attention to process, asking child to do first steps, then last steps.	Verbal prompting in process. Gradual decrease of verbalization.	Verbal attention to coats, pants, boots, zipped by children. Suggesting that child help another.

d,2 plus d,3

Teacher participation continued as long as necessary, to give child idea of the sequence of related movements: a) straightening jacket; b) unlocking tab; c) pulling slide smoothly; d) disengaging ends (of open-front jacket): pulling edges of garment open; e) removing garment.

Verbal attention to purpose of undressing.	Verbal attention to process, describing each movement of sequence as it occurs. Asking child to adjust garment, find tab.	Verbal focus, asking child to do first steps then last steps, then entire sequence.	Verbal prompting in process. Gradual decrease of verbal directions.	Verbal attention to garments removed and hung on hooks or put away. Suggesting that child help another.

1d1. DRESSING: TYING KNOTS;   1d2. DRESSING: UNTYING KNOTS

RATING

THE FIVE LEVELS OF THE CURRICULUM ITEM

1. dependence	2. awareness, will-ingness, interest	3. helping adult	4. independence with direction	5. independence

DEFINITION OF THE TERM: BEHAVIOR UNDER OBSERVATION

d,1.   Child's self-reliance in tying single knots needed in several dressing processes. These were, a) tying single knot preparatory to tying shoe lace bows; b) tying single knot in headscarf or neck scarf, dress tie or sash; and in string used for package wrapping. (Teachers suggested only the single knot because the process, once learned, was useable in tying a double knot.)

d,2.   Child's self-reliance in untying knots (in the same situations as above). Here, observation was made of the single knot, first, and then of the double knot. The untying dealt with the first knot to be untied — treating it as a single knot.

For rating of this item, teachers' interest was in the tying and untying as it pertained to dressing: play materials did not serve as the basis of assessment.

DESCRIPTION OF BEHAVIOR OBSERVED AT EACH LEVEL

d,1. Child did not tie knot in shoe laces, scarf.	Child asked for help. Child twisted ends of laces, scarf, etc., trying to tie; watched Teacher.	Child straightened ends of laces, scarf before asking help. Child held foot, head, arms in positions which helped tying process.	Child tied single knot in response to directions or reminder from teacher.	Child could be relied on to tie single knot in laces, in routine situations.
d,2. Child did not untie knot in shoe laces, tie, sash, scarf: pulled shoe off without untying laces; pulled scarf off over head; tried to put on shoes with knotted laces.	Child pulled at knot or pulled scarf away from chin; asked for help.	Child finished pulling lace, through loop, after teacher had loosened knot. Child finished untying knot loosened by teacher.	Child untied scarf, laces, in response to directions or reminder of teacher.	Child could be relied on to untie knotted scarf, laces, in routine situations.

PROGRAMMING

PREDICTABLE (INTERNALIZED) BEHAVIOR USED IN PROGRAMMING FOR NEXT LEVEL

interest in activity contingent on tying or untying	handles, twists laces watches adult work	does part of process	knows manipulation; follows directions which aid memory	remembers and uses process in situation

TEACHING PROCEDURES TO ESTABLISH READINESS FOR NEXT LEVEL

d,1.   Teacher participation as long as necessary, performing tying as a complete process to give child knowledge of the sequence of movements: a) straightening laces; b) crossing laces; c) threading one end of lace through loop formed by crossed laces; d) pulling to tighten knot.

Verbal attention to activity following the tying. Verbal attention to finished knot.	Verbal attention to process (a-d above) while child watches. Asking child to pull laces straight, and to hold finger on knot for second knot or bow.	Verbal attention to steps. Asking child to straighten laces (start process) and pull knot tight (finish process). Holding crossed laces while child puts end through space.	Verbal direction of steps a-d. Gradual decrease of specific directions (e.g. "You know how to finish," "You can get the laces ready.")	Verbal attention to well-tied laces, sashes, etc. Suggesting that child help another. Use of symbols (e.g. pictures and news sentences, as "Who is ready for juice time? Mary and John and Bobby are ready?")

d,2.   Teacher participation as long as necessary, with teacher untying knots as a complete process to give child knowledge of the sequence of movements: a) locating, adjusting knot; b) pulling at top loop of lace to loosen; c) pulling two ends of lace ap..

Verbal attention to contingent activity (e.g. untying knots to remove shoes for swimming, gym.)	Verbal attention to process (a-c above) while child watches. Asking child to locate and adjust knot for teacher.	Verbal attention to steps. Asking child to pull laces after teacher has loosened knot. Asking child to pull at key loop, then loosen and pull laces apart.	Verbal direction of steps a-c. Gradual decrease in specific directions.	Verbal attention to shoes, scarf, untied before removal. Suggesting that child help another. Use of symbols as above.

Dress-up materials, especially wide satin ribbons, were used to provide practice. The manipulation of the ribbon was easy and provided knots which were quite obvious as well as attractive.

1e1. DRESSING: TIES BOWS
1e2.   UNTIES BOWS

RATING

THE FIVE LEVELS OF THE CURRICULUM ITEM

1. dependence	2. awareness, will-ingness, interest	3. helping adult	4. independence with direction	5. independence

DEFINITION OF THE TERM: BEHAVIOR UNDER OBSERVATION

e,1.   Child's self-reliance in tying bows of shoe-laces, cap-strings, and dress ties.

e,2.   Child's self-reliance in untying bow fastenings. Independence ordinarily meant untying a bow without producing a double-knot. However the child was also rated independent if he could without help or direction undo the double-knot which resulted from a tangling of loops. Play materials were available for practice in this area, but rating was on self-reliance with garments.

DESCRIPTION OF BEHAVIOR OBSERVED AT EACH LEVEL

e,1. Child put on shoes, hood or dress without touching laces or ties; left ends dangling.	Child asked for help; held out ends of laces or ties to teacher; child watched teacher's work.	Child disentangled laces or ties for Teacher; held finger on knot to help; let Teacher guide his hands; tied single knot before asking help with bow.	Child tied bows with verbal directions for steps of process, with verbal encouragement or with reminder.	Child could be relied on to tie own shoes when necessary; tied shoes as part of a situation.
e,2. Child removed shoes without attempting to untie bows; tried to put on shoes which had come off (or been taken off) without first untying bows.	Child inspected shoe bows, etc., before trying to remove garments. Child asked for help and watched teacher; pulled indiscriminately at loops or ends of bow.	Child pulled on ends pointed out by teacher; looked for ends. Ordinarily, child tried to avoid tangling.	Child untied bows with direction or encouragement.	Child could be relied on to untie shoes as part of class situation; helped classmates on own initiative or in response to request.

PROGRAMMING

PREDICTABLE (INTERNALIZED) BEHAVIOR USED IN PROGRAMMING FOR NEXT LEVEL

shows interest in contingent activity or in garment.	watches process; handles laces, ties	does part of process	knows manipulation: follows directions	remembers and uses process in situation

TEACHING PROCESS TO ESTABLISH READINESS FOR NEXT LEVEL (teaching is individual and in meaningful situation).

e,1.   Teacher participation as long as necessary, with teacher performing the tying as a complete process, to give the child experience in the sequence of movements: a) forming loop with one end of lace; b) winding other lace around loop; c) pushing other lace through aperture; d) pulling both sides of bow to tighten.

Verbal attention to contingent activity, and to finished bow. Use of bows for decorations on greeting cards.	Verbal attention to process (a-d above) in addition to single knot. Asking child to hold knot with finger.	Verbal attention to process. Sharing process: child holds first loop while teacher winds and ties; teacher holds while child winds with teacher's help; child starts and tightens knot.	Verbal directions for sequence; gradual decrease in specific directions.	Verbal attention to neat, attractive bows. Suggesting that child help another. Use of symbols.

e,2.   Teacher participation as long as necessary, to give child experience in a) examining bow before pulling at it; b) smoothing bow; c) examining it to locate ends; d) pulling on ends; e) loosening knot.

Verbal attention to contingent activity.	Verbal attention to process (a-e above).	Verbal attention to process: sharing process — child pulls one end. Letting child finish process.	Verbal directions for a-e above. Gradual decrease in directions.	Verbal attention to bows untied (shoes, etc. are ready to be put on again).

1f1. DRESSING: HAT ON;   1f2. DRESSING: HAT OFF

RATING

THE FIVE LEVELS OF THE CURRICULUM ITEM

1. dependence	2. awareness, willingness, interest	3. helping adult	4. independence with direction	5. independence

DEFINITION OF THE TERM: BEHAVIOR UNDER OBSERVATION

Child's self-reliance in removing and putting on his own cap or hat. Headscarfs worn by some of the girls were rated on this item. Rating did not include the child's ability to fasten snaps or buttons or to tie.

DESCRIPTION OF BEHAVIOR OBSERVED AT EACH LEVEL

f,1. Child paid no attention to hat in dressing for out of doors. To suggestion from teacher, child might hold hat but made no move to put it on.	Child handed hat to teacher, asking help; child set hat on top of head; might inspect result in mirror.	Child held head straight so teacher could put hat on, hold chin up for fastening; finished pulling on hat started by teacher; helped adjust scarf.	Child put on hat, etc. with directions, reminders, verbal encouragement.	Child could be relied on to put on own hat, cap, or scarf when necessary, without reminders.
f,2. Child did not remove head covering on arrival: might begin classroom activity with hat still on.	Child asked help with fastenings or with removal of a close-fitting cap.	Child helped with fastenings, helped loosen tight caps.	Child took off hat with reminder or with verbal help.	Child could be relied on to remove own head covering in routine situations: needed no reminders.

PROGRAMMING

PREDICTABLE (INTERNALIZED) BEHAVIOR USED IN PROGRAMMING FOR NEXT LEVEL

shows interest in contingent activity; interest in mirror	attends to process; carries hat, scarf	does part of process	does manipulation, needs cues, suggestions	remembers and uses process in course of regular activity

TEACHING PROCEDURES TO ESTABLISH READINESS FOR NEXT LEVEL (Teacher manipulates fastenings as long as necessary.)

f,1.   Teacher participation: Teacher put child's hat on for him, calling attention to the way hat feels on head, over ears, down cheeks, under chin. The sequence of movements used for putting on a head covering includes: a) straightening out or holding right-side-up the scarf, hat; b) grasping two ends of scarf, cupping hands inside hood, or grasping cap by bill; c) settling cap around head; d) pulling scarf ends or straps under chin.

Verbal attention to contingent activity. Attention to child's headgear; use of mirror for inspection.	Verbal attention to process, describing parts of sequence as they occur (a-d, above); getting child to hold hat in position for putting on, or to smooth scarf.	Verbal attention to process: child to start or to complete process depending upon type of hat. Use of mirror for evaluation of result.	Verbal directions for sequence. Gradual decrease in verbal assistance.	Comments on appearance; types of headcoverings, etc. Readiness work for fastening snaps, tying, and buttoning. Suggesting that child help another child.

f,2.   Teacher participation. Teacher removes child's hat for him, if it is apparent after observation that child has not had experience with process. Steps to be noted are: a) unfastening or untying head covering; b) removing (cupping hands inside a helmet or hood, if it is tight); c) straightening out hat or scarf (putting away or hanging on hook).

Verbal attention to contingent activity. Noticing child's hat, especially a new type of head covering.	Verbal attention to process (a-c above). Asking child to put head covering away.	Verbal attention to process: getting child to start or to complete process, depending on relative difficulty.	Verbal directions for sequence (help with fastening if necessary). Gradual decrease in verbal help.	Comments on hats, caps. Comments on placing caps on hooks. Suggesting that child help another.

1g1. DRESSING: BOOTS ON
1h1.   SHOES ON

RATING

THE FIVE LEVELS OF THE CURRICULUM ITEM

1. dependence	2. awareness, willingness, interest	3. helping adult	4. independence with direction	5. independence

DEFINITION OF THE TERM: BEHAVIOR UNDER OBSERVATION

Child's self-reliance in putting on his shoes (g,1) and boots (h,1) in the appropriate class situations.

DESCRIPTION OF BEHAVIOR OBSERVED AT EACH LEVEL

Child made no attempt to put on own boots or shoes; prepared for home, ignoring boots. In dressing after swimming, or pulling off shoes in process of boot removal, walked away in stocking feet, paying no attention to shoes.	Child brought boots to teacher or to classmate, asked for help. Child stood in coat-corner, holding boots. Child asked for help with shoes, after swimming or when shoes had accidentally come off along with boots. With shoes, child might try to loosen laces and end by removing them from shoes.	Child put toes into shoes or boots; held top of boot or counter of shoe and helped teacher pull; flexed foot or braced foot so teacher could pull boot on; loosened shoelaces according to directions of teacher. Child finished job after boot or shoe was almost on.	Child could put on shoes with help at one or more points: e.g. reminder about loosening laces, or reminder about getting heel into heel of shoe (not standing on counter); reminder about left, right shoes.	Child put on shoes, boots without help or verbal reminder, and could be depended upon to do so in ordinary routine; helped others.

PROGRAMMING

PREDICTABLE (INTERNALIZED) BEHAVIOR USED IN PROGRAMMING FOR NEXT LEVEL

shows interest in contingent activity	watches process	tries part of process	knows process but needs direction	remembers and uses process in daily routine

TEACHING PROCEDURES TO ESTABLISH READINESS FOR NEXT LEVEL

Teacher participation: Teacher helped child as long as necessary for internalizing sequence. For both boots and shoes, the series of movements included: a) loosening or undoing buttons, buckles, laces, or zippers to make the opening of the boot or shoe as large as possible; b) inserting toe in opening; c) pulling boot or shoe on and up over heel (a combination of hand and arm pull and foot thrust); d) adjusting boot or shoe comfortably on foot ready for fastening. Tying and zipping, were not rated on this item. The teacher helped with fastenings, both undoing and doing, as long as necessary.

Verbal attention to contingent activity; to weather; to appearance of well-tied shoes; to shoes, boots as necessary items of apparel.	Verbal attention to process: teacher described steps in the sequence (a-d) as she performed movements calling child's attention to need for bracing foot against movement of boot or shoe.	Continued verbal attention to process. Asking child to start process; then to finish process. Attention to effective body postures, positions, as sitting on floor or chair, lying on floor, standing against wall.	Verbal reminder of steps. a) preliminary summary of steps (a-d) above; b) repetition of directions during sequence. Gradual decrease in amount of verbal help.	Discussion of related aspects: weather, gym, swimming and other activities. Attention to new clothing items, with focus on buckles, ties, fit of item, etc. (Moving toward child's awareness of how shoes feel on feet, (correct size, good style, neatness.)

1g2. DRESSING: BOOTS OFF
1h2.   SHOES OFF

RATING

THE FIVE LEVELS OF THE CURRICULUM ITEM

1. dependence	2. awareness, willingness, interest	3. helping adult	4. independence with direction	5. independence

DEFINITION OF THE TERM: BEHAVIOR UNDER OBSERVATION

Child's self-reliance in removing boots and shoes in the daily routine. On this item, <u>dependence</u> with respect to shoes included inappropriate behavior: as, taking off shoes at odd times during the day.

DESCRIPTION OF BEHAVIOR OBSERVED AT EACH LEVEL

The child did not, on arrival, remove his boots or show any awareness of responsibility; similarly, did not remove shoes in preparation for gym or swimming activities. Child removed shoes when the behavior was not appropriate.	Child did not remove boots or shoes, but asked for help from teacher or another child in appropriate situation.	Child pushed at top of boot, or held foot up so teacher could remove it. Child untied shoe laces and pushed at heel of shoe; held foot so teacher could remove shoe.	Child removed boots and shoes without physical help. He might need guidance in loosening laces, loosening heel of boot or shoe, or working zipper or buckles. Child might need urging to accomplish task or help with snug boots.	Child could remove shoes or boots without help. Child was responsible for removal, without reminders.

PROGRAMMING

PREDICTABLE (INTERNALIZED) BEHAVIOR USED IN PROGRAMMING FOR NEXT LEVEL

shows interest in contingent activity	watches process	tries part of process	knows whole process but needs direction or reminder	remembers and uses process in daily routine

TEACHING PROCEDURES TO ESTABLISH READINESS FOR NEXT LEVEL

Teacher participation: Teacher helped child with complete process as long as necessary to internalize the sequence. For removal of footgear, the sequence included: a) undoing or loosening fastenings of boot; b) pulling boot off of heel; c) removing boot from toe. As in putting on these articles of clothing, the teacher was responsible for fastenings for children needing that help.

| Verbal attention to contingent activity. | Verbal attention to process (steps a-c) as each step is done. Encouraging child to help with loosening boot or shoe. | Continued verbal attention to process. Asking child to finish process; then to start process. Commenting on efficient ways of removal, as child works and after he has completed task. | Verbal reminder of three steps, before child starts removal, and during process. Gradual decrease in verbal help. | Discussion of kinds of footgear, appropriateness for outdoor, indoor wear, home and school wear. Use of symbols; pictures showing settings for wearing shoes, boots, houseshoes; times for going barefooted and in stocking-feet. |

1i1. DRESSING: SOCKS ON
1i2.   SOCKS OFF

RATING

THE FIVE LEVELS OF THE CURRICULUM ITEM

1. dependence	2. awareness, willingness, interest	3. helping adult	4. independence with direction	5. independence

DEFINITION OF THE TERM: BEHAVIOR UNDER OBSERVATION

Child's self-reliance in putting on and taking off his socks in the course of regularly-scheduled class activities such as swimming, or on occasions when clothing change became necessary. Observation was made of ability to put on socks with sock heel properly placed, and of ability to remove socks smoothly at appropriate times.

DESCRIPTION OF BEHAVIOR OBSERVED AT EACH LEVEL

i,1. Child made no effort to put on socks.	Child asked help with socks; straightened and inspected them.	Child straightened socks, held feet flexed so teacher could put them on, finished task after teacher had put socks on over toes.	Child followed directions as to smoothing socks, locating heel, inserting foot, and pulling socks on and straightening them. Usually, reminder as to position of sock heel was needed when child was otherwise self-reliant.	Child put on socks correctly, and needed no reminders or suggestions, i.e., child was self-reliant.
i,2. Child did not remove socks in preparation for swimming, clothing change.	Once child was aware of own role in undressing, sock removal presented no problem.			

PROGRAMMING

PREDICTABLE (INTERNALIZED) BEHAVIOR USED IN PROGRAMMING FOR NEXT LEVEL

shows interest in contingent activity; interest in socks	watches process	tries part of process	knows all steps but needs reminders	remembers and uses process

TEACHING PROCEDURES TO ESTABLISH READINESS FOR NEXT LEVEL

i,1.   Teacher participation: Teacher helped child with complete process as long as necessary to give the child experience with the sequence. Steps included: a) straightening sock; b) grasping by top with thumbs inside; c) inserting toes; d) pulling sock on; e) checking position of heel.

Verbal attention to activity as a whole (e.g. dressing after swimming; changing socks wet by snow or rain; putting on new socks).	Verbal attention to process (steps a-e above). Asking child to shake socks out straight.	Verbal attention. Asking child to start process (a,b,c) then to complete it (d,e). Questions about shape of sock, position of heel, etc.	Reviewing steps before and after putting on socks. Reminder about heel given special emphasis; Gradual withdrawal of verbal suggestions.	Attention to health, weather, appearance concepts. Asking child to help another child.

Verbal attention to effective removal of socks, storing socks in shoes in pool dressing room; hanging wet socks to dry; focus on correct dress for school and swimming pool for children needing direct help in keeping footgear on.

1j1. DRESSING: MITTENS ON
1j2.   MITTENS OFF

RATING

THE FIVE LEVELS OF THE CURRICULUM ITEM

1. dependence	2. awareness, willingness, interest	3. helping adult	4. independence with direction	5. independence.

DEFINITION OF THE TERM: BEHAVIOR UNDER OBSERVATION

j,1. Child's self-reliance in putting on mittens in the ordinary routine.
j,2. Child's self-reliance in removing mittens in the ordinary daily routine.

Dress-up materials included mittens which provided practice, but were not the basis of rating the child's self-help status.

DESCRIPTION OF BEHAVIOR OBSERVED AT EACH LEVEL

j,1. Child did not put on mittens in preparation for going out, or after he had gone out for play. Child did not keep track of mittens.	Child asked help, or brought mittens to teacher; kept track of own mittens.	Child helped pull mittens on; extended hand so teacher could slip mitten on; put thumb in thumb space with help or on suggestion.	Child put on mittens with verbal direction, special direction about thumb, and/or reminder to put on mittens.	Child could be relied on to put on mittens when they were needed for outdoor play.
j,2. Child did not take off mittens on arrival at school: might start activity wearing mittens.	Once child was interested and aware of own responsibility, there was ordinarily no problem with this item. Difficulties posed by pinned mittens were met by teacher, who took the responsibility for undoing fastenings of various kinds.			

PROGRAMMING

PREDICTABLE (INTERNALIZED) BEHAVIOR USED IN PROGRAMMING FOR NEXT LEVEL

shows interest in mittens or in contingent activity	watches process	knows part of process	knows process, needs reminders	remembers and uses process in daily routine

TEACHING PROCEDURES TO ESTABLISH READINESS FOR NEXT LEVEL

j,1. Teacher participation: Teacher puts mittens on child's hands, to present learning experience in the sequence format. Steps included: a) holding mitten by wrist opening with one hand; b) slipping other hand in mitten; c) feeling for thumb opening and inserting thumb. Problems of left and right were minimized when mittens were attached to coat sleeves or shoulders.

Verbal attention to activity, weather. Attention to mittens.	Verbal attention to process: actions described by teacher as they were performed. Verbal attention to need for holding fingers together, for insertion in mitten.	Verbal attention to sequence: asking child to begin process, then to finish it.	Verbal reminder of steps. Gradual decrease in reminders, etc.	Attention to need for mittens, to shape of thumb, hand parts. Attention drawn to left, right in mittens. Suggesting that child help another.

j,2. See Rating, above.

1k1. DRESSING: GLOVES ON
1k2.   GLOVES OFF

RATING

THE FIVE LEVELS OF THE CURRICULUM ITEM

1. dependence	2. awareness, will-ingness, interest	3. helping adult	4. independence with direction	5. independence

DEFINITION OF THE TERM: BEHAVIOR UNDER OBSERVATION

k,1. Child's self-reliance in putting on his own gloves, in the regular daily routine.
k,2. Child's self-reliance in taking off his own gloves.

Several pairs of gloves of different materials, included with dress-up clothing, provided opportunity for practice in managing the glove fingers, but were not the basis for rating.

DESCRIPTION OF BEHAVIOR OBSERVED AT EACH LEVEL

k,1. Child showed no awareness of responsibility for wearing gloves; did not put gloves on before going out or after he had gone outdoors to play. Usually no concern for gloves.	Child asked for help or handed gloves to teacher. Child liked to have teacher talk while helping to adjust fingers.	Child helped pull gloves on; straightened fingers to get them in proper spaces; usually inserted thumb correctly.	Child followed directions to put gloves on correctly; could change glove to correct hand, if on wrong hand, with verbal reminder.	Child could be relied on to put on gloves in course of daily routine.
k,2. Child did not remove gloves.	Removal of gloves presented no problem, after child had become aware of responsibility for removal.			

PROGRAMMING

PREDICTABLE (INTERNALIZED) BEHAVIOR USED IN PROGRAMMING FOR NEXT LEVEL

shows interest in gloves or in contingent activity	watches process	tries part of process	knows process, needs reminders	remembers and uses process in daily routine.

TEACHING PROCEDURES TO ESTABLISH READINESS FOR NEXT LEVEL

k,1. Teacher participation: Teacher puts gloves on child's hands, calling attention to fit of palm, fingers and thumb, and to sequence of movements. Steps involved are: a) shaking and smoothing gloves; b) holding glove by wrist with one hand; c) inserting other hand in glove; d) spreading fingers to go in glove fingers; e) finding thumb space; f) checking finger placement. As with mittens, gloves were fastened to coat so that problems of left and right were not pertinent until kinesthetic aspects were learned.

Verbal attention to activity, weather. Attention to gloves. Handwork tracing around hand and fingers to reinforce kinesthesis.	Verbal attention to process: description of movements and of fitting fingers in glove fingers; asking child to smooth out gloves.	Verbal attention to process; asking child to begin sequence; then to finish it. Special attention to finger placement.	Verbal reminder of steps. Gradual decrease in reminders as child became able to check on proper fitting of gloves.	Conversation about hand coverings; weather aspects; left and right. Suggesting that child help another.

k,2. See Rating, above.

111. DRESSING: OPEN-FRONT GARMENTS ON
112. OPEN-FRONT GARMENTS OFF

RATING

THE FIVE LEVELS OF THE CURRICULUM ITEM

1. dependence	2. awareness, willingness, interest	3. helping adult	4. independence with direction	5. independence

DEFINITION OF THE TERM: BEHAVIOR UNDER OBSERVATION

11. Child's self-reliance in putting on his own coat, sweater or other open-front garment.
12. Child's self-reliance in removing his coat or other open-front.

DESCRIPTION OF BEHAVIOR OBSERVED AT EACH LEVEL

1,1. Child did not attempt to put on own coat. Ordinarily, at dressing time, child paid no attention to coat.	Child asked for help; brought coat to teacher.	Child held coat by collar, when handing it to teacher. Child put arms in sleeves efficiently, while teacher held coat.	Child followed directions of teacher for holding coat (or laying it over chair back); finding sleeve openings.	Child could be relied on to put on own garment in ordinary class routine.
1,2. Child did not remove own coat. Child might begin class activity still wearing coat, sweater, jacket.	Child who showed awareness and interest,was usually self-reliant in this item. Directions or help given by teacher had to do with fastenings or with fit of garment.			

PROGRAMMING

PREDICTABLE (INTERNALIZED) BEHAVIOR USED IN PROGRAMMING FOR NEXT LEVEL

shows interest in contingent activity	interest in process	knows part of process	knows separate movements	remembers and uses process

TEACHING PROCEDURES TO ESTABLISH READINESS FOR NEXT LEVEL

1,1. Teacher participation: Teacher helped with entire sequence, to give child experience with the series of movements. Steps included: a) straightening coat, adjusting sleeves; b) arranging coat in way easiest for child to use; c) slipping arms in coat sleeves; and d) adjusting coat around shoulders ready for fastening. Laying coat across chair back, lining-side up, was often effective.

Verbal attention to projected activity. Comments on children's appearance, readiness for outdoors, etc.	Verbal attention to steps in process (a-d, above); asking child to straighten coat. Comments on efficiency.	Showing child how to arrange or hold coat. Asking him to start, then to finish process.	Summarizing series both before and after process; giving extra reminders. Gradual withdrawal of verbal cues.	Attention to appearance of child. Extension of dressing idea to concepts of weather, health, comfort. Asking child to help another.

1,2. Teacher participation: Teacher helped with process: a) unfastening garment; b) loosening garment from shoulders; c) guiding child's hands behind body to pull sleeve-cuffs over hands; d) shaking or easing coat off.

Verbal attention to projected activity, to hanging up coat.	Verbal attention to steps in process; asking child to do last step and to hang up coat.	Direct work on step b, above, as loosening of cuffs seemed to be the key problem. Asking child to complete removal, then to begin.	Summarizing series before and after coat removal; giving added suggestions when needed; gradual withdrawal of verbal cues.	Attention to child's care of garment after removal.

1m1. DRESSING: SLIPOVER GARMENT ON / 1m2. DRESSING: SLIPOVER GARMENT OFF
RATING

THE FIVE LEVELS OF THE CURRICULUM ITEM

1. dependence	2. awareness, will-ingness, interest	3. helping adult	4. independence with direction	5. independence

DEFINITION OF THE TERM: BEHAVIOR UNDER OBSERVATION

m,1.   Child's self-reliance in putting on a garment which slipped over his head, including T-shirts, undershirts and slipover sweaters.

m,2.   Child's self-reliance in removing garments which slipped over his head.

DESCRIPTION OF BEHAVIOR OBSERVED AT EACH LEVEL

m,1. Child made no effort to put on garment. If dressing to go home, child would omit a slipover sweater.	Child asked for help in putting on slipover; might put garment on head, trying to get into it, or inspect neck opening.	Child brought garment to teacher; shook it out; tried to straighten or turn sleeves. Child pulled garment over head, after teacher started it; pushed arms into sleeves held by teacher.	Child put on slipover, following verbal directions from teacher, or in response to reminder from teacher.	Child was competent, reliable in putting on slipover garment.
m,2. Child made no effort to remove T-shirt.	Child asked for help; might pull at neck or cuffs of garment, trying to dislodge it.	Child pulled arms from sleeves held by teacher; pulled garment over head after process was started.	Child took off T-shirt in response to directions or reminder by teacher.	Child could be relied on to take off slipover garment.

PROGRAMMING

PREDICTABLE (INTERNALIZED) BEHAVIOR USED IN PROGRAMMING FOR NEXT LEVEL

shows interest in contingent activity and/or interest in garment	watches process	tries part of process	knows separate movements.	remembers and uses process

TEACHING PROCEDURES TO ESTABLISH READINESS FOR NEXT LEVEL

m,1.   Teacher participation: Teacher helped with series of movements: a) straightening shirt, ready for putting on; b) pulling shirt over head; c) inserting arms in sleeves; d) pulling shirt down over chest. (Also, where applicable, tucking shirt into band of slacks.)

Verbal attention to projected activity (going outdoors; returning to classroom after swimming). Attention to new or freshly-washed shirts.	Verbal attention to process. Asking child to straighten shirt, helping him turn sleeves.	Asking child to begin process (a & b), then asking him to complete process (c&d).	Reviewing series both before and after dressing attempt; additional verbal clues when needed to maintain sequence; gradual withdrawal of verbal help.	Extension of dressing idea to concepts of health, weather, comfort, appearance; asking child to help another.

m,2.   Teacher participation: Teacher helps with series of movements: a) pulling shirt up from waist or pulling arms from sleeves; b) pulling shirt off over head or pulling shirt up from waist; c) grasping back of shirt and pulling it off over head, or pulling arms from sleeves. (The technique chosen depended upon child's ability and teacher's ease with technique.)

Verbal attention to contingent activity (swimming, classroom activity).	Verbal attention to process; asking child to shake out and hang up shirt after removal.	Asking child to finish process (step c from either series, above, plus hanging up). Asking child to start process (a & b)	Reviewing steps before and after removal; giving additional clues when needed to maintain smooth sequence; gradual withdrawal of verbal assistance.	Extension of undressing idea to concepts of health, comfort; asking child to help another.

1n1. DRESSING: DRESS ON
1n2.   DRESS OFF

RATING

THE FIVE LEVELS OF THE CURRICULUM ITEM

1. dependence	2. awareness, willingness, interest	3. helping adult	4. independence with direction	5. independence.

DEFINITION OF THE TERM: BEHAVIOR UNDER OBSERVATION

n1. Child's self-reliance in putting on dress.
n2. Child's self-reliance in taking off dress.

Dress fastenings were not considered on this item. Blouses, and skirts with side fastenings were, because of processes involved, rated on items for open-front shirts and slacks.

DESCRIPTION OF BEHAVIOR OBSERVED AT EACH LEVEL

n1. Child did not attempt to put on dress, usually waiting for attention of teacher, or finding play activity (waiting not specifically for help with dress).	Child held dress, asked for teacher's help; might put dress around shoulders or try to step into it.	Child held dress up by neck or shoulder seam; spread dress on floor and sat near it; "ducked" into dress held by teacher, thrust legs into dress, spread on floor by teacher.	Child put on dress in response to verbal direction and/or reminder from teacher.	Child could and did put on own dress in regular situation.
n2. Child made no attempt to remove dress.	Child asked help; pulled at dress; tried to pull arm from a sleeve, etc.	Child removed dress after starting help from teacher (either over head, or down over hips).	Child removed dress in response to verbal direction and/or reminder from teacher.	Child could and did remove dress in regular situation.

PROGRAMMING

PREDICTABLE (INTERNALIZED) BEHAVIOR USED IN PROGRAMMING FOR NEXT LEVEL

shows interest in contingent activity	watches process	tries part of process	knows separate movements	remembers and uses process

TEACHING PROCEDURES TO ESTABLISH READINESS FOR NEXT LEVEL

n1. Teacher participation: Teacher helped with series of movements: a) straightening garment; b) determining front; c) slipping dress over head, OR, stepping into it (according to size of opening and apparent habit of child); d) putting arms in sleeves; e) adjusting dress on shoulders, ready for fastening.

Verbal attention to projected activity; attention to new, freshly-washed dresses.	Verbal attention to process. Asking child to straighten dress, ready for putting on.	Verbal attention. Asking child to start process (a-c) then to complete it (c-e).	Reviewing series before and after dressing; additional reminders when needed, to ensure a smooth process; gradual withdrawal of verbal reminders.	Comments on child's efficiency, appearance. Extension to concepts of comfort, appearance (grooming), mutual assistance.

n2. Teacher participation: Teacher helped with series of movements: a) unfastening buttons; b) slipping dress from shoulders; c) pulling arms from sleeves; d) pushing dress down over hips; OR, a) unfastening dress; b) pulling up over shoulders; c) pulling off over head; and d) taking arms out of sleeves. Final step for both, e) folding or hanging dress.

Verbal attention to projected activity; attention to teacher's care of dress.	Verbal attention to process. Asking child to hang or fold dress.	Verbal attention. Asking child to finish process (c-e, above); then to start (a-c).	Reviewing series, as above. Gradual withdrawal of verbal help.	Comments on child's efficiency. Extension to concepts of neatness, mutual assistance.

1o, 1 & 2.   DRESSING: PANTS, SNOWPANTS ON
1p, 1 & 2.   PANTS, SNOWPANTS OFF

RATING

THE FIVE LEVELS OF THE CURRICULUM ITEM

1. dependence	2. awareness, will-ingness, interest	3. helping adult	4. independence with direction	5. independence

DEFINITION OF THE TERM: BEHAVIOR UNDER OBSERVATION

o,1; p,1.   Child's self-reliance in putting on pants, snowpants, slacks.
o,2; p,2.   Child's self-reliance in taking off pants, snowpants, slacks.

DESCRIPTION OF BEHAVIOR OBSERVED AT EACH LEVEL

o1; p1.

Child made no attempt to put on garment; required help with clothing in the bathroom.	Child brought snowpants to teacher for help; sat and held pants; or spread pants on floor and inspected them. Child listened to description of way to hold pants band.	Child held pants by waist band; spread garment on floor and sat in correct position for putting on; put legs in garment held by teacher; helped pull garment up over hips.	Child followed directions about holding pants, inserting legs; child put on garments with reminder.	Child could be relied on to put on snowpants or slacks, in preparation for going out; and to put on shorts, pants, in dressing after swimming.

o2; p2.

Child made no attempt to take off snowpants. Child at this level might need help in bathroom.	Child asked for help with garment; pushed at waist band to indicate need for help; watched teacher work fastenings.	Child pushed garment down over hips after starting help from teacher; pulled foot out while teacher held legs of garment.	Child followed verbal directions given by teacher or took off garment in response to reminder.	Child could be relied on to remove garment in course of activity.

PROGRAMMING

PREDICTABLE (INTERNALIZED) BEHAVIOR USED IN PROGRAMMING FOR NEXT LEVEL

shows interest in contingent activity	watches process	tries part of process	knows separate movements	remembers and uses process

TEACHING PROCEDURES TO ESTABLISH READINESS FOR NEXT LEVEL

o1; p1.
Teacher participation: Teacher helped with series of movements: a) straightening out garment; b) laying it out on floor with waist opening opposite child's feet, OR, holding waistband at knee level of child seated on chair or table; c) directing insertion of feet; d) pulling cuffs or bands over heels; e) pulling garment up around waist ready for fastening or for adjusting.

Verbal attention to projected activity, to garments.	Verbal attention to process. Asking child to straighten out and lay out garment or to hold it up ready for putting on.	Asking child to begin process (a-c, above) then to complete it (d-e).	Reviewing series before and after process; help as needed. Gradual withdrawal of verbal reminders.	Extension to concepts of weather, health, comfort, appearance; place of snowpants in dressing sequence.

o2; p2.
Teacher participation: Teacher helped with series of movements: a) loosening garment at waist; b) pushing down over hips; c) sitting down on chair or floor; d) pulling pants-cuffs or bands over feet; e) pulling legs out of pant-legs.

Verbal attention to projected activity; to hanging garment.	Verbal attention to process; asking child to pull legs from garment and hang garment.	Asking child to finish process (c-e), giving special help to make sure child is not sitting on part of garment; to begin process (a-c).	Reviewing series as above; giving added reminders to maintain smooth sequence. Gradual withdrawal of verbal help.	Extension to concepts of weather, comfort, health; place of snowpants in undressing sequence.

1q1. DRESSING: SCARF ON
1q2.   SCARF OFF

RATING

THE FIVE LEVELS OF THE CURRICULUM ITEM

1. dependence	2. awareness, will-ingness, interest	3. helping adult	4. independence with direction	5. independence

DEFINITION OF THE TERM: BEHAVIOR UNDER OBSERVATION

Child's self-reliance in putting on and taking off his neck scarf or muffler.

The teachers were interested in the child's ability to get the scarf around his neck, in dressing, and to remove the scarf when removing outer wraps. Scarves in the dress-up box provided practice in manipulation, but were not used for rating purposes.

DESCRIPTION OF BEHAVIOR OBSERVED AT EACH LEVEL

q1.

Child made no attempt to put on scarf, when preparing to go out; child would leave scarf on coat hook.	Child asked for help; carried scarf; might try to put scarf on back of neck or tuck it in front of coat.	Child straightened scarf, ready for putting on; held self quiet, chin up so adult could adjust scarf; finished pulling scarf across chest, after teacher had put it around neck.	Child put on scarf, following directions or in response to verbal reminder.	Child could and did put on own scarf in ordinary class routine.

q2.

Child did not remove scarf.	When interest was present, child was ordinarily able and willing to remove own scarf.			

PROGRAMMING

PREDICTABLE (INTERNALIZED) BEHAVIOR USED IN PROGRAMMING FOR NEXT LEVEL

shows interest in scarf; interest in contingent activity	watches process	tries part of process	knows separate movements	remembers and uses process

TEACHING PROCEDURES TO ESTABLISH READINESS FOR NEXT LEVEL

q1.

Teacher participation: Teacher puts scarf on for child, doing whole sequence: a) straightening scarf; b) putting it around neck; c) crossing ends OR tying ends in single knot under chin.

Verbal attention to scarf, ways of wearing and purpose. Use of mirror, use of pictures of children wearing scarves.	Verbal attention to process; asking child to straighten scarf.	Asking child to start process (a,b above); then to finish process (b,c).	Reviewing series, before and after putting on. Giving additional reminders when needed. Gradual decrease in reminders.	Comments on appearance. Extension to concepts of health, comfort, weather. Use of scarf for beginning steps of knot-tying.

q2.   See Rating, above.

2. HAND WASHING

RATING

THE FIVE LEVELS OF THE CURRICULUM ITEM

1. exploration	2. use of soap	3. washing palms	4. washing whole hand	5. consideration of clothing

DEFINITION OF THE TERM: BEHAVIOR UNDER OBSERVATION

Child's self-reliance in washing his own hands, as part of daily routine.

DESCRIPTION OF BEHAVIOR OBSERVED AT EACH LEVEL

Child explored and manipulated wash-room equipment: water, soap dispenser, towel dispenser, waste can; dabbled fingers in water; spilled, splashed, rubbed wet fingers together.	Child used liquid or bar soap to produce suds.	Child rubbed palms together, inspected palms (resoaped sometimes), rubbed palms together with towel held between them to wipe.	Child used soap on whole hand, inspected results. He might still wipe just palms.	Child turned up or pushed up sleeves, was careful about splashing.

PROGRAMMING

PREDICTABLE (INTERNALIZED) BEHAVIOR USED IN PROGRAMMING FOR NEXT LEVEL

shows interest in equipment	shows interest in cleansing process	shows interest in partial result	shows interest in process and result	observes limits, for process.

TEACHING PROCEDURES TO ESTABLISH READINESS FOR NEXT LEVEL

Teachers gave help with sleeves and cuffs before and after washing, until child assumed responsibility; also checked to be sure that backs of hands were dry.

Help with proper use of faucets, soap dispenser, towel dispenser and waste can. Teacher participation or help to child, to show use of soap. Verbal help during washing process. Verbal attention to appearance of palms.	Verbal attention to suds, child's washing movement. Inspection of palms of hands. Suggestion for washing again; suggestions for rinsing.	Verbal attention to palms, fingers, backs of hands. Suggestions for washing part of hand missed; suggestions for wiping hands. Attention to water dripped on floor. Gradual withdrawal of supervision.	Class discussion. Noticing hands, after child's return to classroom. (smelling soap, noting dampness, cleanness). Noticing clothing; reminders about cuffs, sleeves, dress front.	Class discussion. When to wash hands: (after using toilet, after use of clay, paint; before eating and cooking, or handling items apt to get dirty). Discussion of reasons (appearance, hygiene).

3. TOILET EDUCATION

RATING

THE FIVE LEVELS OF THE CURRICULUM ITEM

1. needs reminding	2. knows when and asks for help	3. knows when and partially independent	4. knows when and goes	5. comfortably conforming to group schedule

DEFINITION OF THE TERM: BEHAVIOR UNDER OBSERVATION

The child's ability to care for own toilet needs.

DESCRIPTION OF BEHAVIOR OBSERVED AT EACH LEVEL

Child went to toilet if reminded and helped.	Child told teacher when he needed to use toilet; asked for help; wanted to be accompanied.	Child told teacher; could go to toilet unaccompanied; asked help with belt buckle, zipper, panties.	Child went to toilet, managed ordinary clothing; followed individual schedule.	Child waited for toilet break; used toilet at that time. Could also utilize a need schedule when necessary.

PROGRAMMING

PREDICTABLE (INTERNALIZED) BEHAVIOR USED IN PROGRAMMING FOR NEXT LEVEL

recognizes need if reminded.	recognizes need to go to toilet.	recognizes need; handles some of garments.	recognizes need; manages ordinary garments.	exercises control in usual schedule.

TEACHING PROCEDURES TO ESTABLISH READINESS FOR NEXT LEVEL

Teachers 1) ascertained toilet status of children and followed child's known program; 2) instituted one or more regular toilet breaks; 3) supervised toileting at first to ascertain ability to handle clothing; 4) continued supervision as long as necessary.

Attention to child's correct use of toilet; verbal attention to toilet-break schedule ("We go to the toilet and wash before juice-time." "...before going to the roof." "...before going home.")	Verbal attention to child's independence. Help for girls: attention to holding dress; help with pulling up panties, adjusting dress or slacks. Help for boys: Attention to shorts, slacks, and help with zipper, T-shirt.	Verbal attention to independence; successful handling of dress, panties, shorts, slacks, zippers, and belt. Help with unfastening belts, pulling down panties, shorts. Sending children to washroom singly or in pairs, without teacher.	Asking children to exchange help. Sending children in small groups; inspecting clothing and hands, upon return to room. Verbal attention to toilet schedule, in relation to day's schedule.	Planning trips; going to toilet before departure. Trips to park, neighborhood destinations, home. Using public toilet facilities: cleanliness, consideration of others.

4a. JUICE TIME: SETTING TABLE

RATING

THE FIVE LEVELS OF THE CURRICULUM ITEM

1. dependence	2. awareness, will-ingness, interest	3. helping adult	4. independence with direction	5. independence.

DEFINITION OF THE TERM: BEHAVIOR UNDER OBSERVATION

Child's self-reliance in setting table for juice period.

DESCRIPTION OF BEHAVIOR OBSERVED AT EACH LEVEL

Participated in juice period after table was set; found a place at table.	Watched table being set: chose a place and noted napkin, cup, juice pitcher, cookie bowl. Carried own chair to table.	Accompanied teacher setting table. Carried single items for her. Placed napkins handed him one at a time. Placed chairs as directed.	Carried pitchers, bowls, quantity of napkins, cups to table. Passed napkins, cups to children seated at table for four.	1st year: aware of time schedule. Assumed responsibility for carrying napkins, cups, pitchers, cookie bowls to large tables. Might or might not count place settings.

PROGRAMMING

PREDICTABLE (INTERNALIZED) BEHAVIOR USED IN PROGRAMMING FOR NEXT LEVEL

shows interest in food, drink; child's observation of his own place setting.	shows interest in process; observation of table arrangement.	observes needs of other children	cares for needs of children at one table.	forms a group and provides supplies for it.

TEACHING PROCEDURES TO ESTABLISH READINESS FOR NEXT LEVEL

Teacher participation: providing napkin or paper towel, cup for each child; setting places for individuals (naming children). Pouring juice for and passing cookies to each child. Verbal attention to arrangement of cup and napkin. Attention to teacher's activity in pouring, serving.	Teacher participation: Sitting at table, pouring juice, and passing cups along table, naming recipient of cup of juice. Verbal attention to where child sets cup. Sharing of tasks: first, taking over task started by teacher; then, performing task with direction.	Assigning various tasks, in preparation for juice. Helping with manipulation problems in separating cups, passing napkins. Helping with manipulation problems in pouring, serving juice. Verbal focus on arrangement of tables. Gradual withdrawal of physical help, replacement with verbal.	Verbal focus on table arrangement, matching number of cups, napkins to number of children (i.e., teacher counts children, cups, emphasizing process and number). Planning table groupings. Changes in groupings. Gradual decrease in reinforcement with direction.	Checking supplies for groups. Providing turns at playing host: suggesting number to be included in group, having host set table; planning for refills of pitchers, bowls. Planning table settings and supplies for other situations, as picnics, roof, trip sites.

4b. JUICE TIME: POURING JUICE

RATING

THE FIVE LEVELS OF THE CURRICULUM ITEM

1. dependence	2. awareness, willingness, interest	3. helping adult	4. independence with direction	5. independence

DEFINITION OF THE TERM: BEHAVIOR UNDER OBSERVATION

Child's handling of the pitcher, competence in getting juice into the cup, and ability to stop pouring (not letting cup overflow). Later, focus was on the child's ability to take the pitcher from another child, pour his own juice, and pass the pitcher on to another child.

DESCRIPTION OF BEHAVIOR OBSERVED AT EACH LEVEL

Juice was poured for child.	Child watched pouring, noticed level of juice in cup.	Child helped hold pitcher (controlled tilt of pitcher, juice flow) held own cup while T. poured; carried pitcher to table, handed cup(s) to adult one at a time.	Child poured own juice; poured juice for others at his table. Verbal reminders, physical help given when necessary.	Child poured own and others' juice, filling cups to proper level.

PROGRAMMING

PREDICTABLE (INTERNALIZED) BEHAVIOR USED IN PROGRAMMING FOR NEXT LEVEL

shows interest in getting cup of juice.	shows interest in pouring.	pours own juice.	pours juice for others, under supervision	usually dependable in pouring.

TEACHING PROCEDURES TO ESTABLISH READINESS FOR NEXT LEVEL

Teacher participation: moving around table with pitcher, pouring into cup at each place. Sitting at table, pouring juice and passing filled cups down table. Verbal attention to pouring and to height of liquid in cup.	Teacher participation: moving around table with pitcher, giving each child opportunity to pour own juice. Using opportunities for children to use individual small pitchers. Providing for pouring practice when pitcher contains only a small amount of liquid.	Providing opportunity for carrying pitcher to table; passing pitcher to neighbor at table; passing cups filled by teacher or another child; helping to pour juice for group. Verbal attention to processes: e.g., "I take one cup. I pour juice in it up to here, (the blue line). This is for B____. J____, will you hand it to B____?"	Gradual decrease in accompanying verbal reinforcement. Planning by listing sequence of actions before pouring begins. Review of process, as conversation item. Planning turns.	Verbal attention to cooperative processes. e.g., "B____ could hand the cups to M____ one at a time and M____ could pour." etc. Combining pouring and food sharing as tasks for a "team" of two children. Solving problems of service in other settings, as roof, park, trip sites, snackbars, lunchrooms.

4c. JUICE TIME: PASSING CRACKERS

RATING

THE FIVE LEVELS OF THE CURRICULUM ITEM

1. dependence	2. awareness, will-ingness, interest	3. helping adult	4. independence with direction	5. independence

DEFINITION OF THE TERM: BEHAVIOR UNDER OBSERVATION

Child's handling of the bowl of crackers and in his ability to present it to other children in succession (allowing them to help themselves). Later, focus was on ability to accept the bowl from another child at the table, hold it and take a cracker from it, then pass the bowl on to another child.

DESCRIPTION OF BEHAVIOR OBSERVED AT EACH LEVEL

Child took cracker from bowl passed by teacher or other child.	Child was attentive to passing process. Could hand bowl to another child.	Child carried crack-er bowl to table, helped teacher pass bowl to all children in group.	Child followed di-rections in passing crackers. Needed reminders about holding bowl level, about not missing any children.	Child passed crackers, distributed fairly, did not miss anyone. Could take a cracker and pass the bowl to the next child. "Take one and pass it on."

PROGRAMMING

PREDICTABLE (INTERNALIZED) BEHAVIOR USED IN PROGRAMMING FOR NEXT LEVEL

shows interest in getting cracker.	shows interest in passing bowl.	notices others.	serves others, with supervision.	is dependable in process.

TEACHING PROCEDURES TO ESTABLISH READINESS FOR NEXT LEVEL

Teacher participa-tion: passing crack-ers, with verbal at-tention to taking cracker (e.g., "Will you have a cracker?" "Take one, please?")	Teacher participa-tion: Enlisting help of child in passing bowl; checking for omissions. Verbal notice of process. "You carried the bowl carefully." "B____ came in just now. Would you like to give him a cracker?"	Opportunities for child to carry bowls to table; pass bowl along and across table; walk around table offering bowl. Verbal attention to processes. Giving verbal preparation for process.	Gradual decrease in coaching and verbal reinforcement. Planning turns. Re-view of process as a conversation item.	Cooperative planning. Playing host with treats brought for classmates. Practice in ways of offering. Planning birth-day party menu. Solving problems of service in other settings, such as the park. (Leading to self-direction in strange places.)

4d. JUICE TIME: HELPING SELF TO MORE FOOD

RATING

THE FIVE LEVELS OF THE CURRICULUM ITEM

1. dependence	2. awareness, will- ingness, interest	3. helping adult	4. independence with direction	5. independence

DEFINITION OF THE TERM: BEHAVIOR UNDER OBSERVATION

Exercise of initiative in obtaining more food. Teachers encouraged children to satisfy hunger, since juicetime, for these pupils was the midpoint of a fairly long day. Independence included, besides the ability to obtain more food in acceptable (mannerly) ways, a measure of judgment about overeating.

DESCRIPTION OF BEHAVIOR OBSERVED AT EACH LEVEL

Helped self to more food only at direct suggestion of teacher and when bowl or pitcher was offered.	Indicated wish for more by direction of glance or by moving nearer food. Poured juice for self when handed pitcher.	Answered question. "Would you like more?" by gesture, head movement or verbal response.	Accepted (or de-clined) more food, juice, in response to, "Have another (cracker)if you like." Asked for bowl or pitcher to be passed, when prompted by teach-er.	Helped self when bowl or pitcher was near at hand. Asked for more, verbally or by gesture. Asked for bowl or pitcher to be passed.

PROGRAMMING

PREDICTABLE (INTERNALIZED) BEHAVIOR USED IN PROGRAMMING FOR NEXT LEVEL

Shows interest in food.	Moves toward food.	Responds verbally.	Takes food with encouragement.	Notices others' wants.

TEACHING PROCEDURES TO ESTABLISH READINESS FOR NEXT LEVEL

Offering food likely to be accepted. Pur-poseful selection of children's favorite foods, juices.	Careful attention to small movements and looks of indi-vidual children. Asking children to give a neighbor another cracker, etc. Giving verbal models for asking.	Enlisting children's help in offering to others: pouring, passing to group. Giving verbal mod-els for passing: "Would you like ____?"; "Will you have____?"	Assigning responsi-bilities for passing foods. Commenting on child's responsi-bility for self. Giv-ing models for verbal interchange, "Ask Billy if he would like more. Would you like more, yourself?"	Class planning of juicetime menus: helping to make out cookie orders; help-ing to purchase cook-ing supplies.

4e. JUICE TIME: CLEARING TABLE

RATING

THE FIVE LEVELS OF THE CURRICULUM ITEM

1. dependence	2. awareness, will-ingness, interest	3. helping adult	4. independence with direction	5. independence

DEFINITION OF THE TERM: BEHAVIOR UNDER OBSERVATION

Acceptance of responsibility for clearing tables after the juice period. This included, at first, disposal of paper cups and napkins and carrying of pitchers, bowls, spoons and other dishes to the sink. Later, rinsing dishes was part of the task. (Washing the dishes is discussed in a separate curriculum guide item.)

DESCRIPTION OF BEHAVIOR OBSERVED AT EACH LEVEL

Child apparently unaware of possibility of helping with table clearing.	Child watched process; showed interest in disposal of cups, pitchers, bowls.	Child handed cup, napkin to adult, or dropped them in waste-basket passed by teacher or by another child. Child carried own cup and napkin to waste-basket.	At teacher's direction, child collected cups, napkins to throw in waste-basket, carried dishes to sink and rinsed them.	Child assumed responsibility for collecting cups, napkins; carried cups to sink and rinsed them.

PROGRAMMING

PREDICTABLE (INTERNALIZED) BEHAVIOR USED IN PROGRAMMING FOR NEXT LEVEL

Shows interest in paper cup, sink.	Manipulates cup, faucet.	Tries process.	Takes care of own cleanup.	Helps with group cleanup.

TEACHING PROCEDURES TO ESTABLISH READINESS FOR NEXT LEVEL

| Verbal focus on cleaning done by teacher or another child. Demonstration: the way in which a paper cup could be crumpled. | Providing opportunity for individual practice, help. Verbal attention to completed task. | Suggesting individual cleaning. Asking, "What do you do with your cup? - with the bowl?" Inhibiting repetition of processes such as crumpling cup before juice period was over, playing with water. | Assigning responsibility for collecting cups, carrying dishes. Verbal focus: "Who will get the wastebasket? Who will help? What do you want to do?" Gradual withdrawal of verbal direction. | Planning ahead: purpose of table clearing. Focusing attention on appearance of tables and floor, before and after cleanup. |

4f. JUICE TIME: WASHING TABLE

RATING

THE FIVE LEVELS OF THE CURRICULUM ITEM

1. dependence	2. awareness, will-ingness, interest	3. helping adult	4. independence with direction	5. independence

DEFINITION OF THE TERM: BEHAVIOR UNDER OBSERVATION

Acceptance of responsibility for clean tables at juicetime. At first, focus was on the juice interval itself - wiping up spilled juice and brushing up crumbs: later this task was part of the day's sequence: e.g. cleanup after work with paste was preparation for juice or cooking, while cleanup after juice was preparation for further use of tables.

DESCRIPTION OF BEHAVIOR OBSERVED AT EACH LEVEL

Child apparently unaware of need for wiping up spills, cleaning table before juice.	Child watched teacher washing table; called attention to spilled juice (often at first to juice spilled by another child.)	Child helped to wash table in preparation for juice: noted obvious paste, paint, etc. on tables. Child got sponge or paper for teacher to wipe up spills.	At teacher's direction, child got sponge and soap, and washed table (before or after juice) also got sponge to wipe up spills.	Child assumed responsibility for effective washing of tables before or after juice period; assumed responsibility for own and others' spills.

PROGRAMMING

PREDICTABLE (INTERNALIZED) BEHAVIOR USED IN PROGRAMMING FOR NEXT LEVEL

Notices sponge or paper towels.	Notices spills, his own and others'.	Uses sponge, towels.	Follows directions.	Cleans efficiently.

TEACHING PROCEDURES TO ESTABLISH READINESS FOR NEXT LEVEL.

Tables washed before juice by teacher. Spills wiped up by teacher. Verbal attention to action of sponge and absorbent towels. Providing for experiment with sponge, towels.	Supervised and co-operative use of sponge, towels. Directions to include children.	Directions to include children. Verbal attention to paper towels as placemats. Cooperative washing of tables before and after juice period.	Assigned responsibility for pre-juice washing, for clean-up afterward. Verbal attention to table surface.	Verbal focus on planning aspects. Inspection of table surface by children and teacher. Preparing clean table for juice period. Cleaning table for next activity.

4g. JUICE TIME: WASHING DISHES
4h.   WIPING DISHES

RATING

THE FIVE LEVELS OF THE CURRICULUM ITEM

1. dependence	2. awareness, will-ingness, interest	3. helping adult	4. independence with direction	5. independence

DEFINITION OF THE TERM: BEHAVIOR UNDER OBSERVATION

Child's acceptance of responsibility for washing and wiping dishes after juice. Because paper cups were used for juice, washing was at first confined to pitcher and bowls. Spoons, knives, and cups for hot soup or punch were added at intervals.

DESCRIPTION OF BEHAVIOR OBSERVED AT EACH LEVEL

Child showed no awareness of washing, wiping activity.	Child watched table clearing; followed others to sink; carried dishes to sink; held dishes under faucet; found tea-towel.	Child watched adult wash or wipe dishes; shared task.	Child washed or wiped one or more dishes with verbal help (or request) from teacher.	Child could be relied on to wash and/or wipe dishes, alone or in co-operation with another person.

PROGRAMMING

PREDICTABLE (INTERNALIZED) BEHAVIOR USED IN PROGRAMMING FOR NEXT LEVEL

Shows interest in items (soap, water, sponge, towel) or in persons involved in process.	Watches process.	Imitates process.	Carries out process with verbal help.	Washes or wipes efficiently.

TEACHING PROCEDURES TO ESTABLISH READINESS FOR NEXT LEVEL

Observation of child to determine possible motivation. Verbal attention to process: soaping dishes, rubbing with sponge, rinsing, wiping. Verbal attention to items used, children participating. Suggesting child's participation in parts of process which interests him. Suggesting contributing help.	Observation to determine special interest in child, providing opportunity for him to help with one process. Providing opportunities to watch teacher and classmates (e.g., "Will you take this to John so he can wash it?" or "You could carry the pitchers to the cupboard after Mary wipes them.") Letting child wash and wipe own spoon. Verbal attention to child's participation.	Teacher participation continued. (Gradual decrease in amount done by teacher.) Substitution of verbal help. Turn-taking: a) teacher washing, child, wiping, and vice-versa. b) teacher washing, two or more children wiping. Verbal attention to child cooperation. Attention to effective washing, wiping.	Planning for turns in washing, wiping. Planning process to be used. Verbal attention to results: inspection of dishes; hanging up tea-towel, etc.	Planning for helping at home. Building toward concepts of self-reliance, cleanliness, helpfulness. Use of symbols, things needed for washing and wiping dishes.

4i. JUICE TIME: PUTTING DISHES AWAY

RATING

THE FIVE LEVELS OF THE CURRICULUM ITEM

1. dependence	2. awareness, willingness, interest	3. helping adult	4. independence with direction	5. independence

DEFINITION OF THE TERM: BEHAVIOR UNDER OBSERVATION

Child's acceptance of responsibility for putting away dishes. This task, like the washing and wiping, was facilitated at first by the use of paper cups. It became more complex when cooking utensils and plastic cups for hot drinks were introduced.

DESCRIPTION OF BEHAVIOR OBSERVED AT EACH LEVEL

Child seemed unaware or not interested in putting away pitchers, spoons, etc.	Child watched teacher, classmates (e.g., followed others from sink to cupboard). Child got items from cupboard on request.	Child carried clean dishes to cupboard; handed items to teacher; watched disposal on shelves.	Child put clean dishes away in cupboard, with verbal help.	Child could be relied on to put dishes in correct places on shelves.

PROGRAMMING

PREDICTABLE (INTERNALIZED) BEHAVIOR USED IN PROGRAMMING FOR NEXT LEVEL

Shows interest in some phase or aspect of process.	Watches process.	Imitates process.	Remembers, places dishes with verbal help.	Completes process without help or reminders.

TEACHING PROCEDURES TO ESTABLISH READINESS FOR NEXT LEVEL

Observation of child to note point of interest. Enlisting child's help with part of process which interests him. Teacher participation. Verbal attention to correct shelves, place for pitchers, spoons (Verbal attention to children's work.)	Verbal attention to process as both cleaning up, and readiness for following day. Teacher participation: asking child to bring items; asking child to suggest place for item. Providing opportunities for child to watch others.	Sharing task with child: putting away items brought by child; handing item to child; suggesting place to put it. Gradual reduction of physical help, substitution of verbal help. Verbal attention to appearance of cupboard; work of children.	Planning task: placement of pitchers, turn taking; checking for convenience for following day. Gradual reduction in verbal help. Planning cooperative cleanup: washing tables; washing, wiping, putting away dishes.	Expanding concepts of helpfulness, cooperation, neatness. Use of symbols: pictures of cupboard shelves; cut out items for shelves. Handwork: drawing, coloring, pasting dishes on tables and cupboard shelves.

5a. SKILLS: USING SPOON

RATING

THE FIVE LEVELS OF THE CURRICULUM ITEM

1. Interest in self feeding	2. Finger feeding	3. Semi-solid in spoon	4. Liquid in spoon	5. Solid in spoon

DEFINITION OF THE TERM: BEHAVIOR UNDER OBSERVATION

Child's use of a spoon for handling various foods encountered at juice time, parties and picnics. The teachers were interested in the efficiency (minimum loss of food by spilling) in getting food from container to mouth.

DESCRIPTION OF BEHAVIOR OBSERVED AT EACH LEVEL

Accepted finger foods (crackers, etc.) Dabbled with spoon in ice cream, pudding. Ate directly from cup, lifting cup to mouth.	Handled crackers, cookies, etc. competently. Used fingers for vegetables in salads.	Ate puddings, soft ice cream with spoon.	Ate soup, sipped hot tea, hot chocolate with spoon.	Used spoon efficiently for cake, salad, hard-frozen ice cream. Child might put food on spoon with fingers at first.

PROGRAMMING

PREDICTABLE (INTERNALIZED) BEHAVIOR USED IN PROGRAMMING FOR NEXT LEVEL

Shows interest in food and in situation.	Shows interest in eating with spoon.	Uses spoon for semi-solids.	Handles semi-solids and liquids in spoon.	Handles solids: balancing, cutting with spoon edge.

TEACHING PROCEDURES TO ESTABLISH READINESS FOR NEXT PHASE

Selection of juice-time foods and snacks from list of children's favorites. Conversation about foods. Comments on various preferences.	Use of spoons for cooking activity: stirring instant drinks; stirring and serving jello; instant pudding; dyeing eggs. Variations in party menu: ice cream cups and wooden spoons.	Continued use of play materials. Use of spoons for stirring sugar into tea, making hot drinks, etc. Verbal focus on use of spoon for tasting (testing temperature of hot drink).	Use of spoon for serving dry cereals, nuts, small candies. Use of plastic spoons for play activities with imaginary food. Use of plastic spoons for marking play-dough, clay. Play activity: using spoons to transfer beans, corn, etc. from one receptacle to another.	Verbal attention to correct way of eating: finger foods, spoon foods. Use of plastic forks for imaginary food. Use of forks for marking play-dough, clay, etc. Focus on use of fork for cake.

5b. SKILLS: USING FORK

RATING

THE FIVE LEVELS OF THE CURRICULUM ITEM

1. interest in using fork	2. using fork like a spoon	3. using fork with ease	4. cutting with fork	5. using fork appropriately

DEFINITION OF THE TERM: BEHAVIOR UNDER OBSERVATION

Child's use of a fork in eating. The process of interest to teachers was efficiency in conveying food from container to mouth (minimal loss of food by spilling).

DESCRIPTION OF BEHAVIOR OBSERVED AT EACH LEVEL

Child tried fork. Usually grasped it with fisted hand.	Child "dipped" forkful of cake; might use fingers to keep food on fork, or to put food on fork.	Child scooped or dipped up food with fork, got it to mouth without finger help.	Child used side of fork for cutting cake, pie.	Child used fork for foods usually eaten that way. Child might or might not "spear" food with fork, or might still hold fork in fisted grasp.

PROGRAMMING

PREDICTABLE (INTERNALIZED) BEHAVIOR USED IN PROGRAMMING FOR NEXT LEVEL

Handles fork.	Uses fork to scoop food.	Uses fork to carry food to mouth.	Turns fork; uses pressure.	Selects fork for appropriate use.

TEACHING PROCEDURES TO ESTABLISH READINESS FOR NEXT LEVEL

Play activities; using fork and spoon for imaginary foods, dough play. Teacher participation; Using fork for cake, pie. Verbal attention to holding, handling fork.	Teacher participation: using fork for eating; scooping forward; also scooping with side of fork. Using fork for serving. Verbal attention to: a) loading of fork (bite size), b) holding fork level. Continued play activities: using fork for pricking and marking play dough.	Teacher participation: cutting cake, pie, etc. with side of fork, "spearing" bits of fruit, vegetables. Verbal attention to use of fork for cutting cake. Play activities: cutting play dough with fork.	Teacher participation: cutting food; "spearing" food with fork. Verbal attention to spearing food on tines of fork. Play activities: Using fork tines to prick patterns in play dough.	Verbal attention to uses of fork and spoon, choosing correct utensil. Teacher participation: using tines of fork to hold food for cutting. Use of symbols: pictures of foods, and choosing fork or spoon for imaginary dinner.

5c. SKILLS: USING KNIFE

RATING

THE FIVE LEVELS OF THE CURRICULUM ITEM

1. Interest in using knife.	2. Spreading with knife.	3. Cutting with knife.	4. Using knife and fork together.	5. Using knife efficiently.

DEFINITION OF THE TERM: BEHAVIOR UNDER OBSERVATION

Child's use of an ordinary metal dinner knife in preparing food items. Handling of a vegetable knife for preparation of raw fruits and vegetables was observed after the child could use a metal table knife for cutting soft foods. The handling of the sharp knife was rated as a safety item.

DESCRIPTION OF BEHAVIOR OBSERVED AT EACH LEVEL

Child handled knife; used it to pat butter or spread on bread or crackers; imitated movements.	Child flattened a dab of butter, cheese or jelly on crackers. Used flat side of knife and exerted pressure.	Child held bread or other soft food with fingers of one hand and cut with knife held in other hand.	Child anchored food with fork tines, cut with knife. Cutting could be either sawing or pulling apart.	Child anchored food with fork tines and cut by moving knife back and forth, lengthwise.

PROGRAMMING

PREDICTABLE (INTERNALIZED) BEHAVIOR USED IN PROGRAMMING FOR NEXT LEVEL

Holds knife, tries to use flat side or edge of blade.	Exerts pressure on flat side of knife.	Exerts pressure on edge of knife.	Uses one hand for holding fork; one hand for cutting.	Coordinates two different movements (holding with one hand, cutting with other).

TEACHING PROCEDURES TO ESTABLISH READINESS FOR NEXT LEVEL

Preparation of bread and cracker snacks with butter, soft cheese, peanut butter, jelly. Frosting cakes and cookies.

Preparation of bread shapes for appetizers; cutting cake. Preparation of vegetables and fruits: celery, apples, pears, peppers. Making, cutting fudge, cornbread.

Using spoon, fork and knife for smoothing and mashing food. Verbal attention to holding utensil firmly; turning knife blade. Play activities: use of sand toys for smoothing surface of sand. Tongue blades, toy knives with clay and play dough; soap-suds frosting. Teacher participation: spreading butter on bread, crackers. Starting to spread, then turning process over to child.	Taking soft cheese, butter from bar, and smoothing. Verbal attention to use of edge of blade for cutting off bit of cheese; use of flat side for spreading. Spreading slice of bread, then cutting. Play activities: cutting lines in sand, cutting strips of clay, playdough. Teacher participation: cutting celery, etc. Helping child to cut celery.	Expanding use of knife with various kinds of food. Verbal attention to holding food item with one hand, cutting with the other. Play activities: use of knife and fork with play-dough; house-play; pretending to eat meat. Teacher participation: cutting cheese, lunch meat.	Expanding opportunities for use of knife and fork. Cutting cheese, cold meats, cake with fruit sauce, spaghetti, meat. Verbal attention to cutting with lengthwise movements.	Verbal attention to uses of table knife, vegetable knife, fork, spoon, peeler. Use of symbols: pictures of foods, choice of appropriate utensil for food preparation, and for eating routine.

5d. SKILLS: DRINKING

RATING

THE FIVE LEVELS OF THE CURRICULUM ITEM

1. Can drink with help	2. Can drink from cup with occasional spills	3. Drinks independently	4. Can eat and drink	5. Drinks, eats, talks

DEFINITION OF THE TERM: BEHAVIOR UNDER OBSERVATION

Use of cup or glass in drinking. Provision was made for recording dependence. However, children in the experimental classes showed relative independence in this area. Ability to "drink, eat, talk" meant that handling of drink cup and food was more or less habitual. The child was able to give attention to social aspects of refreshment periods.

DESCRIPTION OF BEHAVIOR OBSERVED AT EACH LEVEL

Needed help in holding cup, guiding cup to lips, tipping up to drink, setting cup on table.	Held cup and drank from it; tipped cup at sharp angle when drinking; spilled occasionally when setting cup back on table.	Held cup, drank, set cups down efficiently with regard to table space, position of other dishes.	Managed drink and food efficiently, gave attention to process.	Entire attention not needed to manage cup and food: joined in table conversation while eating, drinking.

PROGRAMMING

PREDICTABLE (INTERNALIZED) BEHAVIOR USED IN PROGRAMMING FOR NEXT LEVEL

Shows interest in juice, milk, etc.	Watches process.	Handles cup.	Handles food and manages cup.	Manipulates with competence; attends to topics of conversation.

TEACHING PROCEDURES TO ESTABLISH READINESS FOR NEXT LEVEL

Examination of paper cups, discussion of them. Dramatic play with toy dishes, drinking imaginary coffee, etc. Physical help to children needing it; Gradual withdrawal of assistance. Putting in child's cup only as much juice as could be drained in one swallow; refilling to same level often. Gradually increasing amount of liquid in cup.	Focus on pouring and serving juice. (Food kept in background of attention until juice is poured.) Attention to placing cup away from edge of table. Verbal attention to ways of holding cup, drinking from rim, setting on table.	Focus on drinks - kinds, etc. Giving opportunities to refill cup (to interrupt drinking and eating process without disturbing competence). Setting pattern for eating, drinking alternately, e.g. "This juice looks good. I'll try a sip of it first. Then I'll taste the new cookies."	Conversation about foods, drinks, serving processes. Planning future menus, e.g. "We go swimming tomorrow. What would be a good hot drink to fix for juice time?" Recalling previous menus.	Planning events and activities which will include eating as a part of event. (Next step - assumption of responsibility for phases of planning, carrying out plans.)

6a. APPEARANCE: COMBING HAIR

RATING

THE FIVE LEVELS OF THE CURRICULUM ITEM

1. dependence	2. awareness, willingness, interest	3. helping adult	4. independence with direction	5. independence

DEFINITION OF THE TERM: BEHAVIOR UNDER OBSERVATION

Child's self-reliance in combing or grooming hair. There was limited observation of girls' behavior in appropriate situations, since hair styles carefully and securely arranged by mothers usually stayed in place through the school day.

DESCRIPTION OF BEHAVIOR OBSERVED AT EACH LEVEL

Apparently no awareness of need for hair to be combed or pins and barrettes replaced.	Girl looked at hair in mirror; brought barrette or pin to teacher for replacement, called attention to loose braid. Boy put water on hair, called attention of teacher to "part" in hair, hair oil.	Girl held head still for combing, placing of pins. Held comb, pins. Boy slicked hair down or back with water; tried to comb.	Girl looked in mirror, smoothed or combed hair; replaced bobby pin or barrette, at teacher's direction. Boy combed hair straight at teacher's direction.	Girl replaced pins, barrettes when these came loose; combed hair when necessary. Boys combed when necessary.

PROGRAMMING

PREDICTABLE (INTERNALIZED) BEHAVIOR USED IN PROGRAMMING FOR NEXT LEVEL

Shows interest in objects: combs, barrettes, ribbons.	Watches process.	Tries process.	Combs hair with direction.	Practices self-reliance.

TEACHING PROCEDURES TO ESTABLISH READINESS FOR NEXT LEVEL

Verbal attention to new barrettes and hair styles. Provision of ornaments, head coverings for play use.	Providing combs. Suggesting use of mirror. Verbalizing manipulation of barrettes, use of water.	Individual help with fastenings. Suggesting use of comb, mirror. Offering dress-up materials and directing use.	Giving directions for combing. Verbal attention to results.	Adjudging need for combing. Commenting on, evaluating results.

6b. APPEARANCE: BRUSHING TEETH

RATING

THE FIVE LEVELS OF THE CURRICULUM ITEM

1. dependence	2. awareness, will-ingness, interest	3. helping adult	4. independence with direction	5. independence

DEFINITION OF THE TERM: BEHAVIOR UNDER OBSERVATION

Child's care of teeth. Teachers observed the child's use of toothbrush, toothpaste and water for rinsing mouth.

DESCRIPTION OF BEHAVIOR AT EACH LEVEL

Child showed no awareness of process. Let the teacher hold toothbrush.	Child showed interest in wetting brush and holding for use.	Child wet toothbrush, and teacher put paste on brush and demonstrated brushing; child tried to imitate.	Brushed three surfaces of teeth according to teacher's directions. Rinsed mouth. Brushed bicuspids on own initiative.	Child brushed teeth more or less adequately.

PROGRAMMING

PREDICTABLE (INTERNALIZED) BEHAVIOR USED IN PROGRAMMING FOR NEXT LEVEL

Shows contingent interest in tooth-brush, paste.	Watches process.	Tries part of procedure.	Uses procedure with help.	Brushes efficiently.

TEACHING PROCEDURES TO ESTABLISH READINESS FOR NEXT LEVEL

Verbal attention to brush, toothpaste, appearance of teeth. Help with holding brush. Encouraging child to watch others, note results.	Help with wetting brush, brushing outer surface of molars; and grinding surface of teeth.	Help with process; up and down movement; inside and out. (Attention to teeth and various parts of mouth.)	Planning, reminders. Gradual withdrawal of directions. Recall of process, observation of teeth for results.	Group discussion of "dental hygiene," dentist work; appearance.

6c. APPEARANCE: WIPING NOSE

RATING

THE FIVE LEVELS OF THE CURRICULUM ITEM

1. dependence	2. awareness, willingness, interest	3. helping adult	4. independence with direction	5. independence

DEFINITION OF THE TERM: BEHAVIOR UNDER OBSERVATION

Child's ability to use handkerchief or tissue to wipe own nose. Observed were, a) the child's awareness of the need, and b) his efficiency in use of handkerchief.

DESCRIPTION OF BEHAVIOR OBSERVED AT EACH LEVEL

Apparently unaware that nose needs wiping. Adult had responsibility.	Aware of running nose. Asked teacher's help, usually by pointing or gesturing.	Found tissue or handkerchief for adult; helped hold tissue.	Pulled out handkerchief (or went to get tissue) and used it at teacher's direction.	Was aware of running nose and took responsibility for getting and using handkerchief or tissue efficiently.

PROGRAMMING

PREDICTABLE (INTERNALIZED) BEHAVIOR USED IN PROGRAMMING FOR NEXT LEVEL

Shows interest in tissues and handkerchiefs.	Is aware of situation and use of tissues.	Helps with wiping.	Wipes nose with reminder.	Wipes nose when necessary.

TEACHING PROCEDURES TO ESTABLISH READINESS FOR NEXT LEVEL

Focus on feel of nose. Verbal attention to running nose; help with wiping. Verbal attention to opening tissue, wiping nose by pinching tissue together.	Individual help with use of tissue; practice. Verbal attention to process. Showing how to obtain tissues or handkerchief.	Verbal attention to responsibility: "Can you remember to wipe your nose?" "Did you bring a tissue? You seem to need one today."	Recognizing successful self-help. Continued reminders. Gradual withdrawal of directions.	Discussion of colds, coughs, ways of using tissue.

7a. CARE OF CLOTHING: HANGING CLOTHING
7b.   PLACING OVERSHOES

RATING

THE FIVE LEVELS OF THE CURRICULUM ITEM

1. dependence	2. awareness, will-ingness, interest	3. helping adult	4. independence with direction	5. independence

DEFINITION OF THE TERM: BEHAVIOR UNDER OBSERVATION

Child's ability to care for his outdoor clothing, including, a) hanging on a hook coat, jacket, sweater, snowpants, and b) placing overshoes side-by-side on the floor directly under the wraps.

DESCRIPTION OF BEHAVIOR OBSERVED AT EACH LEVEL

Apparently unfamiliar with idea of hanging clothing (wraps) or placing overshoes.	Showed interest in clothing hooks and in place for overshoes pointed out by teacher.	Child carried clothing, boots to coat corner. Watched teacher hang wraps on hook; helped locate loop or buttonhole for hanging. Picked up boots, helped place them side by side against wall.	At Teacher's suggestion, child took off clothing, boots in coat corner, or carried them to coat corner. Found loop for hanging and hung up clothing. Placed boots against wall. Teacher helped locate hooks whenever necessary.	Child was responsible for hanging clothing, placing boots in proper place. Some children recognized own name plate.

PROGRAMMING

PREDICTABLE (INTERNALIZED) BEHAVIOR USED IN PROGRAMMING FOR NEXT LEVEL

Shows interest in clothing, hooks.	Finds loop for hanging garment; holds boots together in one hand.	Tries to hang clothing, place boots.	Puts away clothing, boots, with reminders.	Hangs up wraps, places boots, inspects coat corner.

TEACHING PROCEDURES TO ESTABLISH READINESS FOR NEXT LEVEL

Individual help in finding clothing hook, placing overshoes. Verbal attention, when getting wraps to positions of coat, overshoes.	Individual help in slipping loops or buttonholes over hook and in placing overshoes. Verbal attention to appearance of corner.	Attention to all steps in process. "First, you hang your coat by this loop. Next you put your boots right here." Sharing tasks - "Will you help Billy and Mary hang their coats?" Verbal check of placement, recognition of good work.	Attentiveness to appearance of coat corner. Use of two or three step directions. Summary of steps; inspection of coat corner. Gradual withdrawal of verbal reminders.	Discussing responsibility for appearance of coat corner; responsibility for own orderliness.

8a. HOUSEKEEPING ACTIVITIES: PUTTING TOYS AWAY

RATING

THE FIVE LEVELS OF THE CURRICULUM ITEM

1. dependence	2. awareness, will-ingness, interest	3. helping adult	4. independence with direction	5. independence

DEFINITION OF THE TERM: BEHAVIOR UNDER OBSERVATION

Child's efficiency in putting away toys he had used. Another responsibility was that of deciding whether a toy should be left out, for display or for continuation the next day.

DESCRIPTION OF BEHAVIOR OBSERVED AT EACH LEVEL

Child left toys in play area, moved on to other activities.	Child watched putting away process, stayed in play area during clean-up.	Child picked up toys, handed them to adult; put away toys handed him by adult.	Child followed directions to put toys away; child cleaned up play area when reminded.	Child put away toys when through with them; helped other children on own initiative.

PROGRAMMING

CHILD'S PREDICTABLE (INTERNALIZED) BEHAVIOR USED IN PROGRAMMING FOR NEXT LEVEL

Shows interest in toys; classmates; contingent activity.	Watches pick-up activity.	Helps with process.	Puts away toys with direction.	Takes responsibility for putting toys away.

TEACHING PROCEDURES TO ESTABLISH READINESS FOR NEXT LEVEL

Comments on toys, play activity and storage places, while helping with pickup; comments on next activity in schedule.	Verbal attention to methods of picking up, transporting toys to cupboards. Individual suggestions. Shared processes.	Shared processes continued. "Inspection" of play areas for forgotten toys; comments on room appearance.	Planning clean-up process: "A and B can put away their blocks. C and D can see that the dress-up things are in the drawers. C can get his tinker toys picked up.	Conducting pick-up as part of more inclusive schedule: clearing room for another activity, or for close of school. "Leaving the room neat."

8b. HOUSEKEEPING ACTIVITIES: OPENING AND SHUTTING DOORS

RATING

THE FIVE LEVELS OF THE CURRICULUM ITEM

1. dependence	2. awareness, will-ingness, interest	3. helping adult	4. independence with direction	5. independence

DEFINITION OF THE TERM: BEHAVIOR UNDER OBSERVATION

Child's ability a) to open and close room doors and doors in hallways in the course of daily activities, and b) to manipulate doors of cupboards, in getting out or putting away materials. Independence included knowing when not to open doors; for some it included an understanding of schedules, so that handling of doors contributed to smooth group movements.

DESCRIPTION OF BEHAVIOR OBSERVED AT EACH LEVEL

Child did not open door to leave room, e.g. abandoned trip to restroom if teacher did not open door for him. Child stood in front of closed cupboards.	Child tried knob, moved open door back and forth, shut door. Child tried to get finger in crack of door, experimented with latches.	Child helped turn knob, pushed on door after latch was freed; asked adult or another child to turn knob.	Child followed directions to grasp knob firmly, to close door, or to leave door open; and opened door to visitor's knock; followed directions to place chair and stand on it to open cupboard door.	Child opened and shut doors, without help, in course of daily routine. Child did not play with doors: child interpreting schedule, left room doors open at appropriate times; closed cupboard doors (or opened them flat against the wall to prevent accidents).

PROGRAMMING

PREDICTABLE (INTERNALIZED) BEHAVIOR USED IN PROGRAMMING FOR NEXT LEVEL

Shows interest in activity contingent upon door opening. Interest in materials.	Watches process.	Tries process.	Opens, closes doors with direction.	Handles doors efficiently.

TEACHING PROCEDURES TO ESTABLISH READINESS FOR NEXT LEVEL

Doors opened by teacher as part of routine. Verbal attention to activity which entailed opening of doors. Verbal attention to knob-turning.	Physical help with turning of knobs, working hooks on cupboards; sharing of processes.	Sharing of processes continued. Asking one child to help another. Verbal attention to schedule, when to open, close doors. Help with high cupboards.	Verbal attention to reasons, rules: open doors when entering, leaving school, and at toilet time, closed doors during classroom activities. Assignment of monitors for trips to roof, gym.	Planning. Verbal attention to safety rules, precautions and to responsibility for others in group.

8c. HOUSEKEEPING ACTIVITIES: CLEANUP AFTER ACTIVITY

RATING

THE FIVE LEVELS OF THE CURRICULUM ITEM

1. dependence	2. awareness, will-ingness, interest	3. helping adult	4. independence with direction	5. independence

DEFINITION OF THE TERM: BEHAVIOR UNDER OBSERVATION

Ability to clean up a work area after a handwork construction activity.

DESCRIPTION OF BEHAVIOR OBSERVED AT EACH LEVEL

Child did not help with cleanup after activity (paper scraps, materials, tools, paste and paint smudges).	Child watched cleanup process, listened to verbal description of process.	Child handed paper scraps to adult, put scissors, pencils in box held out by adult or other child, got wastebasket or sponge.	At teacher's direction, child picked up own scraps, or co-operated with others, got soapy sponge to wash tables, collected scissors, pencils, put crayons in box.	Child cleared up own work area, putting away material without reminders; inspected tables and washed tables when necessary.

PROGRAMMING

PREDICTABLE (INTERNALIZED) BEHAVIOR USED IN PROGRAMMING FOR NEXT LEVEL

Shows interest in materials, contin-gent activity.	Watches cleanup.	Tries to help.	Helps, with direction.	Is responsible for cleanup of own work area.

TEACHING PROCEDURES TO ESTABLISH READINESS FOR NEXT LEVEL

Work done by teacher. Verbal focus on "places for things," and to process. Focus on next activity.	Individual help with parts of process. Verbal attention to results. Demonstra-tion of use of tools such as sponge, broom.	Assignment of cooperative tasks. Suggestions for various processes. Inspection of re-sults.	Verbal focus on division of clean-ing job." A and B could pick up scraps, C could wash tables." Gradual withdrawal of verbal guidance.	General discussions of use of tools, and storage places. In-spection and evalua-tion.

9a1. SAFETY IN CLASSROOM: CAUTION WITH SHARP INSTRUMENTS

RATING

THE FIVE LEVELS OF THE CURRICULUM ITEM

1. dependence	2. awareness, willingness, interest	3. accepts and follows advice	4. usually responsible	5. responsible for own safety

DEFINITION OF THE TERM: BEHAVIOR UNDER OBSERVATION

Ability to handle sharp instruments without injury to self or others. Independence meant ability to use items when necessary. Since items were introduced as components of other activities and emphasis was on correct use, deliberate misuse was regarded as dependence.

DESCRIPTION OF BEHAVIOR OBSERVED AT EACH LEVEL

Child showed no caution with pointed scissors, knives, sticks, needles. Also, occasional child regarded sticks and knives as weapons, and was dependent on adults for restraint.	Child commented on pins, knives. "That's sharp." "Be careful." Often pulled hand back from needle, tack, in dramatization of caution.	Child followed directions about use of scissors, knives; accepted rules but needed reminders to conform.	Child usually remembered precautions for use of scissors; brought sticks, pins to adult for disposal. Needed occasional reminders.	Child used sharp instruments correctly and carefully; disposal of sharp sticks and pieces of glass.

PROGRAMMING

PREDICTABLE (INTERNALIZED) BEHAVIOR USED IN PROGRAMMING FOR NEXT LEVEL

Shows interest in using instrument.	Shows awareness of danger, type of injury.	Follows demonstration; accepts advice.	Shows caution, with occasional reminders.	Shows dependable caution.

TEACHING PROCEDURES TO ESTABLISH READINESS FOR NEXT LEVEL

Enforcing the following general rules: a) using scissors and knives at work tables; b) using sharp knives under supervision or direction only; c) inspecting knives to locate cutting edge; d) carrying knives in a tray or box; carrying scissors with hand firmly grasping the closed blades.

Demonstration of use of point or sharp edge.	Help with using instrument safely.	Attention to child's constructive use; safe disposal of dangerous fragments of broken glass or toys.	Attention to child's responsibility in: a) using instruments, b) disposing of fragments.	Expansion of opportunities for purposeful use.

9a2. SAFETY IN CLASSROOM: WITH HOT WATER

RATING

THE FIVE LEVELS OF THE CURRICULUM ITEM

1. dependence	2. awareness	3. accepts and follows advice	4. usually responsible	5. responsible for own safety

DEFINITION OF THE TERM: BEHAVIOR UNDER OBSERVATION

Child's avoidance of injury from hot water and other dangerously hot substances or objects.

DESCRIPTION OF BEHAVIOR OBSERVED AT EACH LEVEL

Turned on water faucets in bathroom full force, without testing. Crowded close to pans used for heating water, foods. Reached to touch corn-popper.	Tested water from faucets, to locate warm, cold water. Recognized meaning of plugged-in cooking unit. Identified steam from hot water. Showed generalized cautiousness.	Needed reminder. Followed directions about trying unfamiliar water faucets, showed caution near cooking appliances, used utensils for testing, lifting foods; blew on hot foods before putting them in mouth.	Usually interpreted situations and was cautious about equipment, materials likely to be hot. Was sometimes overcautious. Occasionally needed reminders. Was able to help use cooking equipment, with direction.	Was responsible for own safety in situations where heat was a factor. Occasionally reminded classmates who became incautious. Helped with use of equipment, as stirring soup in electric pot.

PROGRAMMING

PREDICTABLE (INTERNALIZED) BEHAVIOR USED IN PROGRAMMING FOR NEXT LEVEL

Shows interest in water, cooking, etc.	Notices heat, steam.	Follows demonstration; accepts advice.	Shows caution, with occasional help.	Shows dependable caution.

TEACHING PROCEDURES TO ESTABLISH READINESS FOR NEXT LEVEL

Enforcing the following general rules: a) testing water faucets before using water; b) checking corn poppers and other heating equipment visually for steam and tactually (by holding hand near equipment); c) testing hot foods by holding fingers near or over pan; and d) moving carefully in kitchen.

Directing child's attention to heat of water, appliance; demonstrating how to test heat or detect it.	Demonstrating and helping child to handle hot water faucet, hot utensils.	Verbal attention to child's successful handling of hot water, utensils.	Verbal attention to child's self-reliance in situation.	Expansion of situations using hot materials.

9a3. SAFETY: ON STAIRS
9a4.   HOLDING ON TO BANISTERS

RATING

THE FIVE LEVELS OF THE CURRICULUM ITEM

1. dependence	2. awareness	3. accepts and follows advice	4. usually responsible	5. responsible for own safety

DEFINITION OF THE TERM: BEHAVIOR UNDER OBSERVATION

Use of reasonable caution on stairways and holding on to banisters. Because the two items are so closely related, they are considered as aspects of the same problem.

DESCRIPTION OF BEHAVIOR OBSERVED AT EACH LEVEL

a3.

Child did not estimate height of riser, needed help in negotiating steps when climbing or descending; "walked out into space" going down stairs. Child did not pause before attempting stairs.	Child was aware of problems and asked help from teacher (e.g. took teacher's hand or waited for assistance; sat down and scooted down steps; crawled up stairs).	Child held teacher's hand and followed directions about putting foot on next step; stopped at foot of stairway or at top in response to cautioning by teacher.	Child could usually be depended on to stop and assess a flight of steps to ask help of teacher or classmate.	Child could regulate own ascent or descent, asking help or using banisters when necessary.

a4.

Child could not use banisters or did not hold to banisters when safety required it.	Child tried to use banisters; held to teacher's hand and to banister.	Child followed advice about holding banisters.	With occasional reminders, child used banisters on familiar stairways when necessary; on steep or darkened stairs; on unfamiliar stairways.	Child was self-reliant and dependable in use of banisters.

PROGRAMMING

PREDICTABLE (INTERNALIZED) BEHAVIOR USED IN PROGRAMMING FOR NEXT LEVEL

Shows interest in contingent activity.	Shows generalized caution on stairs.	Follows specific single directions.	Follows rules with reminders.	Remembers and follows rules.

TEACHING PROCEDURES TO ESTABLISH READINESS FOR NEXT LEVEL

Enforcing the following general rules: a) slowing pace at foot or head of stairway; b) inspecting flight of steps, visually, before starting up or down; c) moving to right-hand banister and holding it; d) moving singlefile on stairway; e) walking up or down at a safe pace.

| Observation of individual children to determine need for help: giving physical assistance as needed; verbal attention to child's efforts to maintain safety; verbal attention to destination. | Physical support continued; verbal attention to child's efforts and performance. Verbalizing safety rules while negotiating steps; reviewing behavior afterward. | Briefing on one general rule before leaving classroom; restating rule while negotiating stairs. Gradual substitution of verbal reminders for physical support. | Planning route before leaving classroom; briefing children on rules (a-e) above. Assigning partners, thus arranging child assistance for individuals still needing modified support. Discussion of experiences. Use of picture symbols: Partners; The Roof Book. | Planning trips on and off campus; helping children choose partners. Making picture records of trips. Developing rules for safe play routines on park stairways. |

9a5. SAFETY: PROTECTION OF HEAD FROM BUMPS

RATING

THE FIVE LEVELS OF THE CURRICULUM ITEM

1. dependence	2. awareness	3. accepts and follows advice	4. usually responsible	5. responsible for own safety

DEFINITION OF THE TERM: BEHAVIOR UNDER OBSERVATION

Child's care in avoiding head injury from furniture and equipment in classroom and halls.

DESCRIPTION OF BEHAVIOR OBSERVED AT EACH LEVEL

Children crawled under furniture, bumped head on table, cupboard ledges; ran without watching course for obstacles, stooped and straightened without regard for doors, furniture.	Child recognized that head might be bumped when playing on floor, getting materials from cupboards, but did not avoid situations.	Child followed directions in concrete situations; "Keep your head down while you crawl out from under the table." "You'll have to duck your head to get under here!" "Open the cupboard door wide or shut it so you won't bump your head."	With occasional reminders, child took reasonable precautions when playing or working near ledges, cupboards, furniture. Child adapted speed of movement to a safe level.	Child played near furniture and moved about room safely; closed cupboard doors; or opened them to 180° angle; showed concern about preventing bumps to others.

PROGRAMMING

PREDICTABLE (INTERNALIZED) BEHAVIOR USED IN PROGRAMMING FOR NEXT LEVEL

Shows interest in contingent activity.	Shows generalized awareness of danger.	Obeys specific injunctions.	Avoids ordinary obstacles with reminders.	Remembers to watch for obstacles.

TEACHING PROCEDURES TO ESTABLISH READINESS FOR NEXT LEVEL

Enforcing the following general rules: a) closing cupboard doors after taking out desired materials; b) opening cupboard doors 180° when getting materials; c) walking at a safe pace in classroom: d) placing chairs used to give access to high shelves with chairback against wall; e) exercising care in crawling or reaching under tables and easel; f) confining block-building to assigned area.

| Giving physical help or restriction to children needing support; using follow-the-leader games to develop awareness of obstacles; using small cars for traffic games, screens and chairs for tunnels and bridges. | Physical support continued. Assigning tasks of opening cupboard doors, taking out materials, closing doors; pointing out protruding ledges and cupboards; calling attention to out-of-place equipment and unfamiliar obstacles. | Observing and cautioning children needing specific reminders in dangerous situations. Inspecting room, directing clean-up with attention to safety rules. Gradual withdrawal of physical surveillance. | Inspecting room before and after activities; discussing doors left open and toys improperly stored; discussing safety rules. | Planning with children for clean-up and for follow-the-leader games; helping children to foresee necessary precautions in various situations. |

9b1. SAFETY ON PLAYGROUND: SLIDING

RATING

THE FIVE LEVELS OF THE CURRICULUM ITEM

1. dependence	2. awareness	3. accepts and follows advice	4. usually responsible	5. responsible for own safety

DEFINITION OF THE TERM: BEHAVIOR UNDER OBSERVATION

Use of reasonable caution on slides.

DESCRIPTION OF BEHAVIOR OBSERVED AT EACH LEVEL

Child was careless in climbing steps; stood or played at top of slide; did not test by sliding with hands on side rails first; stood at foot of slide. Dependence in use of slide related to lack of experience or from recklessness.	Child was cautious on steps, held to sides when descending, wanted adult near to give physical support: needed encouragement.	Followed separate directions. Climbed stairs carefully, held sides of slide to test descent, moved away from foot of slide; needed reminders.	Usually remembered precautions for safety of self and group: needed occasional reminders about proper use of slide.	Remembered safety precautions; used slide for sliding; explored safe variations in ways of sliding.

PROGRAMMING

PREDICTABLE (INTERNALIZED) BEHAVIOR USED IN PROGRAMMING FOR NEXT LEVEL

Shows interest in slide.	Shows generalized caution - waits for help.	Follows single directions of supervisor.	Remembers rules with reminders.	Observes rules without supervision.

TEACHING PROCEDURES TO ESTABLISH READINESS FOR NEXT LEVEL

Enforcing general rules: a) waiting turn, b) holding handrail to climb steps, c) sitting down at top of slide, d) using side rails to check descent, e) leaving bottom of slide after descending, f) "spectator" safety - staying away from base of slide, g) cautiousness on an unfamiliar slide.

Teacher help with climbing, descent of slide, returning for another slide. Reminders about waiting turn, sliding correctly, not blocking slide.	Teacher help continued. Verbal attention to success in climbing, sliding, returning.	Verbal attention to observance of safe procedure. Gradual withdrawal of physical help; reliance on sequence of verbal directions.	Conversation about use of slide: planning and recall. Use of sketches, pictures of children on slide. Gradual withdrawal of close supervision, with teacher standing in vicinity, but not next to slide.	Conversation: child planning; child review of play. Verbal review of rules for safety. Supervision at intervals to renew attention to rules.

9b2. SAFETY ON PLAYGROUND: SWINGS

RATING

THE FIVE LEVELS OF THE CURRICULUM ITEM

1. dependence	2. awareness	3. accepts and follows advice	4. usually responsible	5. responsible for own safety

DEFINITION OF THE TERM: BEHAVIOR UNDER OBSERVATION

Care for own safety in use of swings. Early preference was for chair swings at the playground, and safety was the adult's responsiblity. Later, after experiences in making, installing and using small rope swings on the roof playground, preference was for the regulation swings.

DESCRIPTION OF BEHAVIOR OBSERVED AT EACH LEVEL

Did not hold rods or ropes of swing. Walked in swing area without regard for moving swings; used swings recklessly.	Tried to hold rods or ropes of swing. Stayed away from swing or wanted adult near. Preferred chair swings with front bar or wanted to sit on adult's lap.	Child followed separate directions for use of swing.	Child usually remembered and followed composite directions for safety. Needed occasional reminders about proper use.	Child was responsible for proper use of swing. Was aware of responsibility toward others.

PROGRAMMING

PREDICTABLE (INTERNALIZED) BEHAVIOR USED IN PROGRAMMING FOR NEXT LEVEL

Shows interest in swings.	Shows generalized caution; waits for help.	Follows single directions of supervisor.	Follows rules, with supervision.	Observes rules without supervision.

TEACHING PROCEDURES TO ESTABLISH READINESS FOR NEXT LEVEL

Enforcing the general rules: a) Holding ropes or sidebars firmly when getting in, using and leaving swings; b) standing near adult when waiting turn; c) observing "school" rules; d) sitting, not standing; e) swinging to reasonable height; f) stopping swing before getting out; g) governing swing movement when smaller children approach; h) spectator rules; staying or walking along fence, in swing area; skirting swings.

Helping child in and out of swing; pushing swing; giving momentum. Reminders about waiting turn; staying away from moving swing; holding sidebars.	Teacher help continued. Verbal attention to correct use of swing; comments on care taken by children.	Verbal directions given in sequence. Gradual withdrawal of physical help. Gradual movement away from swing by teacher.	Supervision in vicinity of swings. Reliance on verbal reminders; planning and recall activities. Use of picture symbols.	Group planning and listing of rules; comparison with other safety rules. Supervision at a distance.

9b3. SAFETY ON PLAYGROUND: SEE-SAW

RATING

THE FIVE LEVELS OF THE CURRICULUM ITEM

1. dependence	2. awarenes	3. accepts and follows advice	4. usually responsible	5. responsible for own safety

DEFINITION OF THE TERM: BEHAVIOR UNDER OBSERVATION

Child's exercise of caution in use of see-saws.

DESCRIPTION OF BEHAVIOR OBSERVED AT EACH LEVEL

Child showed lack of caution in getting on, off see-saw Reckless use, with danger to self and others.	Child asked for help in getting on, off, asked for support from adult. Showed awareness of heights and danger of bumps.	Child followed advice for getting on, off see-saw, and for operation.	Child was able to use see-saw safely, with occasional reminders.	Child used see-saw safely without supervision; use did not threaten safety of himself or others.

PROGRAMMING

PREDICTABLE (INTERNALIZED) BEHAVIOR USED IN PROGRAMMING FOR NEXT LEVEL

Shows interest in see-saw.	Shows generalized caution.	Follows directions of supervisor.	Follows rules with reminders.	Observes rules without supervision.

TEACHING PROCEDURES TO ESTABLISH READINESS FOR NEXT LEVEL

Enforcing the following general rules: a) pulling see-saw level to get on; b) holding handbars; c) moving see-saw rhythmically; d) limiting load; e) leveling see-saw to get off.

Helping child in getting on, off. Verbal attention to safe procedures. Teacher guidance of board.	Continued help. Verbal attention to getting on. Direct teaching of use of feet for moving see-saw.	Verbal directions about getting off; giving directions in sequence; gradual withdrawal from see-saw area.	Conversation: planning and recall of safe use. Reliance on verbal reminders with teacher at a distance from see-saw.	Group planning and listing of safety rules. Help with setting up roof see-saw. Supervision at a distance when needed. Instruction in "bumping" the see-saw.

9b4. SAFETY ON PLAYGROUND: CLIMBING

RATING

THE FIVE LEVELS OF THE CURRICULUM ITEM

1. dependence	2. awareness	3. accepts and follows advice	4. usually responsible	5. responsible for own safety

DEFINITION OF THE TERM: BEHAVIOR UNDER OBSERVATION

Child's safe use of climbing equipment on the roof and in park playground.

DESCRIPTION OF BEHAVIOR OBSERVED AT EACH LEVEL

Child did not show caution in finding hand and foot holds, in placing ladders, etc. or in choosing activities suitable to climbing frames.	Child refused to try climbing apparatus, or asked help in climbing: child commented on height, chance of falling.	Child tried equipment, accepted physical support, followed verbal directions.	Child ordinarily used apparatus safely: had regard for firm holds, correctly placed ladders. Needed reminders about type of play.	Child climbed safely, arranged or helped to arrange various combinations of climbing equipment for "pursuit" games.

PROGRAMMING

PREDICTABLE (INTERNALIZED) BEHAVIOR USED IN PROGRAMMING FOR NEXT LEVEL

Shows interest in ladders, frames.	Shows generalized caution.	Follows directions of supervisor.	Follows rules with supervision.	Observes rules, without supervision.

TEACHING PROCEDURES TO ESTABLISH READINESS FOR NEXT LEVEL.

Enforcing the following general rules: a) testing apparatus before use; b) checking supports, ground at base of ladders; c) finding good hand holds, foot holds for climbing; d) checking footholds descending.

| Helping child construct and test apparatus; find hand and foot holds. Verbal attention to careful use of ladders, frames. | Continued help. Verbal attention to climbing processes; safety rules about hand and footholds. | Verbal attention to care used by children; help with various ways of using apparatus. Gradual movement away from apparatus by teachers. | Conversation: planning and recall. Use of pictures of activity. Gradual reliance on verbal reminders; withdrawal from vicinity by teacher. | Group planning and recall of safety rules. Comparison with rules for other apparatus. |

9b5. SAFETY ON PLAYGROUND: SANDBOX

RATING

THE FIVE LEVELS OF THE CURRICULUM ITEM

1. dependence	2. awareness	3. accepts and follows advice	4. usually responsible	5. responsible for own safety

DEFINITION OF THE TERM: BEHAVIOR UNDER OBSERVATION

Child's safe use of sand and sand toys.

DESCRIPTION OF BEHAVIOR OBSERVED AT EACH LEVEL

Child played in sandbox but showed no concern for blown or tossed sand, toys - threw sand on self or at others.	Child was cautious or over-cautious in approaching sandbox, protected eyes, mouth.	Child followed advice about use of toys and sand. Accepted restrictions imposed by weather, size of sandbox.	Child ordinarily used sand and toys safely; needed reminders about wind, turn-taking.	Child used sand and toys safely; shared area and toys; helped decide when sand-play was feasible.

PROGRAMMING

PREDICTABLE (INTERNALIZED) BEHAVIOR USED IN PROGRAMMING FOR NEXT LEVEL

Shows interest in sandbox play.	Shows generalized caution.	Follows directions of teacher.	Follows rules, with supervision.	Observes rules without supervision.

TEACHING PROCEDURES TO ESTABLISH READINESS FOR NEXT LEVEL

Enforcing the following general rules: a) waiting for adult help in opening and closing hinged covers of box; b) turn-taking with toys and in playing in sandbox; c) inspection of weather and sand conditions (wind, wet sand, cold); d) Inspection of toys for sharp edges; e) using sand properly and safely (esp. not throwing).

Teacher participation: opening box; helping with sharing of toys; showing constructive activities. Verbal suggestions for careful use of sand.	Verbal attention to child's use of materials: Comments on safe use. Assigning of helping with covers.	Verbal attention to traffic play, cooking, and beach play. Gradual movement by teacher away from side of box.	Conversation: planning and recall of sand play, with attention to safety factors. Gradual withdrawal from vicinity by teacher.	Group planning and recall of play and allied safety factors. Cleanup processes.

9b6. SAFETY ON PLAYGROUND: WHEEL TOYS

RATING

THE FIVE LEVELS OF THE CURRICULUM ITEM

1. dependence	2. awareness	3. accepts and follows advice	4. usually responsible	5. responsible for own safety

DEFINITION OF THE TERM: BEHAVIOR UNDER OBSERVATION

Safe use of wheeltoys on roof and in classroom, also safety as spectator.

DESCRIPTION OF BEHAVIOR OBSERVED AT EACH LEVEL

Child when riding did not avoid obstacles, turn safely, govern speed; did not avoid wheel toys ridden by others.	Child refused to ride wheel toys, kept distance from others riding. Tried to ride, wanted adult support.	Child followed advice about getting on and off toys, about speed and routes; followed advice about watching for toys ridden by others.	Child usually handled toys safely, and was cautious about getting in way of others on vehicles. Needed reminders about speed, choice of games as skill increased.	Child avoided hazards in own or others use of wheel toys.

PROGRAMMING

PREDICTABLE (INTERNALIZED) BEHAVIOR USED IN PROGRAMMING FOR NEXT LEVEL

Shows interest in wheel toys.	Shows generalized caution.	Follows directions of teacher.	Follows rules with reminders.	Observes rules without supervision.

TEACHING PROCEDURES TO ESTABLISH READINESS FOR NEXT LEVEL

Enforcing the following general rules: a) taking turns with wheel toys, b) observing traffic rules as rider or spectator: using care in "cross traffic," and regulating speed; c) using wheel toys for games acceptable in school situation: riding, delivery, gas station, traffic rule observance.

| Helping child to get on and off vehicles, and to ride. Teacher participation in setting up traffic routes, games. Verbal attention to safey observance by child. | Verbal attention to constructive use of vehicles. Attention to condition of toys and need for repair. Planning turns. | Planning in advance all turns for play-period; reminding children about play rules as they claimed turns. Gradual withdrawal from direct supervision. | Conversation: planning for cooperative games; recalling game sequences and traffic rules utilized. Gradual withdrawal from vicinity of wheel toy play. | Group discussion of play: planning, recalling. Conversation about real traffic in travel to and from school. Discussion of care in use of toys: avoiding breakage. |

10. INDEPENDENT TRAVEL IN BUILDING

RATING

THE FIVE LEVELS OF THE CURRICULUM ITEM

1. across hall to washroom	2. return to classroom	3. car to classroom	4. classroom to known destination	5. go and return

DEFINITION OF THE TERM: BEHAVIOR UNDER OBSERVATION

Child's safe independent travel, without loitering or getting lost, between the classroom and various points in the school building.

DESCRIPTION OF BEHAVIOR OBSERVED AT EACH LEVEL

Child could go to washroom unaccompanied.	Child could be relied on to return from washroom.	Child came directly from car to classroom.	Child followed direct route to elevator, gym, office, swimming pool, water fountain.	Child could be relied on to go to a known destination with a message and return with or without a return message.

PROGRAMMING

PREDICTABLE (INTERNALIZED) BEHAVIOR USED IN PROGRAMMING FOR NEXT LEVEL

Knows location of washroom.	Knows return route.	Knows route from entrance to classroom.	Knows route to several points, from classroom.	Knows routes from and to classroom.

TEACHING PROCEDURES TO ESTABLISH READINESS FOR NEXT LEVEL

Verbal attention to location. Verbal emphasis on remembering. Planning for activity to follow washing, toileting.	Group experience in traveling from car to classroom: a) teacher meeting and escorting, b) transportation driver escorting, c) child leading way to classroom.	Experience traveling from classroom to car. Group experience in traveling to other facilities, as to elevator and roof: elevator and small gym; stairway and office. Noting "landmarks"; appointing monitors to lead the way. Verbal attention to going and coming back.	Group experience on return trips: noting landmarks on return route; appointing leaders for return trips. Sending messengers in pairs. Sending messengers singly.	Learning new routes.

CHAPTER **3**

SETTINGS FOR CURRICULUM IMPLEMENTATION

OVERVIEW

The resources available at Columbia Teachers College both provided for and governed the programming of the preschool children's experiences. The major resource in the teaching-learning process was the action possible in the school setting. Modification of this action was dependent upon utilization of four elements common to each of the ten major activity settings: the physical space, time, people and tangible materials. This overview is a discussion of the four elements and will serve as an introduction to the activity settings which follow.

The Physical Space

Highlighted here is not the physical plant per se, but rather, its use in accommodating experiences of the ten major activity settings. The physical structures used regularly by the experimental group included the classroom with its equipment and materials, a lavatory located directly across the hall from one of the classroom doors, the College halls, stairways and elevators, a roof playground, and gymnasiums. The classroom proper served as a center of daily operations for two groups of children. It is described here with reference to the spaces which accommodated continuing experiences. The accompanying sketch depicts the room plan and one arrangement of equipment.

General Plan

The classroom with its adjoining observation booth paralleled the hallway. Entrance was by either of two doors at opposite ends of the inner (south) wall. The observation booth (J) between these doors made the classroom L-shaped. The one-way vision screen of the booth was, in the classroom, a wide mirror set about two and a half feet from the floor. The booth had doors at either

end, one opening into the narrow corridor of the classroom L.

Along the west wall of the classroom were bulletin and chalkboards. In the north wall were two large windows and two additional bulletin boards. On the east was a double bank of storage cupboards (F). The lower shelves were open for child use and the closed upper shelves were supply cupboards for teachers. The narrow passage to the east door contained the sink with running water (G) and the children's coat corner (H).

AREA A WORK TABLES The table grouping (A) was used initially as a central gathering point for the children. With program development, its flexibility and multiplicity of purpose increased.

AREA B DOLL PLAY The playhouse area B was divided by moveable screens into kitchen, livingroom, and bedroom units. The relative size of this play area depended upon the focus of class activities: separate rooms, or the house as a whole, could be made larger or smaller according to the experiences the teacher wished to utilize. Housekeeping appurtenances were based in this area to establish a context of materials connected with home living.

AREA C Area C was used for block play or painting. Either could be amplified for a large group activity by incorporating part of the center area. Moveable front panels on the block cupboards served as supplementary easels. Also in this area were a paint supply cabinet accessible to the children and a wall-cabinet for tools and construction supplies.

AREA D Area D, like Area C above, was multipurpose. Its cupboard held store-play materials. The work bench served for exploratory tool work, cooking or record playing. The bulletin and chalkboards were focal points for preacademic experiences with various kinds of symbols.

2a
Music with consultant

1a, 1b
Discussion Periods

5a, 5b
Free play

4a, 4b
Group handwork

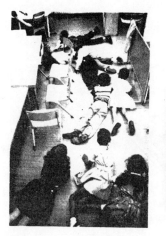

2b
Music with record player

2c
Group singing

3a
Getting ready for juice
3b
Birthday party

6a,6b
Story telling

7
Cooking

8a,8b,8c   Trip to the store

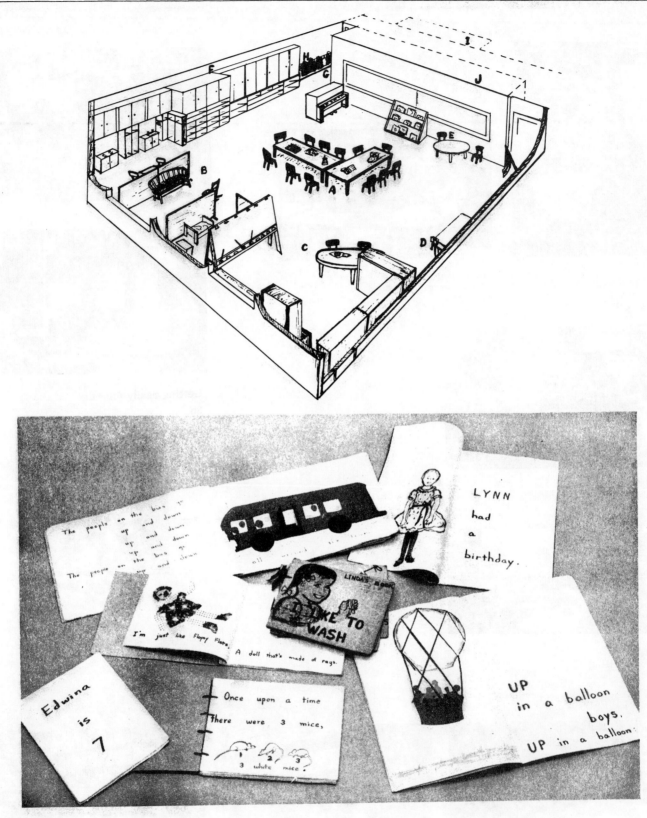

| AREA E | Area E was the library corner. It was a quiet place for individuals or small groups, and was, at times, expanded to accommodate the entire class. The piano, a boundary of the area, was used in extensions of story activities.

| AREA F |
| AREA G | Areas F and G were essentially resource areas for tangible materials and equipment. Attention here was weighted toward children's experiences in locating, taking out, and returning necessary materials and toward their assumption of classroom housekeeping responsibility.

| AREA H | Area H was the focus of work on care and recognition of clothing, on some of the dressing processes, and on elementary approaches to housekeeping practices. Individual name cards were placed over assigned coat hooks.

| AREA I | The lavatory was an extension area for several activities. Toileting, washing, dressing, and grooming activities were handled here, as were special clean-up procedures after work with paint and clay, or in preparation for cooking. Sharing of the lavatory with children from the Agness Russell Center, a nursery-through-sixth grade campus school, highlighted personal and social responsibility for public facilities.

| AREA J | The observation booth served two action purposes. One was social. Children met many visitors and occasionally viewed their classmates from that vantage point. The second purpose related to spatial orientation. The relative positions of the hall, classroom, and booth, with the door placements, made a natural laboratory for investigating space arrangements. Although the area was seldom used by the children, they were given opportunity to notice visitors disappear through one door and appear through another. In relating this to their own use of the adjacent classroom doors, they more accurately referred to the physical position of a visitor or observer.

| ROOF AREA | The Project playground, an area 40' x 84', was located on the roof of Thompson Hall, a building contiguous with Horace Mann Building. To reach the roof, the children traversed halls to the Thompson elevator, rode to the fifth floor, and mounted stairs to a door opening on a lower roof space. From this they climbed a short steep flight of iron steps. The play area was enclosed by sections of board and cyclone fencing permitting a view of the Hudson River and the George Washington Bridge. Wheel toys, sets of large hollow building blocks, and sand box toys were stored in a shed at one end of the roof. Additional equipment included moveable climbing apparatus, the sandbox and a slide. The roof, like the classroom, was divided into focal activity areas by arrangement of the various mobile structures.

| GYM AREAS | Two small gyms and a large one were used by the preschool classes. In the gyms, for the children's use, were wall ladders, rope pendulum swings, a large slide, a climbing frame, and a horizontal overhead ladder. The regulation basketball court of the large gym was used for running, marching, and circle games.

| HALLWAYS |
| STAIRS | Promoted through use of halls, stairs and elevators in the college were experiences in orientation, in a continuation of the process mentioned in connection with the classroom and booth arrangements. In going to and from the roof, gym or other resource areas, children were first familiarized with a basic route, then with alternate routes; later, they assumed responsibility for the group's travel.

| COLLEGE AND |
| COMMUNITY |
| RESOURCES | The College swimming pool and laboratory kitchen were two special resources used regularly by the preschool classes. Each of them provided a physical facility for an important activity setting. Community resources, though not regularly scheduled were an integral part of the school setting. Exploration outside of the classroom included the College snack bar, the cafeteria, the university quadrangle and two student residence halls. Repeated walks around the College block, utilizing the many entrances and exits, afforded spatial orientation and responses to directional signs. In the neighborhood, trips were made to a laundromat and fire station. Parks and public playgrounds supplemented roof and gym activities. Trips to distant resources during the four years included bus, subway and ferry travel as well as visits to an airport, department stores, zoos, and a museum.

Other resources came to the classes. Animals from a traveling zoo were brought to the preschool. Staff members making trips to other states mailed or brought to the children items of interest which extended the limits of their experience. Receiving items from distant places resulted in an appreciation of written communication and use of the mails.

Each physical setting, whether classroom, play area or hallway, presented numerous stimuli, with opportunity for children to choose and attend to one. Choices were the result of preferences, but were also conditioned by elements in the setting. Each physical setting had its corresponding social contexts in which prime consideration was given to the rights of others. In the classroom, classmates, teachers, and visitors were considered; in joint play areas, rights of other classes were respected. Choices in hallways or elevators involved others using the passageways or working in offices along the route. Personal behavior, both deportment and activity, was learned as a response to elements of the settings. For each Project group, teachers prearranged elements of the experiences to ensure desired responses in the majority of the children: reforming or redirecting inadequate behavior in the few was then more practicable. Behavior within the College setting was a gauge of possible responses in outside settings.

The Available Time

Time for school activities was governed by such factors as the double session in one room, transportation company schedules, routine psychological testing, and the age of the children. Within the school day, time in the gym, swimming pool, laboratory kitchen, and other out of classroom space was dependent upon the program sequence as well as the time assigned for the Project's use of all-college facilities.

Time limits set by these external factors were extended on occasion, through cooperative use of facilities and through activities planned to include both groups of Project children. Although the various time allotments were essentially inflexible, the scheduling within these periods was elastic. Expansion and contraction of activity periods depended upon the teachers' immediate objectives, the types of activities introduced, and responses of the children.

Persons as Resources

Other resources included the persons met by the children, such as visitors to their classes, Project personnel, other Teachers College staff, and community members encountered on trips and through use of neighborhood facilities. Children's experiences with personnel other than their teachers developed from carefully planned encounters in which staff members played prearranged roles to spontaneous associations with workers in the community.

The transportation company served the Project throughout the four years as a continuing resource. The owners arranged schedules for off-campus trips, altered their other routes to make the trips possible, and participated in the experiences. The personal interest of the transportation company personnel in the pupils' development made the daily ride to and from school an integral part of curriculum implementation.

Parents, too, had a basic role in curriculum implementation. They were the source of information about children's patterns of activity and about accustomed means of reenforcement and approval. Teachers were not parent substitutes. Rather, they sought to provide and report on school experiences in order to elicit or maintain reenforcement at home. Ways of receiving information included: daily reports from parents; oral or written messages transmitted by the children; parent interviews and visits; and regular parent meetings at six-week intervals. In addition to the oral and written messages, teachers conveyed information to parents through a regular weekly class newspaper and samples of the children's school work. The communication thus established among parents, children, and teachers was in itself a curriculum resource.

The Materials

Tangible materials served as curriculum resources when they stimulated child thought or activity. Materials and equipment were duplicates of those found in most preschool and primary classes. Selection and adaptation of commercially prepared materials were based on the variety of relationships to be employed and established. Teacher-made materials were used for many activities. Not only were they essential to fill gaps when other materials were not available, but they were designed to highlight elements for focus. By making the materials needed for an activity, teachers could more easily direct, control, and maintain attention to a designated stimulus and effect a desirable response. By selection and distribution of color and texture, by arrangement of elements, and by contriving moving parts, children could see the relation of parts to the whole. In de-emphasizing other details, teachers permitted children to interpret on the basis of their experience and to increase their involvement in the functioning of the material in their activity.

The Actions

The physical settings, the time as utilized, the

persons as resources, and the equipment and materials had as their purpose the promotion of child activity. The action of the child was the prime resource of the preschool curriculum. The teachers worked at the action level, providing settings which suggested relationships the child could express through activity. If necessary, the teachers demonstrated or helped to construct the relationships. Teachers also provided experience with the words which expressed actions, that is, the oral language which described relationships produced by the child's activity. The child, in his turn, looked at, handled, smelled, tasted, listened to, put together, took apart, and arranged the materials. He did something in the situations arranged for him.

When familiar with the relationships in fact, the child was ready to deal with symbols for the things and actions. These multi-sensory symbols included three-dimensional representations, textured or raised illustrations, and two-dimensional symbols and drawings, as well as the arbitrary spoken and written symbols. In the Project, language was considered broadly as relationships between person and person, person and things, one thing and another, and a person and himself. The early understanding of relationships, inner language, was the foundation upon which the arbitrary signs used for communication of understandings were built.

The Project curriculum, then was composed of relationships which the child needed to understand; the settings were arranged to make the action level available. Rather than talking or telling or even showing, the teacher's role was one of assuring the activity of the individual child. Verbal telling was a summary of what had been learned, not the vehicle for teaching it.

The teachers used the resources sketched in the overview for maintaining ten major activity settings. These settings, presented in the sections which follow include: Discussion Period, Music, Group Handwork Projects, Free Play, Juice Time, Playground and Gymnasium Activities, Story Telling, Swimming, Cooking, and Trips.

DISCUSSION PERIODS

The two situations specifically designed to promote group discussion were the opening conversation period and the juice period. Since the action contexts of the two periods differed and the development of class participation in each was at first distinctive, they will be described separately. However the underlying purpose of group discussion was, of course, the same for both situations. The teachers sought to promote effective social relationships within the group and to encourage purposeful use of verbal communication.

Opening Conversation Period

As a basis for group processes in early discussion periods, teachers used the daily parent reports which the children brought from home. The reports contained information about the child's rest the night before, his breakfast (or lunch), and any happenings with possible bearing on his school day. Thus, the teachers and children had some mutual information to facilitate genuine communication. Ordinarily, early conversation periods were one-sided: a teacher read aloud an interesting item about each child and asked for confirmation or made a brief comment, and the child answered by a nod, a smile, or by a repetition of the teacher's words. This reading also served to introduce children to one another, by the prefacing use of names: "This is Ted's report. Let's see what his mother has said." The reporting was, at this early stage, selective and rapid in order to refer to each child before restlessness became a factor. The brief period ended with a change to active work or play.

Two classes included in their number several children with scanty or undeveloped speech, as well as one or two who came from bilingual homes. In such classes the more communicative children dominated the conversation at first, with the non-talkers generally listening contentedly. Later, after successful use of speech during the highly structured juice period, the quiet children began to contribute — first with rote items such as songs or story refrains; next with information elicited by questions; then, with spontaneous news contributions. The report sheets were always available in case of need, but eventually the opening discussion included significant news items, reviews of class events of the previous day, and plans for activities for the day ahead. In this discussion were noted general participation and willing attention to individual remarks.

As children became accustomed to classmates and teachers, the opening conversation period was enlarged to include a brief reading period or a story. Tangible objects which could be related to a news item or which illustrated factual and imaginative tales served to draw restless or shy children into the group. The opening discussion period was thus one which provided for alternate listening and participation, but with things which helped to illustrate the spoken word. The parents' reports together with a story required about ten minutes of class time. However, the period lengthened gradually, to accommodate the children's discussions of their own and others' activities.

Although conversation during the first months was mainly teacher stimulated, pupil initiative was noted as children in each group began to reproduce earlier teacher devices. For example, books were brought from home to be read; small toys were offered for classmates' examination; and children volunteered to sing songs for the class. These first contributions were accepted by the teachers as valuable sharing and were given recognition. The first participation opened the way to a general exchange of remarks or objects.

The daily parent report sheets continued throughout the year to be useful in the discussion period. As with the object-centered conversation, the early teacher-oriented use moved gradually toward child expression and assumption of responsibility. For example, pupils picked up teachers' clues to say, "And what time did I go to bed?" or "Read about me." Conversation of this type developed toward the child's answering of questions about menus or morning happenings and, in a few cases, about events of the previous evening. The following teacher-recorded conversation shows an imaginative extension by two second-year children of the use of report information.

Q. What did you have for lunch?
A. Ice cream and soup.

Q. Oh-h. Ice cream?
A. (with a grin) And tea and cookies.

Q. Tea?
A. (wider grin) And pop and milk.

Q. The questioner began to smile, realizing that this was a joke.
A. (smiling broadly) And ice cream. Yeh!

Growth in discussion skills varied according to the composition of a class, but direction was from individualized reception of language to socialized oral expression.

Juice-Time Discussion

The repetitive and familiar circumstance of eating promoted development of discussion. Nontalkers were observed making first attempts at speech during the refreshment period. "More" and "cookie," though articulated in various imperfect ways, obtained the food for which the child asked. First words were rapidly followed by "Please," "No," and "Yes." Teacher participation in the group around the table and the sharing of juice and cookies seemed to add to the relaxation. Likes and dislikes were expressed when cookies and juice were selected from the several available kinds. All seemed to foster speech.

Discussion progressed from monosyllables or phrases about food on the juice table to sentences comparing home menus. While the children ate, teachers introduced questions about the after-juice activity and verbalized plans. Gradually, table conversation moved away from focus on cookies and juice to centers of interest approached obliquely through the food items. Among the topics introduced were television programs, favorite actors or cartoon characters, play activities at home, summer vacation plans and memories of past vacations, and reports on family trips. Consequently, at times the juice period extended into the play schedule which had at first seemed so urgent to the children.

Birthday parties, substituting for the juice period, introduced new discussants and social responsibilities for the children. Oral invitations to guests and arrangements for a parent's or sibling's comfort necessitated certain polite phrases. Other guests invited to share refreshment periods included staff psychologists, observers, and other workers who helped to guide discussion patterns. In these situations, the children learned to talk with increased ease to such visitors, exchanging remarks while they passed cookies or poured juice. The conversation was at first a combination of words, gestures and facial expressions, but the children's intention of promoting the guest's comfort was unmistakable.

In both conversation periods, but particularly at juice time, it was possible for the teachers to observe the ways in which children absorbed attitudes and action patterns which they expressed in fact before they could manage the words associated with them. The activities and tangible materials of the discussion contexts provided the basis for specific learnings such as speech.

Materials for Discussion Periods

Materials were used to facilitate grouping for discussion as well as discussion. Tangible materials of all kinds were used for this purpose.

a) Materials for planning: for example, ingredients for candy making; wood scraps and tools for woodworking; picture patterns for a handwork project.

b) Records of events: calendars, charts, newspapers, parent reports, roll-call sheets, letters, teacher-made books, handwork products.

c) Materials for vicarious experiences: books, newspapers, pictures, word cards.

MUSIC EXPERIENCES

In the Project classes, responses to musical stimuli were used in three kinds of activities which were integral parts of the total program. These were daily singing and rhythms, listening and action sequences with the record-player as focus of attention, and during the third and fourth years of the preschool experiment, weekly programs with a music consultant. Group cooperation and interaction in the various musical settings were planned to promote individual growth in all curriculum areas. Origins of speech skills, social attitudes, muscle control, and informational and conceptual learnings as well as practice in self direction were apparent in the music experiences.

The steps of the process used in the music period under teacher direction include: first, the musical incident or sequence used by a group with a common purpose; secondly, the teachers' work within that group to help individuals achieve that purpose; and, thirdly, reformation of the group by children acting autonomously. The steps, not always clearcut, merged together as expected in a dynamic situation. However, the teacher's awareness of group and individual status was within the framework of the three-step procedure, and changes in approach were made on the basis of children's needs within that framework. The marching, dancing, finger patterns and rhythm ventures were actions set in motion by the teachers and then utilized as teaching materials. The materials were not the percussion instruments, the songs, or illustrative objects, but, as in other aspects of the curriculum, the children's actions: the relationships children set up between themselves and others, between themselves and things, and with themselves.

Singing and Rhythms

Music caught the children's attention and interest and allowed for transfer to other activities with little diminution of that attention. As a closing exercise, it provided relaxation and an easy movement to the task of putting on wraps for the journey home. The length of the period and the complexity of the experiences increased steadily during the year. Progression was from two or three simple songs in a brief period to a series of songs, finger plays, dances and rhythm band activities requiring about twenty minutes. In addition, music in any activity seemed to help clarify or expand a concept, and new songs were often introduced at recreation time when the seesaw, slide, swing and wheel-toys provided meaningful settings.

To establish the regular music period teachers used group singing of a children's classic or a popular song of which a few children knew at least part. Although such contributed music continued as a part of the repertoire, as soon as possible a song familiar in nursery-kindergarten programs, such as Here We Are Together was introduced. This song, illustrated and amplified by actions fitted to the phrasing, accommodated the several verbal levels encountered in each class. The words "all sitting in our chairs" were the cue for turning to pat lightly the chair backs; reference to individual children was accented by a teacher's pointing to each child named. Thus, pupil participation was ensured even though teachers often sang alone for the first days of the session. When children appeared restless, the singling-out process included a teacher's walking around the table to touch each child's head in succession. Eventually children pointed to themselves when named; finally, they fitted their own names into the song. Such variations provided a musical setting for grouping, individuation and regrouping in a quick-moving verbal situation.

The following outline illustrates the method by which key program objectives were continuously amplified in the setting. Bringing the children together for a purpose, drawing attention to each child's contribution, then re-combining the group verbally or physically was a process directing the children's attention to themselves as members of the class and to their responsibility for carrying out a constructive program. Although Here We Are Together was the initial setting, any other greeting song might have been employed.

1. Organization of the group: teacher-child responsibility
   a. Taking places with group when song was started

b. Patting chair when appropriate phrase was sung

c. Noting all persons in room, in naming sequence

d. Responding to song idea in other situations (e.g. "all sitting on the floor", "all putting on our coats", "all ready to go home")

2. Individuation of members: teacher responsibility

a. Naming each member (also a reinforcement for concept 1)

b. Touching and naming each member (also a reinforcement for concept 1)

c. Having children touch themselves when named

d. Having children name themselves

e. Using both first and last names of individuals

f. Using reenforcing songs
   For absentees: Oh, dear! What can the matter be? (_____'s not here today.)
   For children returning after absence: Good morning to you (sung using name of child returning to school)

3. Development of self-direction: child responsibility

a. Remaining with the group

b. Acting with the group

c. Singing with the group

d. Requesting the song

e. Beginning the singing when asked to start the song

f. Assuming responsibility for naming all children (leading song)

g. Naming absent members for 2, f, above

h. Assuming responsibility in Good morning interchange
   (Good morning, dear children. Good morning, dear teacher)

Finger Plays and Body Movements

Finger plays and musical dramatizations provided another means of involving all pupils in a group situation. Old and new songs were adapted for progressive participation of both verbal and non-verbal children. Open, Shut Them, Here's a Ball for Baby, Pat-a-cake, and This Old Man were among the many used. Songs which embodied familiar action-language sequences (The People on the Bus) or which tapped a seasonal enthusiasm (Up on the Housetop; Jingle Bells) usually maintained effectiveness over several months, while single-idea rhymes (Peek-a-boo)

and those fostering a series of movements not parts of an integrated language whole (Open, Shut Them) seemed to diminish in favor once the ideas had been mastered. Development of specific skills in the context of action songs was noticeable. Improved finger dexterity, control and direction of large muscles, refinement of articulation as well as development of speech, and understandings with respect to people, things and events were evident in the successive uses of different songs. The aim of the finger plays and actions, as with the greeting songs was the affording of opportunities to practice progressive self-direction.

Formal Movement Patterns

Rhythmically patterned movements such as clapping, marching and simple folk dancing provided grouping frameworks within which teachers worked. For one group displaying unusual hyperactivity and infrequent responses to speech cues, patterned movements with attention to individuals needing support seemed to promote growth toward self-direction and away from need for undivided adult attention.

Group clapping and marching to music provided an initial setting for action in the program of patterns. Teachers could, within the activity, single out and help one child after another so that individual performances moved from crude and uneven movements toward appropriate rhythm and speech. In marching, partners, experienced in moving through the school building, created mutual reenforcement. Effective partnerships were usually formed by two children, who, singly, had great problems of self-direction.

Simple folk dances with a verbalized chant, to add spoken language to the stimuli, were effective in establishing group cohesion. The chants, actions and organizational steps of the Danish Clapdance and the Shoemaker's Dance are outlined here as a supplementary illustration of the operational method used consciously by teachers to bring about autonomous participation in the class activity.

1. Organization of group: teacher-child responsibility

a. Taking places in a closed circle with teacher in circle next to those needing physical support.

b. Following lead of teacher who stands just outside circle.

c. Following teacher who joins verbally, only.

d. Following teacher playing piano for group.

e. Similar sequence for partner format.

2. Individuation: teacher responsibility
   a. Helping children needing support to remain in circle.
   b. Helping individual children to lead the group
   c. Choosing children in turn as partners of the teacher.
   d. Helping children to choose partners.
   e. Giving verbal acknowledgement of good performances.

3. Development of self-direction: child responsibility
   a. Remaining in the circle.
   b. Participating in movements, chant.
   c. Requesting dance (group already formed in circle).
   d. Leading the group.
   e. Choosing a partner.
   f. Reinforcing partner in execution of dance.

Implied in the foregoing summaries and outlines is formal movements' role in developing ability to stop an action. The Clapdance specifies two claps, a number reinterated by words, music and action. Other songs carrying similar built-in limits are Let Everyone Clap Hands Like Me (two claps), Clap, Clap, Clap Your Hands (three claps), Here's a Ball for Baby (three claps), and Monkey See and Monkey Do (three). When counting was introduced as an element of a song, the reinforcement was increased by virtue of the children's past experience with rote counting. Such body language seemed effective in building number concepts in children with learning problems.

Numerous additional song settings helped to establish ability to start, inhibit and start again. For example, early attempts to introduce very simple circle games such as Roll That Round Ball failed and had to be abandoned until requisite autonomy developed. Later, games such as Farmer in the Dell were apparently understood and played spontaneously after practice in self-guidance in the music learning situations.

Rhythm Band Activities

In use of percussion instruments, the technique of individuation from a group facilitated provision for experience with each instrument by each child. Common action, i.e., practice with fifteen hand bells or fifteen sticks and blocks, created a group from which variations could be drawn. As competence increased, sub-groups were used to start the differentiation process; then individual children were singled out for solo or leadership performance. Rhythm band activities cut across curriculum divisions to provide increased motivation and clear-cut awareness of "equitable distribution." Handwork projects became the source of pupil-made drums and drumsticks, rhythm sticks, harness bells, hand bells and tambourines. Teacher plans ensured each child's use, especially in the weekly program with the consultant, of favorite instruments. Exploration of sound both in and out of the musical setting supplied a basis for appreciation of notes produced by the new instruments. The pupils' proprietary interest in their own drums, sticks and bells aided individualization and the final establishment of situations for a miscellany of instruments.

Activities Using the Record Player

The function of the record player in the pre-school classes was dual. It served in teacher-directed group activities, and as a unifying activity holding the attention of the main group of children while one or more of the group moved in and out for other purposes, or while the teacher(s) worked with one child or another within the group boundaries. In the former, focus of attention was on simple or complicated activities related to the recording. In the latter, the music activity permitted other child pursuits without disturbing individuals or the group as a whole.

Records as a Primary Activity

Action records constituted a primary curriculum emphasis with the teachers setting a pattern for (a) listening, (b) picking up cues from the song tests, and (c) working out actions for group performance. Children's interest was sustained by the opportunity to perform with others sequences which involved whole-body movements. Large group participation was possible, as was also withdrawal from the group by occasional children who worked at other interests. Records first selected for class use consisted of series of short songs or of narratives interspersed with songs. Later, because of the children's evident enjoyment, actions of increasing complexity were practicable. Use of a simple square dance record with calls, at the end of the year, demonstrated the children's acquired behavior pattern of first listening and then attempting to follow directions. Occasionally, in response to cues from individual children, a popular record with Rock and Roll dancing was included under the heading of action music.

Records combining song with minimum story promoted alternate listening and moving. Train to the Zoo, Let's Play Zoo, What Can Baby Hear? provided such opportunities. As the children learned the actions to songs, they improvised movements and developed free interpretations. Often, too, stories were used as illustrated songs with a teacher cutting out paper carrots or cutting up real carrots for The Carrot Seed or with children eating apples and looking for and collecting the appleseeds while listening to Johnny Appleseed. Texts of records transferred known things to new contexts. Where Oh Where is Pretty Little Susie charmed with its familiar things to do — "let's go find her", "picking up paw-paws, put 'em in a pocket," just as one of the music-period songs, Pick a Bale of Cotton found its meaning in the "jump down, turn around". The children seemed well able to manage strange objects when they knew something they could do with them. As relative proportions of music and movement changed with children's maturity and increased skill, instrumental music provided suggestions for action. Brahm's Lullaby, Yankee Doodle and Take Me Out to the Ball Game, illustrate the interpretation range of the children.

Singing along with the records, in the action songs, continued through the year. Growing communication skills were reflected in the music participation, and even minimal participation with a repetitive "choo-choo" or "all aboard" appeared to contribute to speech growth in children with retarded speech development.

Records as a Unifying or Structuring Activity

The group structure of children listening to records was used to facilitate major shifts in activity. With one or two groups, records were used to obtain an initial grouping at arrival-time. For others, the clean-up and wash-up period was a listening period during which individuals or pairs or groups of children left the record-player to prepare for the juice period. In preparation for going home during winter, the music group served as an anchor with children leaving to put on wraps and returning. One teacher assisted the dressing while the other served as attention-center in a listening or action-plus-listening activity.

This period was partly child-directed, with the ultimate aim being child management of the process as the teacher withdraw gradually from the group, maintaining verbal contact while helping individuals with washing, table-setting, or wraps, or moving into the group to assist, when necessary, with the mechanics of phonograph operation.

Some children in each group seemed drawn more by the turntable than by the music, at first. When verbalized for vocabulary learnings, this normal interest in watching was increasingly subordinated to its proper place.

The children learned many songs in this music period, but value of the period was not limited to this single gain. Actions which provided an order for doing things; orderliness which is implicit in following verbal directions of a song; turn-taking; purposeful movement of parts of the body were experiences which reinforced concepts the children encountered in other activities. Language gains carried into regular language periods, in the songs themselves and in independent use of vocabulary items. Rote counting was practiced in number jingles from records as well as from the regular opening song period. Self-direction and control of movement, a part of the listening-movement complex, also was increasingly evident in the music period. Ideas and action processes were apparently carried over into one or more of the other curriculum activities.

Probably most value of the record-player and records, for the pre-school group, was in the flexibility possible in their use: the pattern and structure afforded cooperative activity for the children monitoring the record player; a center of interest for those who left and returned; and also a point of reference for children who turned to individual occupations but who still listened privately to the group music.

It might appear that the question of music appreciation has been set aside in favor of aspects of utilization of music. Experiences such as those described here are, quite simply, based upon an existing appreciation. In the Project program, no period was set aside for listening to and learning to appreciate music. The children liked music when they entered the pre-school; they liked many different kinds of music when they left the experimental program. Hopefully, because of the experiences they had enjoyed, they were ready to add willed appreciative listening to their list of musical activities.

Program with Music Consultant

During the school year (1959-1960) the teachers of the two experimental classes of the Research Project had opportunity to work one hour a week with a music consultant provided by the staff of the Musicians' Emergency Fund. The purpose of the cooperation was to explore the meanings of services of a music consultant for a pre-school program for retarded children. The staffs of both the Musicians' organization and the Project were interested in gathering information on a) the feasibility in a classroom situation; b) use with very young educable retarded children; and c) usefulness as an in-service teacher-education process. There seem to be preliminary indications for each of these three aspects of the inquiry. Although for purposes of discussion this summary considers the three areas separately, in actual operation no lines of demarcation were drawn: the musical approach was through a composite: group situation, pre-school children, and teachers. The teachers felt that the successful use of such a combination of "materials" was dependent upon the interest and the skill of the specialist acting as consultant. The consultant utilized abilities of teachers and responses of children as they existed when she began her scheduled visits, to initiate and to shape a significant part of the program.

The broad aims of the music activities, for teachers and consultant, were personal, social, and intellectual growth of the individual children through group musical experiences. The consultant evidently drew from her experience, kinds of activities which could provide for individual performance and utilized the fluid grouping and regrouping which occurs in children at this level of development as the setting for such activities. Examples of this were the song I'm Going Down to Town, in which all children could sing while one or two children acted out the idea, and There Sits the Monkey, which accommodated a circle of singers and pointers while individual children took turns at being the focus of the song. Early group activities provided for exploration of specified responses, and later activities, as the children acquired a repertoire of musical understandings, allowed for interpretations and improvisations. Cues from the children were accepted as meaningful. For example, failure to respond to introduction of a circle ball game, in one class, led to its deferment until readiness had been established and a succession of circle activities could be introduced.

In analyzing use of developmental factors, it was noted that activities drew on existing abilities and directed children toward "next steps" in performance. Physical activity was utilized in such action songs as Flopsy Flora, Row, Row, Row Your Boat, and Pick a Bale of Cotton. Readiness for control or stopping of a movement was assessed and then practiced in songs such as Tidey-oh and Frere Jacques, which allowed for use of bells, and Flopsy Flora and Fire with their related actions. The idea of waiting, relaxing, then acting on cue was an important concept. Ideas of listening and interpreting were introduced as maturation and musical experience made them useful.

The total effect of the program, so far as it can be assessed at this time, was to give the children in the classes opportunities to practice social skills including sharing, turn-taking, and cooperating with partners and with total groups; to experiment with personal competencies, as self-reliance, self-control, and self-direction; and to add to basic language skills, in the surprising number of song texts which the children mastered, in what was fundamentally a pleasurable activity. The children's movement from imitation to creativity during a nine months' program afforded satisfaction to all concerned. Songs and song contexts were carried into the home situation, orally by the children and via mimeographed copies of song texts and teacher-made "circulating library books." Thus, viewed strictly as a curriculum item, the music program helped to involve parents in curriculum activities.

Similar to findings with respect to the children were those in the area of teacher involvement. The teacher group had the advantage of meeting with the consultant for curriculum discussions throughout the fall and occasionally during the spring. At those meetings, uses of the various musical activities, results in the two classes, and implications for further exploration were studied with the curriculum group. As a result, the teachers gained insight into the place of the music program in the over-all pre-school curriculum. Also, ways and means of carrying over and expanding the activity of the special program during the week were developed. Songs the children had learned prior to the program were discussed so that the consultant could include familiar sequences in her own sequence, and expand applications of the existing music vocabulary.

Most significant was the differential use of teacher abilities, as pointed up by the program. One teacher team included a pianist and the other did not. Work of the consultant in one class was the suggesting and amplification of musical activities; in the other it was literally the teaching of basic chords so that the piano could be used effectively during the week. Similarly, teacher-help in learning a new tune was possible in the one class; in the other, the teachers were convinced of the impossibility of themselves carrying a tune. The consultant attacked this situation also with direct teaching. Experimentation with different pitches discovered a range in which some tunes could be carried. The result was not singers but teachers who could set aside tension in a situation which involved singing.

As can be seen from the foregoing summary, implications for a resource program such as the one enjoyed in the Project are unmistakable. There are tentative curriculum findings and suggestions for teaching processes which merit further study.

Materials for Music

a. Record player and records: Nursery and Kindergarten finger play and motion songs, narrative songs, nursery rhymes; folk, traditional, seasonal, patriotic, popular songs and music.
b. Piano and music books: Children's folk, traditional and seasonal songs; folk and expressive dance music.
c. Percussion instruments: bells, drums, tambourines, maraccas, cymbals; also child-made blocks and sticks, pony bells, maraccas, drums.
d. Auto-harp; 1-octave xylophone.
e. Tangible materials and teacher-made books for action songs.

GROUP HANDWORK PROJECTS

The class handwork project was designed as application rather than exploration of materials and processes. It had a central focus to which the children attended and to which use of materials such as paint, paste or paper was subordinated. Common aspects of the handwork activities included the meaning or purpose which made the projects media for communication, for practice in cooperation, and for the carryover of concepts from trips and other experiences. The wide range of ability found in each Project class was accommodated by a variety of group and subgroup arrangements, as well as by differentiated assignment of tasks.

Handwork projects were of two types: one was an independent enterprise; the other was a contribution to a group unit. In the former, all children had duplicate materials, utilized similar handwork actions, and created individual versions of a product. Activities included the drawing of events or objects, pasting of cutout figures to make a symbolic record of an event

such as a rainstorm or a fire station episode, making of gifts for parents, and cutting Hallowe'en masks. An exhaustive list would cover any year's learnings about holidays, weather phenomena, people, places, and things. The duplicate projects reminded children of previous experiences and suggested future ones. They were symbols which other children, visitors, and parents could interpret, as well as teacher records of the manipulative stages reached by the children who made them. This type of group project served too as communication-with-parents material since, taken home as a trophy, it transmitted news of current class topics and information about individual performance.

The second type of handwork activity included cooperative projects which resulted in a set of related materials. A fire station and fire truck formed one such set. Others were a dollhouse made of cartons, cardboard-cutout foods for the grocery store project, carton drawers for cupboard compartments, and Christmas mobiles and figures which, when folded, assumed three-dimensional form. In such activities, children with high manipulative skill handled scissors and paper fasteners, others wielded paint brushes, and still others watched or experimented with raw materials. In this type of project, although allowance was made for individual absorption in details, teachers kept before the children the meaning of the project as a whole. Also incumbent on the teacher was the assurance of opportunity for the child's refining, expanding and developing his participation in the group project. The tangible toys made by the children as cooperative projects became two-or-three-dimensional records of meaningful group experiences. They served as free-play materials and provided for symbolic review and elaboration of ideas gained on trips. Grocery store items included, for example, articles of dough made by the children. Thus the dough-play process, which functioned as a group handwork sequence, was a natural adjunct to free-play activity.

Preparation of materials for group handwork projects was one of the teachers' out-of-school responsibilities. Materials and equipment readily accessible for the opportune moment of use ensured the child's continued attention to the desired point of focus without loss of momentum or deterioration of the activity. Wherein ideas for projects not anticipated by the teacher and requiring lengthy preparation of materials were elicited from the children during the discussion period, activity was directed toward consideration of necessary materials and procedures.

When a handwork project was postponed by means of such a joint planning session, interest was generally resumed, at a later date, at the level at which it had been interrupted.

As children worked in an activity, teachers had opportunity to study operational patterns. Solitary, paralleled, and cooperative formations in small and large groups were observed, experimented with, and utilized in subsequent projects and in other experience areas. The learnings in the group handwork setting thus seemed to extend beyond the use of basic construction materials: major values were in the social and ideational areas.

Materials for Handwork

a. Drawing materials: pencils, crayons, white and colored chalk. Surfaces: newsprint, smooth and textured drawing paper, cardboard, blackboard, cloth.

b. Painting media: tempera, fingerpaint, soapsuds, water. Tools: longhandled easel brushes; short-handled brushes; 1-1/2" and 2" painter's brushes, sponges. Surfaces: smooth and textured paper mounted on vertical and slanted easels, or spread on table surfaces and floors (as horizontal easels); blackboard; fences and paving (of roof), cardboard construction products; papier maché items.

c. Paper and cardboard construction materials: corrugated boxes, corrugated cardboard, stiff and pliable cardboard, paper towels, colored paper, newspaper (for papier maché). Tools: scissors, paper punches; paste, flour paste; paper fasteners, clips.

d. Wood construction materials: Scrap lumber (soft pine), dowels, woodendisks, wire nails, blued nails. Tools: hammers, crosscut saws, screwdrivers plane, brace and bits, gimlets, vise.

e. Plastic media: clay, plasticene, sand, dough, soap suds, pipe cleaners, wire. Tools: knives, forks, tongue blades, sticks, fluted baking cups, rolling pins, cookie cutters, thimbles, sand toys.

f. Miscellaneous: Rubber stamps and inked pads; crepe paper, tissue paper, serpentine; marker pens.

FREE PLAY

The children in the Project classes did not distinguish between work and play, and anything which really interested them was play. For the five-to-fifteen-minute free-play period, they made choices from several teacher-selected alternatives. Materials for the preferred activities were in evidence; those for undesired activities were intentionally out of sight. The work which went on in this period was the teachers' richest source of information about children.

Materials for free-play were action-centered. They included commercial coordination toys such as pegboards, color towers, mailbox, and tinker toys; expressive materials whose use had been learned in other activity settings, i.e., crayons and paper, books, and clay; and products of group handwork incorporated into free-play upon completion of the units in which they were evolved. Teachers observed that materials, whatever their nature, functioned either as items which were the focus of child attention or as components of sets of objects which formed action contexts. In the one case, actions promoted by an item were an end in themselves: they remained essentially the same, through successive uses, though usually improving in quality. In the contextual use, however, the actions became means for achieving other aims. There was a steady amplification and modification of activity in imitative and creative social sequences. Teachers provided for both material-focused and contextual play by arranging free-play settings which could accommodate both.

Free-Play Settings

Included in the initial free play settings were the play house materials, with furniture, utensils, and dolls; building blocks, with cars, boats and train sets on the same measurement scale; simple table games and the collection of coordination toys mentioned earlier; and several riding toys for modified motor play. Additional "props", however, suggested by the imaginative play or comments of individual children, or brought in experimentally by teachers more than doubled the original number of free-play settings. One by one were added: clothing for dress-up play, equipment and stock for store play, materials for picnic sequences and fishing; and tools for house repair. Later, handwork activities in which children could maintain self-direction were integrated into the existing settings. Doughplay, for example, was transferred to houseplay, and pupil-made food products appeared on grocery-store and cupboard shelves. End-products of trips, such as the toyfire engine and fire station; or of separate handwork projects such as the dollhouse and furniture, became the beginning of a summarizing setting, the community.

Actual household materials were also used in free play. Experimental introduction of some full-size brooms and dust-mops with shortened handles elicited a type of activity different from that shown with toy cleaning equipment. Sturdy short rods and reels, introduced to supplement magnetic and snap-clothespin hooks produced sequences of realistic fishing. After children had actually baked cookies, dough play showed a similar ordering. Apparently, full-sized equipment which children had seen parents use elicited learning qualitatively different from the pretending with toys. For this reason, later additions to store, houseplay and related activities were increasingly realistic.

Other criteria operated in selecting these materials. For example, dress-up supplies were chosen to give experience with different kinds of garments and to meet varying interests, but they were also selected to provide a variety of tactile clues. Lengths of satin ribbon, hats trimmed with velvet ribbon and feathers, scarves of wool and of nylon net, silk head-scarves, crinoline petticoats, a soft dimity apron and a practical broadcloth one, a fur neckpiece, shoes of various kinds were among the textured items the children used. Colors were varied to provide a wealth of visual experiences. High-heeled slippers, Dutch wooden shoes, Japanese pattens, and riding boots were included to promote meaningful auditory experiences. When textures, colors, and sounds were presented in this way, the children could absorb meanings as they used the materials. Teachers called attention to an attribute of an object when children had become familiar with the sight or sound or feel, and could concentrate on the term which described it. Buttons, snaps, apron ties, zippers and buckles were designedly available in the dress-up clothing, to allow experience with fastenings as preparation for teaching of processes. For example, play gloves and mittens, large and easy to manage, facilitated later management of the children's own gloves. The supplies were stored as sets of related objects in designated cupboards or shelves so that "putting-away time" at the end of a free-play period was a natural exercise in sorting and arranging.

Use of Materials

Ordinarily, with introduction of a unit of materials, children were encouraged to explore the possibilities of the items. The play was thus within unit limits at first, as each child sought out the items which appealed to him and with which he could work profitably. For example, the first play with dress-up clothing was one of trying on, parading, and trading of items. The children then incorporated the clothing into their dramatic play. Use of the play-store materials followed a similar pattern. The first reaction was an examination of food containers, cash register, and bags. This was followed by manipulative play: children filled bags with groceries and emptied them, until they mastered the process to their own satisfaction. After that, the grocery store became a center of shopkeeping and shopping and a contributing sequence in house-play. The second-year use of the store setting included making items to be sold, utilizing the handwork skills described in another section of this report.

Occasionally, play sequences were stimulated by individual items in the sets of materials. A red-fox neckpiece was at various times a Davy Crockett hat, the fox that ate the gingerbread boy, and Santa Claus's beard. Interestingly, one child who ordinarily played quietly alone and who spoke seldom, but who evidenced delicate pantomime, was discovered to be the source of much imaginative dramatic play. The fur also suggested to one of the girls a visit to the principal of her "son's" school; this enactment of a parent whose child was in difficulty was reproduced in various guises by others. A length of veiling also suggesting a wedding with many play sequences. The activities and the reactions were as numerous and as varied as the children in the group.

At free-play time, were often seen one subgroup playing in the doll-corner, another small group building with the blocks, a third at a worktable busy with puzzles or crayons. A single child might be looking at books in the library corner, another riding on the small tractor, watching the others yet mainly interested in his own physical activity.

Teacher Participation

The teachers, during the free-play period, had opportunity to move from one center of activity to another, giving help where needed, joining dramatic play occasionally, talking briefly with the solitary children, but always watching the use of materials, the direction of play, and the ideas expressed by individual children. In this kind of play the children reaffirmed the situations and the relationships which they knew. It was possible to note gains from class handwork processes, and to get an estimate of abilities which had previously found no expression in the regular curriculum activities. Leadership skills and special interests were observed as well as areas in which individual children needed reinforcement or encouragement. Short as the free-play period was, it supplied many of the ideas for further work with the classes. The teachers built their plans on the firm base of what the children already knew. They could, during this period, begin to enlist the children as active curriculum planners: a child, putting away the tractor or trundling the shopping cart back to the store, might say, "Tomorrow I'm going to play this again." Such casual remarks were steps in effective classroom planning, by children whose previous planning was limited to making choices.

Related Learnings

The scope for expression of past knowledge, and the basis for planning ahead were two contributions of the free-play activities to the general curriculum goals. Gains were also noted in concept development and in communication. The imaginative games as a form of role-playing permitted children who might evade participation in regular class discussions to talk freely and effectively to others. For example, a quiet child who preferred to play alone in the kitchen corner assumed the role of nurse for a boy who pretended injury when his elevated train structure collapsed on him, made the spoon in her hand serve as a thermometer, and cleared the hospital room of visitors firmly and efficiently. Yet, in other curriculum activities she assumed no noticeable leadership function. Even though the leadership might be long in transferring to actual situations, the teachers' observations showed the direction which this child's program might take. Communication among the children and between teachers and children, relative to the materials including games and puzzles was free and purposeful. There were time and opportunity to talk with or read to a child who had a speech problem and to elicit verbal behavior.

The difference between the real and the make-believe emerged in many of the activities. At first a role seemed to linger after toys had been put away, and the "pretending" would be noted as such, with a suggestion that the child remember to play the same game the next day. The children's echoing of this kind of remark has already been mentioned. Part of the concept of time, including past, now, and tomorrow, was built upon free-play experiences. Increasingly larger blocks of time figured in the planning in the same way. Time within the school hours also came to the children's attention: one day, when a handwork project continued past the usual time and it was discovered that the hands of the clock already

indicated juice time, one little girl moved about, picked up materials and repeated, "Shucks! No free play!" It is noteworthy that the materials themselves supplied openings for talk about other children in other places, as well as for review of settings the class had visited and which they could locate as belonging to their own city environment.

On the surface, the free play seemed to be a period of relaxed limits. But a paradox observed on the roof and in the gymnasium was also observable here. The responsibility for action was transferred to the children, who were governed by their own knowledge of the materials they used. This self-discipline seemed more powerful and the limits more evident than in any teacher-directed situation. Also, the limits operated because the children were working in familiar language contexts; they knew what to do with dress-up clothing, or groceries, or brooms because they had seen the complete action hundreds of times. The settings transferred from other curriculum areas were also familiar and practiced, so that children knew how to use the materials for their own ends. A negative affirmation of this observation on self discipline comes from an experience with blocks. These materials were unfamiliar to some of the children. Left to draw on their own experiences they used them as make-believe cars, as things to throw, or as tools to reconstruct the block-building they had encountered in psychological-test situations. It was necessary to demonstrate what could be done with a cupboard full of blocks, and to use blocks as handwork material, until the children had enough experience to enable them to make original structures. Blockbuilding was a suitable free-play activity only for those children who had learned to use them.

Similarly, activities first regarded by the teachers as work became, with experience, favorite play items. Easel painting and clay work were two of these, as were many of the handwork objects. The distinction between work and play seemed, under the circumstances, to be a technicality of which only the teachers were aware. Toward the end of their experiences in the Project, the children were introduced to the idea of a "work period". Choices in such a period were limited to the materials ordinarily found in grade-school settings as distinguished from the kindergarten-nursery setting. The children found that they were choosing as work the things they chose also as play, and discovered that their liking was for the activity, by whatever name it might be called.

Materials for Free Play

a. Houseplay. Kitchen: stove, sink, cupboard, table, chairs, cooking utensils, dishes, facsimile foods, hot pads, tea towels; living room: settee, cushions, rocker, rugs; bedroom: bed, chest, bedding doll carriage; miscellaneous: broom, dustpan, dustmop, mop, shopping cart, ironing board and iron, telephones, mailbox.

b. Construction sets. Polished maple blocks all shapes, wooden boat set and train set, rubber animals and people, plastic figures, tinker toys, snapblocks, car construction sets.

c. Manipulation materials. Color towers, cubes, nested cubes; keyboard, color-shape insets, sewing boards, beads of all sizes; mailbox, lock garage, number pegs, abacus; inset and jigsaw puzzles, parquetry, puzzle pegboards, spelling frames, rubber band frames, magnetized letters and numbers; hammerboards, hammers and nails; stamp printing sets.

d. Games. Lotto: picture match and language match; bingo, dominoes, picture dominoes, checkers, color wheel "Let's face it."

e. Dress-up. Women's clothing: dresses, skirts, blouses; men's clothing: pants, shirts, coats; foot-wear: riding boots, wooden shoes, Japanese sandals, high heeled shoes, button spats, fur slippers, bath clogs; headgear: women's and men's dress hats, bonnets, costume and "occupation" hats, scarves, veiling, caps; handcoverings: large and small mittens, gloves, gauntlets; miscellaneous: necklaces, bracelets, rings, ribbons, belts, fur piece, aprons, shawls.

f. Store play. Papier maché foods, plastic and wooden eggs, wax fruits, food cartons and cans; cash register, balance scale, paper bags, shopping bags, play money, canned juice.

g. Soapsuds play, dough play. Soap-flakes, flour, salt; rotary beaters, egg whips, rolling pins, spoons, knives, cookie cutters, fluted paper cups, tooth picks, candles, thimbles, pans.

h. Fishing. Fishing poles; rods and reels; plastic hooks and fish; magnets, metal fish; snap clothespins; shells, small boats; plastic pail, pans.

i. Teacher-made "box books." Story settings: family, traffic, farm, fire-truck, picnic, cowboy, nursery tales, Indians, boats; activity sets: bubble pipes, whistles, feathers, balloons; table settings, color boxes, nested toys, boxes of various shapes; vibration toys: metal chains, coil springs, box puzzles with rolling pieces, rattles; miniature tools, cars, windup toys, friction toys, rubber tools; magnetic toys; magnifying toys; ribbon, thread, and yarn collections; matched sets of metal, wood, plastic, and rubber toys; weights for balance scale.

JUICE TIME

A juice or refreshment period was scheduled for the children, who were away from home five to seven hours. Ordinarily, this period occurred at about the mid-point of the daily session, and became part of an interlocking sequence of activities. In a sample program, juice time was preceded by opening exercises, a discussion period, a handwork activity, and a free-play period. Putting toys away, toileting, and hand-washing, which were clean-up activities, were, in essence, preparations for juice time and merged naturally into table setting and arrangement of food. Similarly, clean-up after juice was preparation for the play or gym period, music, story or project work which comprised the second part of the day's program. As children learned the position of juice time and maintained themselves within the routine, the action processes, including the preparation of classroom, of self and of tables, the pouring of juice and the casual table conversation, appeared as much a part of the refreshment, as were the cookies and juice. Children's focus was on whose turn it was to pour juice as well as on the kind of juice available. Obviously hungry, children were willing to postpone eating for the apparent satisfaction of pouring or of passing out special-occasion treats.

Program alterations including the extension of a planned activity into the regular juice period and unusual expenditure of energy, resulted in behavioral changes. Frequent were children's verbalizations about time and their being very hungry. However, overt impatience was rare; they expected and seemed to prefer usual preparations even when juice time was delayed.

Manipulative and Motor Activity

The juice period afforded opportunity for coordinated physical actions. Eye and hand worked together in fine movements to manage a spoon, a cup, or a pitcher; gross movements of the body or body parts were restricted by the nearness of other children, the table, or the juice pitcher. Practiced through the year were carrying, lifting, tilting without spilling, pouring and the stopping of pouring and relinquishing the pitcher to others. Carrying a full bowl of crackers, washing pitchers and bowls, lifting a paper cup to the lips or handing it to another child without crushing it presented problems to be solved by the four-and-five-year-olds. Variations in refreshments promoted their experimentation in use of spoons for stirring and tasting, as well as for handling hot drinks; of small wooden spoons for ice cream; of dull knives for spreading; and of forks for eating cake and other foods.

Throughout the Project years, teacher attention was required when children miscalculated distance in pouring juice or deliberately disregarded the comfort of others. But daily practice enabled the children to move confidently toward physical competence and toward management of the physical components of the juice time activity while their social interactions, particularly conversation, were increasingly noted.

Sensory Discrimination

Food offered at juice time provided experiences with varied flavors, textures, and odors, in addition to the usual crisp cookies and fruit juices. Refreshments after swimming included instant soup, hot milk, hot punch or "spice tea." Other flavors and textures included marshmallow cookies, popcorn, matzos, juice mixtures, birthday cakes, pastries, and ice cream. Juice time also, because it was a nucleus for later cooking activities, afforded opportunities for handling, discussing, preparing, and eating "simple" items such as carrot sticks, carrot curls, celery, peas in the pod, nuts, jelly, peanut butter, coconut, and instant pudding.

To foster taste discrimination, children sampled different items. Obvious dislikes were respected, and marked preferences were noticed and elicited comments. Children were guided toward equitable sharing of favorite foods. Experimentation with combinations was encouraged. To most pupils, however, common adult preferences for sweet foods with fruit juice or milk and bland or salty foods with tomato or vegetable juice were already in evidence.

Communication Skills

In the juice time setting, development of communication skill seemed to follow two directions. One of these was toward increased vocabulary; the other was toward the use of speech to relate to others. The teachers noted that the context, i.e., the known process of eating, the relaxation of pupils and teachers gathered together around the table, as well as the familiar and the unfamiliar food items, apparently promoted verbal activity. Several children without functional speech or with extremely limited vocabularies evidenced initial use of words and increased ease in communication during the juice period. The situation evidently provided a comfortable speech setting.

Vocabulary expansion areas included food names, number and space terms, and qualitative words, as well as names of utensils and equipment. Introduction of terms at the action-language level and in sentence format seemed to promote sentence and paragraph understandings and subsequent use by the group. The usual formal expression of "More," "Thank you," "I want . . .," "May I have . . .?", "Please pass . . ." were augmented by comparisons of taste, statements about favorites, and comments about similar foods at home. Verbal responses included comments on the food being tried or general conversation about similar foods and references to television commercials. Vocabulary development per se occurred as an element of the communication process in the meaningful eating activity. Use of new terms and expressions occurred in and was explained by the related activities.

Similarly, patterns of social behavior evolved through the juice period. Passing, dividing, and sharing of food could be experienced and practiced, since sharing extended from food to school activities. The coveted pouring process, for example, was shared both verbally and physically, as one child held cups for the pourer and others passed the filled cups. Mishaps also were shared. Early in the class experience spilled juice was handled by a teacher as she demonstrated use of paper towels and sponges as well as an attitude of accepting accidents. Later, a child was directed toward the sponge or towel and helped to mop up spilled juice. Still later, the child who spilled took care of the situation independently or with the advice of a classmate. Eventually, some children assumed responsibility for wiping up spilled juice, regardless of who had spilled it. The focus of their attention had moved from the spilling and spiller to the general comfort of the group and the restoration of that comfort. This was active socialization.

Juice time provided a situation base for introducing visitors to children wary or timorous of strangers. In this context children imitated teacher patterns and invited family members, observers and other Project workers to share refreshments. Children's personal responsibility on such occasions seemed to extend to their making the brief visit entertaining and pleasant. They shared ideas as well as food.

Concept Development

Particularly noted among the conceptualizations expanded in the juice period experiences were those of time, of spatial arrangements, and of quantity. The children's expectation of juice appeared with reference to the scheduled position of the period. At first, the teacher's announcement tied together two ideas, i.e., "It is time to wash your hands." and the getting out of the record player, or the warning that materials should be put away which resulted in anticipation of lavatory preparations, table-setting and the refreshments. By the first year's close, children located events as "before juice" or "after juice." They also recast the day when a special event altered the routine and adjusted to postponement in time or change in location of their refreshment period. Evidence of interest in clock-time was noted as children used in casual conversation the teachers' phraseology such as "It's time for juice," "Look at that clock!," "It's almost time," "Harry will be here," "What time is it?"

Opportunities to deal with space in various ways were inherent in the juice time sequence. A notable example was the process of setting the two long tables, given the exact number of napkins and cups. When chairs were not yet in place, first attempts usually resulted in a non-functional close line of napkins and cups on each table. Proper placement of chairs, comments and help from the teacher, and subsequent observation of appearance of the tables with children seated for juice, brought about more adequate table setting by a few children. Calculation seemed to be based on "one for Tom and one for Bill and one for Patty" rather than a concept of "three on each side."

Juice pouring presented a space and manipulation problem. After considerable teacher demonstration of filling cups at each place, the children were given opportunity to pour. A major difficulty came in stopping the flow of liquid: cups were filled to overflowing. Attention had to be drawn to the cup and the in-coming liquid in contrast to the "pouring till empty" process of other activities such as sand play. Children were shown how to fill the cup to a designated level or to "half full." In response, they at first poured only a small amount and stopped, then increased the amount gradually. Toward the end of the first year,

overfilling occured only in cases of sudden or major distraction.

Cookies, crackers and other foods provided daily number experience. Introduction was through the basic idea of extremes; i.e., a bowlful of crackers or no more crackers, a handful of pretzels or one pretzel, and "another" as an additive term. Children showed awareness of different quantities and of serial quantities, when able to choose one, two or three items as suggested, to designate those quantities and to ask for "more" represented by four, five, or six. Quantitative concepts were expanded through use of children's notions of relative size. For example, when confronted with a plate of irregular bits of chocolate, children usually selected the largest piece. Children, sharing a cracker or an apple, at first broke or cut it into many tiny pieces; later a more realistic division matching vaguely the number of children was realized.

The juice-time setting also provided one of several daily opportunities for turn-taking. For coveted duties, assignments were made regularly. Setting the table, passing unusual treats, making sure that each child got his sample of new or special cookies, clearing the table, and carrying the wastebasket around the tables to collect used napkins and cups were all processes involving order. Performances, with anticipation and remembrance of other "turns," seemed fruitful in helping children to discover and reenforce meanings of future and past.

Other curriculum settings resulted in learnings similar to the juice time behavior changes, but the relaxed situation, with children and teachers participating in a familiar recurring activity, seemed to foster the early development of many skills and relationships.

Supplies and Equipment for Juice Time

a) Juice concentrates: frozen and canned juice, instant drinks (chocolate, fruit, carbonated), lemons; b) hot drinks: instant milk, instant cocoa, whole sugar, spices, instant soup, salt; c) crackers, pretzels, dry cereals, cookies, popcorn, potato chips and fruits of all kinds; bread, rolls, spreads, canned foods; d) pitchers, bowls, cups, plates, cutlery, picnic basket, table-cloth; paper cups, plates, napkins, towels, placemats; can opener, electric cooker, corn popper; sponges, tea towels, scouring powder, soap.

PLAYGROUND AND GYMNASIUM ACTIVITIES

The roof area and its equipment provided extensive opportunity for the types of play the small children enjoyed; the gymnasium facilities were used when weather conditions precluded roof play. When classes gained a degree of group cohesion, play activities were sometimes transferred to the larger playground area of a nearby park. Although similar behavioral learnings were promoted in both the roof playground and the gymnasium, children's activities varied in accord with the physical features and kinds of equipment appropriate to the differing settings.

The Roof

The roof equipment was planned to provide several activity settings. Personal motion was fostered through wheel toys including a pedal tractor, tricycles (two sizes), wheel-barrows, luggage truck, scooter, and Irish mail. Large hollow blocks, planks, climbing frames and boxes, ladders and wooden horses offered materials for building and large-movement games. A sand box with numerous play items, small trucks and toy animals afforded manipulation experiences. A rocking boat, metal rocking tubs and rocking frames for see-saws provided for still other activities. The water fountain and faucet, nails, tubs, washboard, large paint brushes, clothespins and clothes line, mop and broom were provided for carry-over house-play. A slide and jumping ropes were available for children to practice familiar activities. The assortment of materials assured each child of at least one activity in the range of his experience or readiness and at least one set of materials with intrinsic motivation for his constructive play.

Major consideration was given to readiness for the roof itself as well as readiness for getting there. The most important preparation for use of the roof was for the trip through the halls of the college building, the elevator ride, and the final stair climbing. The prospect of roof play, once experienced, acted as strong motivation to climbing and to orderly progress through the halls. Used largely in the framework of this physical activity period, the stairways and halls were teaching materials through the year. Four children, extremely timid about the roof or roof equipment, were helped to develop varying degrees of self-reliance through continued physical reassurance and verbal encouragement.

The roof area provided for free movement, motor activity of various kinds, and for vocal play not comfortable in the classroom. Choice of activity was made by the individual child, with limits to behavior supplied by the interpersonal situation. Early use of the sand-box included both individual and parallel activity, with a fluid participating group. The youngest and most timid children continued to prefer sand-box play; others moved gradually to a variety of games and to establishment of small group relationships through the year. The sand-box served as a base from which children moved to try other activities and to which they frequently returned. Early use of wheel toys was ordinarily exploratory and individual. Turn-taking and sharing were reenforced by establishing schedules for use of one-of-a-kind vehicles and procedures for use of blocks, climbing equipment, and the slide. A major social responsibility was the neat arrangement of the shed for use by another group. This activity concluded each play period.

The early exploratory and learning processes became part of later development of group games and processes. Climbing frames, ladders and boxes were turned into zoo cages in which to act out animal games, "stages" for singing and dancing, pirate ships or fishing boats, circus ladders and trapezes, or settings for houseplay of various kinds. The wheel toys, serving as cars or trucks, stopped for traffic lights, pulled into gas stations, or became parts of parades. The sandbox allowed for filling, pouring and modeling, in an imaginative context of cooking, truck-loading, or simply "playing at the beach." The roof's fountain promoted the carrying of small pails of water and experimentation with elementary mixing.

The cooperative play was essentially a carry-over from story and conversation periods in the classroom as well as from actual experiences. Particularly noteworthy were the numerous opportunities for acted-out problem solving. Among these were the use of hollow blocks and boards to construct benches for juice time, when that event was transferred to the roof, or of the wheelbarrow, shovels, and a board-ramp to sweep up spilled sand and return it to the sand-box.

The roof setting as a whole lent itself to the development of various concepts through action with its contents. Number and order, for example, were implicit in the use of single toys, the parade games, and the storing of toys. The panoramic view of the George Washington Bridge, the hills along the Hudson river, the rooftops stretching north from the college, and the closer view of college buildings and streets were all part of a concept of distance discussed from time to time. Use of the slide, in a favorite game, provided practice in listening to names of classmates and self. Later, fantasy entered and children assumed roles of various animals in learning to come <u>safely</u> down the slide prone or backward. Finally, a "set" for problem solving was noted as children transferred classroom processes to the roof situation.

When the park playground was the site of play activities, comparisons of size, quantity, and number of pieces of equipment could be made by the children. They commented, for example, on the difference between the roof sand-box and the park sand-box area and the comparative adequacy of space for specified group games. The slide "game" helped to overcome timidity on slides and swings which dwarfed the roof equipment. Established regulations for staying in a group with partners, routines for stair-climbing, and habits of safety also were paralleled in the hazardous trek across Broadway to the public park.

Gymnasium Activities

Two gymnasiums were available to the Project classes at various times. One was a large gym with basketball court, a balcony for track-practice, and along one wall vertical ladders, horizontal bars, and tumbling mats. It was used when large motor activity, swift movement, and strenuous climbing seemed to be in order. Activities for this setting were discussed in advance to establish the purposes to be accomplished there. Otherwise the wide floor space, and the echoes from high ceiling and walls resulted in a scattering and a loss of self-direction. The large, bare room seemed to suggest random behavior to these small children.

In the smaller gym, equipped with a slide, tumbling mats, a climbing frame, a horizontal ladder, and rope swings, small-group activities occurred naturally, and large-group games fitted into the sequence of activities. Beginning experiences in foot-races, in use of tumbling mats, and in folk games were part of the small-gym activity. Balls carried to the gym provided practice in bouncing, tossing and catching, and song games such as <u>Farmer-in-the-Dell</u>, <u>Looby-loo</u>, and <u>London Bridge</u> were either introduced or re-experienced here.

Unusual opportunities for experience with other children also occurred. The project group watched children in the Agness Russell Center's elementary school perform intricate folk dances, and saw them line up to go through the hall. In other words, they observed from the standpoint of their own experiences, similar experiences in an older group, and drew generalizations.

General Observations

The roof, public playground, and gym appeared to be settings for a lessened control and a freer movement, but in the situations personal limits of turn-taking, responsibility for play not encroaching on rights of others, and responsibility for leaving on command a satisfying play situation had to be comprehended by each child and acted upon by him. The small gym and the roof, with focal apparatus, were more suited to internal control than the large gym which promoted activity and movement sometimes difficult to manage.

The routine playtime warning "Five more minutes" helped to quiet the children before equipment was gathered up and the activity redirected. In the acquisition of useful gross motor-skills was also found development of the self-direction necessary for this kind of play.

Equipment and Materials for Roof and Gym

Roof:

a. Sandbox: pails, shovels, spoons, molds, sifters, funnels, small cars, boats, sticks, pails, brooms for clean up.
b. Hollow blocks, boards.
c. Climbing frames, ladders, rocking boat, seesaws, slide, rocking saucers.
d. Tricycles, wagons, wheelbarrows, scooter, pedal car, Irish mail, trucks.
e. Jumping ropes; rope swings (made by children) croquet set (plastic).

Gym:

a. Slide, vertical ladders, ladder trapeze, parallel bars, horses, pendulum swings, climbing frame.
b. Beach balls, basketball, small ball, wooden hoops, jumping rope.

STORY TELLING

In the Project classes "story telling" assumed various forms; the stories ranged from the factual to the fantastic. The list of stories used in the pre-school classes was long and varied. It included many of the contemporary books for children and classic nursery tales, in addition to teacher-made booklets which turned curriculum happenings into stories. Certain stories, however, held the interest of all four groups of children, and books containing them were worn out and replaced during the four years. Such stories generally had meanings which extended curriculum interests and activities, family associations, and common experiences. Another factor not to be minimized was the teacher's enthusiasm for a story. The force of interpersonal relationships was evident as children's listening enjoyment seemed in direct ratio with the teacher's preference in telling.

Three "top favorites" were studied to determine criteria for story selection. Caps for Sale, in repeated readings and tellings, seemed to be liked because of its strong plot with swift movement, its details which matched details of child life; the clear pictures illustrating incidents of the plot; and the simple text modified when necessary to an even simpler level. Re-readings were pleasurable, because the critical phases of the plot allowed for audience participation. Added to the above qualifications was the content relative to monkeys, amusing ones. This factor seemed to be the initial point of interest.

Another universal favorite was The Carrot Seed. Added to the factors noted in Caps for Sale was a parallel phonograph record which increased the story's detail. Readings of this book were half musical, with children interpolating the refrain from the recording, "No, no, it won't come up," at the proper places. A third contemporary book, The Little Cowboy, although it lacked a tight plot, had so many connotations for children who watched TV westerns and who coveted cowboy hats that it maintained a four-year popularity. The separate incidents were meaningful; the sequential pictures increased understanding. A supplemental record for this book also enhanced its enjoyment. Of the nursery tales, The Three Bears seemed to be the favorite, with a shortened version of The Three Little Pigs ranking second.

The stories described above, were adaptable to dramatization, to the child's story telling, to conversation, and to related handwork activities. Teacher-made books such as Flopsy Flora and Eensie-weensie Spider, made illustrating favorite songs, withstood many tellings and singings. So also did Billy's Hat, The Roof Book, and other true stories of the children's day-to-day activities. Interest in these varied tales seemed positively related to the extent to which they reiterated and gave utterance to experiences of the children.

The story-telling process varied from group to group and from story to story. In some classes, the activity assumed the traditional aspect of the story hour, with children sitting in a close circle around the teller. At other times, it was a conversation group around a table, with the book or with tangible props passing from hand to hand as the plot unfolded. Narrative records provided another kind of setting in which the teacher also was a listener or a leader when listener-participation was indicated. Finally, the music consultant's weekly visit was occasionally a story experience in which the consultant wove rhythmic dramas, absorbed and then enacted by the children.

Each story presentation minimized the story time as a way of telling and emphasized it as a way of listening. The form of the teller-listener situation was determined by the kind of response wanted from the children. Listeners in the circle about the teacher sought one thing; children with book in hand saying "Read this to me" wanted another; the group at a record player expected a third outcome. The essential feature of any listening arrangement was the extent to which the arrangement furthered the purpose of the experience. Enforced attendance in any arrangement guaranteed little more than bodily attention. On the other hand, freedom to withdraw from the group, which seemed necessary occasionally for a child or two in the various groups, did not preclude sharing in the story. Children appeared to listen in many ways, and were taught new attitudes of attention as teachers recognized these ways as related to the concept of listening.

Learnings from the story experiences were reflected in the other curriculum areas. As some stories drew upon the children's experiences, so other stories could be transformed into experiences by way of dramatization, imitation, paraphrasing, and finally criticizing. Children sought distinctions between the real and the make-believe, a concept which was reinforced in many other experiences. They told or "read" stories to small-group audiences or to puppets, composed oral dramas for their free-play, compared TV programs and films they had seen, and brought books from home to be read and discussed. Interest in Alice in Wonderland, for example, was not in the story, which apparently had been absorbed from a film, but in the puzzling quick changes, the magic. They sought help in relating magic to the developed ideas of real and make-believe.

A major value of the story program appeared to be the development of this critical faculty. One class's final interest in The Three Bears was in a comparison of versions of the tale. The items compared seemed to indicate the story's attraction for children. Comments included, "My story says 'porridge,' not 'soup'"; "My story says she jumped out of the window and ran home"; "Oh, no! My story says she ran down the stairs"; "My story says she ran home to her mama". The reiterated "My story says . . .", appeared to show realization of the "make-believeness" of stories. Comments indicated that interest was in familiar objects such as beds, bowls, spoons, and chairs. The bears apparently were interesting as Father, Mother, Baby, but as bears they elicited the comment, "Oooh! I'm afraid of bears!"

A second large concept drawn from the use of books was of the value of books per se. Some children came from homes with an appreciation of books as sources of enjoyment and information; others apparently acquired this appreciation during their attendance in class. Interest in symbolic media developed steadily, so that the older groups, the six-year-olds, began to look at and to study pictures, to locate pages they wanted read because of the illustrations, and to inspect newspaper magazine sections for meaningful symbols. A few of the children tried also to decipher print letters and words. The story program was thus a part of the route toward reading readiness. It served to identify first pictures and then printed texts as expressions of things the children knew from their own experiences.

Materials for Storytelling

Books: factual (real-life, science); folk tales; animal stories; children's rhymes; number, color books, fingerplay, teacher-made song and story books, experience books.

Tangible materials: sets of small toys illustrating stories; punch out books; illustrative items; class-made 3 dimensional materials; real fruits, vegetables, other foods; stand-up cut outs and silhouettes; maps, room plans.

Flannel board and cut outs: Blackboard and large sheets of paper, colored chalk; marker pens for "chalk-talk" stories.

SWIMMING

"Swimming" in the College indoor pool provided an unusual curriculum opportunity in a highly-motivating setting. It was designed to familiarize the children with the water, to help them to become comfortable and reliable in water, to enable them to appreciate swimming as recreation and to afford opportunity for application of other school learnings. Some children learned to swim a few strokes although swimming instruction was not the essential purpose. More important, children learned to dress and undress efficiently, to use a hairdryer, and to utilize inner control. The teachers focused on development of habits of enjoyment and of security in the situation.

Use of the pool required both the staff arrangements for the children's safety and the preparation of the children themselves for what would be, for most of them, a new experience. A doctoral student in the Department of Health Education, Physical Education and Recreation at Teachers College served as life guard during the first years; a professor in that Department gave her time during the final year. The two teachers and either the language developmentalist or the Project observer participated in the weekly swimming, with substitutions by teachers of the alternate group when necessary. Early in the year the ratio of one adult to four children was necessary, later, one to six was deemed adequate.

The children's preparation was comprehensive and began in advance of actual pool use. During the first two years, only the six-year-olds participated in the program, the younger group visiting the pool in the Spring to become familiar with the setting. During the first weeks of the Fall session, plans for swimming were discussed and all children were taken to see the pool and to watch other groups swim. They inspected the dressing rooms, met the pool attendant, and were shown how to walk in the pool area. Thus, prior to their first swimming day, they had practiced some of the necessary routines and knew that swimming privileges were contingent upon acceptance of teacher guidance. Other instructions were developed as the children entered the situations in which the directions were needed. These were reinforced when necessary by suspension from the pool for a stated interval. The rules were:

1. Walk at all times in the pool area (dressing rooms, corridor, etc.)
2. Stay outside the pool gate until the teacher gives the signal to enter.
3. Stay in the shallow water marked by the rope and floats.
4. Be careful of others in the pool with you.
5. Follow teacher directions instantly, when in the pool.

Teacher direction of this activity seemed accepted as a natural element of the situation. Similar parent direction in previous experiences probably formed the base of partly established habits on which teachers were building.

Children who were uneasy upon first entrance into the water were included by teachers and by more competent children in the varied activities while they sat on the steps which led into the water. Timid children entered the pool step by step, over several weeks. A child was given support in entering the water if he wanted to try; he was not forced to enter the pool. The general atmosphere was one of relaxation and close association with the teacher, a swimming participant. With this approach, children gradually developed confidence and a measure of judgment and self-reliance in the pool.

Play in the pool included splashing, blowing bubbles, catching a large ball, holding the nose and ducking under water, and clinging to handrail or to a surfboard held by a teacher. Some children learned to jump into the water from the side of the pool; the lifeguard, watching individual children from her vantage point, suggested variations from time to time. Children experimented with prone floating, floating on their backs, and diving. They imitated arm strokes of various kinds, while walking about the pool, and many efforts were made to keep afloat. The few children who began to swim used an easy "frog" stroke developing from the prone float and at first swam a few inches under water.

Related Learnings

As a curriculum setting, the swimming program provided a variety of opportunities for children to excel. Competence in the water drew the admiration of children and teachers; skill in dressing or in gathering up towels and suits for the pool attendant was recognized and appreciated. A major gain was in an unanticipated direction toward oral communication. On swimming days, the juice time discussion dealt primarily with experiences in the pool. An early attempt at sequential accounts, by several children with little speech was the recitation of the swimming experiences. Communication seemed fostered by the shared experience: every person in the group knew what was being said, even though articulated words might be imperfect and the sentences fragmentary. During the week, accounts were volunteered to others, for example the music consultant, who had not been present. Also, the first real appreciation of time stemmed from this experience. The swimming day was known by name and seemed to be located absolutely, within the week. "Tomorrow we swim," became "Today is _____. We swim today!" The concept was carried from week to week, and provided a basis for other time concepts.

Equipment for Swimming

Large balls, wood floats, plastic floats.

COOKING

The cooking activities in the Project classes seemed to fall into three stages. The first, preparatory activities, included group handwork and free-play which, in their increasing complexity, fostered refinement of manipulation necessary for cooking processes. The second stage, group processes, was the development of autonomous activity in small groups, as part of a larger group activity. The third stage, the cooking project, was actual food preparation requiring a) skill with aids such as knife, spoon, egg-beater, fingers, and b) self-direction by individuals or small-group units. This step-by-step process, which moved from preparation of simple foods to the staging of a buffet tea, was a progression only to the teachers. For the children, each activity occurred as a complete and meaningful project. Preliminary steps were not necessarily related to cooking though some were imitative or imaginative cooking. The teacher's purpose in all cooking activities, was the development of the child's independent functioning within and contributing to a group.

Preparatory Activities

Work with modeling clay and with play dough provided several of the needed pre-cooking experiences. Rolling and patting of both media, cutting with dull knives, marking with forks or tongue depressors, cutting with cookie cutters, and arranging materials on pans for cooking were actions later utilized in complicated processes. Similarly, experimentation with soap suds of varying consistencies gave practice in using mechanical egg-beaters and spoons for stirring, as well as flat knives for spreading make-believe icing.

Dough play and soapsuds play also allowed for preliminary experiences in mixing raw ingredients. Initially, activity was with materials prepared before the session by the teacher. Later, the children's activity included making as well as playing with the materials.

Experiences with actual foods also formed part of the preparatory activity. Children shelled peas, scrubbed carrots and celery, broke up cookies to share with others, pulled grapes from a bunch, stemmed and ate strawberries. They also cut celery, made carrot curls, and sliced apples to share at juice time.

Instant pudding, instant milk, chocolate milk drinks, instant soup, and hot fruit juice to which sugar could be added provided experiences in which all used beaters and spoons and saw that adding one ingredient to another made an interesting food item for juice time. Other preparations for the refreshment period included spreading butter, peanut butter and jelly on crackers or bread, and cracking or shelling walnuts and peanuts. Use of thumb and finger, hammer, or nutcracker for this latter activity was a particularly absorbing experience for the small children.

Group Processes

In all of the preparatory activities, the materials and actions were selected because each child could perform them. The similar products for individual movements created multiple reinforcement when a child needed the added clue of observation to work effectively. The preparatory group processes, on the other hand, worked toward a single unified end but provided for a delayed end-product. The delay, as materials hardened, roasted or jelled, was used as part of the teaching plan: children were a) directed toward free-play or work activities, b) encouraged to check upon the stages of the cooking, and c) recalled into a unified group as the project neared completion.

Cooking Projects

Corn popping was the first major cooking project since its introduction included inspecting ears of popcorn, husks, and silk; shelling the corn; washing it; and helping with the measuring of oil and corn. Full attention was given as children shelled and helped to gather up corn scattered in the process. Several children participated in setting up the "popping area" and monitored the bowls of washed corn, while others brought individual small bowls and cups from the kitchen area and juice cupboard. Those selecting other activities retained the focus on cooking as they moved back and forth from the circle around the popper. All children put away materials and gathered at the tables when the popped corn was ready to eat. After this first experience, use of the popper for corn was real. It became the object of anticipation: children could shell extra corn, or wash it, as they chose, or could select other waiting activities. The first experience with chestnuts was also a full-attention enterprise for part of the period, the slitting of the shells became a focal activity until chestnuts were ready to taste.

When the children had become reliable in the simple basic activities and were also responsible for working neatly, some cooking activities were transferred to a laboratory kitchen of the Home and Family Life Department of the College. Here,

applesauce, corn-bread, tossed salad, and other foods were prepared within a classroom time-schedule, with the children taking turns and sharing activities. They managed the deferred result element by means of a conversation period, singing, or story-telling. Activities in two of the more complicated projects are listed below to illustrate the extent to which previously learned skills were used in the later cooking program. One is a simple process, making pudding, involving use of heat; the other, preparing canapes, a process with several separate, simultaneous activities.

Cooked pudding:

a. Trip to the store for ingredients:

b. Pouring:

Bottle to cup
Cup to pan
Pudding to bowl

c. Measuring:

Milk in measuring cup

d. Opening package:

Pudding boxes
Wax envelope

e. Stirring:

Watching thickening process

Canapes for buffet lunch:

a. Mixing:

Cream cheese and olive
Sour cream and onion
Cream cheese and cherry

b. Cutting:

Bread shapes with cookie cutters

c. Spreading:

Decorating with olive circles and cherry rings

d. Arranging on trays:

e. Final steps:

Selecting canapes for own plate, from buffet
Getting juice from a second serving table
Returning for refills (taking "conservative" amounts)
Offering trays to visitor

Learnings

Learnings in the sense-training areas of taste and smell were implicit in the cooking program. Children sampled all items, commented on new tastes, revised former reactions to some tastes, or discovered dislike for certain strange flavors. They learned that appearance and odor were at times misleading, as in the case of roasted chestnuts and coconut milk, or surprising, as in the case of the cinnamon sticks used for making spice tea, or helpful, as when green onions (scallions) were identified not by name but by odor.

There was a noticeable increase in vocabulary, paralleled by gains in information about combinations of foods. Tossed salad with crackers, cocoa with marshmallows, sliced cucumbers for bread-and-butter sandwiches, cornbread with butter and applesauce, are a few of the combinations evoking the children's appreciation and comments.

Larger concepts of turn-taking, sharing and cooperating were also part of this activity. The delayed-result element of some of the projects resembled the start-stop element of certain of the music activities, since both demanded self-management and alternating activity and inhibition on the part of the child.

In the total program, cooking seemed to be an experience area well adapted to strengthening parent-child-teacher relationships.

Materials for Cooking

a) Readymix cookies, cake, fudge, soup, cornbread, jello, pudding; fresh vegetables, fruits, nuts; bread, rolls, crackers, potato chips; butter, peanut butter, mayonnaise, jelly, sour cream; cream cheese, shredded coconut, decorettes, lump sugar, salt, whole spices.
b) Bowls, spoons, peelers, paring knives, forks, knives, rotary beaters, ladles, food coloring, rolling pins, cookie cutters, cake pans.
c) Corn popper, hot plate, electric cooker. Laboratory kitchen equipment: stoves, sinks, work tables.

TRIPS

In selecting and planning trips, consideration was given to the appropriateness of resources to the preschool level, and to the apparent and expressed interests of the children themselves. Their attention to transportation processes, play equipment, and animals determined choice from the many possibilities of nearby playgrounds and parks, the fire station, the subway, the bus, boat docks and ferry, the airport, and the city zoos. Interest in home and school events prompted shorter excursions to the school food services and to a college residence facility; among the frequently repeated trips were those to neighborhood stores and to parks. After serving as primary experiences, they became subordinate parts of increasingly complicated activities such as cooking projects or special parties. The transportation-based excursions provided series-type experiences. Still others, such as trips to various zoos, were regarded as preparation or follow-up to one another. Scheduling of the trips was similarly flexible. Ideally, it was felt, a spacing of trips to allow for the children's absorption of ideas was indicated. However, series-type and mutually-dependent experiences in quick succession were found to fit comfortably into a schedule when classroom preparation for the sequence of trips extended over a long period of time. Trips varied with each new group, during the four years. Both scheduling and selection of experiences depended upon the specific class and the specific situation.

General Preparation

First in importance in preparation for trips was the children's ability to assume a measure of responsibility for their own behavior. Thus, prior to off-campus or out-of-the classroom ventures was action preparation, including learning to move through the halls of the school building safely and with consideration for others; practice in negotiating stairways, elevators, and doorways and practice in safety procedures for street-crossing. Instructions relative to behavior for trips focused on broad areas of motor efficiency, language response, and safety concepts which included a personal responsibility for staying with partners and in contact with others.

The total group of fifteen children moved safely in explorations of the community. The most competent children were relied upon to help the accompanying adults in maintaining group cohesion. The one or two children slow in absorbing the idea of cohesiveness received special attention from teachers or others. More than three adults, unless children were subdivided into small groups, seemed to lessen application of personal responsibility, either because attention of individual children was directed toward one of several "centers," or because they automatically resumed prior habits of irresponsibility, dependency, and disorganization in the presence of several responsible adults.

In addition to the general readiness requirements, preparation for specific trip content was essential. The following examples of preparatory sequences for visits to a fire station by two different groups, are presented as possible approaches. One group, in preparing for the experience, surveyed the topic in class discussions, listened to stories and to phonograph records, and learned an appropriate song. Handwork periods before and after the trip were devoted to coloring pictures of fires and fire engines. Another group built on a fortunate opportunity to observe from their classroom window a fire drill at a neighboring school, then the evacuation of the building because of a real blaze, and the appearance of a fire engine. The teachers commented on what had been seen, and suggested that a visit to the fire station would be possible later in the spring. The plans were added to regular or calendar conversation, and were mentioned casually from time to time since this group was still in process of building necessary self-reliance. The planned trip was anticipated as one of a sequence but received no further advance notice. During the trip itself, questions and comments of group members referred to the school-building fire, as well as to other past experiences of individual children. Also, the calendar concept received unexpected reinforcement: from the deliberate building of the idea of scheduling a series of trips. As in selection and timing, the manner and extent of preparation seemed to be a function of the class composition and temper.

For the children's trips an advance teacher visit was required to make arrangements, assure a welcome, and determine emergency provisions. A trip to a park or zoo, or a ferryboat or subway ride, necessitated preliminary scouting and rehearsal of the trip by a teacher. For these groups of small children, fore-knowledge about escalators, turnstiles, ticket formalities, and restrooms was essential. This preliminary information, introduced into class discussion by means of drawings, photographs and samples or miniatures, formed part of the group preparation. Children knew ahead of time about certain procedures to be fitted into the trip when it occurred: the actual happening was reinforcement of the symbolic preparation, as well as an important experience in its own right.

Competence-Area Learnings

Learnings in the trip context seemed to fall into four major competence areas: motor and manipulative, language including both action and symbolic aspects, social, and conceptual. Objectives in each experience were appreciated in various ways by children and teachers: a trip was not merely "going someplace" or "seeing something," although the variety and novelty were undoubtedly important to the effectiveness of the experiences. As a result of earlier developed ideas, children had plans of things to do and ways to do them. The actual happenings during the progress of a trip were the spontaneous results of the earlier preparations.

Motor Learnings

The teachers knew the location of such obstacles as stairs, escalators, turnstiles and railings, and prepared the children for them. The school trip provided, even for children who had experienced the obstacles with their parents, opportunity for practicing skills of climbing, balancing and walking under rather exacting conditions. In a busy subway station there was no time for a timid child to decide whether or not a turnstile was "safe." Recorded by one teacher was a child's triumphant, "I did it!" One problem, a long step from a passenger plane to a temporary landing stage, offered each child an unexpected challenge. The exigencies of these situations raised performance levels for each child.

Similarly, small manipulative skills had to be comprehended and executed within seconds or minutes. Putting a token in a turnstile was, at first, a major problem. Subsequently the glimpse of a turnstile ahead evoked "sets" for the sequence of getting a token, putting it in a slot, and pushing through the stile. Being responsible for hats or sweaters, managing lunch bags, and balancing against the wind on a ferryboat were other instances of motor and manipulative adjustments apprehended and accomplished while attention was centered on activities such as looking at ducks, feeding elephants, and commenting on the pose of the Statue of Liberty. The situations were rich in child learning; they were deemed even better for teacher learning, as each occasion helped their assessments of individual children and their planning in appropriate motor and manipulative areas.

Social Learnings

Social relationships in general were also, on the trips, placed in the context of actual necessity and responsibility. Juice time, transferred perforce to the public situation, became a way of learning to eat a home-packed lunch, to buy a cold drink or box of crackerjack, to take a place at a table and maintain public decorum, to gather up and dispose of papers, napkins, cups and scraps. Conversation skills too were practiced. Listening was essential as a guide described a jet plane or a teacher commented on tugboats seen from a riverside dock. Answering the generalized, "And now, are there any questions?" with appropriate queries was a social as well as a conceptual response. The child who said "Thank you," or "We liked it," or smiled at an adult who made room for him at a railing was practicing socialization. Contact with practical problems of community living, such as correct use of water fountains, restrooms, checkout counters, and sidewalks, was turn-taking applied at the citizenship level.

Concept Development

Concepts of geographical space, time, quantity and self emerged from the trip activities. The halls of the Teachers College buildings, routes to stores and to parks, the paths laid out in the zoo grounds, and larger units such as the river and the New Jersey hills on the opposite bank were apparently meaningful to the children, since follow-up discussions and activities included questions about distant places, or about the homes of the teachers, and comments on sketch maps of neighborhood or zoo. One extension of concepts to a vicarious experience occurred upon recipt of a postcard map from a teacher.

The idea of time as a governing factor was inherent in the trip setting because of the involved transportation arrangements; some children altered habits of lagging behind or dashing ahead in order to stay with the group and maintain the schedule. The effect of time "habits" showed itself in hunger, which on several trips appeared at the customary refreshment hour. There was also interest in the actual plotting of a day's schedule, the expected sequence of events.

Ideas of number, quantity and size were explored in a variety of trip situations. Bears or chimpanzees, elephants or tiny monkeys, money to buy lunch-time drinks, big lunches or little ones, cookies sent by mothers for sharing at lunch-time, coins for the ferryboat ride, the long way back to the zoo gate and the long wait for Harry, the driver, plus the idea of partners and total number of children in the group are a few of the fact applications of how many, how big, how do they compare, and what do they mean for us.

Finally, the ideas of self-reliance, dependability, and social responsibility developed from

the social learnings noted above were felt to be important conceptualizations in the context of neighborhood and community.

Follow-up Activities

Derivative activities assumed many forms. They ranged from the more familiar drawing and pasting to three-dimensional mementoes, records and activity rehearsals in dramatic play. Details of the fire-station visit will serve as illustrations. Follow-ups by the two classes included drawing pictures of the fire station, equipment, and firemen; pasting cutouts to produce the fire-station scene; wording a letter of thanks and preparing pictures to send to the firemen; finding books containing related stories; singing with renewed interest the familiar fire song and listening to a supplementary phonograph record; helping to construct and to paint a model firehouse and fire-truck which, with dolls dressed by the teachers, provided a new free-play activity; and finally working out dramatic sequences with the aid of firemen's plastic hats. Since the two groups worked in the same room, materials prepared by one group were observed, imitated, or played with by the other. Conversation about materials of both groups thus provided a reaffirmation of the learnings gained from the trip.

General composition of follow-up activities showed a definite pattern. There were two- and three-dimensional symbolic records, social responses, related activities in music, usually further extending the learnings, and reporting to parents through a mimeographed newsletter, by a telephoned or child-delivered message, or by means of handwork carried home. Also, using tangible properties, the trip content moved into free-play activities, and dramatic or construction play. The trips were part of the year's program sequence, with memories reinforced by subsequent trips. The pattern, viewed in retrospect, showed a movement from the teacher-guided initial experience toward the child's autonomous activity and expression.

Materials for Trips

    a. All tangible items relevant to particular trips.
    b. Materials for laying out 3-dimensional routes
    c. Maps and route drawings showing locations
    d. Pictures showing travel activities: walking, riding on vehicles of different kinds, sightseeing, studying maps.

CHAPTER 4

CROSS-SECTIONAL CONSIDERATIONS

INTRODUCTION

The Curriculum Guide (Chapter II) and action settings (Chapter III) were parts of a three-dimensional design. The third component was the manner in which settings were used to implement the Curriculum Guide items. It has been noted that neither Guide items nor experience areas were designed to serve as a course of study. However, both teachers and children needed, for effective work, a continuing intention or direction. For the children's direction, reliance was upon natural action sequences where relationships were determined by space, time, materials, ideas and people. For maintaining their own direction, the teachers had first the six long range behavioral goals formulated in the initial phase of the curriculum study, and later, the itemized goals of the curriculum guide. These, running through all activities, could be identified for focus in relevant situations. The present chapter deals with the two sets of directions: those followed by the teachers, the behavioral goals, and those followed by the children, the activity-sequences of time, subject matter, conceptualization and personal relationships.

The Behavioral Goals

The teachers kept in mind as general goals six habits of functioning. These had to do with (1) motivation, (2) attention, (3) perseverance (work habits), (4) problem-solving, (5) concept development, and (6) oral communication. These goals were not mutually exclusive. Motivation was viewed as the determinant of attention and perseverance, these three promoters of successful problem-solving and conceptualization. Language understandings were as a result of contributory problem-solving and conceptualization. Teachers concentrated on one or another in the

relevant situations in the same manner as they concentrated on a detail such as buttoning. These goals ran through the sequences in all settings.

The teaching method, as implied in this curriculum employing a cross-sectional approach, was a unit method. However, the units were the habits and ways of functioning. More familiar units, whether subject matter, core or skill, became the means by which behavioral units were mastered. Each of these six goals is discussed briefly here, to serve as reference base to the four subsequently described sequences of time, subject matter, conceptualization and personal relationships.

Motivation

Just as experiences were presented "whole" to provide meaningful activity at all levels of competence, motivation also was offered in a qualitative range. To a large extent, the five-level activity provided intrinsic motivation, but the teachers' goal was the child's internalization of motive. Therefore they called to the child's conscious attention his response even though some children were very little above a stimulus-response (perception) level. To realize the goal of the child's understanding of his motive, the teachers needed a practical scale of motives. One of the Guide items supplied a general sequence of motivation.

In the section on intellectual development (A, 17) an item on "self-concept" or autonomy summarizes teachers' observations of general child functioning. The five levels of development were phrased as follows:

1	2	3	4	5
Realization of external objects	Can do to get	Can refuse to get	Can make a choice	Can assess

A restatement of the item, emphasizing the details to which a child at each level might respond provides a hypothetical motivation scale:

1	2	3	4	5
Responds to tangible objects: holds, carries, manipulates.	Responds to activities; imitates, explores and responds to spaces to explore.	Responds to persons: uses his refusal to elicit new action opportunities.	Responds to opportunity to choose.	Responds to opportunity to consider several aspects.

Analyzed further, this scale shows the child responding at each level to a new combination of variables. The order of inclusion seems to be as follows:

1	2	3	4	5
Objects	Actions in space	Persons	Past time (memory)	Future time (planning)

The teachers noted that a child's willed participation in an activity was positively related to his response to the element(s) he comprehended. Therefore, plans were checked to ensure the presence of necessary motives, and, in the course of the activity, to call attention to the connection between motive and response. They were also ready for shifts in motivation. The child was not just able to respond to one or two or five elements; he seemed to respond best to the highest level he could comprehend.

Transition from one level of motivation to the next apparently involved, for the child, a reordering of his personal situation to encompass one more element of the total situation. For the teachers, it involved planning for increasingly-complex responses. The child responding to the person offering a toy was ready for action choices. With help from additional tangible and action lures, positive personal motivation increased in strength and reliability. Many of the Project pupils responded at entrance to complex motivations. Others, the tracing of whose progress enabled the teachers to chart the apparent sequence, worked their way up from level one.

A series of maneuvers resulting in progressive motivation with one group is summarized as follows:

(a) Tangible stimuli (crackers)
(b) Imitative action (sitting with the group at the table and eating - because the bowl of crackers was on the table)
(c) Response to personal reference ("I think we could have crackers today. Alfred and Max are especially fond of them. Alfred, Max - will you sit down, please?")
(d) Response to known alternatives ("We can have crackers or pretzels or cookies. It is Max's turn to choose this morning.")
(e) Response to a problem ("We are almost out of food. Will you help me to make out an order? We can order only four boxes of cookies and crackers, so you'll have to choose things that everyone can enjoy. We can save some ideas for the next cookie order.")

When a child chose to sit with the group, even though his reason for doing so was crackers and not conversation, his response at the level meaningful to him placed the motivation within him, rather than in extrinsic motivation or prodding of the teacher.

Attention

Attention implies a continuing motivation or purpose. It is effective, that is, the child attends to the experience the teacher has in mind, to the extent that the child has a real interest in some aspect of the experience. In the earlier illustration of the discussion group, a child motivated by food joined the group and remained attentive as long as he was busy with crackers. Although temporarily satisfied with response at an object level, the teachers wanted, eventually, a sustained attention to discussion topics. Therefore it was necessary to develop attention to persons and to parts of discussion. As the child sat with his classmates, conversation about crackers served as a worthwhile beginning to probing for other interests of the child in question.

Conversation about crackers ranged far. For example, the brief daily discussions touched upon likes and dislikes (crackers); supermarkets (brand names and kinds of crackers); plans for future after-swimming snacks (crackers and kinds of soup); arithmetic and line-drawing (eating can be delayed to break a double cracker along the perforated line, to bite out shapes, and to sketch crackers on the board); alternatives to crackers ("Would you like to taste cookies?") and, finally, planning for something besides crackers for the benefit of others in the class. Each of these topics was explored by children interested in ideas; the child attentive to food combined crackers with another element. Each topic that caught his interest carried him a small step beyond food-centered attention. If it elicited a comment, it was strong enough to substitute momentarily for a cracker. The teachers' task was noting the response, eliciting it again, calling the child's attention to his receptivity to old and new interests, and helping him to maintain the new level.

The child's physical presence in the group could be exacted when presence in the group was the experience under consideration. Although efforts to force attention were essentially unproductive, it was possible to call attention to aspects of the situation, which were then made so interesting that the attention bond was between the child and the new thing he could grasp. Attention mediated by a teacher was divided attention, at best, and lasted only as long as the teacher exacted it.

Work Habits

Work habits referred to ability to stay with and finish a task, perseverance and attention span. Prerequisites sought were an interest in the task and a purpose which sustained attention. Capacity for sustained work was evident in many of the pre-school children. During the first exploratory days of a school term, and thereafter in free-play periods, children stayed with, and worked hard at, self-chosen tasks. By incorporating the child-selected activities into planned experience sequences, teachers sought to bring perseverance into focus and turn it into a tool for other activities.

To clarify the process the following illustration is presented. A child consistently used Tinker Toys at an uncomplicated level, constructing and naming chance structures, working for extended periods. Putting the toys away, however, after completing his play was most distasteful to him. By stages, the teachers introduced the following variations which built upon the existing capacity for sustained activity:

(1) Structures were admired and "saved" to be finished on the following day. Thus, the number of pieces to be picked up was reduced.
(2) Available time was discussed in advance. The child was told that a "long time" was available because he used time well.

(3) A second child, skilled in producing "working models" was encouraged to work with the first child. Pickup was shared.
(4) The set was divided to enable the boys to work side by side. Communication about building was observed.
(5) A third boy with an "idea" was introduced into the group. All structures were saved, and reworked on several consecutive days.
(6) The group progressed to work with blocks and to construction of traffic routes. Other children moved in and out of this group.
(7) The three-boy nucleus was used as a subgroup in handwork, music, gym, and conversation periods.
(8) The first child was singled out for separate activity in new areas.

The net gain for the child in question was the shift away from a very small work sphere, object and action motivated, toward more complex motives. His capacity for sustained attention had carried to several situations, and he worked at tasks which included clean-up. He was aware of his ability to concentrate in the new situations and was less confined to tangibles here and now for continuous work. The boy whose competence served as leavening had meanwhile moved toward confident self-direction and planning of work.

Teacher planning for the development of work habits involved using the capacity observed in the child, making provision for the activity which would hold his attention, and expanding that activity until it could be separated into several processes. Minor behavior threads including relatedness to children, manipulation, creativity, working with a group, were used as a means, while the free play setting was a major tool.

Problem-Solving

In comparing the Curriculum Guide item on problem-solving with other Guide items, the parallel structure is noticeable. For discussion purposes, the five observed stages of the item are reproduced here, with sample items from other sections of the Guide.

PROBLEM SOLVING (A, 16)

Sees problem and withdraws	Asks for help or attracts attention without trying for solution	Random trial and error	Trial and error based on previous experience	Assesses situation before moving and acting

CLAY (E, 3)

Interest at a distance	Touching and exploring	Patting, rolling, squeezing, pinching off bits.	Imitative handling of material	Participation with originality

DRESSING: putting on boots (G, 1g)

Dependence	Awareness, willingness, interest	Helping adult	Independence with direction	Independence

The items on clay and dressing were selected because many of the preschool children unfamiliar with the material or unaware of the problem, invariably withdrew. Once interest and attention had been elicited, there appeared obvious stages of handling materials and asking for help, trying out parts of processes, using processes, and choosing appropriate movements to obtain the desired result.

Each Guide item was a separate problem recurrent in one of the seven curriculum areas. Solution for children was in terms of the materials handled, and the observed pattern of attack resembled Piaget's levels. There was a stage of producing random results; then a trial and error phase of noticing correspondence between action and result; finally a stage of remembering and using the action necessary to solve the problem. The child at level five had mastered an operational solution; he had the experience underlying verbalization to enable him later to form hypotheses and choose solutions.

Observation of this pattern of problem solving made feasible an economical programming of behavior items. Time was allowed for manipulation and experimentation, usually in free-play periods. Teachers made accessible to the children materials that would later be used for a purpose. Individual children were observed testing operational hypotheses; teachers provided additional situations and pointed out results. Thus, when separate processes were needed for solution of a problem, all or nearly all of them had been tried out and were ready for use. It was possible to concentrate on the problem without delay for mastering contributory skills.

Concept Development

In the development of the Curriculum Guide items, a similarity in sequence of item levels was noted whenever the behavior dealt with something presumably unfamiliar to the children. That is, the recurrent pattern strongly suggested a way of learning. Items dealing with concepts presented a clear pattern. A sample reproduced here is the color concept item (A, 11a).

1	2	3	4	5
Interest in color	Interest in one color	Matching	Selection for pattern	Appropriate selection for pattern

The process shown by the children involved experiences with the group of colors, a focus on one color, a duplicate notice of the color item, a selection of it for use, and the appropriate use of the color — that is, matching it to its appearance in a familiar object. The third level of this item is expanded in color matching (A, 12c).

1	2	3	4	5
Participation in activity	Recognition and awareness	Putting together	Selecting likes at at random	Generalizing discriminations

In this item, the materials were pairs of colors, rather than single colors. Yet the process was the same: (1) generalized participation or handling, (2) focus on one sample (pair), (3) selection of a pair, (4) duplication of pairs, still selected at random, and (5) generalized ordering of available pairs. The reiterated pattern might be summarized:

1	2	3	4	5
Undifferentiated exploration of collections of elements	Focus on an element	Duplicating the element	Using the element	Rearranging the elements in accord with the new insight

Teachers found it profitable to use this sequence in planning for mastery of concepts. Materials to illustrate color, quantity, extension, and quality of objects as well as objects and actions, were provided for, (a) familiarization and random use, (b) experience with selection, (c) duplication of selection, and (d) rearrangement of the materials. The four sequences followed by the children were a way of handling large concepts such as time; in class work and free-play periods were settings for work with particular (smaller) concepts.

The preschool children responded to activity series directed toward concept development. The reading readiness sequences, the subject matter units, and the time sequence reported in the present section revealed high motivation and self-direction in the children. Within each sequence, it was possible to observe the isolation of details and their inclusion in new and progressively more complex arrangements of reading materials, language understandings, food categories and time blocks. Observable also within the sequences were more specific experiences tending toward development of contributory concepts. These experiences were reinforced by similar but non-unit activities. The classroom materials used for the latter activities are of special interest for the way in which they helped to build transferable ideas.

Materials included both commercial and teacher-made equipment such as construction toys, matching sets, and games. Supplies included single examples of some toys; pairs or three or more of others. The single toys embodied in themselves a transferrable idea or comparison, for example, a lock garage to which were affixed different kinds of locks. The duplicate materials such as pegboards, color towers, nested blocks and beads, presented single processes. Used as single toys, they provided experience with simple manipulative processes; for later phases of concept development the processes were mirrored or repeated. Teachers noted that reconstruction of a graduated color tower seemed easier if two children with similar materials were seated opposite each other and compared results, or if one child worked with and compared two towers. In such situations, the concept of a series was under study. Similarly, it seemed easier to select the red crayon needed to color an apple, or four petals to paste on a flower, if several classmates were selecting red crayons and four petals. It was easiest if the real apple and the real flower were there too. The child's propensity for imitation and copying was used to advantage.

Part of the teaching process in use of tangible materials was teacher participation in reconstructions, and teacher verbalization of a child's status. The child moved from the manipulation level, at which he put disks on the color tower, through the next level, by saving a particular ring until the last, and continued through the next level, where he copied a neighbor and put the big ring on first. Supplying the words for his actions helped with mastery of the concept.

Teacher-prepared materials included giant dominoes for floor play, letter-matching sets, story pictures for matching, varied "idea" materials in "box books," utensils for real and play cooking activities, and stamp printing sets. Their use, in either group hand work or free play activities, gave children opportunities to match, compare and produce shapes, sizes, color and kinds of objects. The box books contained self-regulating sets of toys, again with opportunity for arrangement according to attributes of different kinds. Sets of miniatures provided stepping-stone experience with symbols which was part of the reading-readiness foundation.

The materials used by the children were kept in order, arranged according to the ideas they embodied. For example, the color book contained five colored plastic boxes, each of which held three colored toys (a doll, a ball, a top). The dolls could be grouped for play, as could balls and tops. When the child reassembled the set to put it away, toys went back into the matched color boxes. Any set of materials made available for work or play was a conceptual whole. The child took it apart for use, then recombined it, with help as needed, before returning it to the cupboard. Parts were rarely lost when the child had the whole idea for reference.

Direct attempts to develop concepts brought out additional information about the retarded children in these particular classes. They entered school with and were able to develop concepts of many kinds. They did not always have the verbal language for them, but could express in various ways simple transferrable understandings. They evidenced management of inclusive concepts, but had uneven supplies of subsidiary concepts. Preschool teaching called attention to details such as red and blue, one and two, now and later, drawn from the broad categories. The preschool program seemed to help in clarifying details and in reordering bodies of knowledge within useful and useable frameworks.

Language and Speech

The Curriculum Guide includes no separate section on language and speech. Language goals for the preschool children were comprehensive, a part of each area of development. The teachers were interested primarily in the children's mastery of language relationships at the action level. For example, children learned that books communicated meaningful ideas, such as, that rabbits like carrots; that three can be applied to bears and bowls and spoons, and children can mix paint; that real fruits can be cooked, and models of fruit can be made from papier mache; that parents like valentines and class newspapers and will contribute stock for a grocery store. These and similar relationships were understood and worked out by children who could not produce the corresponding oral symbols.

Action language, as the foundation for spoken language, cuts across curriculum areas. General speech goals were ability to communicate information or to relate experiences; to ask and answer oral questions, to express and compare ideas, and to participate in the group activities involving spoken words. Since a criterion for admission to the Project was ability to communicate needs and no stipulation was made regarding speech, each entering class contained one or more children with delayed or defective speech. The teachers worked for their speech development within the classroom situation. Understandings about speech were built in the same way as other language understandings.

Oral communication was based on non-oral communication. Gestures or pantomime were accepted as legitimate communication from children who did not talk. In return, teachers used verbal forms supplemented with action or gesture when essential for communication. They described and discussed experiences; asked questions and, at times, supplied the words for the children's responses; and took the lead in expressing ideas. Children without speech could watch and absorb the speech patterns; those who did speak imitated the teachers' efforts with non-talkers. Individual children learned first vocabulary related to favorite activities. One child, for example, learned broke, "busted", cracked, fix it, wire and hammer from his preoccupation with things needing repair. Another, interested in print forms, said letter names and numbers first. A third learned a song text. In general, in the action sequences and subject matter units, single words had verb force at first. The teachers accepted communication in early sentence fragments and poorly-articulated words, as they had the gestures, to ensure the fixing of the communication habit.

In descriptions of settings, log records, and in the programming sequences for Guide items are frequent references to associated language and speech processes. These processes seemed basic to work in all curriculum areas.

THE ACTIVITY SEQUENCES

The teachers found that the children could learn to operate within the following patterns utilizing the various activity settings.

(1) Time Sequences: arrangements of activities within the day, from day to day, week to week, and month to month.
(2) Subject matter sequence: arrangements of activities which explored sets of materials.
(3) Conceptual sequences: arrangements which followed a notion from one subject matter sequence to another and through varying time intervals.
(4) Personal relationship sequences: developed with reference to time, subject matter, and conceptual sequences.

The sequences were interdependent and each was useful, to some extent, in every situation. The teachers identified the continuities as they identified the Guide items, by observation of the preschool children: the children were, on entrance, acting in terms of time, materials, ideas, and personal relationships. For example, time was for some children "here and now," for others, "now" and "after awhile," for others, longer expanses, but time was something understood and ready for use. Similarly, they already functioned with respect to space, materials, ideas and people. The teachers utilized and expanded what already existed in the new space of the preschool.

Presented in this chapter as illustrations of the four continuities are five sample sequences. The first describes the way in which time limits within which children could account for their own activities were expanded during the year. The second and third present two subject matter sequences, a long-term unit on fruits and vegetables and a short-term unit on a nursery tale. The fourth deals with the development of the reading readiness concept of visual, interpretable symbols. The fifth summarizes a sequence which was concerned with development of parent-child-teacher relationships. Noticeable in the sequences focusing on one or another of the designated patterns are the interweaving threads of the Curriculum Guide items which appear and reappear in meaningful ways. So far as possible, the cross-sections are given in the form or excerpts from the teachers' and observers' records to reconstruct as nearly as possible the sequences which they represent. The conceptual sequence, represented by the section on reading readiness, is based on a student teacher's report.

TIME SEQUENCE AS A CROSS-SECTIONAL UNIT

The general pattern of daily programs included alternating group and individual occupations, with a balance, determined by class make-up, between opportunities for movement and quiet. Children learned the sequence by participation, and eventually recognized cues, endings and transitions of the major activities. To extend the children's "frontiers" of time sequence awareness, teachers used the children's concrete experiences. Non-school hours were included as children were asked about breakfast and the trip to school, as they carried messages or handwork home, and as they discussed weekend and after school activities. Following is a summary of daily building in a first-year class from the teachers' annual report. (An observer's report on activity during one day in this class will be found in Chapter V.)

Starting with a group of five children, a program was set up to become routinized enough to give the children a feeling of security. It was arranged so that the children were helped with undressing upon arrival and then encouraged to get books to look at for the first few minutes while waiting for the rest of the group.

In the first ten or fifteen minutes, group activity was either a story selected by a child from those at the table or a well-structured, highly-motivated group table activity such as coloring, pasting, clay modeling or drawing. The motivation for these experiences was built around the children's own experiences: the weather; their trip to school; or, later, an outside experience shared by the group.

The children then had some choice for a short free play period. Early in the year this time block included also a return to a brief table activity. In good weather, the second activity was roof play or a walk to the park or playground.

When the children returned to the room,

the record player was set up for a transition activity. Children went to the washroom in small groups for toileting. The teachers prepared the tables for juice.

Juice time in the first few months was mainly an eating time for children; they ate heartily. Social conversation consisted essentially of the teachers' discussion of class activity.

Music time followed juice. The children were responsive to the use of rhythm instruments and to learning songs, especially action connected ones.

As a final activity in preparation for home, story time or music were most effective. Children brought their wraps from the coat corner to their chairs, and prepared for departure.

Variations in daily schedule during the week were introduced gradually. For example, on Tuesdays, beginning in October, music was scheduled at the regular time, but for a longer period with a music consultant; on Thursdays, beginning in November, swimming in the College pool was included. At this time too, names of juice pourers were posted and a slot calendar was used on a regular basis.

The activities throughout the year made possible an expanding process of references backward and forward through time. Experiences on special trips, holiday and birthday events, weather details, and individual and group handwork or construction projects provided factual bases for recalling and anticipating. Illustrated in the following excerpts from the teachers' annual report on a second year group is the building of a time continuum from September to June. An observer's report on one daily session of this group will be found in Chapter V.

The structure attained the preceding spring was reestablished in the first weeks. The schedule was as follows:

1. September

M	T	W	Th	F
R	R	R	R	R

R: The regular daily schedule included the following:

1. Book period. 2. Home reports, conversation 3. Music 4. Handwork 5. Free play, records, toileting 6. Juice 7. Recreation - roof or gym 8. Return to room;

gathering of materials to take home; departure.

1. October

M	T	W	Th	F
R	R+M	R	R	R

M: Music with consultant began; period changes to follow book period in daily schedule. Calendar introduced. Music highlighted on calendar.

3. November

M	T	W	Th	F
R$_n$	R+M	R	R	R+S

S: Weekly swimming began.

n: Weekly newspaper introduced.

4. December (PP)

M	T	W	Th	F
R$_n$	R+M	R	R	R+S$_{nd}$

PP: Pre-planning of December activities.

nd: Dictating newspaper items begun.

5. January (PP)

M	T	W	Th	F
R$_n$	R+M	R	R+C	R+S$_{nd,1}$

C: Cooking program regularly scheduled.

1: Circulating library introduced.

6. February (PP)

M	T	W	Th	F
R+T$_n$	R+M	R+P	R+C	R+S$_{nd,1}$

T: short trips regularly included.

P: Construction projects scheduled.

7. March (PP)

M	T	W	Th	F
R+T$_n$	R+M	R+P	R+C	R+S$_{nd,1}$

8. April (PP)

Su	M	T	W	Th	F	Sa
H,Pl Ch	R+T$_n$	R+M	R+P	R+C	R+S$_{nd,1}$	H,Pl

H: Home

Pl: Play

Ch: Church

Saturday and Sunday included in preplanning and conversation. Pre-planning for two months. Trips to distant points.

9. May

Su	M	T	W	Th	F	Sa
H,Pl Ch	R+T$_n$	R+M	R+P	R+C	R+S$_{nd,1}$	H,Pl

Checking off events of planned schedule.

Planning end-of-school picnic.

10. June

Su	M	T	W	Th	F	Sa
H,Pl Ch	T	R+M	R+P	R+C	R+S$_{nd,1}$	H,Pl

Tentative summer plans: three months' calendar.

Conversation about new school in the fall.

By the end of the second year, children were conversant with the daily and weekly class schedules in terms of activities assigned to specific days. They recalled the principal events of the school year just past, and speculated on probable events of the year to come. They were familiar with calendar terms as summarizing names learned after they had mastered the meaning through their own activities.

The work on time sequences, through the two years of preschool, was, then, in terms of childrens' experiences. Recall and anticipation of events, construction of tangible records of experiences; and use of written and oral messages and of newspaper reviews of activities helped to motivate attention to time and calendar details. Growth in language understanding was evident in the ability to follow sequential accounts. Problem-solving was recognized in activities such as arranging travel, planning regular weekly events, constructing three-dimensional records of happenings, and in sharing experiences with parents. Perhaps the understanding of time in terms of the things done and in terms of memory and planning was the principal gain of the daily and yearly programs viewed as cross-sectional activities.

Reproduced on the following pages are two newsletters, one recording a week's events, the other showing planning for a large block of time.

SUBJECT MATTER SEQUENCE AS A CROSS-SECTIONAL UNIT

The following illustrations of two subject matter sequences depict a long-term, recurrent

Project News

Friday   April 14

MONDAY

We made cages for mice.

TUESDAY

Diana had a birthday   party.

WEDNESDAY

We went to the store.

THURSDAY

We made play dough.

FRIDAY

We fished.

Page 1

Project News

June 3

Afternoon

VACATION NUMBER

JUNE 1960

SUN	MON	TUE	WED	THU	FRI	SAT
			1	2	3	4
5	6	7	8	9	10	11
12	13	14	15	16	17	18
19	20	21	22	23	24	25
26	27	28	29	30		

Stevie will have a birthday in June.

JULY 1960

SUN	MON	TUE	WED	THU	FRI	SAT
					1	2
3	4	5	6	7	8	9
10	11	12	13	14	15	16
17	18	19	20	21	22	23
24	25	26	27	28	29	30
31						

Richard will have a birthday in July.

AUGUST 1960

SUN	MON	TUE	WED	THU	FRI	SAT
	1	2	3	4	5	6
7	8	9	10	11	12	13
14	15	16	17	18	19	20
21	22	23	24	25	26	27
28	29	30	31			

Dorothy will have a birthday in August.

Stevie and Richard and Dorothy had parties and treats in school this week.

Coney Island

We could not go on a picnic to Coney Island last week. It rained all day. We had a make-believe picnic in the classroom. We all went to the store and bought some food. Everyone was hungry. We played with the beach balls and had a good time.

Chicken Pox

Mary Ann and Judy and Junior and Ken and Billy and Richard all had the chicken pox. They are all better now and everyone is back in school.
Mary Ann had a birthday while she was sick. She celebrated it this week.

And now school is over,
It's time to go home.
Good-bye! Good-bye!

We hope you all have a good vacation.
We have had a pleasant year.

The teachers.

SEPTEMBER 1960

SUN	MON	TUE	WED	THU	FRI	SAT
				1	2	3
4	5	6	7	8	9	10
11	12	13	14	15	16	17
18	19	20	21	22	23	24
25	26	27	28	29	30	

unit on fruits and vegetables and a short-term unit of action on a nursery tale, The Three Bears. The presentation is three dimensional: first is a pictorial overview of sequences highlighting various episodes, second are excerpts from the teachers' anecdotal records relevant to each of the pictured episodes; third is an analysis of the activities for each episode including, (a) an indication of the group's previous performance, (b) the anticipated performance in the episode, (c) the Curriculum Guide item in focus, and (d) the teachers' methodological rationale or base.

A short-term subject-matter unit:
THE THREE BEARS

The new book:
The Three Bears

Attention-getting materials arranged by the teacher: spurs to activity and participation of children.

A concrete problem

Creativity in action.

Making the three bowls: size, form, number.

A child directing group singing with teacher-made materials.

Free play: the teacher's opportunity to assess learning of individuals.

Parent involvement in the curriculum.

Dramatization: a creative review.

Excerpts from Teacher's Log:

1-9 . . . At reading time, T said, "We have a new book. I found it at the store yesterday. It is a story about the three bears. It is really a very good book because it has good pictures about the story. Would you like to hear it?" T, as she talked was leafing through the book, holding it up for the children to see. Attention of the group was continuous through the whole story. . . . At free-play time, the book was in demand.

1-10 D hurried to take off her wraps. She went to the book rack, saying, "Where is the new book? I want to read that book." Others, arriving and looking for a book to settle down with, had the same idea. They tried to hurry D. At a suggestion, D held the book so neighbors could see the pictures, and there were comments on the bears, with more than one squeaky "Someone's been eating my porridge and ate it all up." The book was in demand at free-play, as it had been yesterday, as only two children had turns during reading period.

ANALYSIS OF THE PLANNED ACTIVITIES:

a Previous level	b Planned Augmentation	c Curriculum Guide Items in focus	d Rationale
Asking Answering questions about pictures, action sequence	Noticing actions, details, in illustrations	(A,4d) Listening to story (A,6) Visual discrimination	Linking new story to familiar one. Focus on selected relationships.
Anticipating action	Anticipating voice tones, actions.	(A,7) Auditory discrimination (A,13b) Size discrimination	Internalization of a vicarious experience
Participating: comments on "next step."	Participating by comments on size, number.	(A,11a,b) Concepts of color (A,3) Picture symbols	Focus on concepts of real, make-believe.

EXCERPT FROM TEACHER'S LOG:

1-11 When the children came in, three toy bears, three chairs made of cardboard, and a yellow-haired doll were lying on the table. The children identified the items with the new story, and looked for the "new book." When all children were settled at the table, they were shown the three bowls T had made of papier mache. These, with the chairs and dolls, made the children speculate on ways of playing with them. The house made for Christmas was suggested as a house (after T had pointedly looked about the room and let her gaze linger on the house). There was a question as to its suitability. T said, "There's no upstairs." "Is it big enough?" D said, "We'll need spoons for these bowls. I'm going to play with these later and I'll have to have some porridge." As she talked, her eyes moved from the small house to the kitchen area. She evidently was planning later activities because at free-play time she occupied herself for quite a while with the new materials, and T found (after school) that she had brought three plastic spoons, all the same size, from the kitchen. When D left the toy house to play in the doll house, A played with the bears, etc., arranging and rearranging. She tried to get the bowls to stay on the fireplace mantel in the house. D returned, came to ask T about a table. She answered her own question, remembering, "There's one in that apple." She went to the cupboard and took out the hollow apple which contains a table and tea set. She did not know how to put the table together, got help

from T. She put the large bowl on the table, arranged the others on the work table — since the big bowl is almost the same size as the tea table —, put the tiny apples from the tea set in the three bowls, then left. A continued to play with the toys. D returned again and walked off with Goldilocks, carrying it with her as she played house. T suggested that she return it to A, saying that it must remain with the bears. A did no verbalizing through all this: she was playing a game which included language meanings but used no words. (The game was miniature house play, so far as T could tell.) . . . R asked for paint and did two or three pictures, then painted one of the cardboard chairs when T asked him if he would like to do so.

ANALYSIS OF PLANNED ACTIVITIES:

a Previous level	b Planned Augmentation	c Curriculum Guide Items in focus	d Rationale
Free choice of play materials	Directing at- tention to new materials from which to choose	(A,6) Visual discrim- ination (A,13b) Size discrim- ination	Interpretation of verbal symbols. Recognition of a problem situa- tion.
Painting		(A,3) Symbolic behav- ior	
Houseplay	Cooperative painting	(A,16) Problem solv- ing	Focus on relationships.
	New houseplay setting		

EXCERPTS FROM TEACHER'S LOG:

1-12 P said, "I will paint chairs tomorrow." T said, "That will be fine. You remember that and be sure to ask about painting." D repeated P plans. She automatically included A in her planning, and A smiled assent.

1-13 D, A and P reminded T about the painting, when handwork was completed, and went directly to the cupboard to get smocks. They painted contentedly, and T had time to make an additional bed for them. D watched while T showed how to add a little water to thin the paint. She then took the initiative and led P and A to get water in paper cups. The paint was thinned so that it left little pigment on the furniture. Evidently the remedy decided on was more water, as the three paraded again to the bathroom to fill their cups. This time, T intervened and explained what was happening to the paint. As it was then time to clean up, T promised to show how to mix better paint, next week.

1-18 R came to T, after surveying the various free-play activities of the others, and asked, "How about painting? Will we have painting today?" He assumed responsibility for the activity, at T's suggestion, got a smock, and traded buttoning with C, who decided she wanted to paint, too. He, C, and three others shared in final steps of paint mixing. Four painted furniture (the things which had received the dilute coat on Friday), but R painted bowls, admiring them as he worked. Others transferred to the easel, eventually, but R stayed with his clay bowls.

ANALYSIS OF PLANNED ACTIVITIES

a	b	c	d
Previous level	Planned Augmentation	Curriculum Guide Items in Focus	Rationale
Supervised use of materials	Self-direction in painting and mixing of paints	(G,1a,1) Self-help (G,1; C,3) Interaction in self-help (C,3) Cooperative planning (A,11a,b; 13a,b) Color, size, and shape discrimination	Recognition of problems in self-help. Planning and reaching objectives.

EXCERPTS FROM TEACHER'S LOG:

1-13 . . . Following free play, there was a brief period of work with clay. T had the children inspect the papier-mache bowls, then showed how she had shaped them, using clay. The children all tried to imitate, then began to make snowmen and offer them for T's approval. T began to roll balls, then use a finger to make a depression for a bowl. R made "a tiny one for baby bear," and went on to make a middle-sized and a big one. The others shaped bowls, then named the size after they had finished. They evidently matched sizes to the pattern bowls, to get the right term. E pieced together figures of bears and of Goldilocks sitting in a chair.

1.18 . . . During conversation, T brought the clay bowls to the table and the children looked at them critically, identifying them as big, middle-sized, little, and asking who had made certain bowls which they admired as being "very nice bowls" and "right" for the baby bear, etc. They talked about painting them. D asked, "Did you make those other bowls that way, too?"

ANALYSIS OF PLANNED ACTIVITIES:

a	b	c	d
Previous level	Planned Augmentation	Curriculum Guide Items in focus	Rationale
Manipulation of clay, exploration of material	Purposeful use to produce a wanted item	(E,5) Manipulation of clay (A,13b) Size discrimination	Concretation of verbal symbols
Cooperative setting, individual work	Cooperative work for common purpose	(C,3) Group relationships (A,16) Problem solving	Purposeful use of a manipulation process
Recognition of items made	Evaluation of performance. Use of size criteria		Extension of turn-taking concept to conversation

EXCERPTS FROM TEACHER'S LOG

1-18 . . . The newspapers were passed out and children looked at the news items carefully. T was
doubtful about interpretation of pictures, since three had to do with the various handwork activities
related to the Three Bears story. However, D said of the first item, "That's the new book;
and R looked at the third, said, "That's painting." T then pointed to the clay pail and asked,
"What's this?" Two children said, "Clay?" D said, more firmly, "That's clay." Children
asked about and lingered over the item about boots, since T had introduced riddles here, and asked,
"Who has big black boots?" Later there was an incipient argument. Since D seemed to have
been allotted possession of big boots, someone concluded that he was sole possessor and twitted
M about his "little boots." M asked T about this and was mollified when told that his boots
would probably be called "middle-sized." D said, "Listen. I want to tell about this." He
pointed to the pictured bowls and worked hard to get out the sentences, "The big bowl is for the
Father Bear. The middle-sized bowl is for the Mother Bear, etc." His interest was in the word
"middle-sized," seemingly. He repeated it several times until he no longer stumbled over the
articulation, then repeated the ideas, "The Mother Bear's middle-sized bowl. That's the middle-
sized bowl. etc." T asked the children to color Goldilock's golden hair. She asked what color
gold was. D said, "That's like Mrs. Busch's hair." All except Al selected yellow as the color:
Al selected orange. T also asked that the tree be colored green. (She suggested that the other
pictures be colored as the children liked.)

ANALYSIS OF PLANNED ACTIVITIES

a	b	c	d
Previous level	Planned Augmentation	Curriculum Guide Items in focus	Rationale
Interpreting pictures in news	Recalling, by reference to pictures in news-paper	(A, 13b) Size discrimi-nation	Interpretation of ideas in a new form
Coloring pictures	Coloring according to directions	(A, 13a) Number dis-crimination (A, 12) Matching (C, 3) Relatedness	Looking for optimum source of help
Noting familiar ideas	Noticing new items, asking help to interpret	(A, 16) Problem solving (A, 17) Self-concept	Experience of picture symbols

EXCERPTS FROM TEACHER'S LOG

1-17 ... Song book to match lines of song presented as part of conversation period.

1-18 ... (The bear song). Major interest was again in the way bears really go for a walk. The children repeated their counting of trees on the last page and found all the trees. D emphasized, "That one away off, back there," indicating awareness of perspective. She also said, "The forest! Indians." and others used woods, forest (suggesting to T the possibility of leading from the bear story to exploration of the Indian sequence from Mrs. L's music period). Al got the book, climbed up on the table to hold it, and led the singing.

1-23 ... Conversation turned to the Three Bears story. The six children who arrived first got the song book and began to try to point to words as they said them. Cards were brought out and phrases put on them. M withdrew from the group as soon as he saw that print words were being noticed, but stayed on the edge of the group. When cards were passed out, he took one, held it, and smiled when he handed it back to be slipped between the pages of the book. The other five children looked at their cards and tried to match them to the right pages. Phrases were ** Father Bear ** Mother Bear ** Baby Bear ** too ** went out walking ** as ** Bears often do **. (M had been given the card saying "too".)

ANALYSIS OF PLANNED ACTIVITIES

a Previous level	b Planned Augmentation	c Curriculum Guide Items in focus	d Rationale
Singing, guided, by picture: child holding book	Noticing print forms of text, pointing to successive words	(A, 12) Matching symbols (A, 13) Numbers (A, 6) Visual Discrimination	Interpretating verbal symbols via action Focus on idea of perspective

a	b	c	d
Previous level	Planned Augmentation	Curriculum Guide Items in focus	Rationale
Dramatizing	Dramatizing, w. number clue from song	(A, 3) Use of books	Direct experience of print symbols
Noting scenes in sequence	Noting details in scenes	(A, 5) Singing	
		(B, 7a) Dramatization	

EXCERPTS FROM TEACHER'S LOG:

1-24 Mrs. L worked a dramatization of the story into the music period ... all children had to be in whatever was going on, and there were actors moving into scenes at several points, also actors moving onto "sets" which had just been vacated. L and N got extra chairs and joined the three bears at the breakfast table. C and E climbed into beds as soon as the designated actors had left them. M tried to mix a western of some sort into the script and was firing six-shooters (H was made camera man at this point.) D hovered over the actors after her turn was done, absorbed in what was going on, prompting and suggesting words and actions, The children brought the toy bears and other items to the breakfast table, and put the toys through the actions while acting out parts themselves. They pretended to taste porridge and exclaimed, "It's too hot! I almost burned my tongue!" E after doing this, picked up a toy bear and started spooning porridge into its mouth. Mrs. L. asked, "What are you doing?" E said, "I'm going to feed the baby." All children enjoyed sequences where they walked through the woods, skipped through the woods like Goldilocks, or walked up the stairs like the three bears. Evidently they still need more of the imaginative sequences which allow the group to participate as a whole.

Project News

Tuesday   **January 17**

THE THREE BEARS

We have a new book about the ~~three~~ bears and Goldilocks.

We have three toy bears.

We have a Goldilocks doll.

THE THREE BOWLS

We made three bowls.

We made big bowls and middle-sized bowls and little bowls.

THE THREE CHAIRS

Some of us painted chairs.

We painted a big chair and a middle-sized chair and a little chair.

CATHY'S BIRTHDAY PARTY

Cathy had a birthday party.

She had a **big, big** cake.

Her mother came to school for the birthday party.

Cathy is 7 years old now.

HAPPY BIRTHDAY CATHY

SOMETHING TO GUESS

WHO has big black boots?

WHO has red boots?

WHO has boots with zippers?

ANALYSIS OF PLANNED ACTIVITIES

a	b	c	d
Previous level	Planned Augmentation	Curriculum Guide Items in focus	Rationale
Taking in story, participating	Expressing entire story sequence	(F, 1-7) Motor activity. Skipping, etc.	Interpreting musical clues
Responding to straight rhythmic clues	Responding to musical clues - modulation	(B, 7b, c) Group dramatization (A, 7) Auditory discrimination	Expressing ideas which have been internalized

EXCERPTS FROM TEACHER'S LOG:

1-26 E got the <u>Three Bears</u> book, and started to tell the story after morning conversation. D wanted to tell it and was reminded that she had had the first turn. Later, T heard E say to D, "I listened to you tell the story. You should listen to me." E recounted the sequence with the aid of some interested prompting from the others. At reading time various children collected small participating audiences and recounted all or part of the story.

2-14 N turned pages and pointed to details of pictures as he talked. When the story reached the porridge-eating part, N began to skip Mother Bear references. He jumped from "big" details to "little," (giving "kweeky" variously for squeaky, teeny, and wee). He almost skipped, "And she broke the chair." D, leaning over his shoulder, made a movement and N interpreted it, turning the page back and correcting his omission. D said, "And she broke a leg." N added this and rushed on to the return of the bears. He put down the book to put hands on hips (like the picture in the book) and give Mother Bear's "somebody has been eating my porridge." He barely took time for Baby Bear and the chair; he smiled when he reached the picture of Goldilocks waking up and detailed this carefully. He and D ended the story as a duet (D had been interjecting sentences throughout the recital, and he was promised the next turn.) N closed the book, looked up and smiled.

A long-term (recurrent) unit:

Fruits and Vegetables

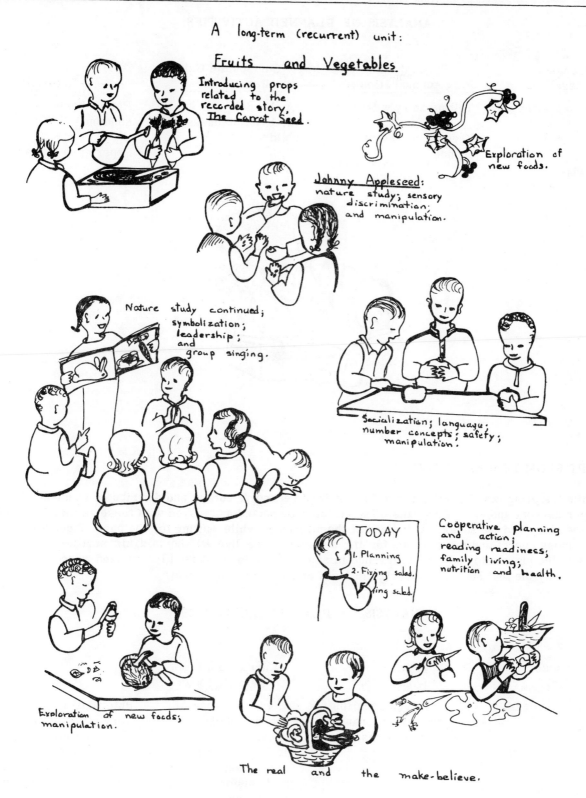

Introducing props related to the recorded story. *The Carrot Seed*.

Exploration of new foods.

Johnny Appleseed: nature study; sensory discrimination; and manipulation.

Nature study continued; symbolization; leadership; and group singing.

Socialization; language; number concepts; safety; manipulation.

TODAY
1. Planning
2. Fixing salad.
3. Eating salad.

Cooperative planning and action; reading readiness; family living; nutrition and health.

Exploration of new foods; manipulation.

The real and the make-believe.

ANALYSIS OF PLANNED ACTIVITIES

a Previous level	b Planned Augmentation	c Curriculum Guide Items in focus	d Rationale
Listening to a story	Telling story with book	(A, 17) Self-concept (C, 1) Relatedness to children (C, 3) Sharing	Remembering a learned sequence
Participating	Keeping correct se- quence		Experience in leadership
Anticipating			Sharing leadership

EXCERPT FROM TEACHER'S LOG:

9-28   While the group was listening to the Carrot Seed record, T cut out and distributed construction-paper carrots and sprinkling cans. The children inspected and played with these as they listened to the story and the songs. At the end of the afternoon, while waiting for the cars, T cut out an enormous carrot and made leaves for it. Ju wanted one like it: he laid his smaller carrot beside the big one to show the difference in size. All children wanted leaves, and were interested in the way the leaf stem was inserted in a slit at the end of the carrot.

ANALYSIS OF PLANNED ACTIVITIES

a Previous level	b Planned Augmentation	c Curriculum Guide Items in focus	d Rationale
Listening to records	Listening and recalling recorded story; hand- ling related items.	(A, 4c) Listening to records. Story with props. (A, 6) Visual dis- crimination (A, 7) Auditory dis- crimination (A, 13b) Size dis- crimination	Internalization of audi- tory stimulations 1) Interpretation of ver- bal symbol 2) Concretation of symbol 3) Focus on selected ob- jects 4) Relevancy of objects to situation

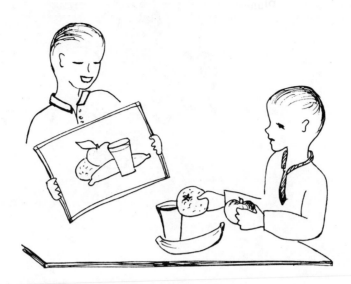

EXCERPT FROM TEACHER'S LOG:

10-10 The fruit puzzle (orange, apple, plum, banana and milk) was reconstructed with real fruit as the children had been having trouble with the placement of pieces.

ANALYSIS OF PLANNED ACTIVITIES

a	b	c	d
Previous level	Planned Augmentation	Curriculum Guide Items in focus	Rationale
Work with jig-saw puzzles	Reproducing the puzzle arrangement in three dimensions	(A, 16) Problem solving (A, 6) Visual discrimination	Translation of the symbolic into the concrete objects within child's experience Reinforcement of earlier sensory experiences.

EXCERPT FROM TEACHER'S LOG

10-17 A new <u>Johnny Appleseed</u> record made a setting for cutting up apples, eating the slices, and looking for the seeds to save. This was evidently the children's first experience in looking at apple cores: they are accustomed to eating slices with skin and seeds cut away.

ANALYSIS OF PLANNED ACTIVITIES

a	b	c	d
Previous level	Planned Augmentation	Curriculum Guide Items in focus	Rationale
Eating foods	Sharing foods from home	(C, 3) sharing (C, 4) Consideration of others (C, 1) Relatedness to children (A, 9) Taste discrimination (A, 10) Smell discrimination (A, 8) Tactile discrimination (A, 13a, b) Concepts of quantity: number, size (A, 17) Self-concept, autonomy	Firsthand experiences becoming base for later vicarious experiences Self-concept expanded through recognition of other persons in actual setting.

EXCERPTS FROM TEACHER'S LOG:

9-29   F showed the group a grapevine which she had brought from the country. The children inspected
        vine and grapes and picked one. S, B, and Ju liked them, took small bunches of them.
        . . . Sn had brought some apples to share with the class: these we took to the roof. T
        cut them up so that Sn could pass the pieces.

10-29   Children took turns helping with the jack o'lantern. Sn said that she wanted to cut <u>alone,</u> but
        accepted the rule that with such a sharp knife she needed the teacher's hand over hers to guard
        against slipping. The seeds were collected and saved. Children tasted the raw pumpkin.

12-1   Carrots, celery, lettuce, bananas, and apples were brought from time to time, to be included in the
to   juice-time menu. One by one, children had a chance to use the knife and the vegetable peeler,
1-18   first with hand held and gradually with a minimum of supervision. Me could, when it was her
        turn, be expected to cut any of the vegetables to the size of mince-meat.

ANALYSIS OF PLANNED ACTIVITIES

a	b	c	d
Previous level	Planned Augmentation	Curriculum Guide Items in focus	Rationale
Eating foods	Enlarging knowledge of characteristics of common foods	(A, 15a) Nature study	Relating all sense impressions to the object, leading to concept.
Passing food		(A, 6) Visual discrimination	
		(A, 9) Taste discrimination	
Watching T use knife	Helping to hold knife	(A, 10) Smell discrimination	Reinforcement through experiencing the elements of common objects in the situation.
		(G, 5c) Use of knife	

EXCERPT FROM TEACHER'S LOG

1-18   We discussed buying apples with the nickels that S, Ju, and R had brought to school. T and the
       three boys went to the store. T told the man that each boy had five cents and wanted to know how
       many apples he could buy with it. The storekeeper gave each one an apple, and the boys gave their
       nickels to the cashier. The boys took turns with the knife. R cut up his apple first, then . . . tried
       to take the knife from Ju, who had the next turn. He said, "He's using the wrong part of the knife."
       S needed to have his hand guided. The apples were cut into many small pieces, which were passed
       to the other children who were grouped around the record player, listening to music.

ANALYSIS OF PLANNED ACTIVITIES

a	b	c	d
Previous level	Planned Augmentation	Curriculum Guide Items in focus	Rationale
Watching while T uses knife and helping to hold knife	Handling knife with minimum supervision	(G, 5c) Use of peeler and knife	Combining familiar elements in a new process
Sharing a food activity	Dividing an item so it can be shared	(A, 13b) Number concepts (A, 12b) Money concepts	Relating numbers to activity
	Planning for a food activity	(A, 16) Planning ways and means (C, 1) Turntaking (C, 3) Sharing plans	Cutting an object into pieces (factoring of a whole).
			Taking account of relevant information
			Verbalization

EXCERPTS FROM TEACHER'S LOG:

1-28   T outlined the various parts of the day's cooking project (stuffed dates). S said, "I don't like walnuts," then asked, 'Are they soft?" The word walnuts evidently sounded too much like <u>chestnuts</u>, which S had not liked . . . Ji stuck to the nut-cracking for a long time, using both hammer and nutcracker. K struggled with the nutcracker, trying to get force with his hands, and when he cracked the nutshell said loudly, 'Teacher, I got it!" All children tried both tools.

2-25   The children listened to the milk slosh about in the coconut, helped to pound holes in the eyes and pour out the milk, then helped to crack the nut itself. They admired the whiteness of the meat, tasted, and expressed various degrees of disapproval. L said, "It tastes ugly." . . . There was interest in the coconut size. Children seemed to wonder at the idea of this big thing being a nut. They suggested using a hammer to crack it but someone specified, 'Take a big hammer." S said, referring to the fibers, "Oh, you got grass on them and now you can't get it off."

ANALYSIS OF PLANNED ACTIVITIES

a	b	c	d
Previous level	Planned Augmentation	Curriculum Guide Items in focus	Rationale
Use of hammer as primary play activity	Use of hammer, nutcracker as means to an end	(A, 6-11) Sense impressions - taste, smell, temperature, color	Combining familiar elements in a new process
Eating prepared food		(A, 16) Vocabulary problem-solving	Attending to new sense impressions
	Preparing foods	(C, 3) Cooperating in a complicated task	
Identifying familiar foods	Learning to recognize idea that food is prepared	Sharing results	Comparing ideas
Eating preferred foods		Offering verbal and physical help	Cooperative planning.
	Tasting unfamiliar foods	(G, 5c) (E, 9) Use of hammer, knife, nutcracker	
	Comparing flavors		

EXCERPT FROM TEACHER'S LOG:

2-17   During the music period, T got out the song book with John, the Rabbit in it, and the children looked
        closely at the black and white drawings. T drew special attention to the pictures of carrots and
        cabbage. Do led the others in singing. B pretended to be a rabbit: he hunched on all fours
        eating an imaginary carrot . . . At the close of the sequence, children returned to the tables to
        work on "books" — folded sheets with drawings of a rabbit, a carrot, and a head of cabbage. The
        handwork held attention for a long time. Children chose correct colors for the three pictures
        (from orange, brown, and green crayons ready in a separate tray) and colored the three objects
        according to directions. There was a brief preliminary focus on orange, since this color had not
        had special attention before . . . The "poorest" coloring represented the most important advance,
        since three children who had so far done no representative coloring marked the pictures with the
        correct colors and did no random scribbling.

ANALYSIS OF PLANNED ACTIVITIES

a	b	c	d
Previous level	Planned Augmentation	Curriculum Guide Items in focus	Rationale
Singing response song, "John, etc."	Noticing pictures connected with text of song	(A, 23) Relating song words to experience with vegetables	Familiar elements in fictional setting
Noticing drawings	Interpreting pictures and applying color learnings from cooking experiences	(A, 15b) Exploring ideas about foods for animals Picture symbols	Absorbing vicarious experience
Spontaneous leading, following.		(A, 11a, b) Applying color concepts	Follower-leader practice
	Leading of group, following leader, at request	(E, 3) Staying within outline or recognizing outline as pertinent	Translation of symbolic concrete activity
		(C, 1) Comparing products	
		(A, 4a, 5) Conscious cooperation in group singing	

EXCERPTS FROM TEACHER'S LOG

5-12   R said "You know that big paper you wrote about what we do?" (He was referring to a chart
list of daily activities.) "Well, are we going to do another one today?" . . . The work of washing and
preparing celery, radishes, lettuce, carrots, and green onions was efficient. Jy was especially
vigorous in washing celery and breaking it into pieces. A, wiping off a table to help tidy up,
spent a long time drawing her sponge across the black surface and watching the moisture evaporate.
In the kitchen, all had a turn at cutting leaves from radishes with a sharp knife. Back in the classroom, all worked with plastic knives, cutting up vegetables for salad. They sampled as they cut,
then put salad bits in cups, got salad dressing, crackers and cheese, and settled down to eat. The
intent had been to mix bowls of tossed salad, but the cutup materials no sooner got into the bowls
than they were dished out into the cups and eaten. Jy and Me worked long after the others
stopped. Jy had a half carrot beside her cup, and she ate it, bite by bite, as she cut up the other
vegetables. Me industriously reduced one stalk of celery to tiny pieces.

5-13   R said, "You remember I tasted those (radishes) yesterday and didn't like them" . . . "I think
I'd better taste them. They might be different today."

ANALYSIS OF PLANNED ACTIVITIES

a	b	c	d
Previous level	Planned Augmentation	Curriculum Guide Items in focus	Rationale
Preparing one or two vegetables for class use	Preparing several vegetables for class use	(G, 5) Use of knife, scrub brush, sponge, fork, serving spoon	Familiar objects, sensations, actions in a new situation
Working with one or two children	Combining vegetables	(A, 12) Language—vocabulary review Grouping—vegetables	Making symbolic plans
Carrying out a simple plan suggested by T	Working as part of a large group	(A, 3) Use of symbols	Following written plans
	Preparing a comprehensive plan and following it		

EXCERPTS FROM TEACHER'S LOG:

5-13 One group of children arrived early and settled down to class planning. Some cutout vegetables and leaves were ready to work with, and attracted attention. Children became interested in manipulating paper fasteners to attach leaves to carrots, celery, and radishes and to fasten lettuce leaves together.

5-19 The children were attracted by the papier-mache vegetables, once they had examined the peppers and cucumber Ju and J had painted last week. T had more forms ready to work with, today, before time to start cooking. Radishes, celery, green onions, strawberries, oranges, apples, and bananas were included in the shapes. (Children have sampled and worked with all of these during the years.) The finished products were added to the grocery store stock.

5-19 T brought in some artifical (wax) fruit, and also some real items, and children enjoyed comparing
to   and identifying the real and "make-believe".
5-31

ANALYSIS OF PLANNED ACTIVITIES

a	b	c	d
Previous level	Planned Augmentation	Curriculum Guide Items in focus	Rationale
Painting, assembling hand-work items	Assembling pieces to produce a planned result	(A, 1-3, 12) Symbolic learnings two-dimensional three-dimensional	Producing symbols
	Painting to match an experienced item	(C, 3) Planning Summarizing (A, 12) Grouping (E, 3) Coloring	Experiencing review and recall process

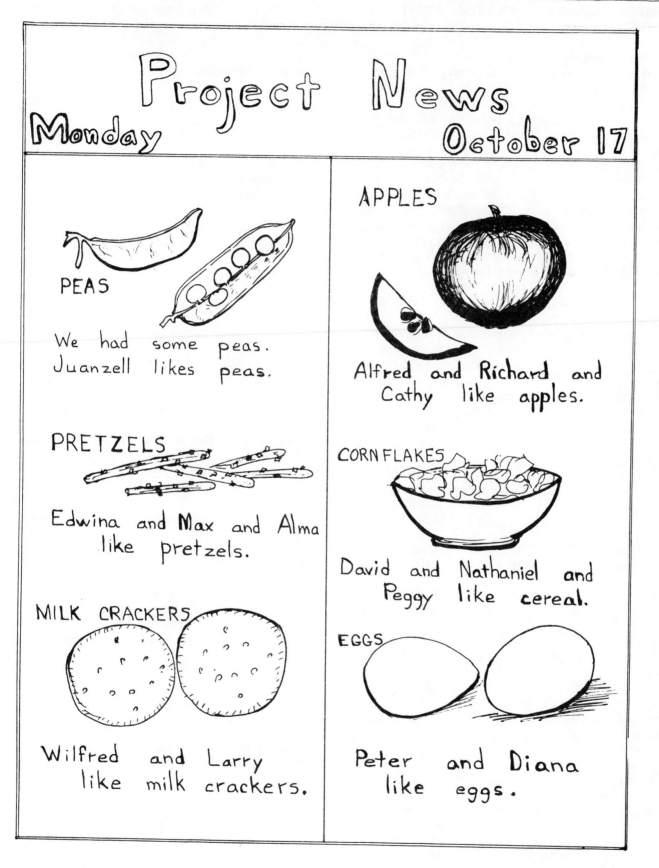

Project News

Monday
October 17

PEAS

We had some peas.
Juanzell likes peas.

PRETZELS

Edwina and Max and Alma
like pretzels.

MILK CRACKERS

Wilfred and Larry
like milk crackers.

APPLES

Alfred and Richard and
Cathy like apples.

CORNFLAKES

David and Nathaniel and
Peggy like cereal.

EGGS

Peter and Diana
like eggs.

READING READINESS AS A CONCEPTUAL SEQUENCE

The preschool program as a whole was regarded as a reading readiness program; it was designed to provide a foundation of factual information and language understandings deemed essential to successful reading. Activities with books, pencils, crayons and other school materials were part of the general program, as evidenced by items on manipulative, creative and intellectual use of the materials included in the Curriculum Guide. One or two children in both the younger and older groups, were found to be functioning at or near symbolic levels, while others were still at manipulative levels. The following table showing first and fifth steps of a few relevant Curriculum Guide items, indicates the spread of behavior in the classes.

Curriculum Guide Item	1	2
(14) Time concept	Apparent lack of awareness	Can plan for for future
(1) Listening to oral language	Listens for directions	Can remember and carry an oral message
(2) Using books	Listening while story is read	Ready for reading (discriminates print forms)
(3) Handling of books	Not destroying	Use of books as a resource
(6) Visual discrimination	Diffuse visual activity	Symbolic behavior

To make provision for further development of children already at the symbolic level, within the general readiness program, experiences were framed to allow for the individual child's participation in a manner to ensure his forward movement. Described here are illustrative activities which seemed particularly effective for wide-range participation.

The method used was the same as for other activities: symbolic material was a part of every experience for the benefit of children at the upper reading readiness levels. There were no formal reading lessons or testing. That is, children were not asked to read. Specific reading readiness work included visual and auditory discrimi-

nation, work on concepts and use of art materials, as well as the handling of books and pictures or print symbols. The examples included illustrate motivation techniques, specific auditory and visual training, and ways of developing useful concepts.

Curiosity and Desire To Read

Curiosity about words and letters was deemed essential for creating a desire to read and for promoting attitudes necessary to effective learning. The children's interest in words and letters was manifest in their pointing to or asking about signs, notices, and labels on packages or food cans. At times, the teachers called attention to the words written on clothing (a Mickey Mouse shirt) or food packages (the letter K on Kellogg's K cereal), but more often, the children asked about them. The curiosity, recognized as the same motivation to read exhibited by all children exposed to print forms and adult reading activity, was encouraged, and children asked questions freely. This casual or indirect emphasis on words and their meanings fostered the child's awareness of the importance of words. The attention was not initiated by the teacher but picked up by her from the questions of the children; the experiences were the result of the child's curiosity.

The desire to read involved the idea that reading was valuable. The children were given opportunity to observe the teacher's use of reading, and to imitate the process. Soon after arrival at school each morning, they took books and sat at the tables looking at them unless something else was presented for their consideration. During the day, a story might be read, or songbooks were used by teacher or music consultant, with opportunity for the children to inspect music notations, text, and pictures. Books were an integral part of their day in school. Reading was something that helped answer independently the questions asked of the teachers, about words and letters. Children felt free to ask their questions and therefore the value of reading was reinforced when the teacher read to find the answer. Many of the experiences with symbols were put into free play time. A stimulating tangible material was a teacher prepared word wheel with names and pictures of things familiar to the children. Some children used this independently, studying meanings of the words from pictures and asking the teacher for definitions. Also included in free play were the writing of the children's names and of the word today, thus introducing the idea of spelling. Children wanting to copy books or make their own did so during free play.

Reading Materials

Reading materials were not limited to books, experience charts, magazines, bulletin boards or other conventional materials. They included various activity and sense-stimulating items. The word wheel mentioned earlier was originally a revolving card index for telephone numbers. Each word put in for the children was on a separate card and was illustrated by a picture. The child turned the wheel at will, reading his way around; the wheel provided activity and manipulation, as well as reading experience.

In using teacher-made books children stood before their classmates and turned the pages for the songs, while the group sang. Some books contained things to move or to feel. For example, the rag doll songbook contained dolls made of colorful cotton print; the mouse in Hickory, Dickory Dock moved; for I've Been Working on the Railroad, banjo strings could be "played" and a train moved. A book written about the classroom white mice had a cage with a moveable door and mice to be taken out and returned. These captured interest and also provided for manipulative activity.

After purchasing fruits for juice time, the children's attention was called to a jigsaw puzzle picture of these fruits in a certain perspective. Some of the children had opportunity to arrange the real fruits on a model of the picture. Children were learning to match one thing to another, to notice perspective, and to see details.

When a book of action silhouettes was shown to the children, the teacher mentioned casually that many words started with the letter s, such as slide, skip and sit. After the actions were performed in the classroom and in the gym, two pictures of each action were cut from identical books. The children enjoyed matching the pairs and placing them side by side on the observation booth ledge. As opposed to mechanical work in a workbook or passive listening, the children were actively involved in the learning process; their bodies, for example, were utilized in learning the concepts of sit, skip and slide.

Teachers presented symbolic experiences of various kinds: blackboard sketching and printing, songs, artwork, play themes, and craft projects which reinforced and extended the concepts learned through action.

In selecting materials for children's activities, teachers anticipated need for recognition and differentiation of forms, sizes and colors for beginning reading work. In working with alphabet letters attention was given first to capitals because many of the parents were using upper case letters with their children. Gradually, however lower case letters were introduced in teacher-made books and attendance charts and in words written on the board; similarities of the two forms received comment. Later, upon the introduction of a set of alphabet puzzle cards, some children fitted capitals to the corresponding lower case letters. Children playing with these were told the names of the letters when they asked. By calling their attention to the names of the letters and pointing out various letters, differences among various symbols were identified.

To teach colors, effort was made to help children attend to a color and use its name. One color at a time was taught by its use in numerous contexts. Ordinarily the primary colors were learned first, then black and white, then the shades. The description of techniques used to teach orange will illustrate the approach to color discrimination for a group which had difficulty with the concept and the word. On the daily attendance sheet checked by the children, the teacher underlined or circled the child's own name with an orange crayon as he watched; the name of the color was mentioned. Pumpkins, oranges and carrots, brought to class, were used in a variety of action settings. The teachers added "my orange carrots" to John, the Rabbit, a folk song being learned, and included it in an illustrated book. Since the children liked the song and sang it many times, they were exposed to the word and idea, and eventually most learned it. Subsequently, variations such as light and dark were called to the children's attention for recognition that all shades of a color could be called by the generic name. Generalizations such as this and the work on discrimination of details were the two aspects or goals of visual training.

Auditory Factors

Distinguishing sounds, as the basis for later work in phonics, was part of auditory training. Children's attention was drawn to the sounds of letters with easily distinguished visual characteristics and constant phonetic value. For example, when one child noticed the final y in several names, and the children responded to comments on the way it sounded, the teacher, with the children, found all the names that ended in y. She then asked the children to listen carefully for the sound of the letter. A similar procedure occurred with M and the words Miss, Miller and Mary. Most children at roll call, simply said "I here today." rather than "I'm here today." The result of the teacher's verbal approbation upon the inclusion of a clear "I'm" was the child's assumption of increased responsibility for self improvement.

Focus was directed to initial sounds. The letter z and its sound were of interest when, in response to a child's report on his airplane trip, the teacher mimeographed a picture of the plane and the word "z-z-z-zoom," the plane's take-off sound. Children recognized the sound and later the letter in the word zoo. Several repetitions of this analysis of familiar words for initial sounds (p, s, b, o) emphasized the listening process and the matching of printed forms.

Enrichment of Backgrounds

For a variety of reasons, the children had special need for an enrichment program. Enrichment was interpreted as expansion of an idea, rather than addition of materials to provide extra activities. A description of the use of one piece of material which helped to develop and expand several concepts will show its relationship to the reading readiness program.

The song John, the Rabbit mentioned earlier, was introduced by the music consultant. The text is as follows:

Oh, John, the Rabbit,	Yes, Ma'am
Had a mighty habit	Yes, Ma'am
Jumping in my garden,	Yes, Ma'am
Eating up my cabbage,	Yes, Ma'am
My sweet potatoes,	Yes, Ma'am
My fresh tomatoes,	Yes, Ma'am
My orange carrots,	Yes, Ma'am
My nice green onions,	Yes, Ma'am
Well if I live,	Yes, Ma'am
To see next fall,	Yes, Ma'am
I ain't gonna have,	Yes, Ma'am
No garden at all.	YES, MA'AM

The children first joined in on the words, "Yes, Ma'am," then learned the whole song. Later, a book was made with one line and an appropriate picture on each page. In addition to serving as an added book for children to explore, follow, and enjoy, it provided a symbolic representation and re-enforcement of their classroom experiences with the real vegetables at juice time.

The book was drawn so that the rabbit was seen to move, through pictures on successive pages, further and further away from the farmer and up a hill. From this children were introduced to per-

spective; it was one more experience in following the pictures, testing the reality, seeing the relationship between pictures and facts and looking carefully at details.

John the Rabbit was a favorite and well-worn "library" book. During free play children would, on their own initiative, repeatedly and quietly sing John the Rabbit, turning the pages and looking at the words. Throughout the preschool program, the teachers fostered situations for child-motivated repetition of activities learned in the more teacher-structured settings.

The development of the concept orange illustrates the use of many materials to promote one idea. The same materials were used to teach other concepts, but care was taken to focus on only one concept at a time with a given piece of material. Many ideas came from an item such as John the Rabbit, but these came over a period of time. The symbolic representations of interest to the children were those which recorded previously developed ideas and concepts.

In the Project, no formal demands to learn to read or to understand an idea were made. The children were provided experiences to enrich and expand their backgrounds and which, because of their enjoyment, they wanted to repeat. Teachers focused on the value of reading and its conceptual bases, noting that readiness for print symbols was developing in such a context.

CHILD-PARENT-TEACHER RELATIONS AS A CROSS-SECTIONAL UNIT

The regular meetings of parents and teachers served two purposes: for the parents, counseling was provided in educational areas; for the teachers, the meetings were a curriculum tool, an additional means of attaining behavioral goals.

To illustrate the usefulness of parent meetings as a cross-sectional curriculum activity, excerpts from teachers' records are presented. The focus here, as in other cross-sectional illustrations, is on the children's activity. With reference to the behavioral units, effect of the child-parent-teacher relationship on language and speech, conceptualization, planning, and self-generated interest can be seen. Teachers and parents gained, too, from this situation as they concentrated on the activity of the children.

Interpretation or comment	Anecdotal report of a child's first day in school
Relationship between parents and teachers reflected in the child.	Child L came in with her mother and was smiling broadly as she entered the classroom carrying a small stuffed dog and her bag of clothing. She showed me her dog and told me he was Lassie and then

Interpretation or comment	Anecdotal report of a child's first day in school (Cont.)

followed the other children over to the clothing hangers. She had trouble unbuttoning her coat and came over calling me Mommy and asked me to unbutton it for her.

The first parent meeting, October 21

Written and oral messages carried home by pupils.

Invitation to the parents

Dear Parents: The first parents meeting of the year will be held on Wednesday, October twenty-first in the classroom, Room 111, Horace Mann Building.

Children were told that movies would be shown, and supplemented the invitation with an oral message.

One of the staff members took several reels of films during the class sessions at the beginning of the term and will be at the meeting to show the films. We hope you will be able to come, as we feel you will enjoy seeing your children as they go about their daily school affairs.
Yours sincerely, The teachers.

Date: October 21, 1960
Place: Room 111, Horace Mann
Time: 8:00 p.m.

Excerpts from teacher reports of the meeting

Exchange of factual information useful for school planning.

The movies were shown amidst much gleeful comment on the part of the parents at seeing their own children playing and being able to get some first-hand knowledge of the program at school. P's mother was pleased at the extra emphasis put on manipulative skills in terms of individual work with him. R's mother

Information about activities carried from school to home. Behavioral information.

commented on the film. "R was the only child who gave you any trouble." J's parents reported that he now talks much more at home and that he sings all the songs at home. (At school he is doing neither.) J's brother plays the accordion and J sings to it.

Ju's mother, seeing the children doing the Shoemaker's Dance, said, "What do you call that? Ju showed me what you did and I told him that that was 'Round and round, the shoemaker,' but he said, 'No, that isn't it.' " She noted the words, evidently so she would be able to respond to Ju another time.

Parent experience with use of piano for signal.

The small parent groups were still busily talking at 10:10 p.m. A teacher went to the piano and played "Goodnight, Ladies." One of the parents laughed and said, "A gentle hint."

Follow-up in class

Children asked about the film, the next day. Parents had told their children about it. The reels were shown in school and the children reported this event to parents. Careful attention was given by the children and teachers to words for the folk dance.

Interpretation or comment	Second parent meeting, December 8

Invitation

Invitation carried home by children with oral news.

Dear Parents: The second meeting of the year will be held on December eighth, in the classroom, Horace Mann Building, Room 111.

This will be a "back-to-school" night, with a chance for you to examine and try out the materials your children work with in school.

If it is at all possible, we will have some short reels of the swimming experience to show.

We hope you will be with us. Sincerely, The teachers.

Date: December 8, 1960
Time: 8:00 p.m.
Place: Horace Mann, Room 111.

Teachers reports - excerpts

Parent experience with school materials.

Feedback of planning

Material for future class planning; for future communication.

The groups were impressed with the movies of swimming. Four parents were fiddling with clay, not really doing much with it but using it to keep their hands busy while they were chatting about future placement.   P's father asked about the teachers in the public school classes. S's excitement about both parents attending was apparently not limited to behavior in school since her mother said that S told her siblings to be good that evening so her parents could leave. Her father seems quite interested in the construction of the tables and chairs and other materials. L's mother finished icing the play birthday cake with soapsuds icing. She is interested in taking part in L's birthday party on January 3. Me's mother expressed interest in the Christmas party and offered to come to school to help. She spent time with store materials and said, "Me is always collecting things for the store. I have to get back some things because she collects things we haven't emptied." Parents suggested activities with soapflakes to follow up bubbles and cake icing. They also asked for song texts.   Teacher played, and we sang songs and showed movements. Parents who had missed copies of the newspaper asked for them.

Follow-up in class; follow-up with administrative head.

Feedback of parents' (factual) reporting to children; factual response to expressed concerns of parents.

Inspection of clay, painting, etc., done by parents. Children elaborated on soapsuds play.

The Curriculum Study group discussed the song texts and decided to prepare and send home words for all songs.

Children talked in class about parents' reports of the meeting. Newsletters mentioned both.

Because of parents' concern about future placement, their questions were referred to an official and processes already under way were rechecked.

Interpretation or comment	Final Parent meeting, May 26

Invitation

Invitation carried home by children, with message as to topic of conversation.

Dear Parents: The fifth parents meeting will be held on Thursday, May twenty-sixth.

The Assistant Director of the Special Education Research Project, will be the guest speaker, and there will be some general discussion on the topic of educational planning for children with learning problems.

As this is the last meeting of our group this year, we hope that all of you will be able to arrange to come. Yours sincerely, The teachers.

Date: May 26
Time: 8:00 p.m.
Place: 256 Thompson (This is on the second floor in the building attached to Horace Mann Building. It is reached by using the same entrance as is used for Horace Mann.)

Teachers' reports

Attention to placement problem.

Although the problems of public school placement are not immediate for some of these parents, they are very much concerned and the talk seemed to alleviate many areas of concern for them in just supplying them with information about the process.

After the speech there was time for coffee and many discussions of next year's schooling with some of the parents being concerned with the change of teachers. We attempted to assure them that the children would make an adequate adjustment, that it was part of normal school experience.

Discussion of current activities and plans.

Twelve of the fifteen older children's families were represented at the meeting, evidently because of concern with placement. Details given by the Speaker, on the Project, and also on procedures for placing children seemed to answer questions which had arisen. Parents seemed to be satisfied to learn of procedures they could follow. The discussion gradually turned to questions about the closing of school and the reopening next fall. Parents of the younger children were interested in next year's program.

Requests for reactions to an end-of-school picnic, to include parents and siblings, led to tentative plans.

Follow-up of final meeting

Feedback of consideration of school problem.

Conversation in classes about the meeting, next year's schools and teachers.

Letters to parents, from the Project office, about tentative placements.

Newspaper about parent meeting, picnic plans.

Interpretation or comment   Follow-up of final meeting (Cont.)

Participation of families in   End of school party for younger class. A.M.
school event.
                                    End of school picnic for older class. P.M.

                                    Newspaper about summer vacation, school plan for fall.

The impetus given to classroom work by the parents' familiarity with classroom materials and activity plans was noticeable in performance of the children and in their increased verbalization about prospective and past parent meetings. Newspaper announcement and reporting of parent activities, plus reporting of the children's volunteered news about parent reactions, enabled children to experience the force of written symbols. A final benefit, which had not been sought, was the children's beginning appreciation of vicarious experience. On the morning following a parent meeting, children walked about the room looking at chairs and tables and searching for tangible evidence of parent attendance: "Did my mother sit here?" "Whose father painted that picture?" were some of the questions. It became expedient to provide ample refreshments for the parent meetings to ensure left-overs for the children's juice break the following day; the classes particularly enjoyed this sharing of the pastries or other refreshments.

The newsletter reproduced here illustrates the way in which news items served to stimulate and reenforce three-way child-parent-teacher communication based on the children's activities.

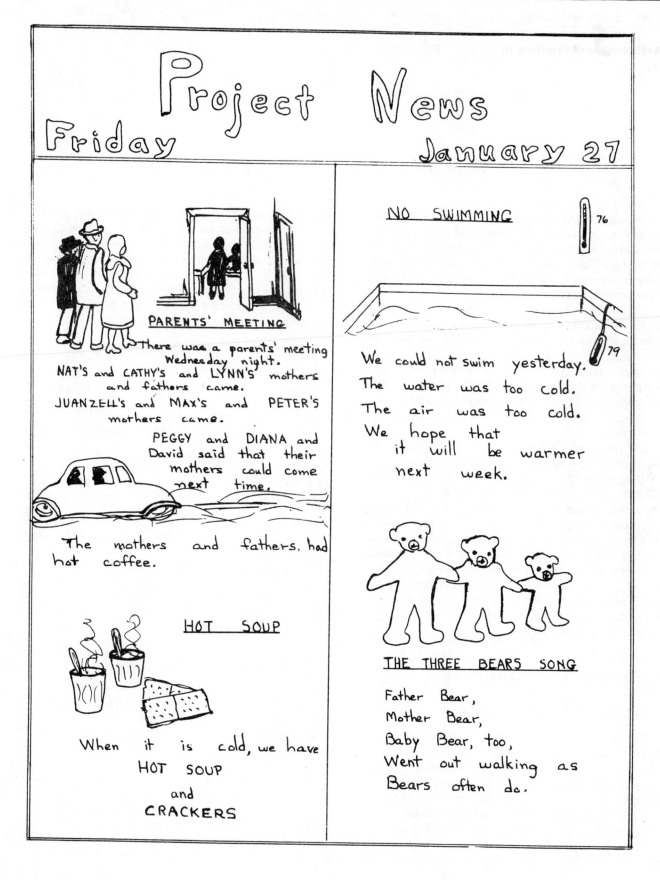

Project News

Friday   January 27

PARENTS' MEETING

There was a parents' meeting Wednesday night.
NAT'S and CATHY'S and LYNN'S mothers and fathers came.
JUANZELL'S and MAX'S and PETER'S mothers came.

PEGGY and DIANA and David said that their mothers could come next time.

The mothers and fathers had hot coffee.

HOT SOUP

When it is cold, we have
HOT SOUP
and
CRACKERS

NO SWIMMING

76

We could not swim yesterday.
The water was too cold.
The air was too cold.
We hope that
it will be warmer
next week.

79

THE THREE BEARS SONG

Father Bear,
Mother Bear,
Baby Bear, too,
Went out walking as
Bears often do.

CHAPTER 5

PROGRAM ORGANIZATION AND MANAGEMENT

Although the teachers' central task was developing and implementing the preschool curriculum, they were also concerned with related management problems. These dealt with the organization of the classes themselves and adjustments to the purposes of cooperating groups.

Within the province of the teachers were: adjustments to transportation company schedules, ways and means of arranging a double session in a single classroom; adjustments to requisitions for children's time and for research processes; and rearrangement of schedules for special program experiences. These matters were in addition to planning for daily class programs and use of recreation areas.

The teachers also work as a committee to establish effective in-class structures. Particularly pressing were questions of grouping children for activity; studying transitions between activities and balances between kinds of activity; solving problems of classroom management; and working out effective procedures for the two-teacher setting.

A third management concern was arrangement of parent meetings. Since parent meetings were part of the over-all home-school relationship, the programs were planned to fit into a year's sequence. The present chapter summarizes adjustments made in the college setting.

SCHEDULING ARRANGEMENTS

Adjustments to Transportation

Transportation arrangements set the time limits of the school day. Pupils came from Manhattan, the Bronx, and Queens and were en route for periods ranging from ten minutes to about an hour and a half. The transportation company officials gave priority to the preschool children, routing two vehicles to ensure the shortest possible travel time and computing a combination pick-up and return schedule for the between-sessions (noon) exchange of pupils. The

teachers, setting up morning and afternoon preschool classes within this schedule, had to consider, also, children's ages and susceptibility to fatigue. Since several children had a normal daily travel time of three hours, a two and a half hour school day was deemed the maximum. Below are sample class schedules illustrating the need for dovetailing school and transportation company arrangements.

Morning class

Earliest Pickup	School day	Return Home
6:45	8:00-10:30	Approx. 12:00
7:00	8:30-11:00	Approx. 12:30

Afternoon class

Earliest Pickup	School day	Return Home
11:45	1:15-3:45	Approx. 5:30
12:15	1:30-4:00	Approx. 5:45

Schedules varied from year to year as new children with new addresses were fitted into the itinerary. School activities were planned so that opening activities could be adjusted to delayed arrival of either car.

A Double Session in a Single Classroom

Although teachers could have used additional time to advantage, they learned to operate economically in the allotted two and a half hours. The scheduling and other arrangement for dual room use depended less on time than on intergroup relationships. Physical arrangements and rearrangements of the work and play areas, disposition of equipment, and storage of materials and supplies replanning adjustment. Examples of physical arrangements which facilitated program operation were reversible bulletin boards, removable covers for cupboards and equipment which could be dismantled quickly. Time was a factor in the reordering of the room for the next session of the alternate group.

Adjustments to Research Schedules

The design of the Mental Retardation Project included periodic testing of the children enrolled in the preschool. Twice during the year, for periods of a month or more, class schedules were altered to facilitate administration of the test batteries. Minor rearrangements were made at other times to permit psychologists to work with children missed during the regular series. Initial adjustments were needed since the teachers came from situations where teaching was the prime focus, and were not accustomed to new roles in helping the children to anticipate visits to testing rooms and adapting to the schedules. Upon realization of the problem, procedures were devised to ensure, first, a minimum of traffic in the classroom; second, a schedule to be utilized effectively for curriculum as well as for testing purposes; and third, inclusion of research staff members in activities immediately before and after their sessions with the children. This approach was adapted from that of the language developmentalist who, in his early program, worked in the classroom and thus was able to make the necessary transfer to a conference room easy and natural. Program management in the last two years of the experimental preschool included curriculum use of testing schedule and a planned utilization of visits from research personnel.

Rearrangements of Schedule for Special Experiences

Swimming schedules, regular sessions with the music consultant, visits by the traveling zoo and other special activities which involved both classes were also discussed in advance by the teacher committee to eliminate encroachment on the time of resource people. For example, for work with the music consultant, the morning group scheduled its music at the end of the session while the afternoon group arranged for music as an opening activity. Thus the consultant ate lunch with the teachers and arranged her schedule to avoid unnecessary expenditure of time in traveling or waiting.

Trips were scheduled according to their objective and length of time required. An all-day expedition by one class was made possible through modification of the second class' hours to permit the necessary transportation adjustments. Teachers of both classes discussed trip arrangements even when these affected only one group since a solution for one was ordinarily useful for the other.

Inherent in arranging a trip or expedition was its function as a parent-relation detail. Times, schedule changes, destination and purposes of the trips were the subjects of letters and news announcements as well as of conversations among parents, teachers, children and drivers. For curriculum goals, this communication was highly valued.

IN-CLASS STRUCTURES

Grouping for Activity

The term grouping as used in preschool classes refers to centers of activity rather than to the more usual ability-level grouping. Teachers took advantage of the intrinsic motivation of materials and ideas to plan activity centered work. The number of groups and the extent of physical movement were controlled by the materials made available at any particular period of the day. The program was exploratory at first, taking the form of offering to the class a choice of two activities. Expansion of the procedure followed one of two directions, depending upon the composition of individual preschool groups. If the limited choice program was continued, changes were made at times in the two activities offered. When patterns of interest and attention were clearly evident in a class, the number of choices was increased. Teachers took cues from the interest patterns for their teaching control.

General techniques for setting up and maintaining multiple groups in a class included the following steps, or variations of them:

1. Presenting initially an activity in which most children were competent, and using that as a focal group. Dollhouse play and eating are examples of such activities.
2. Attracting a sub-group to a second activity by means of new materials or materials children had previously only explored. For example, a tangible toy such as the mailbox, or an idea-based set, such as miniature cars creating a traffic context, was set up for one or two children.
3. Expanding the second activity, giving children a chance to reach a moderate level of proficiency. Duplicate sets of miniatures or other tangible toys were used.
4. Drawing a new nucleus by expanding some aspect of one of the first two groupings. A new set of dishes in the dollhouse, some new dress-up items, or a book showing pictures of the tangible toys were supplied.
5. Observing children's use of materials for clues

to acceptable further expansions, sub-
groups and finally, regrouping to bring
several related activities together into a
new whole-class group. Picnic play,
grocery shopping, mail delivery to children
playing in the dollhouse, restaurant sequences and many other group experiences
were the outgrowth of this process.

Except in the initial observation of children in free
play situations to determine profitable settings for
grouping, the activities in a room were as related
and interrelated as possible. They supplemented or
developed from one another. Children who held
themselves aloof from the settings received individual help when class attention was held by materials and self-directed activity.

Materials employed for drawing a nucleus of
interested children were designated as baits. The
teaching procedure, however, was a circular one of
observing, selecting and introducing stimulus to a
child or children, observing the resulting activity,
guiding it to a competence level, then leaving it to
maintain its own momentum and to reveal possible
motivations for a more complex activity. The bait
changed imperceptibly, from week to week. Children whose attention was attracted and held briefly
by tangible lures in September, responded later to
such symbolic bait as spoken ideas or the announcement that planning needed to be done.

The development of multi-group activities is
given in some detail in the sections on cooking, discussion groups, and hand-work in Chapter III. The
long-term and short-term units (Chapter IV) illustrate the way in which one activity was drawn from
another and the way in which separately learned
processes were fed into cooperative class activities.

Transitions and Balances Between Activity

Efficient transitions from one activity to another,
and the balancing of quiet periods with physically-
active periods were matters of concern to the teacher group. The preschool children were able to
maintain a busy schedule without tiring when the
day's plan allowed for an ebb and flow of activity.
Energy seemed to be drained by inefficient transitions, by juxtaposition of periods of motor activity,
or by successive periods of sitting. Daily programs
in general were planned to provide for alternating
quiet and active occupations.

The program was developed in a sequence format
rather than a clock-time schedule. Children learned
that their day included the specified general activities. First year pupils or children who were added

to the groups during the year were given help by the
teachers in learning the sequence. Pupils who had
learned the general sequence were ordinarily able
to move from one process to the next without expli-
cit instructions. Their knowledge of the schedule
facilitated self-direction in transitions. Changes
in the daily program were made when the group was
ready to learn an alternate arrangement. Older
children followed the weekly plan with its five different schedules.

Transitions were considered to be formations of
new groups. Anticipation of an activity, whether
awakened by presenting a tangible bait or a verbal
one, was the force used to move children from one
activity to the next. They learned gradually to assume responsibility for clearing up one process and
beginning another. The teacher's role in a transition began in advance of the child's movement. Verbal cues, holding in abeyance an activity begun pre-
maturely by a child, and exchange of remarks between teachers were preparations for transitions,
setting the stage for purposeful movement to another
occupation. The ultimate goal of this kind of transition was the children's foreseeing and planning their
own movements with minimal cues within the context of a school day, then successive days, and
finally, a longer span of time. Ability to defer
activities first for several minutes, then for a period,
and eventually for a day or a week was developed
as an aspect of the planning.

Problems of Classroom Management

Ideal classroom management was self-direction
of the children in activities, which, over two years,
moved toward cooperatively-planned experiences.
The materials provided by the teachers determined
the content of activities. For the preschool retarded
children who entered between ages 4-9 and 5-9 and
left between ages 6-6 and 7-6, the range covered
nursery school, kindergarten and pre-academic
experiences. All entering children exhibited some
kind of self-direction, but their choices of activities
and their purposeful behavior were ordinarily referrable only to themselves; they were, with a few
exceptions, self-centered as well as self-directed.
In this respect, they resembled their age mates in
other nursery schools and kingergartens. Teachers
wished to establish in them an awareness of an active
respect for the rights and interests of others, in their
choices of activity and their performance. To promote
movement toward such goals, teachers utilized the self-
direction observed in the children. Teachers created
settings for that purpose, set up mechanical controls to
provide for group formation, and attempted to steer individual behavior little by little into a group context.
When necessary, teachers used personal controls to

ensure, if not participation in a group process, awareness of a group whose rights took precedence over the wishes of an individual child.

Techniques differed from class to class and teacher to teacher. The size of a class, the behavior patterns of children composing it, the relationships which developed between individual children and between teachers and individual children, needed to be considered in determining the management of a class. Classes which reached full size slowly generally attained effective interaction in the small group within a few weeks. Those which began at or near full size required a disproportionate amount of time. Each child introduced into an existing group changed the composition of the class and necessitated change of routine to absorb the new element. The number of hyperactive children in a group affected consolidation.

One of the first project classes was the subject of much discussion by the teachers. Of twelve children first admitted, half showed undue stress under the stimulus of the school setting. One of these six was released when it appeared that his major problem required other educational provisions. His replacement upon admission also responded to the school setting with excessive activity. The management problem was solved by dividing the class, with children in each section matched carefully to provide effective, but not similar, pairs. The sections came to school on alternate days, were given similar programs, and were helped to form effective relationships in the smaller, less-stimulating group. At the end of two weeks, the groups were merged, day by day and child by child, until the class was again at full strength. It was possible to maintain an efficient class by assuming that children drew some support from their well-knit sub-groups. At signs of extra stress, the class was divided for separate activities for a brief period of lessened stimulation. For example, half of the group went to the roof, while the others remained in the classroom; generally the overactive children were retained in the classroom, since their problems seemed to be a function of the new situation. The result of the experimental regrouping was interesting, and warrants further investigation.

Procedures in a Two-teacher Classroom

Just as addition of a child changed the composition of a class, the presence of two teachers in a classroom produced a group different from the usual one-teacher classroom. There were several combinations of teachers during the four years of experimental work. From discussion and study of problems which developed when neither teacher was in charge of procedures, a way of operating was devised. The adjustments applied to the techniques of conducting a class, to the ideas of interpersonal relations, and to the means of communicating without disturbing children's activity.

In general, two teachers who worked together effectively held similar purposes in their teaching and respected each other's basic personal tenets. Teaching purposes with reference to the goals for the children, careful observation of individual pupils, joint planning for the accomplishment of aims and attention in the classroom to the child's response to the opportunities opened for him were apparent in the most congenial teaching teams. The activity concept underlying the curriculum aided adjustment of individualistic teachers to a co-teacher process. When the aim was child experience and when the teacher functioned as much as possible outside the action nucleus, there was no central didactic role. Verbal presentations were summaries of what the children had experienced, and the teacher closest to the experience had the responsibility for summarizing. Management problems were handled similarly. The teacher in optimum position for dealing with a conflict or adjustment problem dealt with it. Each member of a teaching team treated the classroom as a composite which for her contained the other member of the team. To determine her own movements, she gauged the probable activity of the other teacher. The complementary movement is best illustrated by the handling of general activities. If one teacher was occupied with one or two children, the other took on the task of general surveillance or direction. The roles were reversed, at need, by a casual comment or by a movement such as bending over a child's work. Teacher signals were sometimes obvious to an observer; at other times they passed unnoticed. Interestingly, children in the classes interpreted and used with skill some of the teacher communication techniques. The general exchange of roles was usually planned as was the lesson content. In specific cases, as with the over-active group described earlier, the two teachers avoided risk of failure by scheduling each program together with each one's role prior to the children's arrival.

When it was necessary for a single teacher to handle the group, as in the case of unanticipated absence, a cohesive group was maintained by selecting experiences which the children knew well and in which they were relatively self-reliant. New activities were introduced with careful preparation, and with all materials at hand, or in the cupboards, ready to be taken out with a minimum lapse of time. The lone teacher sometimes increased her direct control to avoid disturbing the two-teacher activity habits.

The classroom, which allowed for movement of children and was equipped with abundant materials, was structured by the continuous insistence that children direct their own behavior, by the arrangement of materials, and by the teacher support which forced them toward responsible behavior. They had freedom to move, to talk, and to explore, but they were held responsible for infringements on the freedom of others. They were accorded respect, and in return had to respect others. Teacher purposes, which made possible cooperative teacher-function, derived from respect for one another and for the children.

Parent Meetings

Regular meetings of teachers and parents were held at six-week intervals during the year. Each school term, the sequence of meetings as reviewed in Chapter IV, included one evening for inspecting classroom and materials; one at which parents were asked to help with teacher problems in obtaining materials or in understanding physical difficulties of particular children; one when the children's work was exhibited or their experiences shown by means of films or snapshots; one in which suggestions for home activity or descriptions of curriculum were offered by teachers; and the final one at which the Project's Assistant Director discussed post-nursery school placement. At each meeting opportunity was provided for exchange of practical information about the children.

Parents, among themselves, as coffee was served at each meeting, discussed individual problems, doubts, and discoveries. From one another, they seemed to derive personal satisfaction and help in home problems, more directly and much more effectively than could be anticipated from the teachers.

Parents unable to attend meetings because of family responsibilities or travel problems were informed of the programs and encouraged to visit the classroom during the day. Again, the aim of the teachers was communcation to the parents of information on their child's school experiences.

Illustrations from Observer's Reports

From his observation post in the booth, the Project staff observer took notes or recorded on tape the different classroom procedures. Two running accounts, excerpts from taped records, are given here to illustrate several organization and management problems of the two-teacher classroom, and of one teacher working alone with a class in the absence of the second teacher. The two records were made on the same day. On that day, the music consultant made her regular weekly visit. Psychologists were administering tests and long sessions with individual children in the morning group and short sessions with afternoon children were scheduled. Major or minor alterations in routines permitted adjustment to the variations.

The first account refers to the morning group of five-year-olds. The ninth child was added to the group the day before the observation was made, and the observer comments occasionally on the activities of the new pupil.

The second account describes the afternoon group of six-year-olds. This is the second day of a three-day interval in which one teacher is reforming the group in preparation for the introduction of a new second teacher. Three children of the fifteen enrolled are absent. A relatively new pupil is still establishing relationships with classmates.

Included here are details relevant to transitions, movement in and out of the classroom by pupils and staff members, movement of the newest pupils, and, in the two-teacher classroom, communication between the teachers. Omissions marked by dots are details within activities, essentially highlighting occupations of individual children and are not immediately relevant to the processes of organization and management. The observation excerpts, together with comments from teachers' program outlines, illustrate the planned activity as it is carried out in the repetitive class context.

OBSERVATIONS

8:30 Arrival
   Coat removal
   Quiet time with books,
   as transition to next
   activity.

   Children select own
   books from rack and
   carry them to table.

The first group of children come in at 8:29. T_1. was waiting for them and greeted them at the door - and took the parents' reports from the driver. There were four children . . . T_2. went over toward the clothing area . . . T_1. and T_2. both helped. The children came over and sat down at the tables . (At 8:34) P. comes out and T_2. tells him to get a library book, etc. J. says, "Come on everyone; bring your books over here." . . .T_2. discusses the books with the children . . . At 8:44 the second car arrives with five more children . . . T_2. greet them and takes the parent reports from Mrs. B. Each child says "hi" to T_1. and she sends them over to the clothing

They get up to exchange one book for another, from time to time.

area. T_2. helps them and sends them to the table. After all the children are seated at the table, T_2. begins to look through the parents' reports. She looks up and says, "Now I think everyone can put their books up and come back and sit down." (The second group have only a minute or two of looking at the books.)

8:50 Work with puzzles

Children P. and S. walk over to T_2 . . . *S wanders to the record player . . . to the mail box. T_2. goes over and takes him by the hand and sits him down at the table. All the books are put away and the children are sitting down waiting for the next activity. T_2. says, "We are going to do puzzles this morning." T_2. supervises this at table . . . S.'s attention has wavered from time to time, but even he is able to sit in one place and work on a puzzle. T_1. (working at a cupboard) has been observing the children from time to time . . . T_2. goes around and helps the various children. T_1. finishes . . . comes over and sits down at table 2 and helps the children. T_2. is giving a lot attention to S., trying to keep him attentive. Then she turns and helps Ja. C. is helping D. and L. T_1 sees at 9:05 that P. was losing attention . . .

Individual transitions to free play.

9:10 Free play.

Clean-up of puzzles by one teacher.

He doesn't seem able to finish his puzzle. She called him to her . . . helped him. At 9:07 T_1. turned to T_2. and asked her if P. could play in the house area. T_2. said yes. T_1. asked A. if she would like another puzzle. She didn't seem very interested, so T_1. asked her if she would like to play in the house area. She said yes very excitedly and ran over. This was the beginning of free play. T_2. went over to get out some blocks. T_1. begins to put some puzzles away - those that the children have worked on. Two of the children have remained . . . K. gets up. At 9:15 the psychologist took D. out. Thus all except one are engaged in free play activity. S. went and got the telephone and is carrying on conversations, first calling daddy, then P. Ja. is working by herself, still on a puzzle . . . At 9:22 T_2. looks at her watch . . . at 9:29 S. is back playing by the sink. T_1. restricted him and told him he couldn't. She had to take him (away from the sink).

5-minute warning of clean-up

Individual transitions to record period-lavatory arrangement.

9:40 Record period

At 9:34 T_1. announced to the children that in about five minutes they were to go and clean up and then have juice. T_2. was helping P. with a puzzle and T_1. was helping Su. The free-play activity seemed to slow down. Some of them began cleaning up. Ja. wanted to go to the bath. T_1 let her go. T_1. suggested that those who were through playing come and sit down at the record player. She directed those in the kitchen and block areas to clean up there. T_2. went over at 9:36 and set up the record player for the children. T_1. went to help put the blocks away. By 9:39 the free play activities were all cleaned up and children going to the bath. As they came back in, they came over and sat by the record player. T_2. is there. T_1. began to get ready for juice . . . she was aware (watching through the east door) of those children still in the bath. At 9:46 all the children had come in from the bath and T_2., seeing that T_1. was ready, said, "juice time." The record was playing Supper Time. This was the signal for the children to go to the tables.

Movement of whole group of tables.

9:50 Juice time

Transition to prepare for work with music consultant: individual movement with music

C wanted to sit at T_2'. table, but T_2. sent her to other table to even out 4 at each. D. and A. poured. P. left with psychologist. At 10:00 T_1. said, "Come over to the piano." Mrs. L. was not there yet. T_1. sat down at the piano and told the children to throw away their cups and come over. She began to play and the children began to throw their cups away. They didn't go over to the piano, however, T_2. began guiding them in the direction of the piano.

stimulus, plus
teacher help.

Chairs moved, to
leave tables free for
use as "barns" in
Little Gray Ponies.

10:15 Music Period
with consultant

(Drivers have arrived
and are waiting for
children.)

1:30 Arrival
Coat removal
Looking at books,
as transition.
(Second group is late,
which delays program.)

Psychologist begins
taking children.

1:41 Second arrival time
to be worked into
schedule.

1:45 Music

2:15 Handwork materials
brought out to
children at tables,

T_1. tried a Thanksgiving song . . . it seemed too complicated. So after
playing it once through, T_1. asked them what they would like to sing.
(Children marched to music, moving chairs back against walls as they
marched.) S. . . . began jumping up and down. P. returned to
classroom. They started Little Gray Ponies. Steve did participate in this
somewhat . . . T_1. asked T_2. if they could push the tables away and play circle
games. Mrs. L. came in at that moment . . . the children got in a circle
and T_1. suggested Mrs. L. play Bluebird.

After Bluebird was over, T_1. said that all the children should "go sit by
the piano and see what Mrs. L. has for you." She turned the activity over
to Mrs. L. The children did the hair cut song . . . another motion song,
then Flopsy Flora. Then she said, "Do we have time to do Grey Pony?"
T_1. told her they had already done that, and that it was time for children to
get their coats. So Mrs. L. played a marching song for them to march
out and get their wraps. (T_1. helped Mrs. L. helped also as she ended
playing.) Several were banging on the piano and T_1. called them to come
and get their partners. They did and all had left by 10:47.

Mrs. L. and T_3. are here. The books are on the tables before the children
come in, about five books on table 1 and about eight on table 2. At 1:29
the first group arrives. T_3. greeted them and took the parents' report from
Mrs. B. and directed the children to go take off their wraps. The Psychologist came in. T_3. is busy helping the children remove their wraps. L.
and Ae. go over by the piano, looking at the music books on the piano.
Psychologist gave T_3. the list of children she would be taking out this afternoon. S. went and sat down at the table. T_3. did go over to Ae. and
put her hand on her shoulder and asked her to go sit down at the table.
Ae. did go over and stand by the table and looked at a book for a few
seconds, then sat down. T_3. also had to urge B. to sit down. T_3. sat
. . . All except two were sitting at the tables with a book. Mrs. L. was
singing over by the piano for these two. L. came over and touched
piano. Mrs. L. said "Let's go sit down and tell me what you are reading
about." T_3. took L. on her lap.

At 1:41 the second group arrived . . . T_3. directed M. over to the
clothing area, then sat L. in her chair and greeted and talked with them,
sent them to clothing area, calmed Ae. who had gotten up excitedly to
greet the other children. T_3. went to the clothing area, helped . . . goes
round and gathers Ae. and B. who had begun to run around room
at arrival of others. She tells them to find chairs . . . asks J. to say
hello to Ae. who sat down there.

At 1:45 all children are seated; Mrs. L. and T_3. talk; children are excited,
talking loudly. At 1:46 T_3. says, "All right, children, Mrs. L. is going to
start music." Children get up and go over to piano as Mrs. L. begins to
play. T_3. gathers books, then allows Ae. to finish. Mrs. L. takes over
and tells children to go sit down, as they had gathered around her. Ae.
brought a book, put it back when Mrs. L. asked her to.

Mrs. L. plays, Here we are together. Then asks children. D. men-
tions Fire and several others are mentioned . . . loudly in excitement. . .
R. came back. Psychologist takes Jm. out . . . Mrs. L. presented a
new song, then . . . made a big circle, all children except J. for Bluebird.
A . . . . directed children . . . . Psychologist brought Jm back, took
By. . . . at 2:15, Mrs. L. played the good-bye song and said, "It's time for
me to go home." T_3. began to put the tables back in place and . . . gets out
paper and cut-out turkeys. Began to tell children what they would do. Some

as Mrs. L. terminates music period.

2:20 Handwork
    Thanksgiving posters. Children put posters on tray as they finish, go to wash paste from hands, move to free play.

    (The class had looked at posters of other group, the previous day, and asked to make similar ones.)

2:30 Free play
    House play or small tangible toys at tables.

    New: magnetic numbers, food chart.

    Putting away free play materials, starting wash-up, for transition to juice. Children assist in the preparation.

2:50 Juicetime

3:00 Discussion

    (Ordinarily at 1:40; postponed because of music.)

3:05 Table clean-up by teacher, while children throw away cups, move about, return to table.

3:10 Materials passed for soap suds: rotary beaters, plastic bowls, soap, water, straws. Soap suds

of the children begin to bring chairs and T_3. helps set them. Mrs. L. is over at piano with several children. She goes to get her coat. T_3. begins to pass out paper, etc. More children gather around table . . . D. is over pointing to a turkey on the bulletin board. Jm goes to get the telephone. T_3. takes it, tells him to get a chair. Same for L.

Mrs. L. left at 2:20. All of the children are at the tables. T_3. is going around writing their names on the papers. The chldren are singing as they work. Di. asks something about a purse. T_3. told her she could play with it during free play period, as well as L. with the telephone. She discussed what they might do during free play. Jm. finished, held up the picture, took it over to set along chalk tray. Other children followed . . . Some began to wander . . . T_3. took down telephones, gave one to J., one to L. They she went around to check hands, to see if children had washed. T_3. gets out various things, then goes back to help the few children who are left at the table. T_3. asks M. to pick up the paste cups . . . helps Ae. to put her picture up . . . sends S. to wash . . . gives Di. the purse.

2:27 and all are now engaged in free play . . . several still out at the bath cleaning up.

Children choose house, dress-up, store play or ask for small toys. Two children try out new magnetic numbers offered by T_3., also food chart.

At 2:41, T_3. looked up at the clock and said, "Oh, look at the time." Someone said, "Can we go to the roof?" T_3. said, "On a day like today?" She begins to clean up some of the items . . . starts some children.

At 2:43 she called out, "O.K. it is putting away time." B. ran away from cleaning up T_3. asked Ae. to help, gets B. by hand, helps him start, only a few children are cleaning up. T_3. goes to each area, encouraging them to begin. At 2:45 directs some children to the bath. Ae. wasn't helping, D. puts away but yells for M. J. went over to the record player. (This was ordinarily the transition activity during wash-up) . . . At 2:50 most of the children had been out to the bath and T_3 was settling them at the table for juice. She took J. out to wash, came back and with help of D., Ae., B. and L., tables were set with food, cups, etc.

2:53 T_3. poured juice into the pitchers. She poured into the cups, telling the children they could pour their second cup if they wanted to . . . T_3. talked with the children about making soapsuds . . . At 3:00 she said, "Let's look at our calendar while we eat." Discussed dates, party yesterday and the Thanksgiving holiday, noted absentees. As the children finished their juice, T_3. went around cleaning up a bit at a time. They get up on their own and throw the cups away. T_3. went to retrieve B.; brings a few more crackers. Some of the children are banging piano, some leaving table . . . looking out windows. T_3. is cleaning up. At 3:07 she asks the children to come away from the window. Gets out bowls.

All of them come to table . . . children put bowls on their heads and shouting and laughing and banging bowls . . . T_3. restricts those who are banging their bowls against table . . . 3:12 she went to pour water. L. comes running. J. is pushing grocery cart. At 3:16, after all children were settled and engaged in the activity she went and got J. . . .

T_3. decided suds were right consistency, got the cake they had been working

play used as tran-
sition to process of
putting soap-icing
on cake.

Clean-up transition.
Children go to
record corner as
they return from
lavatory.

3:40 Records

Putting on wraps,
one or two at a
time.

3:50 Preparation for trip
home.

on the day before and brought it to the table. Jm. didn't want the cake,
several girls did. Jy. got smock for painting. T_3. brought her to table. Jy began to help frost the cake. At 3:30 T_3. told the children they would have to
clean up and then they would listen to records. The children have been at
this activity for about 20 minutes. They are still going strong . . . beginning to be weary of it. T_3. started to clean up. Children help with clean-
up, go to lavatory and get soap off their own hands, etc.

At 3:57, T_3. went out and brought the children back in who were out at the
bath . . . She tells the children to take a chair and go to the record player.
Most of them do.

She goes over at 3:38 to the record player and asks the children what they
want first. They say "Take Me Out to the Ball Game." She is arranging
their chairs in a semi-circle around the player. T_3. got the record out
as the children begin to sing it . . . she puts it on. All the children are
back . . . and settled in the record player area except L., in the kitchen . . .
Ae. goes to wipe off a table. At 3:40 T_3. gets out gum-drops, then
balloons left from preceding day's party. L. and Ae. wipe tables.

At 3:44, she told B. to get her coat and take M. with her. B.
stopped and said, "Hey! Where are we going?" Then, "Oh, are
we going home?" Other children began to talk. T_3. took record off, said
no record if they talked so loudly. B. was still talking sadly about
going home. T_3. said it was almost time . . . children quieted down. At
3:50 she turned record off again and said, "I'm going to turn it off again
until we get all settled." . . . As the children need help, they come over
and T_3. helps them. At 3:57, Hy came and T_3. sent one group out.
D. resisted going for some reason.

The second car left at 4:00

CHAPTER 6

EVALUATIONS

The basic teacher records were the anecdotal accounts of daily sessions. The two teachers for each group pooled their observations in a running account of group and individual child activity. To keep the daily log within bounds, events relevant to the planned program ordinarily provided the framework; supplementary happenings and incidents which referred to continuing problems were also included. Teachers' observations were focused directly on individual children under two special circumstances: first, each child's first day in a class was recorded in detail; secondly, whenever the suitability of the school placement was questioned, the child was checked through several days' activities. The consecutive log, then, contained information which could be utilized in teachers' records of both individual and group behavior.

Individual Records

Three kinds of individual records, based on the anecdotal reports, were used. They were:

1) The ratings on curriculum guide items. Items were checked at the beginning of a year, at mid-year, and at the end of the term.
2) A year-end summary of each child's progress during the year. In this summary, progress was in terms of the long-term curriculum goals.
3) A year-end report to parents, which was a condensation of the individual summary. The reports were the concluding phase of the year's child-parent-teacher relationship. Older children ordinarily were shown and had an opportunity to discuss their own reports, while younger children were given whatever information they seemed ready to use.

Composite Records

For each class, a comprehensive annual report, summarizing briefly the year's curriculum study and classroom activities as described in Chapters III, IV and V of the present report, was prepared by teachers for their respective groups. A resume and evaluation of group progress toward long range and short range curriculum goals were part of the survey. Information on progress in the various areas was drawn from anecdotal records and from the Curriculum Guide ratings of individual children.

At the end of the experimental classwork (June, 1961), the accumulated Guide ratings of children in preschool groups during the 1958-59, 1959-60, and 1960-61 were recorded and tallied. Scores for groups were combined, and September, January and June means were computed. The resulting mean scores, presented here in linear charts, show some interesting trends. Child improvement was noted in all categories, but certain areas showed continuous growth. Whether that growth was a function of school experience, or home experience, or maturation, the fact of its occurrence indicates value in concentrated effort or opportunity for children of this chronological age. Although the intervals on the Curriculum Guide five point scales are not equated, growth in manipulation areas shows a consistent lag as compared to mean ratings in most areas. The scores may indicate the existence of special kinds of problems in children diagnosed at an early age as educable-retarded children. It is suggested that additional preschool programs, experimenting within the curriculum framework summarized in this report, would yield valuable additional information on curriculum content and methodology suitable for young children exhibiting — for whatever reason or combination of reasons — learning problems and retardation when compared with their peers.

A Child's Status and Progress: Teacher Logs and Curriculum Guide Ratings

The following illustrations are intended to show the teachers' use of daily logs and

Curriculum Guide Ratings in viewing one child. The first presentation shows the process by which performance on Guide items was identified in the anecdotal records for the purpose of rating the child. The second shows the child's status and progress profile using Guide ratings. Depicted in the latter are: 1) the child's functioning on entrance as compared with other Project pupils; 2) his growth from October of the first year to June of the second year; and 3) his comparative functioning in the various items reported at the end of preschool attendance.

Immediately following the illustrative profile are the tables of summarized ratings. The clustering of exit scores near level five, noticeable on many items and on the individual rating, indicates the need for extension of the five-point scale.

INDIVIDUAL LOG EXCERPTS AS BASES FOR CURRICULUM GUIDE RATINGS

Child D. C.A. 5-7 on entrance

Curriculum Guide Items	
F8a	September 16 (First day, first year). D. arrived with his mother in the station wagon. He greeted T. with a rather hesitant smile as T. opened the door of the station wagon and he handed me his school bag. He took T's hand and his mother's and walked up the stairs without a word, one step per tread, to the classroom. He refused verbally to enter the classroom but slipped through the door and looked around, holding onto his mother.
E1a	Although the three other children were sitting around the table pasting, cutting and drawing, D. sat off on the other side of the room with his mother. Even when she got up and joined us at the table, he stayed where he was and answered "no" to all requests to join us. T. told him he could sit on her lap if he liked . . . he came and sitting down on T's lap, picked up a figure of a boy and with some help from T. pasted it next to a picture he had identified as a car.
C1	
E6	
A6	
F16	D.'s first spontaneous response came when he say the large tractor-trailer and, when encouraged, rode around the room. This started M.'s interest and S.'s. However, the three went their own separate ways.
C1	
A4a	He joined the group at the piano but sat to one side by himself and did not participate in the singing. At juice time, he waited for everybody to start before he took a bite out of his large oatmeal cookie. He drank no juice and said little except to answer questions T. was asking in reviewing the day's program.
G5	
A4d	At storytime, D. drew his chair close to T's to sit and listen. After the first sentence, he was anticipating verbally . . . he brought over Red Light, Green Light to be read.
A14	When told it was time to go, D. got his coat readily and ran to his mother to tell her how he was coming back tomorrow.
G1n	Sept. 17 He put on his jacket, but upside down, so T. helped him by putting the jacket over the back of the chair, and showing him how.
A14	Sept 30. D. has picked up the routines in which he had been included (transportation was a problem and D. was consistently tardy) rapidly, and to the point where he reminds both teachers and children to anticipate coming events. On the roof the only equipment he has not used has been the slide.
F10	
E1a,1b	Oct. 30 D. does not tend to concentrate too well in structured manipulative activities. He does not care too much for coloring, or pasting, and needs teacher support to finish these activities.
E3,E6	
g1n1,n2	In self-care . . . he still needs much help in both putting on and taking off his outer clothing but likes the idea of trying first himself.

G1
E1,2,3,6

May Report. D.'s most obvious and important area of progress this year has been in social relations. He was frustrated by his lack of manipulative skills and by his lack of desire to communicate with the other children, not learning to use any of the manipulative materials with ease.

C1
F10

At the playground this month, D. laughs excitedly as he bumps the child on the other end of the see-saw or is bumped by him. He comes down the slide with gusto. When a new boy, N., entered just three weeks ago, D. showed intense interest in the child and by the third day was bosom pals with him. They play together all during free play, carrying on conversations and sharing materials easily. D. insists on N. for a partner always and is actually hurt if Nat snubs him occasionally.

Second year   C. A. 6-7

G1

Oct. 31. The children went Trick or Treating to two offices. D. lost pieces of his costume from time to time and soberly retrieved them and put them on properly before walking on.

A2
A4a

D., N. and E. each monitored songs, turning pages of the books so the class could sing.

E1b

D. tried to cut out a gingerbread boy, freehand, and came out with something which looked very much like a dinosaur.

C1

Nov. 5. On the roof D. was in a group playing monster. He still seems to be enjoying the physical contact this entails, when the children tumble over one another.

A14

A1
C1

Nov. 18. D remembered that before his absence on Friday he had been promised the next turn at asking about breakfast. He took possession of the parent report slips and held them until time to lead the conversation. He needed some prompting in commenting on menus, but a few began to say "Oh-h. Cornflakes!" etc., imitating T's intonation. He also asked, at each sheet he uncovered, "Whose is that one?" and thus actually followed the order of the sheaf of reports.

B7b
A1
C1

B7d

D. got out his airline set, put on the cap, got his pad and a pencil, and asked T, "What is your name?" then, "Where are you going?" and "What do you want for breakfast?" Several children watched him with admiration . . . T. got out hand puppets for the group gathered around D. when the plane sequence palled, and they joined in some "make-believe" conversation.

A4d

B7c
B4

A2

April 27. N., reading the story of the Three Bears, skipped relevant details. P., D., Di. did not allow the omissions, so the story reading was interspersed with comments and sometimes simultaneous narrations of events. Later, dramatizing the story, D. ad-libbed beautifully, playing a full role as Father Bear and making suggestions for his co-actors. D. helped with painting of the little clay bowls for the bear's house. Others painted furniture. The painting was different from January work on furniture. Children inspected for bare spots, then applied paint as needed. D. played with "the boxbook" of pipes, and gradually edged into Kathy's work with the word-wheel. He ended by using the other word-wheel alone.

June (Excerpts from final report to parents, regrouped according to six long-range goals).
C. A. 7-4
(Daily Living Skills)

G
C

Is competent in all areas of eating, drinking and dressing. Is slow in dressing, apparently liking occasional help from an adult.

(Cognitive sensory-motor skills)

A   Contributes to discussions involving time concepts, spatial relations, and elementary
nature and science facts. Shows understanding of complex language structures. Interprets
E   pictures. Has just begun to attempt line drawings. Shows only beginning interest in use
B   of pencil and crayons. Likes working with paints on large surfaces.

A   The disparity between language ability and use of pencil and crayon for written
E   expression suggests some problem. Since coordination with very small construction toys
is good, it might be profitable to have an ophthalmological examination to check.

(Communication skills)

A   Has done well in all oral language activities, including singing, group discussion,
B, C   story experiences, news periods. Helps with planning.

(Sustained attention)

A17,18   D. can be relied upon for self-direction. Does his part in carrying out plans.

(Acceptance of teacher values)

A17,18   From an initial shyness and inclination to withdraw, D. has changed slowly to an
C, D   attitude of interest. He can be relied upon for good conduct in all situations.

(Extracurricular social adjustment)

G   D. has been responsible for his own safety on the trips in which he has participated.
A, C, F   Early lack of interest in swimming experience changed to strong interest and effort.

MEAN SCORES ON SELECTED CURRICULUM GUIDE ITEMS FOR YOUNGER AND OLDER GROUPS (THREE PER YEAR)[1] AND FOR CHILD D (ENTRANCE AND EXIT)[2]

Guide Items	Ratings on Curriculum Guide Items	Mean Scores	
		Younger .-.	Older o-o
E1a Cutting		S 1.42	2.60
Tchr holding		Ja 2.28	1.75
paper		Ju 3.00	4.32
1b Cutting		3.00[3]	3.41
Independent		4.00	3.34
w. paper		4.00	3.82
E2 Drawing		1.39	3.22
		1.49	3.43
		2.00	4.35
E3 Coloring		2.17	3.72
		4.23	3.87
		3.33	4.23
E6 Pasting		2.00	4.25
		2.91	4.31
		3.95	4.78
F9 Running		2.83	4.41
		3.24	4.32
		3.64	4.65
F8a Stair Climbing		2.91	4.10
		3.29	4.31
		3.83	4.85
F10 Sliding		3.06	4.93
		3.81	4.96
		4.29	5.00
F16 Cars, trucks (Carriers)		3.89	5.00
		4.11	4.83
		4.78	4.91
F17 Musical Instruments		3.50	4.29
		4.20	4.81
		4.78	4.94
G9b Safety 3 on seesaw		3.14	4.87
		3.52	4.86
		3.65	4.91

[1] Vertical lines represent mean performance levels 1 to 5 on the curriculum guide items. In each case, the broken (-----) line depicts the children's growth from September to January; the solid (_____) line indicates their movement from January to June. Successive scoring for the younger group is depicted either on the upper line or to the left for each item; the older group's ratings are to the right or on the lower line. Where regression was noted, the broken and solid lines are concurrent.

[2] Connected points (X) on the left refer to Child D's ratings at entrance; those (O) on the right represent his rating at exit from the two-year program.

[3] Only two children rated on the item.

Mean Scores on Selected Curriculum Guide Items for Younger and Older Groups
(three per year) and for child D (Entrance and Exit) (Continued)

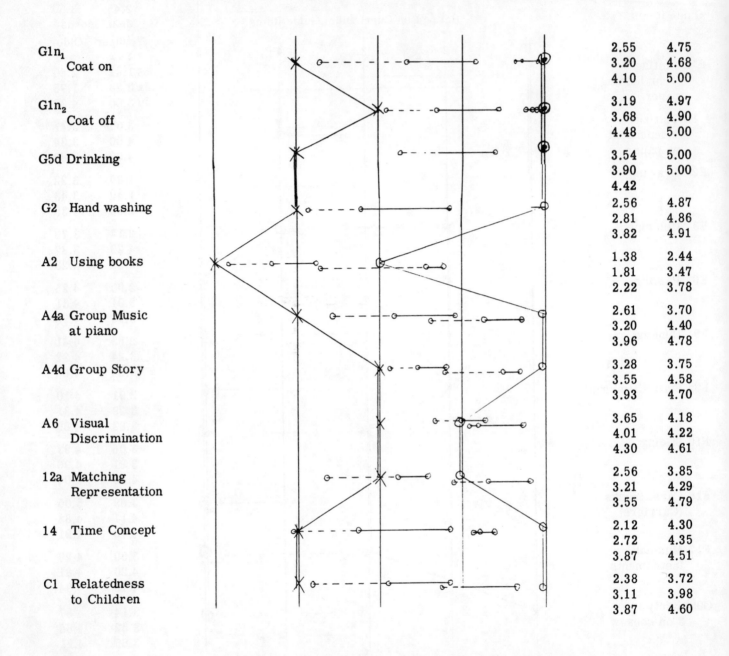

G1n$_1$ Coat on	2.55	4.75
	3.20	4.68
	4.10	5.00
G1n$_2$ Coat off	3.19	4.97
	3.68	4.90
	4.48	5.00
G5d Drinking	3.54	5.00
	3.90	5.00
	4.42	
G2 Hand washing	2.56	4.87
	2.81	4.86
	3.82	4.91
A2 Using books	1.38	2.44
	1.81	3.47
	2.22	3.78
A4a Group Music at piano	2.61	3.70
	3.20	4.40
	3.96	4.78
A4d Group Story	3.28	3.75
	3.55	4.58
	3.93	4.70
A6 Visual Discrimination	3.65	4.18
	4.01	4.22
	4.30	4.61
12a Matching Representation	2.56	3.85
	3.21	4.29
	3.55	4.79
14 Time Concept	2.12	4.30
	2.72	4.35
	3.87	4.51
C1 Relatedness to Children	2.38	3.72
	3.11	3.98
	3.87	4.60

MEAN CURRICULUM GUIDE SCORES FOR YOUNGER AND OLDER GROUPS
AT ENTRANCE, MID-YEAR, AND EXIT

A. Intellectual Development

	Younger x—x	Older o—o
1. Listening to oral language	S 2.39	3.26
	Ja 2.95	4.31
	Ju 4.07	4.46
2. Using books	1.38	2.44
	1.81	3.47
	2.22	3.78

A. Intellectual Development (Continued)

Item	Value 1	Value 2
3. Handling books	2.45	3.50
	3.00	4.33
	3.35	4.59
4. Participation in structure or grp. a. Music at piano	2.61	3.70
	3.20	4.40
	3.96	4.78
b. Records	2.95	4.23
	3.50	4.76
	3.90	4.81
c. Story with props	3.28	4.17
	3.65	4.62
	3.98	4.81
d. Story	3.28	3.75
	3.55	4.58
	3.98	4.70
e. Singing	1.49	3.26
	2.07	4.16
	3.31	4.48
6. Visual Discrimination	3.65	4.18
	4.01	4.22
	4.30	4.61
7. Auditory Discrimination	2.87	4.55
	3.22	4.47
	3.94	4.67
8. Tactile Discrimination	2.32	3.93
	2.96	3.88
	3.32	4.31
9. Taste Discrimination	2.72	4.50
	3.03	3.92
	3.53	4.50
10. Smell Discrimination	2.40	4.33
	2.45	3.97
	2.70	4.41
11. Color Recognition a. Concept	1.72	3.57
	2.56	3.83
	2.99	4.00
b. Language	1.82	2.44
	2.12	2.85
	2.71	3.73
12. Matching a. Shapes 1. Objects	2.83	5.00
	3.47	4.83
	3.82	4.82
2. Geometric shapes	2.82	5.00
	3.32	4.83
	3.61	4.82
3. Representation	2.56	3.85
	3.21	4.29
	3.55	4.79

A. Intellectual Development (Continued)

b. Size, coins	2.65	4.20
	2.82	4.43
	2.00	4.20
12. c. Primary colors	2.49	3.97
	2.91	4.48
	3.09	4.80
d. Numbers 1. 1 - 5	1.80	3.09
	1.90	3.26
	2.12	4.12
2. Pictured groups	2.00	3.27
	2.00	3.90
	2.25	3.85
3. Symbols	1.84	2.95
	1.84	3.11
	1.84	
13. Concepts of quantity a. Numbers	1.55	2.74
	1.88	3.04
	2.69	3.83
b. Size	1.66	3.15
	2.25	3.73
	2.92	3.78
c. Time	1.61	3.20
	2.15	3.31
	2.87	3.89
14. Time concept	2.12	4.30
	2.72	4.35
	3.87	4.51
15. Nature study a. Plants	1.15	4.00
	1.67	3.00
	1.80	3.80
b. Animals	1.22	3.20
	1.96	3.18
	2.08	4.10
c. Weather	2.00	4.43
	2.65	4.16
	3.08	4.37
16. Problem solving	2.55	3.59
	3.20	3.98
	3.98	4.41
17. Self-concept or autonomy	2.34	3.88
	3.17	4.06
	3.70	4.57
18. Obeying rules	2.63	3.71
	3.23	3.94
	3.71	4.44

B.   Imagination and Creative Expression

1. Sand play	2.12	3.99
	3.00	4.13
	3.36	4.63
2. Water play		
a. Water painting	2.38	
	2.90	4.43
	3.23	4.48
b. Soapsuds	2.13	3.73
	2.57	4.09
	3.12	4.64
c. Fishing	2.75	
	3.00	4.00
	4.08	4.83
d. Swimming	1.57	3.00
	2.00	3.60
	2.60	4.44
e. Bubbles	2.32	
	2.30	3.94
	2.98	4.96
f. Washing clothes, dishes, dolls	2.51	3.62
	2.78	3.59
	3.20	4.39
3. Drawing	2.19	3.10
	2.50	3.41
	2.88	4.03
4. Painting	2.00	3.12
	2.15	3.80
	2.35	4.37
5. Finger painting	1.84	
	2.05	3.79
	1.95	4.26
6. Clay	1.90	2.87
	2.50	3.48
	3.03	4.13
7. Dramatic expression		
a. Individual	2.38	3.66
	2.80	3.94
	3.46	4.73
b. Group dramatic play	1.96	3.50
	2.75	3.83
	3.41	4.73
c. Structured dramatic play		3.57
		3.88
	4.46	4.47
d. Puppetry	1.50	2.43
	2.09	3.23
	2.09	4.21

B. Imagination and Creative Expression (Continued)
C. Social Development

8. Creative rhythms a. Individual	2.10	3.49
	2.56	4.04
	3.50	4.62
b. Group	2.55	3.41
	3.11	3.98
	4.21	4.56
c. Structured	2.17	3.41
	3.88	3.93
	3.97	4.72
9. Rhythm Band	2.54	
	3.14	4.11
	4.12	4.38
C.		
1. Relatedness to children	2.38	3.72
	3.11	3.98
	3.87	4.60
2. Relatedness to adults	2.60	3.86
	3.31	4.11
	3.92	4.63
3. Sharing	2.43	3.86
	3.07	3.99
	3.71	4.63
4. Consideration of others	1.89	3.47
	2.43	3.62
	3.13	4.39
5. Receiving help	2.35	4.82
	3.13	4.50
	3.88	4.82
6. Respecting property rights	2.07	4.48
	2.72	4.18
	3.74	4.51
7. Expressions a. Adults 1. Please	2.37	3.07
	3.16	3.42
	3.66	4.18
2. Thank you	2.72	3.50
	3.15	3.98
	3.71	4.49
3. You are welcome		
4. Apology	1.93	3.19
	2.41	3.79
	3.05	4.39

C. Social Development (Continued)

7. a. 5. Greeting	3.48	4.50
	3.98	4.56
	4.43	4.91
6. Offering	2.14	3.43
	2.85	3.50
	3.27	4.67
b. Children 1. Please	1.87	3.18
	2.71	3.46
	3.21	4.15
2. Thank you	1.97	3.93
	2.75	3.79
	3.26	4.41
3. You are welcome		
4. Apology	1.85	3.79
	2.27	3.56
	2.76	4.32
5. Greeting	3.37	4.84
	3.61	4.56
	3.98	4.91
6. Offering	2.10	3.50
	2.38	3.77
	2.82	4.73
8. Juice time a. Attitude	2.93	4.79
	4.08	4.76
	4.59	4.97
b. Participation	2.50	4.25
	3.27	4.15
	3.89	4.78
9. Food preparation	1.11	2.50
	1.50	2.50
	1.85	4.00
10. Group games	3.17	3.47
	3.40	3.67
	4.02	4.92
11. Trips a. Participation	2.73	3.54
	2.90	4.29
	2.91	4.93
b. and c. new		

D.   Emotional Development
E.   Manipulative Development

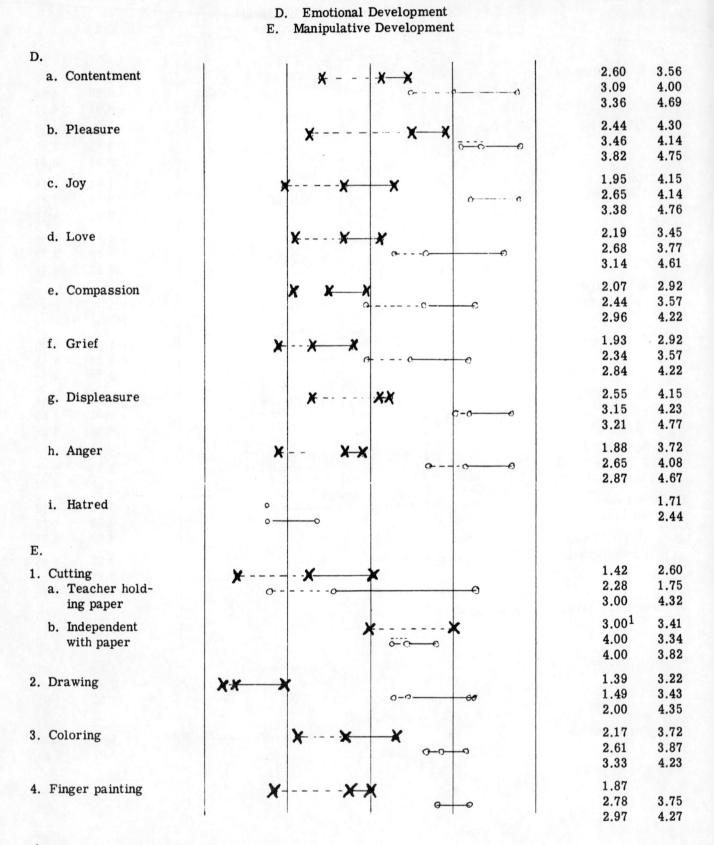

D.

a. Contentment   2.60   3.56
                                                    3.09   4.00
                                                    3.36   4.69

b. Pleasure   2.44   4.30
                                                    3.46   4.14
                                                    3.82   4.75

c. Joy   1.95   4.15
                                                    2.65   4.14
                                                    3.38   4.76

d. Love   2.19   3.45
                                                    2.68   3.77
                                                    3.14   4.61

e. Compassion   2.07   2.92
                                                    2.44   3.57
                                                    2.96   4.22

f. Grief   1.93   2.92
                                                    2.34   3.57
                                                    2.84   4.22

g. Displeasure   2.55   4.15
                                                    3.15   4.23
                                                    3.21   4.77

h. Anger   1.88   3.72
                                                    2.65   4.08
                                                    2.87   4.67

i. Hatred   1.71
                                                            2.44

E.

1. Cutting   1.42   2.60
   a. Teacher hold-   2.28   1.75
      ing paper   3.00   4.32

   b. Independent   3.00[1] 3.41
      with paper   4.00   3.34
                                                    4.00   3.82

2. Drawing   1.39   3.22
                                                    1.49   3.43
                                                    2.00   4.35

3. Coloring   2.17   3.72
                                                    2.61   3.87
                                                    3.33   4.23

4. Finger painting   1.87
                                                    2.78   3.75
                                                    2.97   4.27

[1] Only two children rated on item

E. Manipulative Development (Continued)

Item		
5. Clay, dough, plasticene	2.27	3.68
	3.01	4.10
	3.81	4.55
6. Pasting	2.00	4.25
	2.91	4.31
	3.95	4.78
7.		
8.		
9. Hammering	2.95	3.74
	3.45	4.17
	3.93	4.55
10.		
11.		
12. Bead stringing	2.00	3.34
	2.45	3.54
	2.45	4.39
13. Pegs	2.51	3.00
	2.92	3.61
	3.14	4.13
14. Cars, trucks, trains (miniatures)	2.88	4.00
	3.25	4.27
	3.70	4.72
15. Trains and tracks	1.59	3.54
	2.32	4.14
	3.35	4.42
16. Block building	1.32	2.92
	1.66	3.54
	2.60	4.37
17. Tinker toys	1.60	3.50
	2.21	3.97
	2.72	4.33
18. Tops		
19. Puzzles		
a. Coordination board	3.57	5.00
	3.93	4.67
	4.37	4.94
b. Two-piece	2.80	
	3.45	4.50
	4.18	4.82
c. Three-piece	2.00	
	3.00	4.50
	3.55	4.73
d. Five-piece +	2.80	3.88
	3.61	4.13
	3.96	4.50
e. Non-insert	1.33	
	1.67	4.00
	5.00	3.81

F.   Motor Development

1. Walking		3.19	4.93
		3.60	4.50
		3.82	4.82
2. Running		2.83	4.41
		3.28	4.32
		3.64	4.65
3. Marching		2.78	4.24
		3.18	4.34
		3.56	4.82
4. Jumping		2.69	4.13
		3.04	4.41
		3.27	4.71
5. Hopping		2.50	4.50
		2.82	4.18
		3.42	4.62
6. Skipping		1.00	4.00
		1.27	4.44
		3.32	3.90
7. Dancing		2.15	4.27
		2.47	4.33
		3.03	4.58
8. Stairs			
a. Climbing		2.91	4.10
		3.29	4.31
		3.83	4.85
b. Descending		2.06	3.32
		2.24	3.96
		3.24	4.47
9. Jumping rope			2.00
			2.07
			2.37
10. Sliding		3.06	4.93
		3.81	4.96
		4.29	5.00
11. Ball playing		1.67	2.27
a. 1. catching large ball		2.05	2.13
		2.06	2.42
a. 2. catching small ball		1.00	2.13
		1.00	2.07
		1.00	2.60
b. 1. Throwing large ball		1.68	2.55
		1.95	3.15
		2.45	3.46
b. 2. Throwing small ball		2.00	2.63
		2.22	2.97
		2.67	3.31

F.   Motor Development (Continued)
G.   Self Help

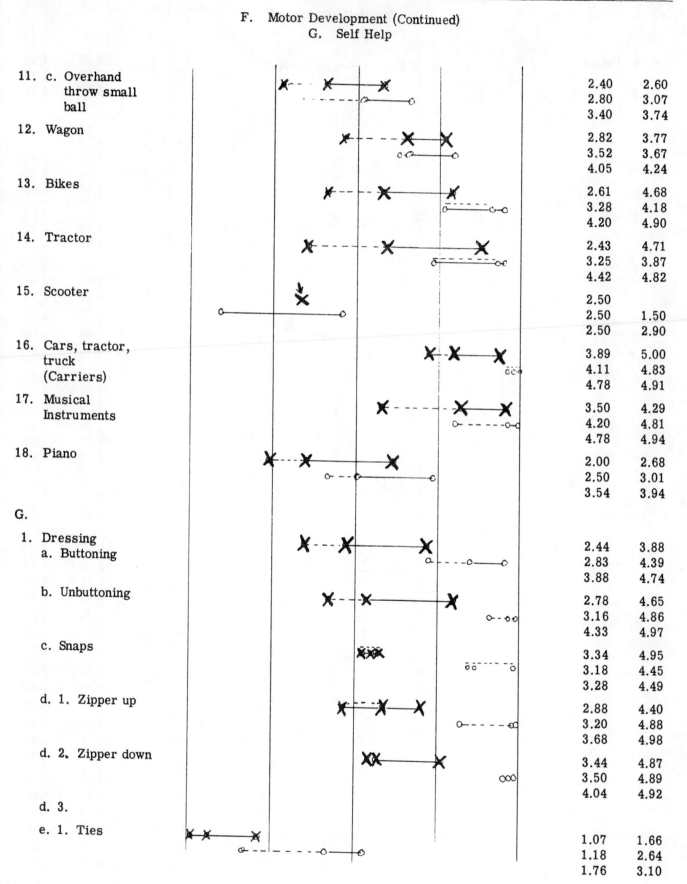

11. c. Overhand throw small ball	2.40	2.60
	2.80	3.07
	3.40	3.74
12. Wagon	2.82	3.77
	3.52	3.67
	4.05	4.24
13. Bikes	2.61	4.68
	3.28	4.18
	4.20	4.90
14. Tractor	2.43	4.71
	3.25	3.87
	4.42	4.82
15. Scooter	2.50	
	2.50	1.50
	2.50	2.90
16. Cars, tractor, truck (Carriers)	3.89	5.00
	4.11	4.83
	4.78	4.91
17. Musical Instruments	3.50	4.29
	4.20	4.81
	4.78	4.94
18. Piano	2.00	2.68
	2.50	3.01
	3.54	3.94

G.

1. Dressing a. Buttoning	2.44	3.88
	2.83	4.39
	3.88	4.74
b. Unbuttoning	2.78	4.65
	3.16	4.86
	4.33	4.97
c. Snaps	3.34	4.95
	3.18	4.45
	3.28	4.49
d. 1. Zipper up	2.88	4.40
	3.20	4.88
	3.68	4.98
d. 2. Zipper down	3.44	4.87
	3.50	4.89
	4.04	4.92
d. 3.		
e. 1. Ties	1.07	1.66
	1.18	2.64
	1.76	3.10

G.   Self Help (Continued)

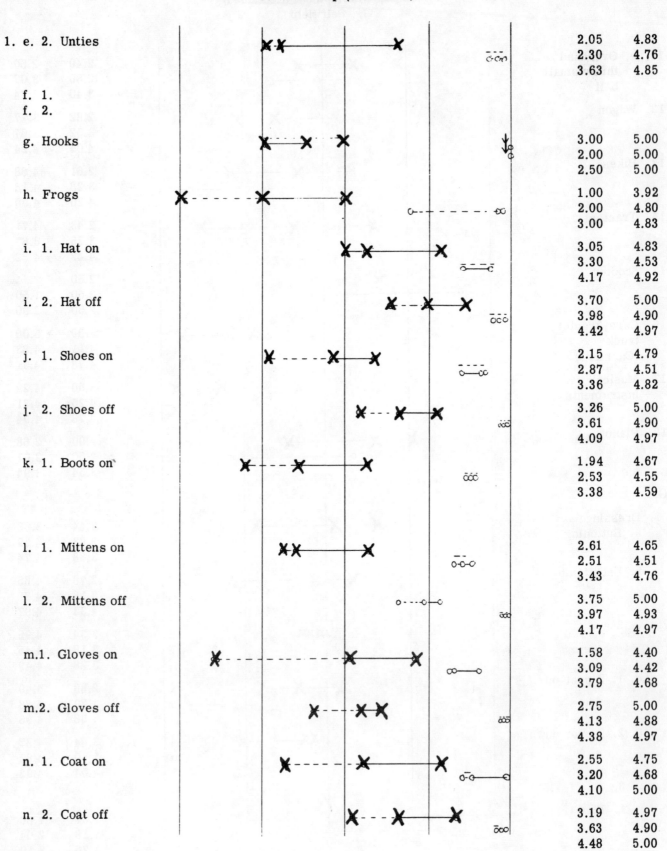

1. e. 2. Unties	2.05	4.83
	2.30	4.76
	3.63	4.85
f. 1.		
f. 2.		
g. Hooks	3.00	5.00
	2.00	5.00
	2.50	5.00
h. Frogs	1.00	3.92
	2.00	4.80
	3.00	4.83
i. 1. Hat on	3.05	4.83
	3.30	4.53
	4.17	4.92
i. 2. Hat off	3.70	5.00
	3.98	4.90
	4.42	4.97
j. 1. Shoes on	2.15	4.79
	2.87	4.51
	3.36	4.82
j. 2. Shoes off	3.26	5.00
	3.61	4.90
	4.09	4.97
k. 1. Boots on	1.94	4.67
	2.53	4.55
	3.38	4.59
l. 1. Mittens on	2.61	4.65
	2.51	4.51
	3.43	4.76
l. 2. Mittens off	3.75	5.00
	3.97	4.93
	4.17	4.97
m.1. Gloves on	1.58	4.40
	3.09	4.42
	3.79	4.68
m.2. Gloves off	2.75	5.00
	4.13	4.88
	4.38	4.97
n. 1. Coat on	2.55	4.75
	3.20	4.68
	4.10	5.00
n. 2. Coat off	3.19	4.97
	3.63	4.90
	4.48	5.00

G.   Self Help (Continued)

1. o. 1. Pants on	1.75	4.72
	2.00	4.77
	3.94	4.97
o. 2. Pants off	2.17	5.00
	2.25	4.90
	4.23	5.00
p. 1. Snowpants on	1.84	
	2.53	4.64
	3.52	4.85
p. 2. Snowpants off	2.67	
	3.12	4.70
	3.75	4.93
q. Scarf	3.00	
	3.40	3.99
	3.50	4.59
r. Bow ties	1.10	5.00
	1.23	4.39
	2.41	4.65
2. Hand washing	2.56	4.87
	2.81	4.86
	3.82	4.91
3. Toilet education	3.13	4.57
	3.77	4.85
	4.43	5.00
4. Juice time a. Setting table	2.22	3.26
	3.24	3.87
	3.83	4.64
b. Pouring juice	2.42	4.75
	3.28	4.61
	4.06	5.00
c. Passing crackers	2.86	4.00
	3.29	4.83
	4.32	5.00
d. Helping self to more food	3.82	5.00
	4.36	4.90
	4.50	5.00
e. Stacking dishes (clearing table)	2.34	3.65
	3.07	4.21
	3.95	4.88
f. Washing table	2.15	3.28
	2.97	4.21
	3.87	4.82

g., h., i.

G.   Self Help (Continued)

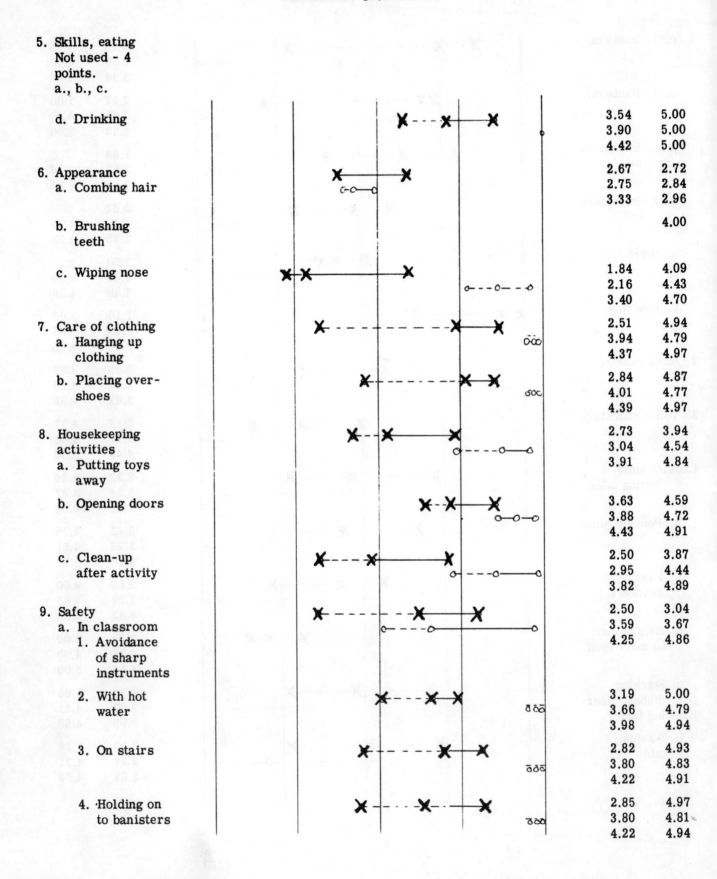

5. Skills, eating
   Not used - 4
   points.
   a., b., c.

   d. Drinking   3.54   5.00
                              3.90   5.00
                              4.42   5.00

6. Appearance   2.67   2.72
   a. Combing hair   2.75   2.84
                           3.33   2.96

   b. Brushing   4.00
      teeth

   c. Wiping nose   1.84   4.09
                           2.16   4.43
                           3.40   4.70

7. Care of clothing   2.51   4.94
   a. Hanging up   3.94   4.79
      clothing   4.37   4.97

   b. Placing over-   2.84   4.87
      shoes   4.01   4.77
                           4.39   4.97

8. Housekeeping   2.73   3.94
   activities   3.04   4.54
   a. Putting toys   3.91   4.84
      away

   b. Opening doors   3.63   4.59
                           3.88   4.72
                           4.43   4.91

   c. Clean-up   2.50   3.87
      after activity   2.95   4.44
                           3.82   4.89

9. Safety   2.50   3.04
   a. In classroom   3.59   3.67
      1. Avoidance   4.25   4.86
         of sharp
         instruments

      2. With hot   3.19   5.00
         water   3.66   4.79
                           3.98   4.94

      3. On stairs   2.82   4.93
                           3.80   4.83
                           4.22   4.91

      4. Holding on   2.85   4.97
         to banisters   3.80   4.81
                           4.22   4.94

G.   Self Help (Continued)

9. a. 5. Protection of head from bumps		3.12	4.66
		3.66	4.74
		4.08	4.85
b. On playground 1. Sliding		2.84	4.93
		3.79	4.74
		4.00	4.94
2. Swinging			5.00
		4.00	4.55
		3.09	4.56
3. See-saw		3.14	5.00
		3.52	4.39
		3.65	4.94
4. Climbing		2.99	4.59
		3.57	4.52
		3.68	4.94
5. Sand box		3.05	4.94
		3.64	4.79
		4.18	4.94
6. Wheel toys		2.78	4.79
		3.26	4.45
		3.98	4.90
10. Independent travel bldg.		2.12	4.15
		2.75	3.90
		3.89	4.47

A CONCLUDING STATEMENT

SUMMARY

The curriculum presented in this volume was designed and implemented by the in-service teachers in preschool classes established as part of the research design of the Teachers College - U. S. Office of Education Mental Retardation Project. The classes were composed of children diagnosed at an early age as educable mentally retarded and referred to the Project on the basis of their functioning which was noticeably different from their chronological age-peers. The purpose of the curriculum was to prepare these boys and girls to live more effectively and to facilitate their subsequent adjustment in the New York City public school program.

During the four years of the experimental preschool, seven classes, including four different groups of children, were operated at Teachers College, Columbia University. The class sessions held five days weekly were approximately two and one-half hours in length. For each group, there were two teachers.

Both a younger and an older group, with approximately fifteen children attended during the first three years; only an older group participated during the fourth year. Upon entering the program, children ranged in age from four years nine months to five years nine months in the younger group, and from five years nine months to six years nine months in the older group. In addition to stipulations as to age and retarded functioning, criteria for admission included freedom from gross physical or emotional deviation and ability to communicate basic needs. Enrollment in the preschool was, for the most part, the direct result of recommendation by community agencies.

The teachers' activities consisted of developing a curriculum design, methodology and materials; implementing the curriculum in an on-going program; observing and reporting child behavior, and recording results. Major long range focus was on child attention, motivation,

problem-solving, work habits, concept development, and speech and language growth.

The resultant three-dimensional curriculum design reflected interrelationships among the three components: 1) the Curriculum Guide, 2) the Action Settings and 3) the Cross-sectional or unit approach.

The Curriculum Guide, with the seven subcategories of intellectual development, imaginative and creative expression, social development, emotional development, manipulative development, gross motor development and self-help contained 190 items arranged in five-point developmental scales for the teachers' use in viewing teaching-learning processes. On the basis of observed behavior in the Action Settings, teachers rated each child on each item three times annually. The ratings were designed to provide 1) teacher direction, 2) program balance, and 3) assessment of child and group status. Utilizing cumulative classroom records, each recurring experience or item was programmed; sample teaching procedures based on the child's predictable or internalized behavior have been presented in Chapter II of this volume.

The Action Settings in which the Guide items were implemented included: discussion periods, music, group handwork projects, free play, juice time, playground and gymnasium activities, story telling, swimming, cooking, and trips. The physical settings, the time as utilized, the persons as resources and the equipment and materials were the promoters of child activity. The child's action, deemed the prime resource of the preschool curriculum, was used by the child to construct and experience relationships suggested in the settings. Upon these early understandings of relationships, comprehension of pictorial, three-dimensional and print symbols was to be established.

The Cross-sectional Approach was the manner in which the Action Settings were used to implement the Guide. The teaching method utilized in this approach was a unit method wherein the units were habits and ways of functioning. Continuing intention was provided through two sets of directions: one for the teachers and one for the children. The teachers' directions were the long range behavioral goals and the itemized goals of the Curriculum Guide; the children operated within patterns of time, subject matter, conceptual sequences, and personal relationship sequences which were interdependent and useful in varying degrees within each situation.

Evaluations made by the teachers included: 1) ratings recorded in September, January, and June for each child, on each detail of the Curriculum Guide; 2) annual reports of individual child progress toward behavioral goals; and 3) monthly and annual reports of teacher activity in curriculum development and implementation. The source of ratings and reports was the behavior of the preschool children, observed and recorded in the teachers' continuous anecdotal accounts.

Successive composite ratings made during the second, third and fourth years of experimental classwork and summarized by means of line graphs in Chapter 6 indicate the direction of growth of children diagnosed at an early age as educable mentally retarded and included in a program of planned enrichment. Refinements in the children's intellectual, creative and imaginative, social, emotional, manipulative, motor and self-help behavior over a two year period, suggest a relationship between the three-dimensional curriculum design and the observed development. Similar indications are found in the results of adjustment measurements subsequent to the children's admission to public school programs. Both the teachers' ratings made on a scale afforded by the Project developed Guide and the later assessments which utilized standardized instruments point to particular areas for which the preschool curriculum has pertinence. These congruences, together with tentative generalizations and suggestions for more definitive study are offered in this concluding chapter.

CONCLUSIONS

The effects of the curriculum indicate a significant increment in Stanford Binet scores from time of entrance to exit from the preschool program. However, except for the 1958 group, the scores on follow-up did not show the significant increment although it continued in a positive direction. Kirk's study of effects of a preschool enrichment program reports significant IQ increments throughout the follow-up period. Two questions are raised here:

1) Kirk and his co-workers mass-tested community children for subject identification; the present study's subjects were referrals from various social and medical agencies, who, when informed as to purposes of the Project, reported children who had, because of their deviations, called attention to themselves. The extent to which the populations differed merits investigation. 2) Direction of teacher efforts in the present program was toward the child's internal control, self-reliance, and creative expression as well as toward removing ceilings on growth through action. The degree of follow-up acceptance of the resultant behavior pattern and the ability of the child to adjust to a more teacher-oriented classroom environment merit further study.

Results of the Wide Range Achievement Tests showed encouraging academic growth of the children who attended the experimental preschool program. Those placed in both special and regular classes yielded significantly higher reading scores than their peers, i.e., they were approximately five months superior on this subtest. There were no significant differences in either spelling or arithmetic although slight numerical superiority was noted. Suggested here is value in studying further the approach which introduced children to symbols through an enriched action program. Study should also be made of the differentiation between reading and arithmetic achievement. Was the arithmetic lag a consequence of inadvertent inequality of focus in the Action Settings; a function of child maturation; or a reflection of an achievement test which did not differentiate skills acquired in this developmental arithmetic program? Of particular interest would be a three to five year follow-up of the experimental group's academic achievement.

Although intervals of the Curriculum Guide scales were not equal nor the instrument standardized, growth in items relating to manipulation was less prominent than in other areas. Continued attention to manipulation problems in children diagnosed as mentally retarded at an early age is indicated.

Of particular value would be a study of the patterns of growth in the various areas of development and a test of the present curriculum to observe the suitability of its content and methodology with other young children exhibiting learning problems and retardation.

The potential of the children participating in the experimental program was somewhat underestimated by the preschool teachers as revealed by the number rated at the top of the scale by the end of the second year. There is need to extend the Guide upward and to test the patterns of learning with similar preschool groups as well as with school age retarded children.

Question is raised concerning the relationship between teaching and learning. Knowing generally how children learn is not sufficient to ensure an effective learning process; children's responses to teaching approaches differ. There appears to be need to study further means of obtaining maximum educational results through determining and utilizing the child's movement and direction.

Children in the experimental preschool manifested unanticipated growth in attending to a task. Further study should be made of the situational variables of time, the action and its elements, and personal resources of both the child and the adult in the process of increasing attention span and improving work habits.

The teaching method apparently effective in the preschool was the maintenance of conceptual wholes while directing attention to components of the wholes. The components were included in differing contexts for the child to experience. On the assumption of the presence of inclusive concepts and certain categorical understandings of preschool children, it seemed possible to develop and refine other concepts. A depth study of developmental ordering of conceptualization is recommended.

As a result of the productive curriculum involvement of non-professional personnel, including parents and transportation staff, study is needed of the amounts and kinds of participations most valuable in even the youngest child's learning. To be pursued is the development for parents and children of home action curriculum different from the school program to prevent possibly irreparable cumulative learning barriers in school life.

Question has been raised regarding the number and kind of repetitions, exposures and experiences needed for learning and retention. Study needs also to be conducted on the effectiveness of various teaching practices in developing imaginative and creative expression with attention to the status and potentiality of retarded children in fluency, flexibility and inventive level of such expression.

Finally, from the results of the varied admission policies in scheduling children to enter the preschool classes, and in the utilization of subgroups to develop total group cohesion, it is possible to infer the relevance of social psychological theory to teaching methodology. Further experimentation with individual and sub-group interactions and motivations as tools for establishing class efficiency, that is, as disciplinary tools, is indicated.